# Fantastic Four

## The Herald
## of Doom

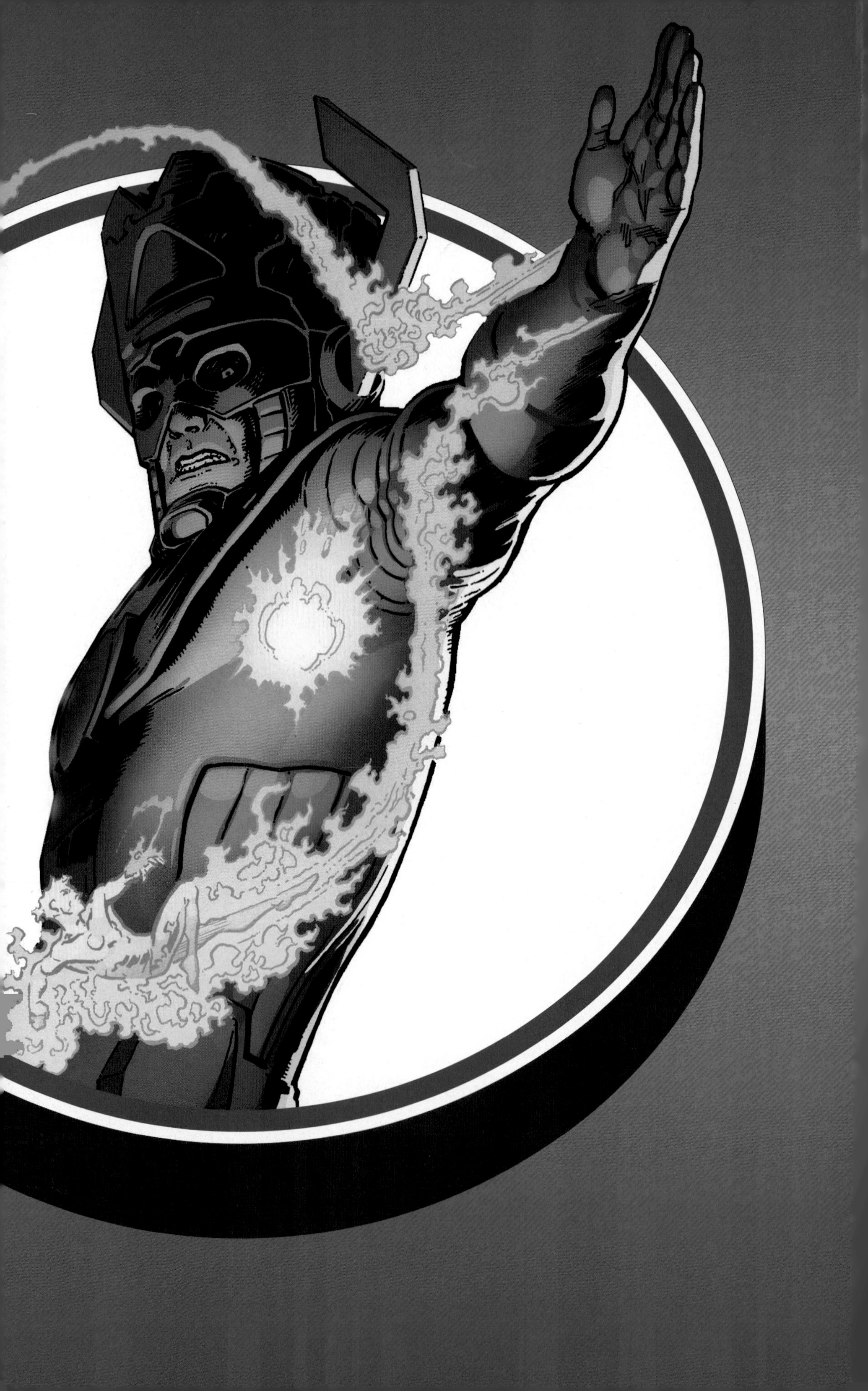

A brilliant scientist — his best friend — the woman he loved — and her
fiery-tempered kid brother! Together, they braved the unknown terrors of outer space
and were changed by cosmic rays into something more than merely human! They became the...

# FANTASTIC FOUR

The long-awaited wedding of Ben Grimm and Alicia Masters came to an abrupt end when
a massive hologram of Doctor Doom appeared in the sky, announcing that Galactus had made
landfall in Latveria but that Doom alone would deal with the World-Eater. Reed stopped time long
enough for Ben and Alicia to tie the knot, then the team jetted off to Latveria to investigate!

## The Herald of Doom

**Dan Slott**
WRITER

**Aaron Kuder** (#6-9), **John Lucas** (#7), **Stefano Caselli** (#8-9),
**David Marquez** (#8), **Reilly Brown** (#8), **Paco Medina** (#9-11),
**Kevin Libranda** (#10-11), **Paolo Villanelli** (#11) & **Juanan Ramírez** (#11)
ARTISTS

**Marte Gracia** (#6-7), **Erick Arciniega** (#6, #9),
**Rachelle Rosenberg** (#7), **Matt Yackey** (#8) & **Jesus Aburtov** (#10-11)
COLOR ARTISTS

**VC's Joe Caramagna**
LETTERER

**Esad Ribić** (#6-9 & #11) AND **Matteo Scalera** & **Moreno Dinisio** (#10)
COVER ART

**Alanna Smith**
ASSOCIATE EDITOR

**Tom Brevoort**
EDITOR

The Fantastic Four created by Stan Lee & Jack Kirby

COLLECTION EDITOR **Jennifer Grünwald**
ASSISTANT EDITOR **Caitlin O'Connell**
ASSOCIATE MANAGING EDITOR **Kateri Woody**
EDITOR, SPECIAL PROJECTS **Mark D. Beazley**

VP PRODUCTION & SPECIAL PROJECTS **Jeff Youngquist**
BOOK DESIGNER **Adam Del Re**
SVP PRINT, SALES & MARKETING **David Gabriel**
DIRECTOR, LICENSED PUBLISHING **Sven Larsen**

EDITOR IN CHIEF **C.B. Cebulski**
CHIEF CREATIVE OFFICER **Joe Quesada**
PRESIDENT **Dan Buckley**
EXECUTIVE PRODUCER **Alan Fine**

**FANTASTIC FOUR VOL. 3: THE HERALD OF DOOM.** Contains material originally published in magazine form as FANTASTIC FOUR #6-11. First printing 2019. ISBN 978-1-302-91442-4. Published by MARVEL WORLDWIDE, INC., a subsidiary of MARVEL ENTER-
TAINMENT, LLC. OFFICE OF PUBLICATION: 135 West 50th Street, New York, NY 10020. © 2019 MARVEL. No similarity between any of the names, characters, persons, and/or institutions in this magazine with those of any living or dead person or institution is
intended, and any such similarity which may exist is purely coincidental. **Printed in the U.S.A.** DAN BUCKLEY, President, Marvel Entertainment; JOHN NEE, Publisher; JOE QUESADA, Chief Creative Officer; TOM BREVOORT, SVP of Publishing; DAVID BOGART,
Associate Publisher & SVP of Talent Affairs; DAVID GABRIEL, SVP of Sales & Marketing, Publishing; JEFF YOUNGQUIST, VP of Production & Special Projects; DAN CARR, Executive Director of Publishing Technology; ALEX MORALES, Director of Publishing Oper-
ations; DAN EDINGTON, Managing Editor; SUSAN CRESPI, Production Manager; STAN LEE, Chairman Emeritus. For information regarding advertising in Marvel Comics or on Marvel.com, please contact Vit DeBellis, Custom Solutions & Integrated Advertising
Manager, at vdebellis@marvel.com. For Marvel subscription inquiries, please call 888-511-5480. **Manufactured between 7/26/2019 and 8/27/2019 by LSC COMMUNICATIONS INC., KENDALLVILLE, IN, USA.**

10 9 8 7 6 5 4 3 2 1

6

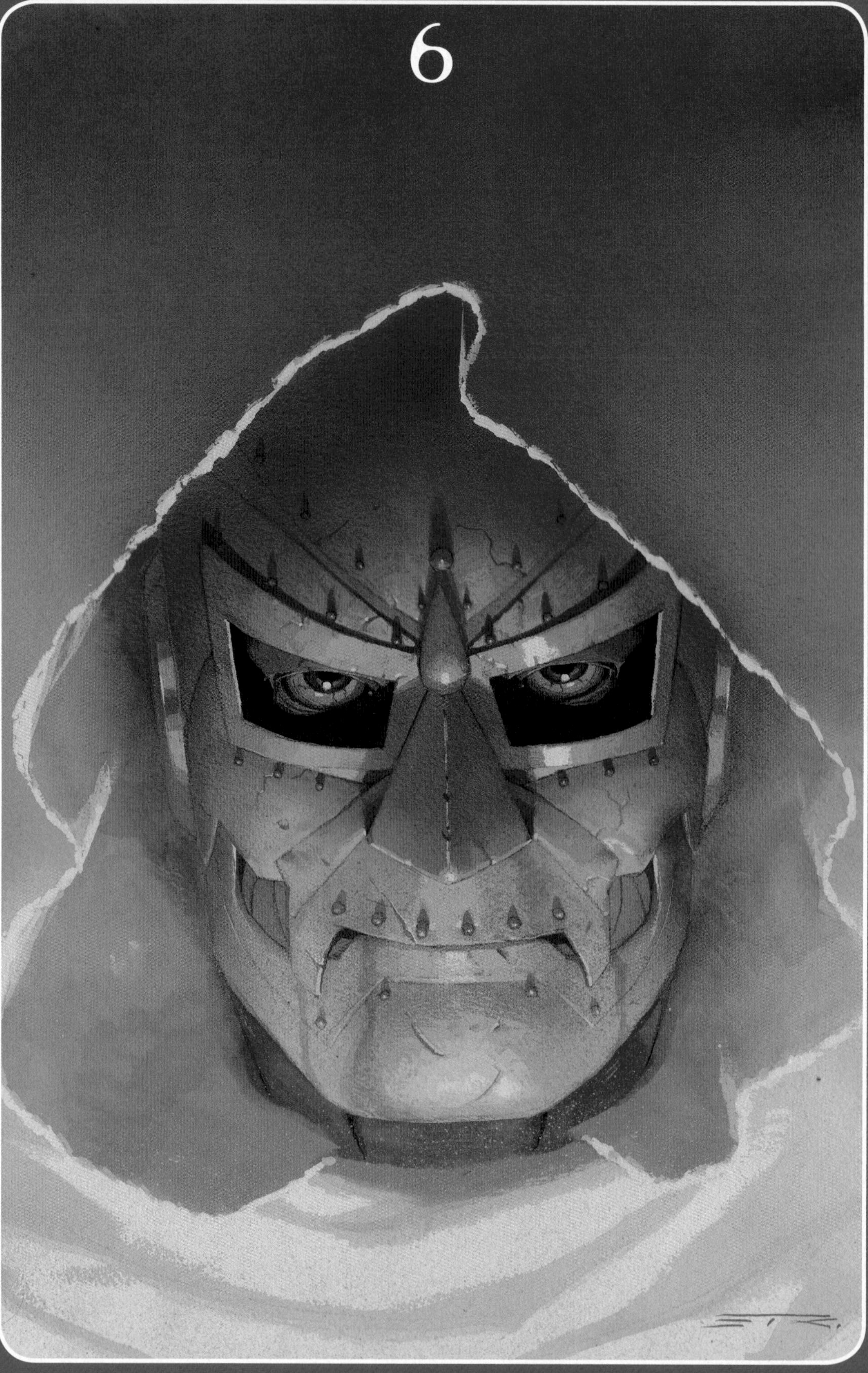

"Herald of Doom"

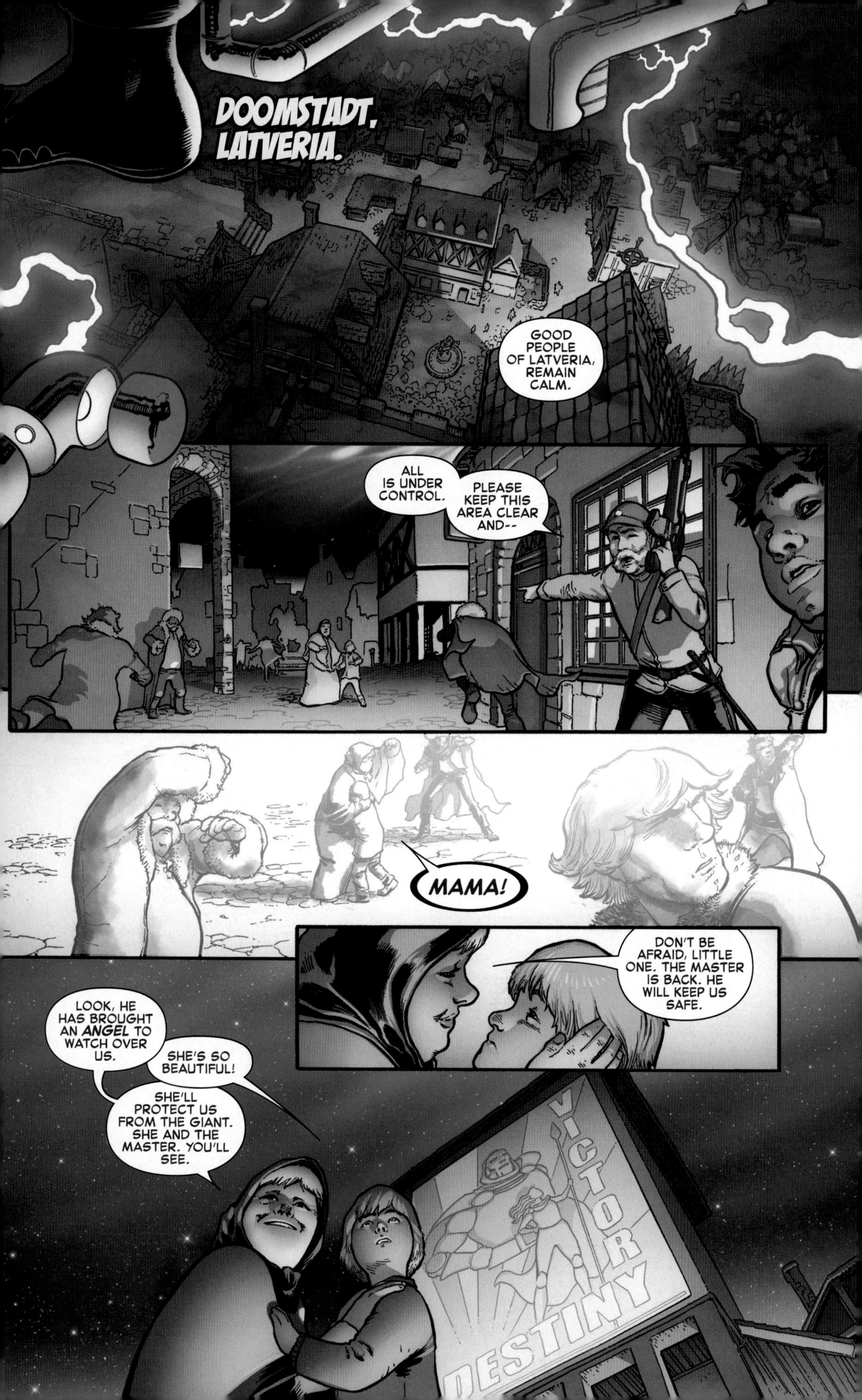
DOOMSTADT, LATVERIA.
GOOD PEOPLE OF LATVERIA, REMAIN CALM.
ALL IS UNDER CONTROL.
PLEASE KEEP THIS AREA CLEAR AND--
MAMA!
DON'T BE AFRAID, LITTLE ONE. THE MASTER IS BACK. HE WILL KEEP US SAFE.
LOOK, HE HAS BROUGHT AN *ANGEL* TO WATCH OVER US.
SHE'S SO BEAUTIFUL!
SHE'LL PROTECT US FROM THE GIANT. SHE AND THE MASTER. YOU'LL SEE.
VICTORY
DESTINY

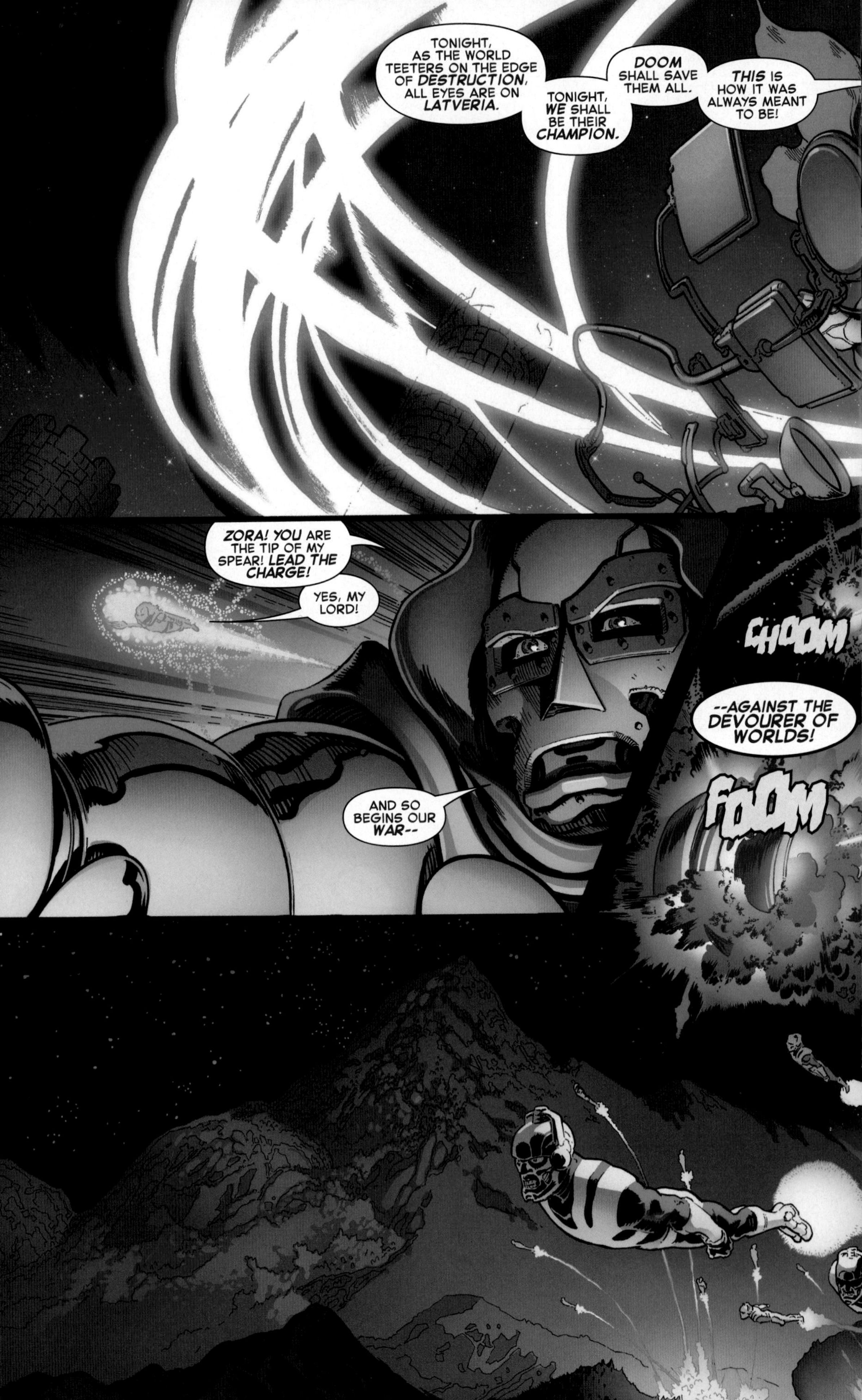
TONIGHT, AS THE WORLD TEETERS ON THE EDGE OF DESTRUCTION, ALL EYES ARE ON LATVERIA.
TONIGHT, WE SHALL BE THEIR CHAMPION.
DOOM SHALL SAVE THEM ALL.
THIS IS HOW IT WAS ALWAYS MEANT TO BE!
ZORA! YOU ARE THE TIP OF MY SPEAR! LEAD THE CHARGE!
YES, MY LORD!
CHOOM
AND SO BEGINS OUR WAR--
--AGAINST THE DEVOURER OF WORLDS!
FOOM

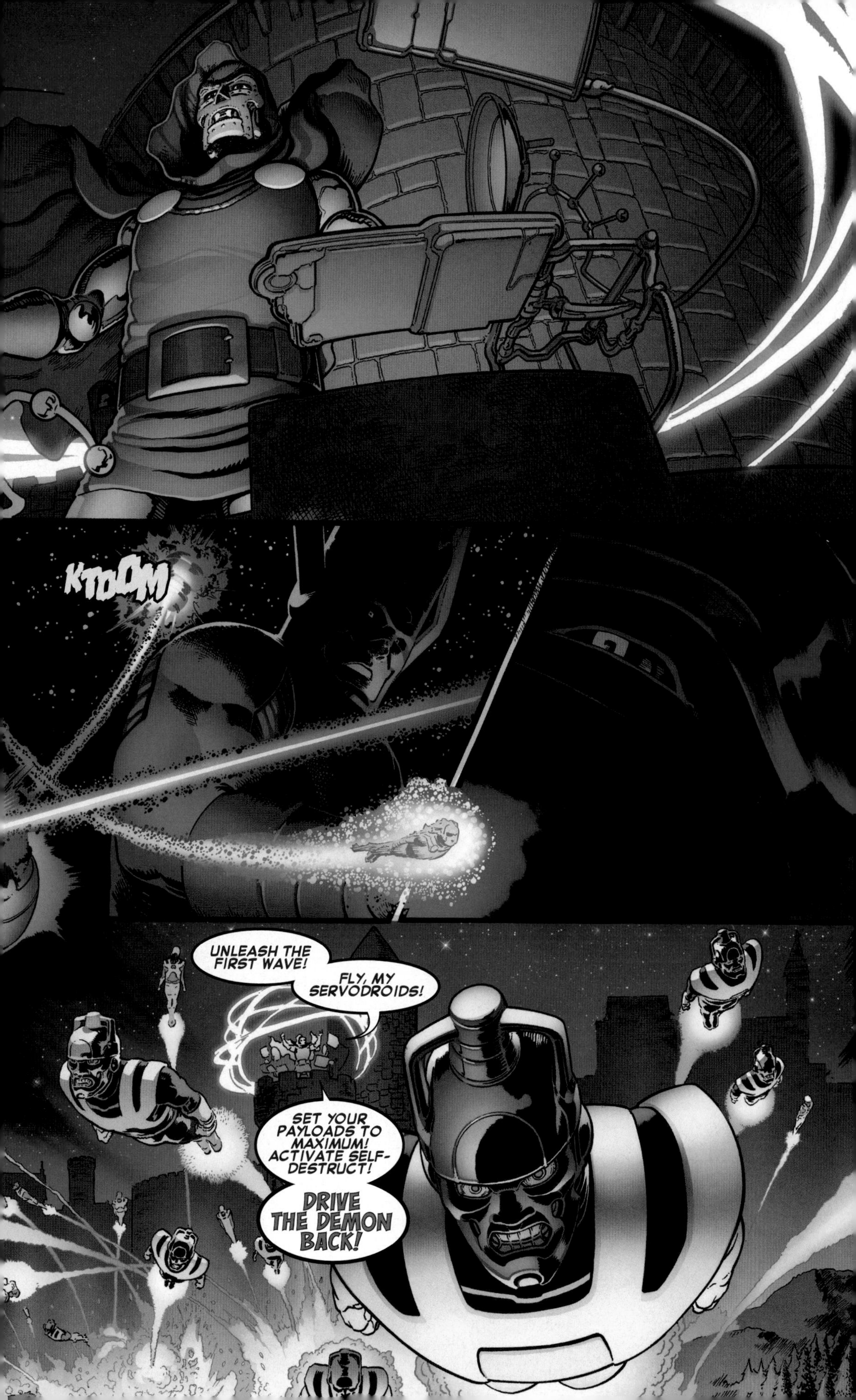
KTOOM
UNLEASH THE FIRST WAVE!
FLY, MY SERVODROIDS!
SET YOUR PAYLOADS TO MAXIMUM! ACTIVATE SELF-DESTRUCT!
DRIVE THE DEMON BACK!

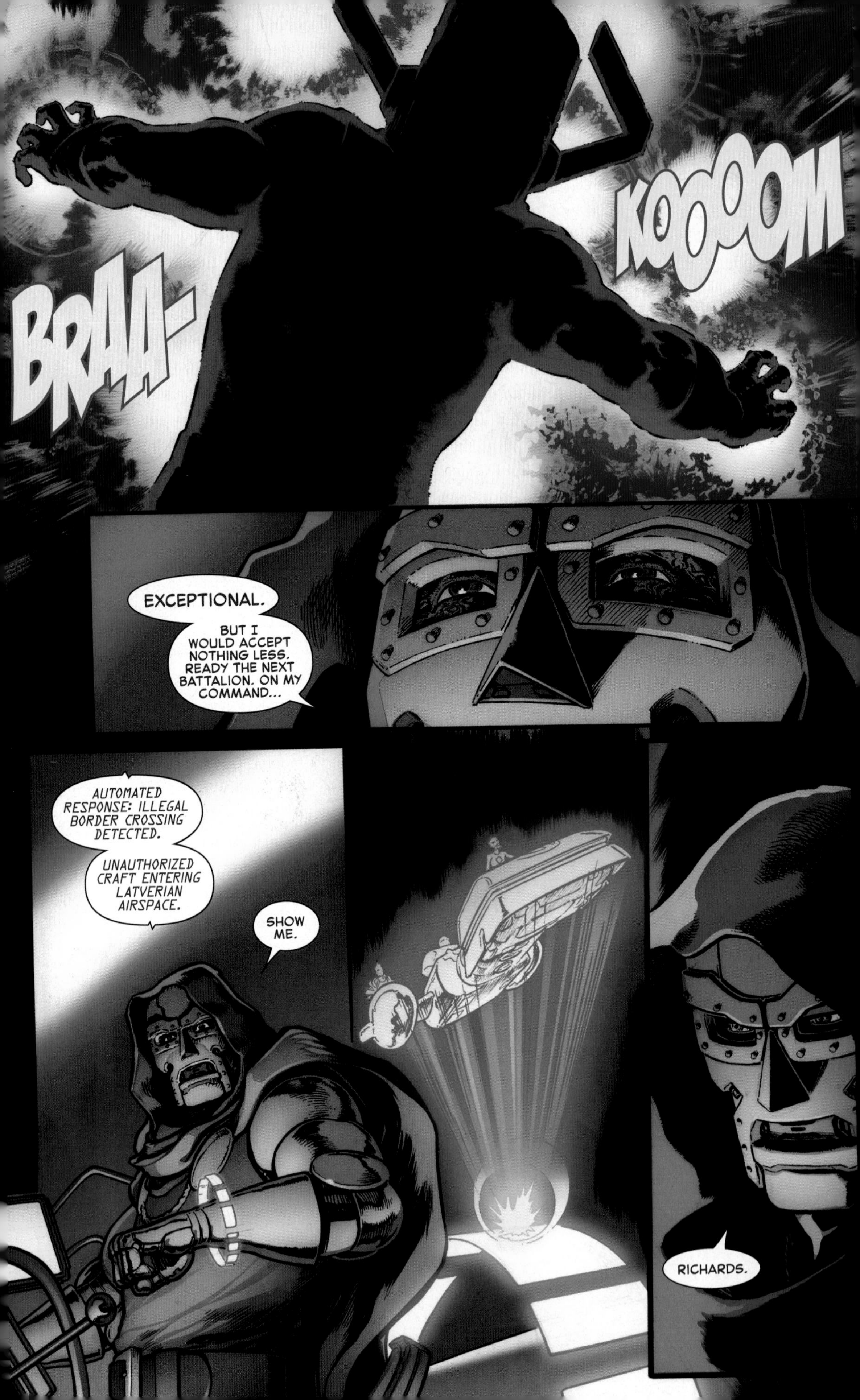
BRAA-
KOOOOM
EXCEPTIONAL.
BUT I WOULD ACCEPT NOTHING LESS. READY THE NEXT BATTALION. ON MY COMMAND...
AUTOMATED RESPONSE: ILLEGAL BORDER CROSSING DETECTED.
UNAUTHORIZED CRAFT ENTERING LATVERIAN AIRSPACE.
SHOW ME.
RICHARDS.

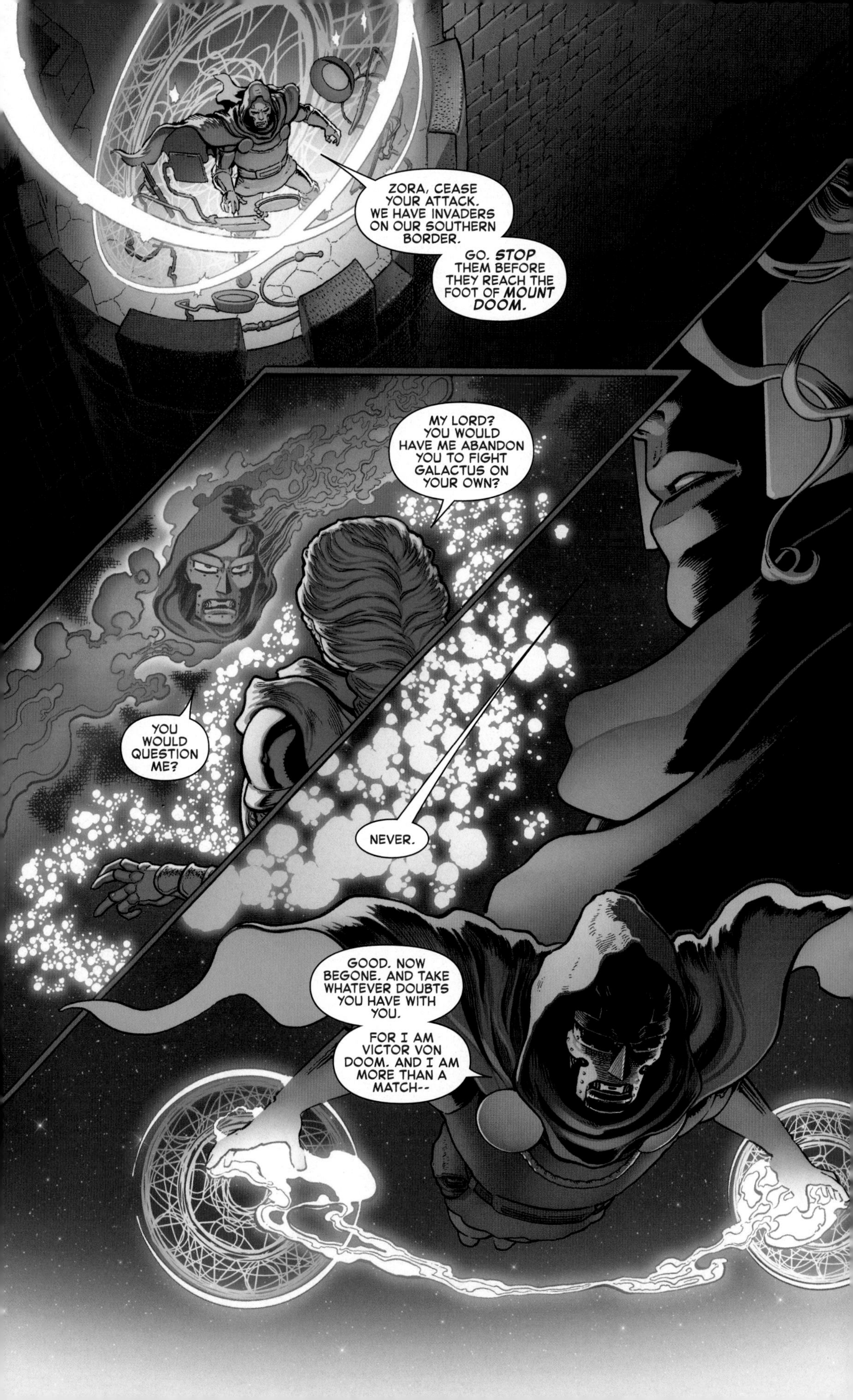
ZORA, CEASE YOUR ATTACK. WE HAVE INVADERS ON OUR SOUTHERN BORDER.
GO. STOP THEM BEFORE THEY REACH THE FOOT OF MOUNT DOOM.
MY LORD? YOU WOULD HAVE ME ABANDON YOU TO FIGHT GALACTUS ON YOUR OWN?
YOU WOULD QUESTION ME?
NEVER.
GOOD. NOW BEGONE. AND TAKE WHATEVER DOUBTS YOU HAVE WITH YOU.
FOR I AM VICTOR VON DOOM. AND I AM MORE THAN A MATCH--

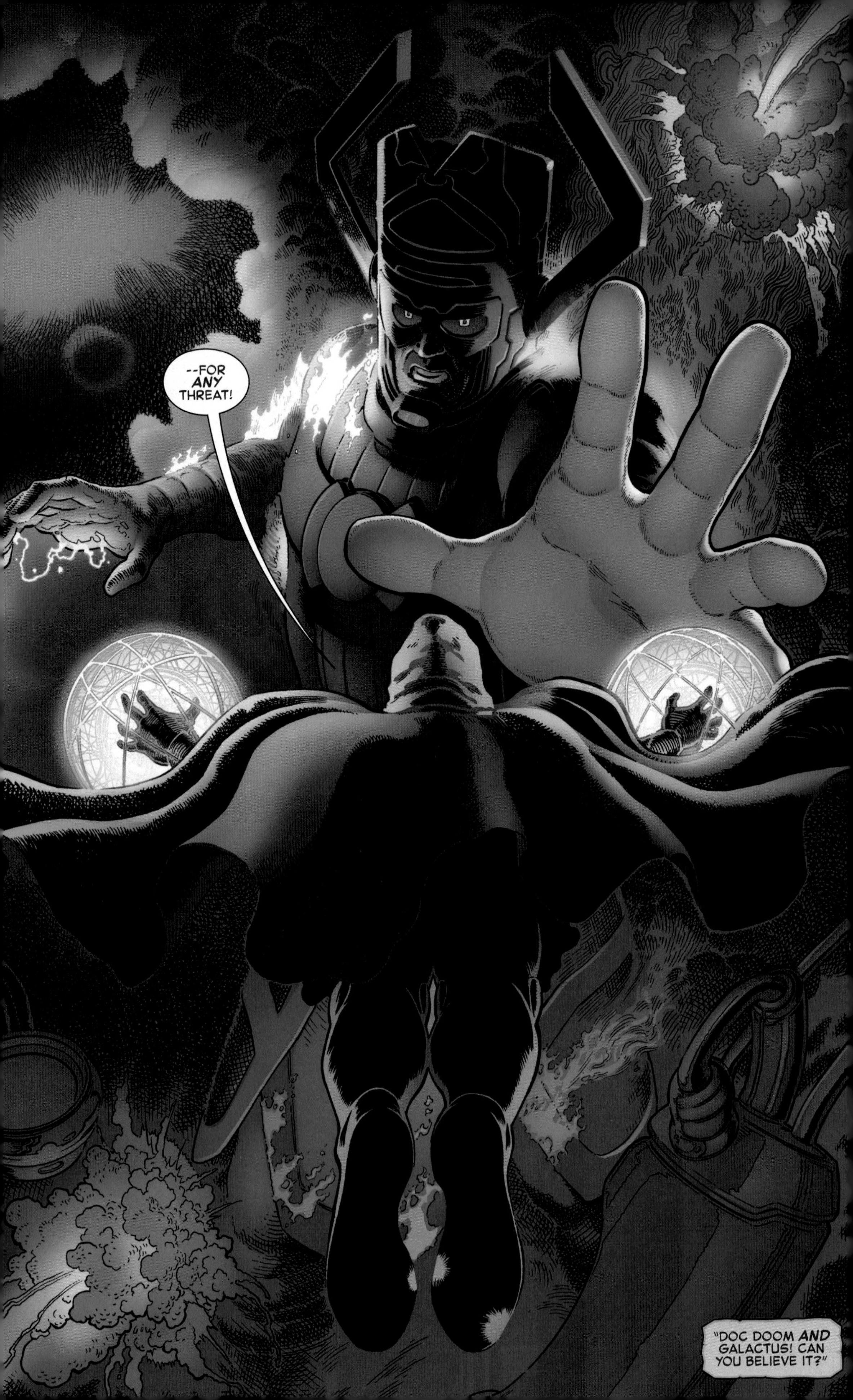
--FOR ANY THREAT!
"DOC DOOM AND GALACTUS! CAN YOU BELIEVE IT?"

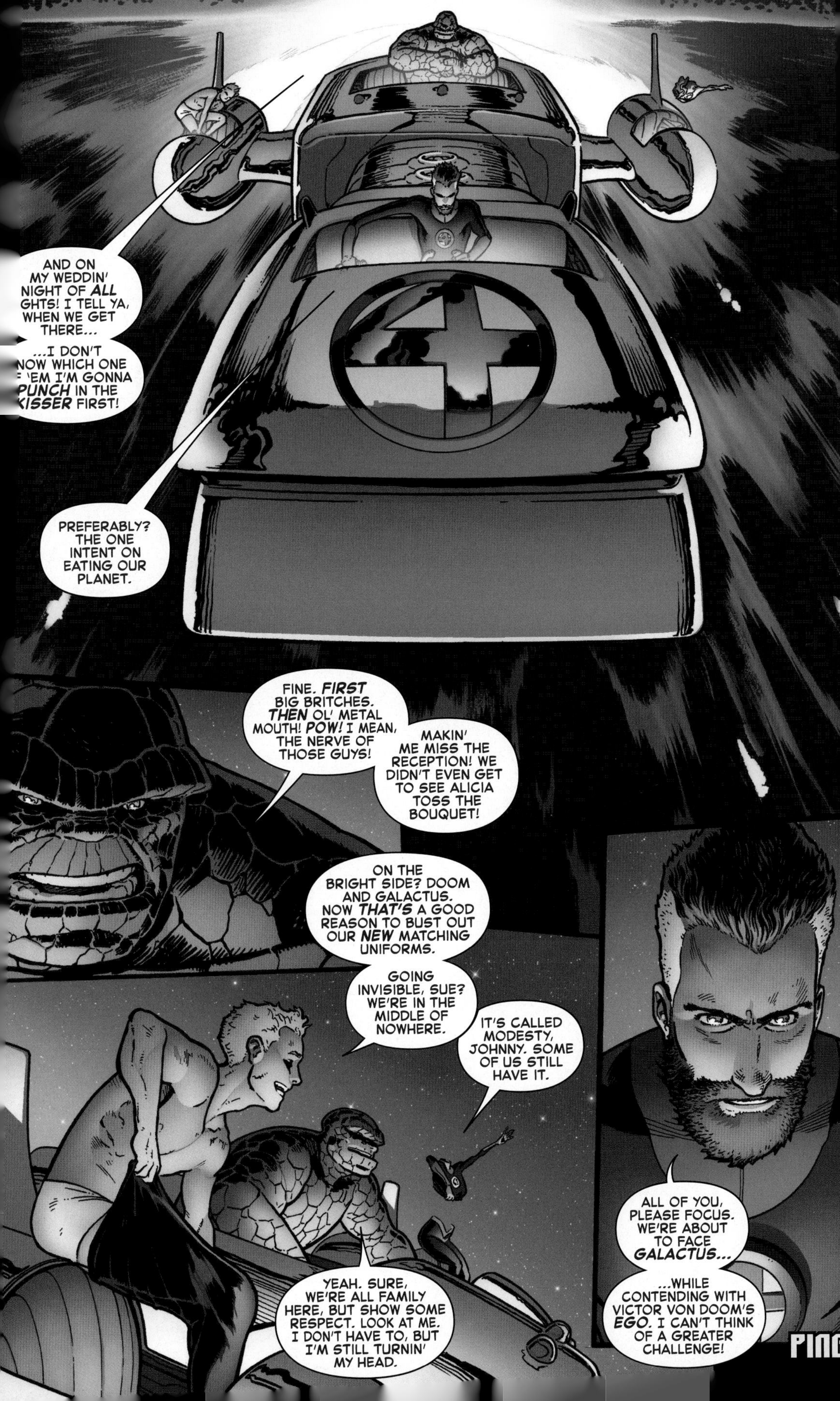

AND ON MY WEDDIN' NIGHT OF ALL GHTS! I TELL YA, WHEN WE GET THERE...
...I DON'T NOW WHICH ONE 'EM I'M GONNA PUNCH IN THE KISSER FIRST!
PREFERABLY? THE ONE INTENT ON EATING OUR PLANET.
FINE. FIRST BIG BRITCHES. THEN OL' METAL MOUTH! POW! I MEAN, THE NERVE OF THOSE GUYS!
MAKIN' ME MISS THE RECEPTION! WE DIDN'T EVEN GET TO SEE ALICIA TOSS THE BOUQUET!
ON THE BRIGHT SIDE? DOOM AND GALACTUS. NOW THAT'S A GOOD REASON TO BUST OUT OUR NEW MATCHING UNIFORMS.
GOING INVISIBLE, SUE? WE'RE IN THE MIDDLE OF NOWHERE.
IT'S CALLED MODESTY, JOHNNY. SOME OF US STILL HAVE IT.
YEAH. SURE, WE'RE ALL FAMILY HERE, BUT SHOW SOME RESPECT. LOOK AT ME. I DON'T HAVE TO, BUT I'M STILL TURNIN' MY HEAD.
ALL OF YOU, PLEASE FOCUS. WE'RE ABOUT TO FACE GALACTUS...
...WHILE CONTENDING WITH VICTOR VON DOOM'S EGO. I CAN'T THINK OF A GREATER CHALLENGE!
PING

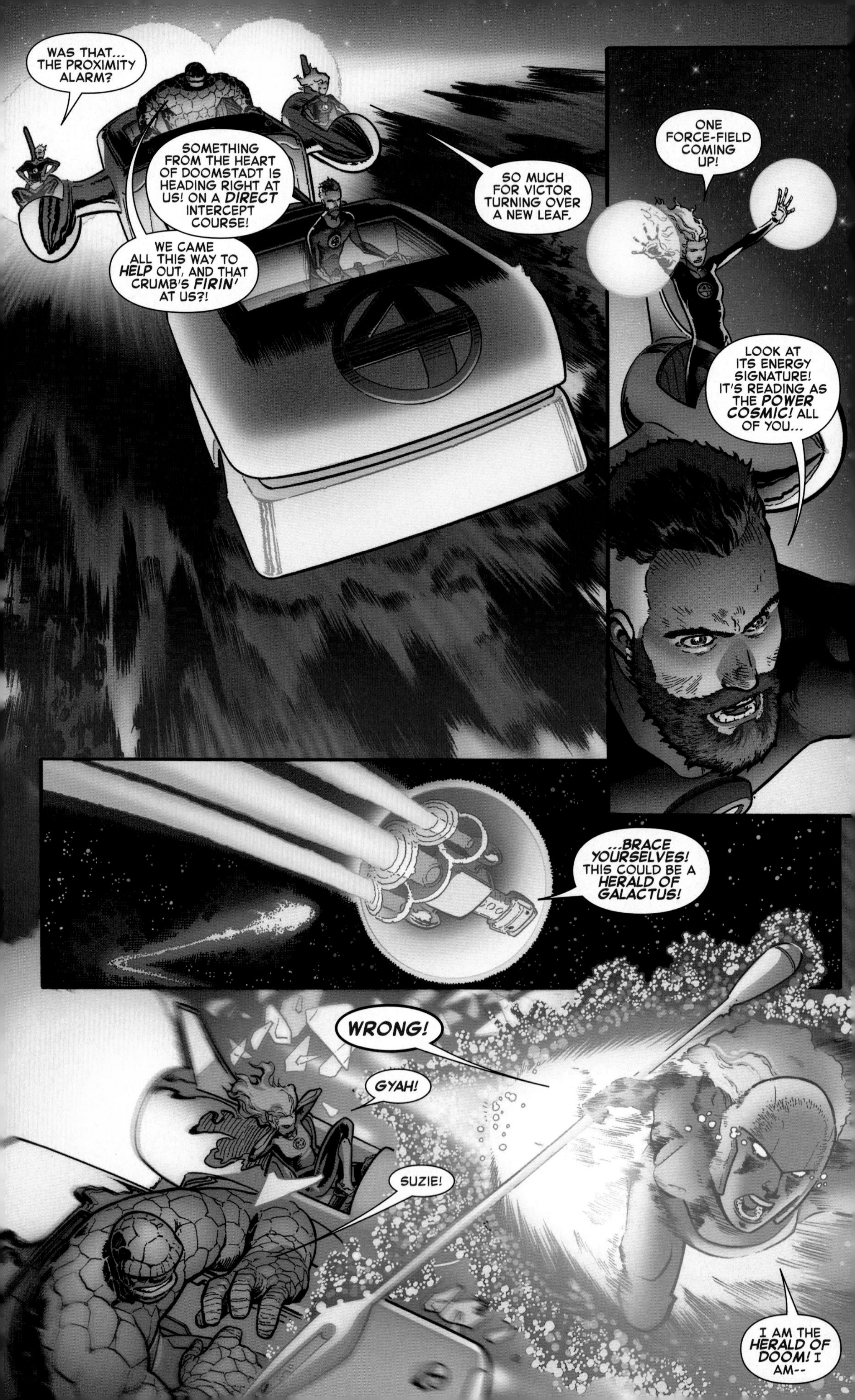

WAS THAT... THE PROXIMITY ALARM?
SOMETHING FROM THE HEART OF DOOMSTADT IS HEADING RIGHT AT US! ON A *DIRECT* INTERCEPT COURSE!
WE CAME ALL THIS WAY TO *HELP* OUT, AND THAT CRUMB'S *FIRIN'* AT US?!
SO MUCH FOR VICTOR TURNING OVER A NEW LEAF.
ONE FORCE-FIELD COMING UP!
LOOK AT ITS ENERGY SIGNATURE! IT'S READING AS THE *POWER COSMIC!* ALL OF YOU...
*...BRACE YOURSELVES!* THIS COULD BE A *HERALD OF GALACTUS!*
*WRONG!*
*GYAH!*
SUZIE!
I AM THE *HERALD OF DOOM!* I AM--

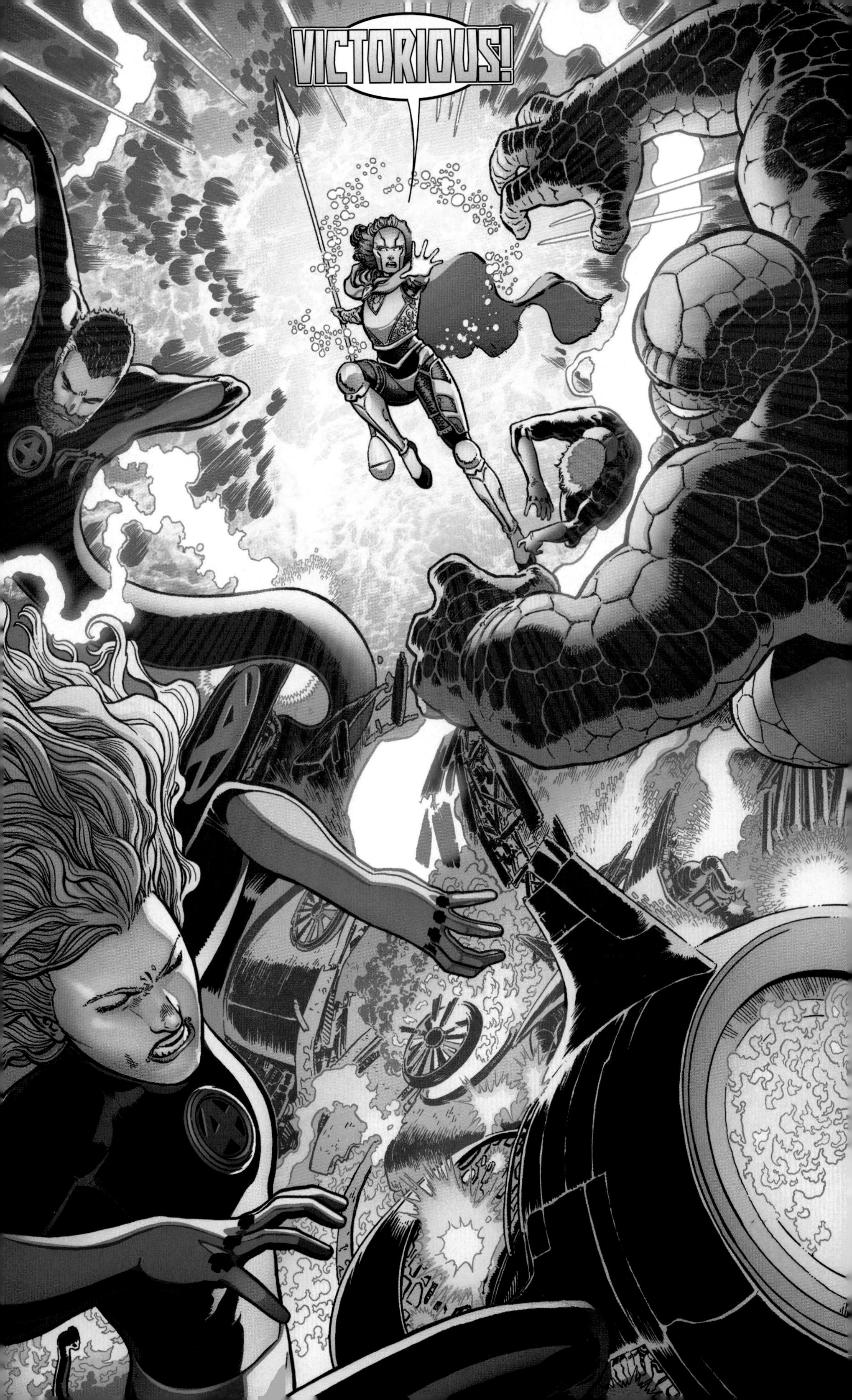
VICTORIOUS!

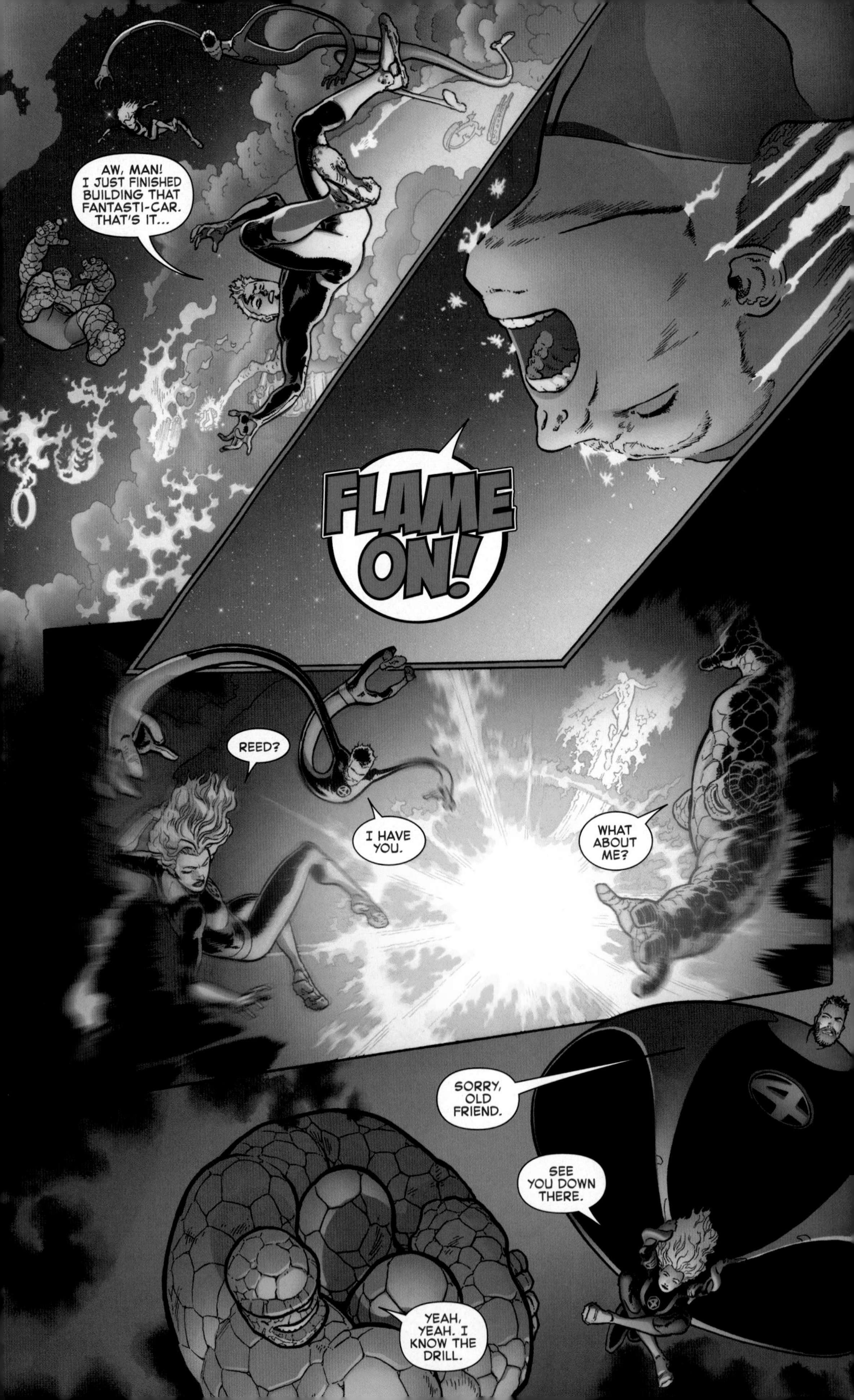
AW, MAN! I JUST FINISHED BUILDING THAT FANTASTI-CAR. THAT'S IT...
FLAME ON!
REED?
I HAVE YOU.
WHAT ABOUT ME?
SORRY, OLD FRIEND.
SEE YOU DOWN THERE.
YEAH, YEAH. I KNOW THE DRILL.

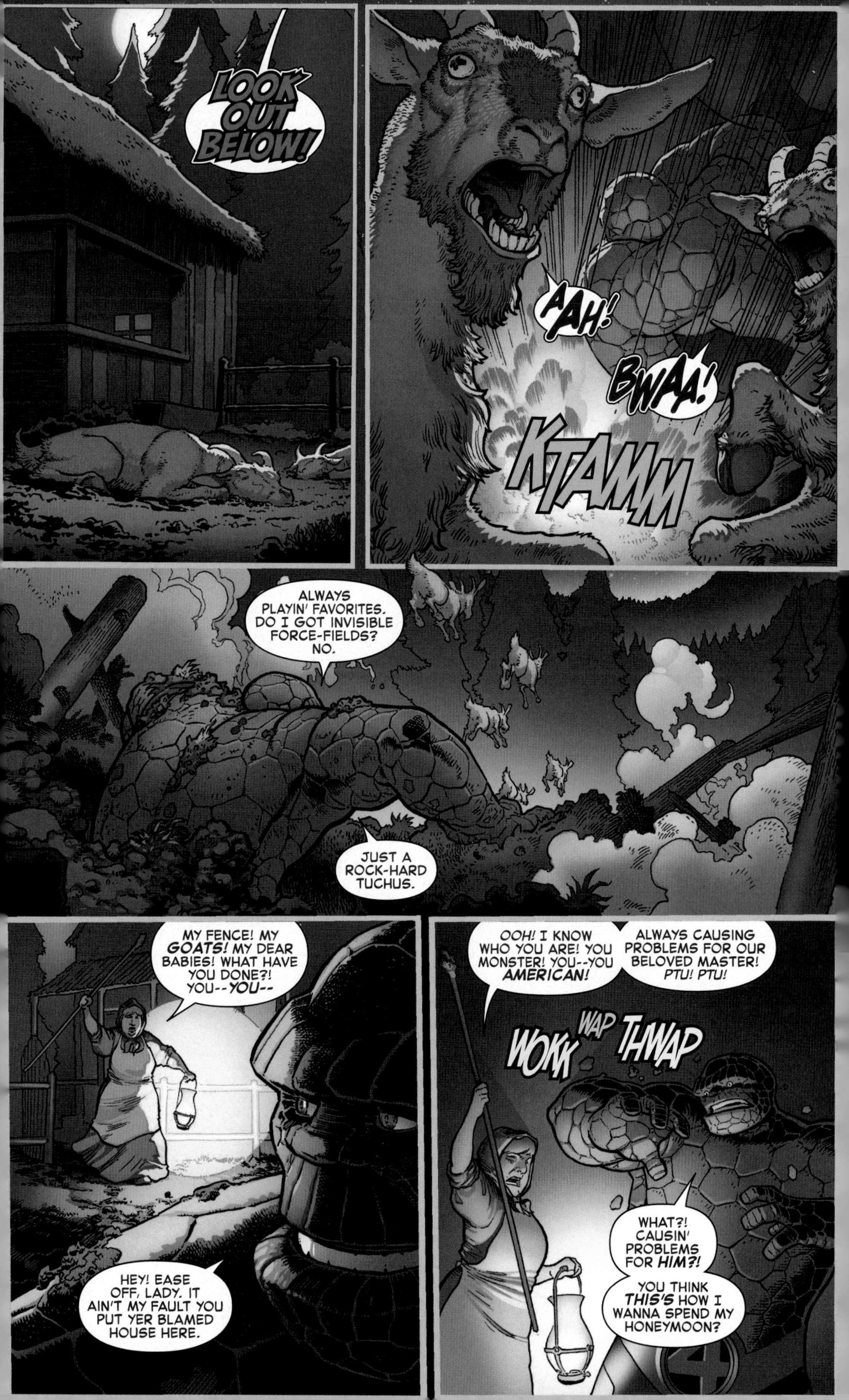
LOOK OUT BELOW!
AAH!
BWAA!
KTAMM
ALWAYS PLAYIN' FAVORITES. DO I GOT INVISIBLE FORCE-FIELDS? NO.
JUST A ROCK-HARD TUCHUS.
MY FENCE! MY GOATS! MY DEAR BABIES! WHAT HAVE YOU DONE?! YOU--YOU--
HEY! EASE OFF, LADY. IT AIN'T MY FAULT YOU PUT YER BLAMED HOUSE HERE.
OOH! I KNOW WHO YOU ARE! YOU MONSTER! YOU--YOU AMERICAN!
ALWAYS CAUSING PROBLEMS FOR OUR BELOVED MASTER! PTU! PTU!
WOKK WAP THWAP
WHAT?! CAUSIN' PROBLEMS FOR HIM?!
YOU THINK THIS'S HOW I WANNA SPEND MY HONEYMOON?

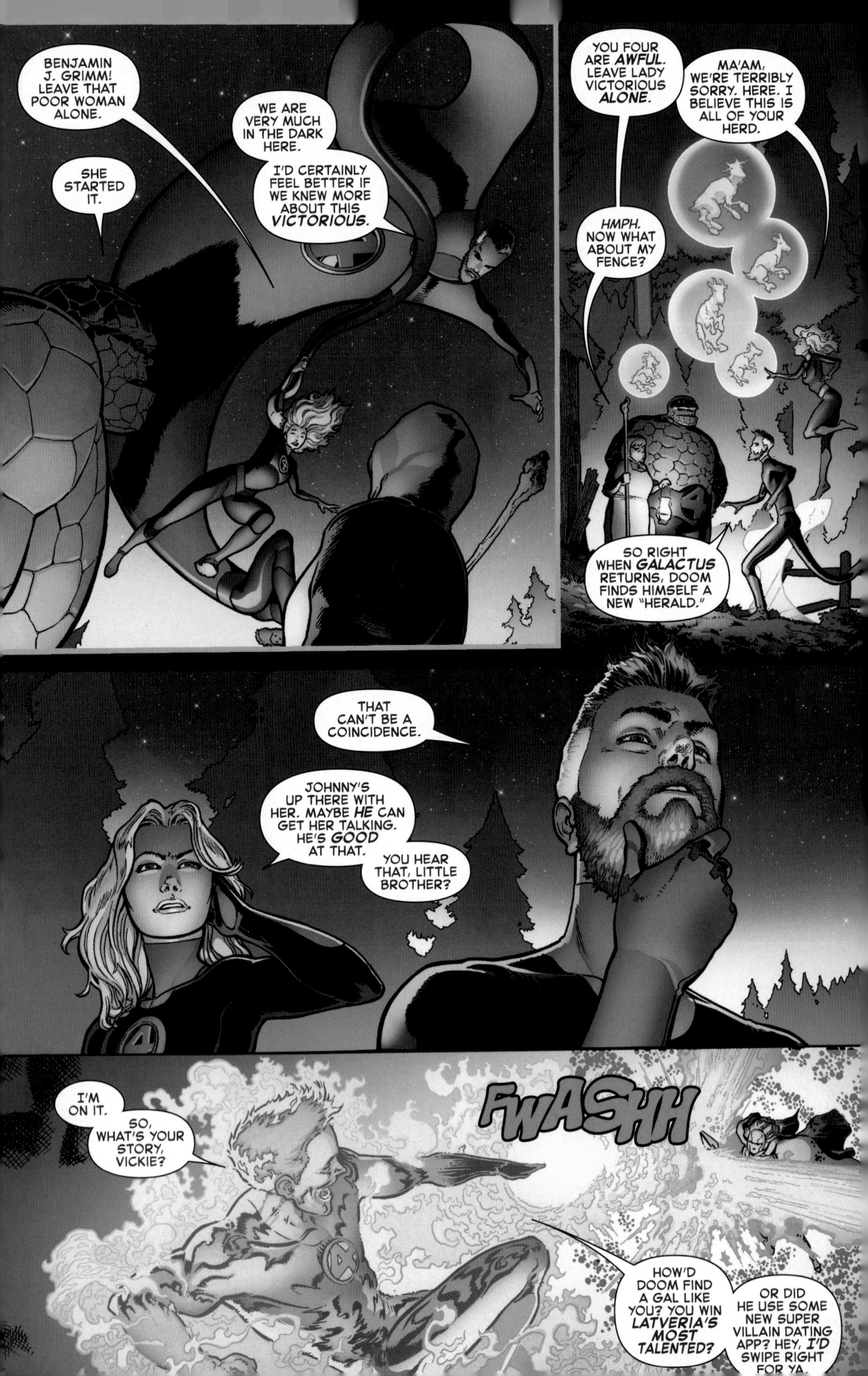
BENJAMIN J. GRIMM! LEAVE THAT POOR WOMAN ALONE.
SHE STARTED IT.
WE ARE VERY MUCH IN THE DARK HERE.
I'D CERTAINLY FEEL BETTER IF WE KNEW MORE ABOUT THIS VICTORIOUS.
YOU FOUR ARE AWFUL. LEAVE LADY VICTORIOUS ALONE.
MA'AM, WE'RE TERRIBLY SORRY. HERE. I BELIEVE THIS IS ALL OF YOUR HERD.
HMPH. NOW WHAT ABOUT MY FENCE?
SO RIGHT WHEN GALACTUS RETURNS, DOOM FINDS HIMSELF A NEW "HERALD."
THAT CAN'T BE A COINCIDENCE.
JOHNNY'S UP THERE WITH HER. MAYBE HE CAN GET HER TALKING. HE'S GOOD AT THAT.
YOU HEAR THAT, LITTLE BROTHER?
I'M ON IT.
SO, WHAT'S YOUR STORY, VICKIE?
FWASHH
HOW'D DOOM FIND A GAL LIKE YOU? YOU WIN LATVERIA'S MOST TALENTED?
OR DID HE USE SOME NEW SUPER VILLAIN DATING APP? HEY, I'D SWIPE RIGHT FOR YA.

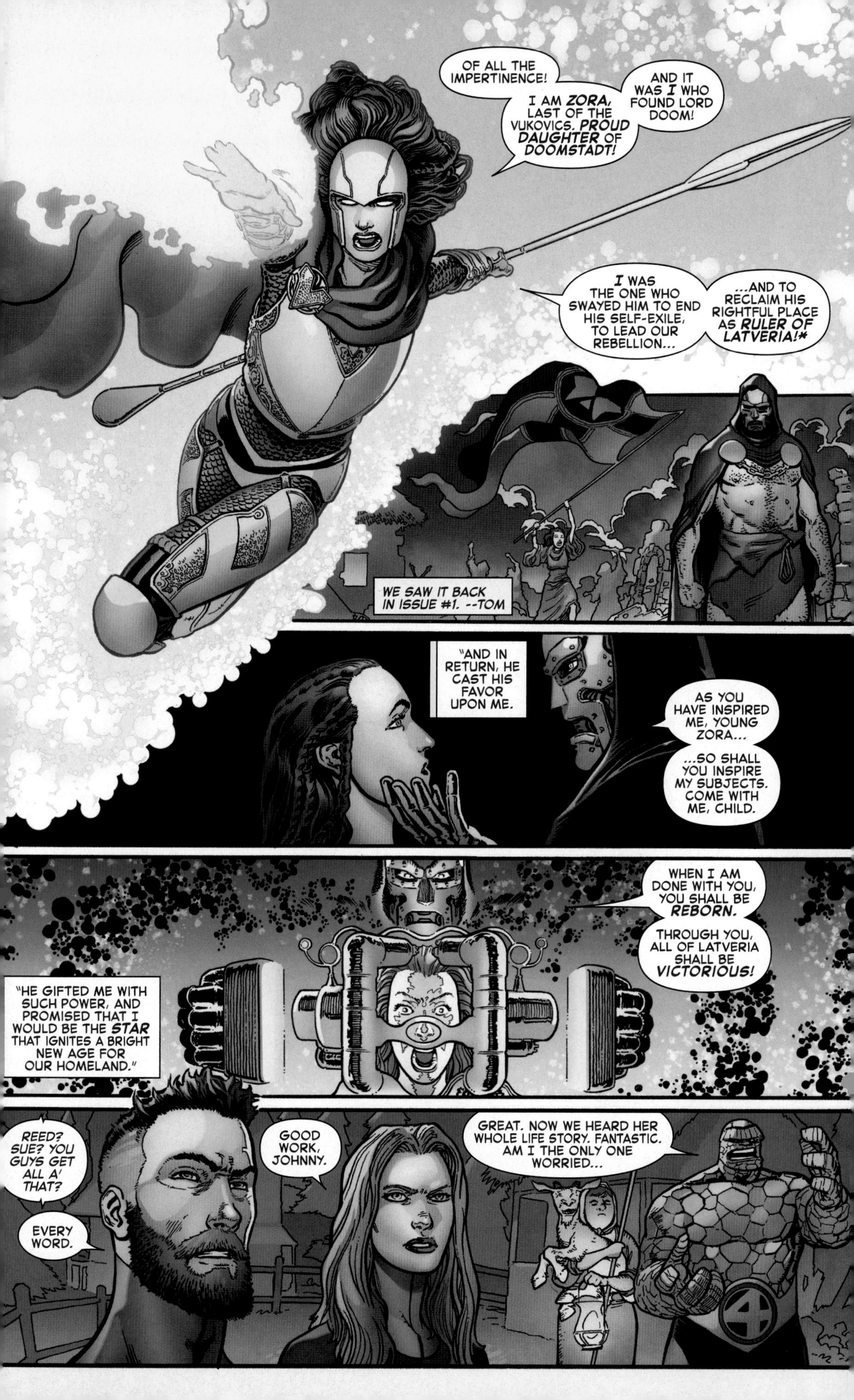

OF ALL THE IMPERTINENCE!
I AM ZORA, LAST OF THE VUKOVICS. PROUD DAUGHTER OF DOOMSTADT!
AND IT WAS I WHO FOUND LORD DOOM!
I WAS THE ONE WHO SWAYED HIM TO END HIS SELF-EXILE, TO LEAD OUR REBELLION...
...AND TO RECLAIM HIS RIGHTFUL PLACE AS RULER OF LATVERIA!*
WE SAW IT BACK IN ISSUE #1. --TOM
"AND IN RETURN, HE CAST HIS FAVOR UPON ME.
AS YOU HAVE INSPIRED ME, YOUNG ZORA...
...SO SHALL YOU INSPIRE MY SUBJECTS. COME WITH ME, CHILD.
"HE GIFTED ME WITH SUCH POWER, AND PROMISED THAT I WOULD BE THE STAR THAT IGNITES A BRIGHT NEW AGE FOR OUR HOMELAND."
WHEN I AM DONE WITH YOU, YOU SHALL BE REBORN.
THROUGH YOU, ALL OF LATVERIA SHALL BE VICTORIOUS!
REED? SUE? YOU GUYS GET ALL A' THAT?
EVERY WORD.
GOOD WORK, JOHNNY.
GREAT. NOW WE HEARD HER WHOLE LIFE STORY. FANTASTIC. AM I THE ONLY ONE WORRIED...

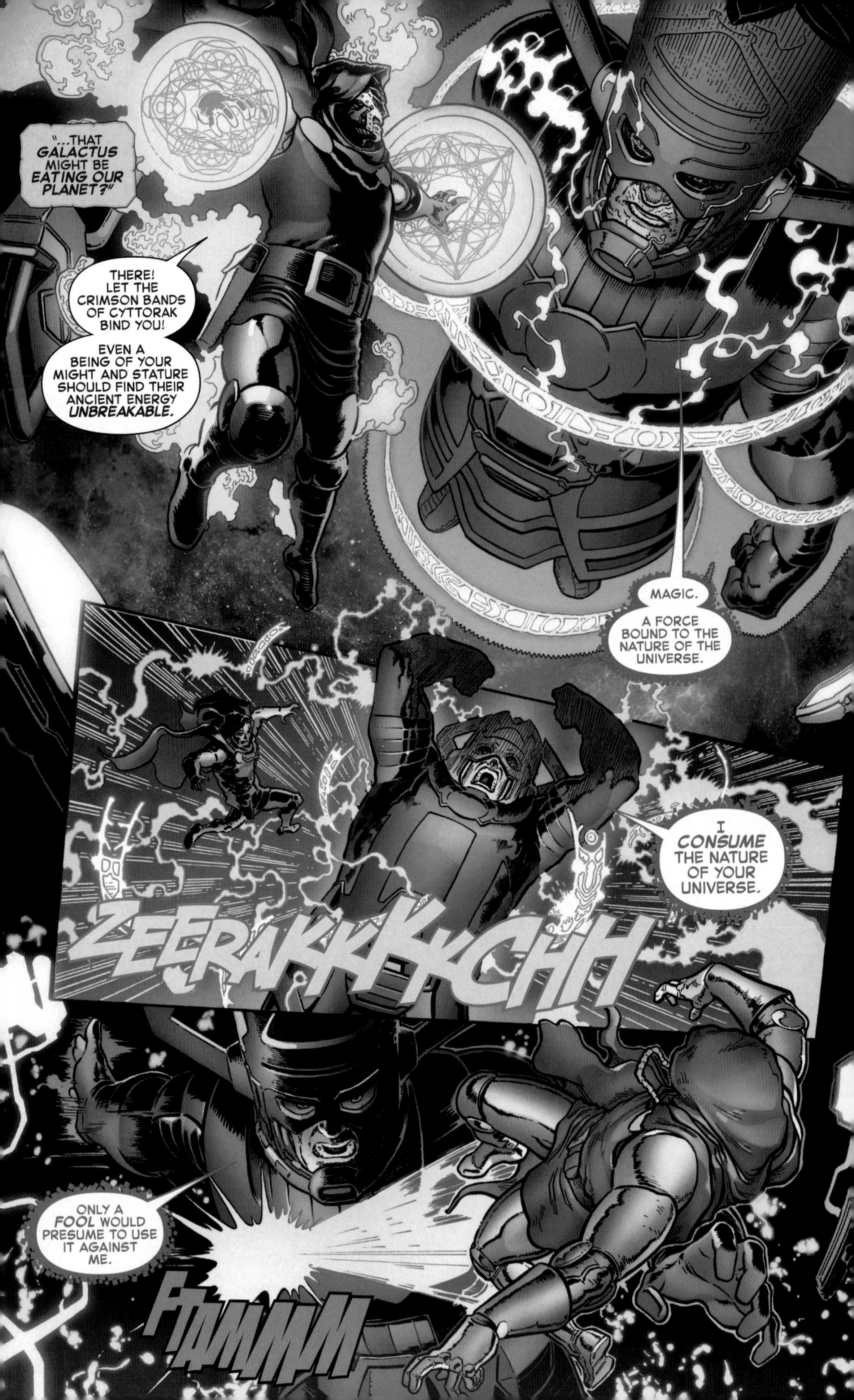
"...THAT GALACTUS MIGHT BE EATING OUR PLANET?"
THERE! LET THE CRIMSON BANDS OF CYTTORAK BIND YOU!
EVEN A BEING OF YOUR MIGHT AND STATURE SHOULD FIND THEIR ANCIENT ENERGY UNBREAKABLE.
MAGIC.
A FORCE BOUND TO THE NATURE OF THE UNIVERSE.
I CONSUME THE NATURE OF YOUR UNIVERSE.
ZEERAKKKCHH
ONLY A FOOL WOULD PRESUME TO USE IT AGAINST ME.
FTAMMM

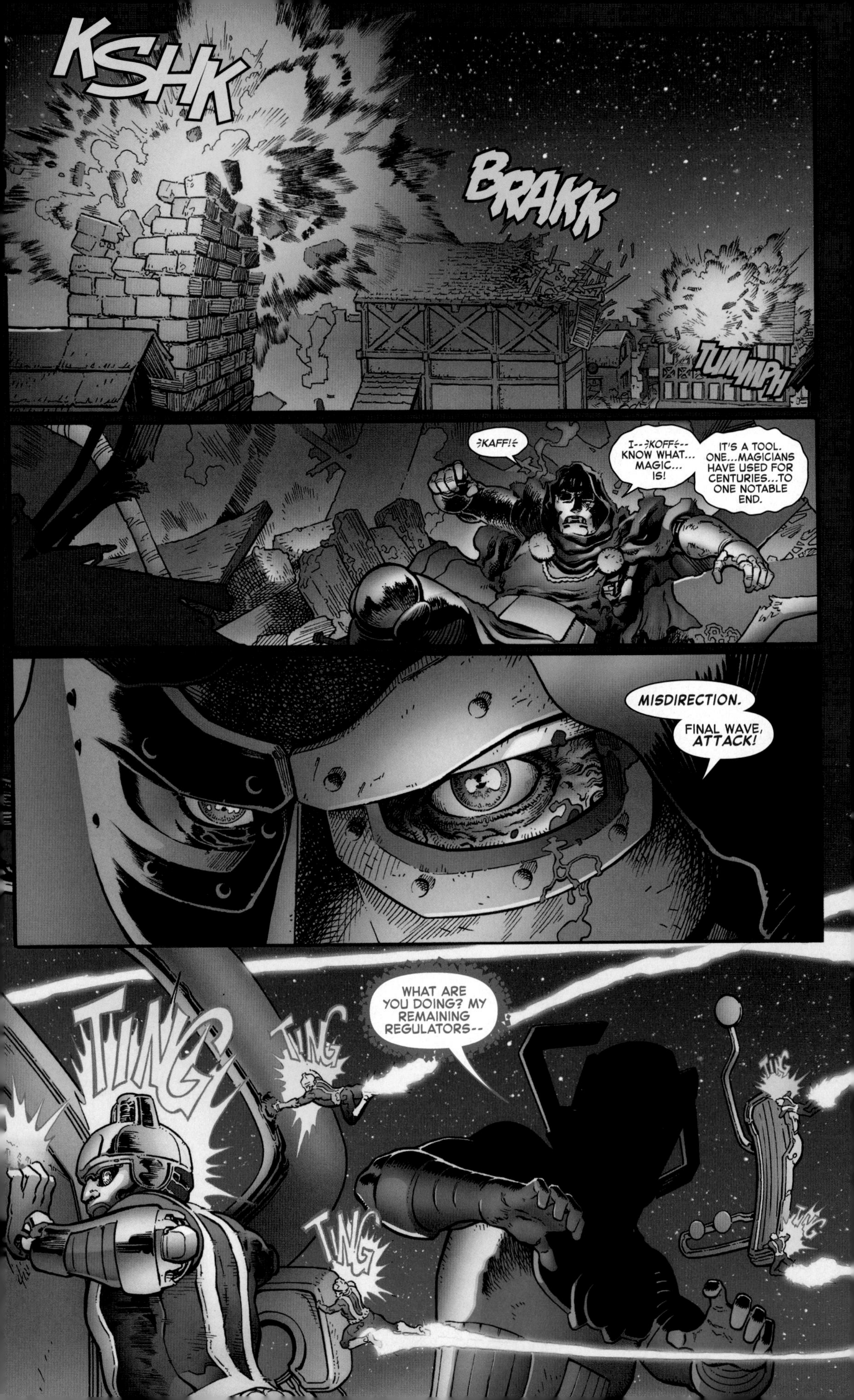
KSHK
BRAKK
TUMMPH
*KAFF!*
I--*KOFF*-- KNOW WHAT... MAGIC... IS!
IT'S A TOOL. ONE...MAGICIANS HAVE USED FOR CENTURIES...TO ONE NOTABLE END.
MISDIRECTION.
FINAL WAVE, ATTACK!
WHAT ARE YOU DOING? MY REMAINING REGULATORS--
TING
TING
TING
TING
TING

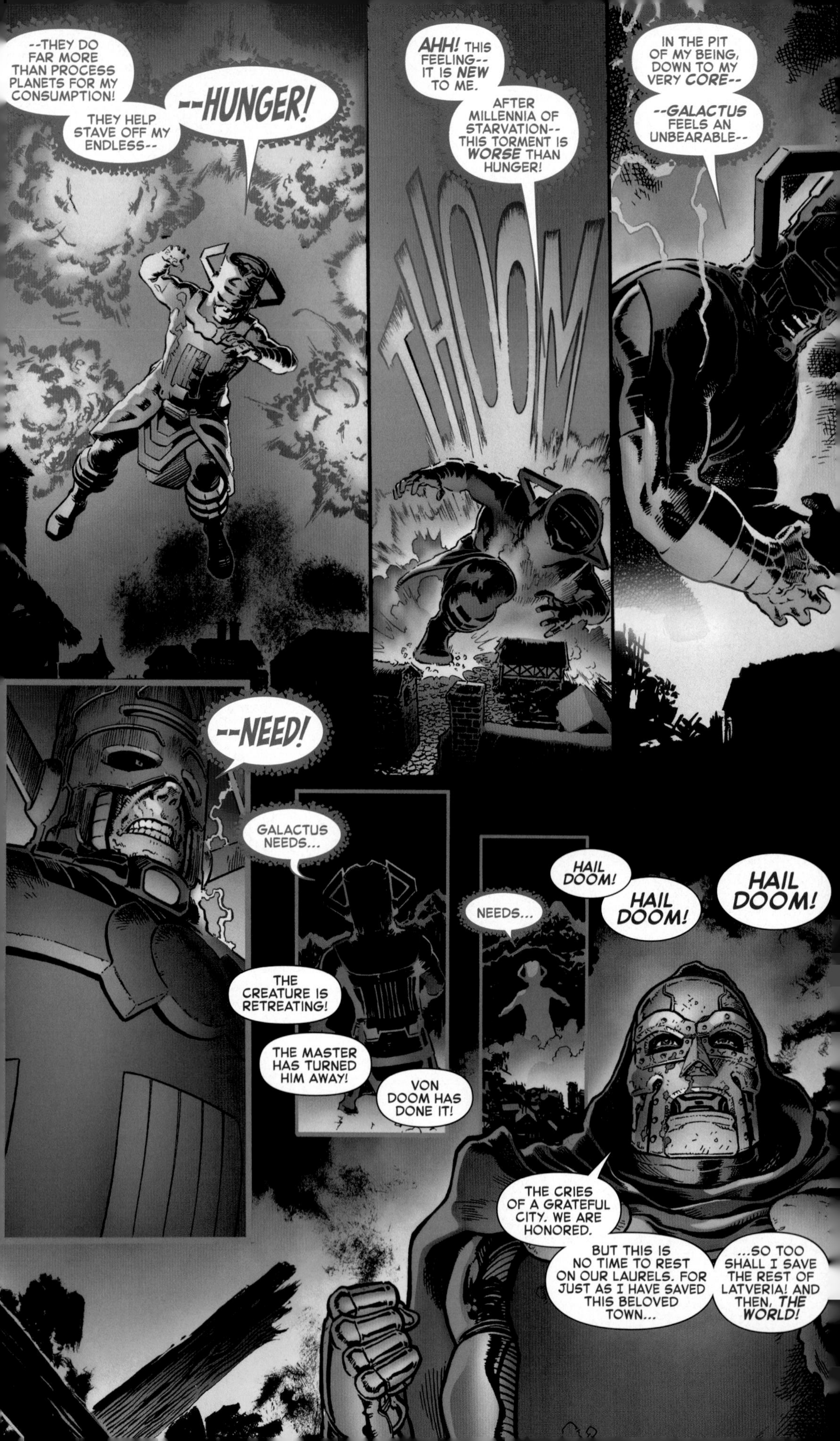
--THEY DO FAR MORE THAN PROCESS PLANETS FOR MY CONSUMPTION!
THEY HELP STAVE OFF MY ENDLESS--
--HUNGER!
AHH! THIS FEELING-- IT IS NEW TO ME.
AFTER MILLENNIA OF STARVATION-- THIS TORMENT IS WORSE THAN HUNGER!
THOOM
IN THE PIT OF MY BEING, DOWN TO MY VERY CORE--
--GALACTUS FEELS AN UNBEARABLE--
--NEED!
GALACTUS NEEDS...
THE CREATURE IS RETREATING!
THE MASTER HAS TURNED HIM AWAY!
VON DOOM HAS DONE IT!
NEEDS...
HAIL DOOM!
HAIL DOOM!
HAIL DOOM!
THE CRIES OF A GRATEFUL CITY. WE ARE HONORED.
BUT THIS IS NO TIME TO REST ON OUR LAURELS. FOR JUST AS I HAVE SAVED THIS BELOVED TOWN...
...SO TOO SHALL I SAVE THE REST OF LATVERIA! AND THEN, THE WORLD!

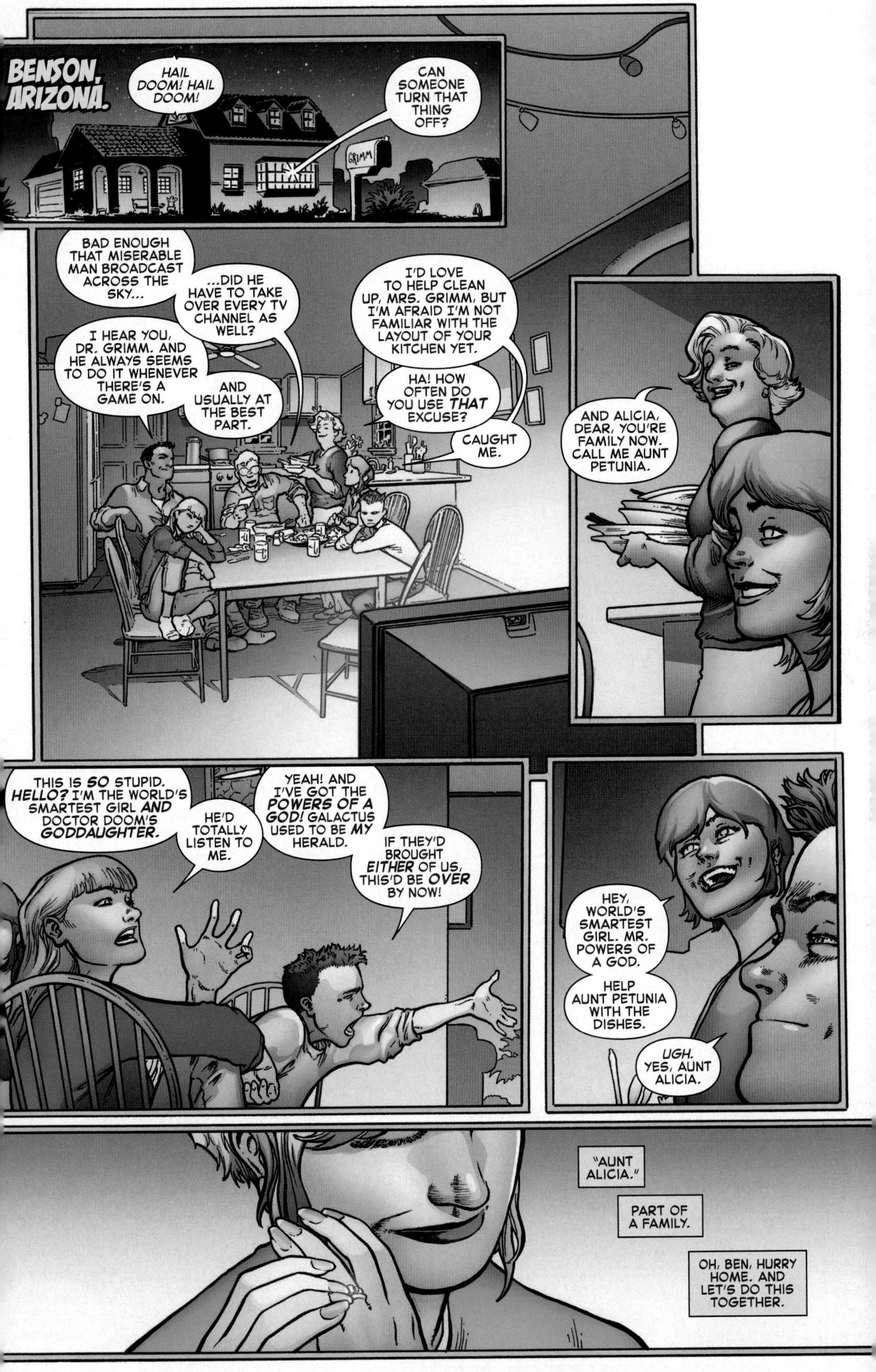

BENSON, ARIZONA.
HAIL DOOM! HAIL DOOM!
CAN SOMEONE TURN THAT THING OFF?
GRIMM
BAD ENOUGH THAT MISERABLE MAN BROADCAST ACROSS THE SKY...
...DID HE HAVE TO TAKE OVER EVERY TV CHANNEL AS WELL?
I HEAR YOU, DR. GRIMM. AND HE ALWAYS SEEMS TO DO IT WHENEVER THERE'S A GAME ON.
AND USUALLY AT THE BEST PART.
I'D LOVE TO HELP CLEAN UP, MRS. GRIMM, BUT I'M AFRAID I'M NOT FAMILIAR WITH THE LAYOUT OF YOUR KITCHEN YET.
HA! HOW OFTEN DO YOU USE THAT EXCUSE?
CAUGHT ME.
AND ALICIA, DEAR, YOU'RE FAMILY NOW. CALL ME AUNT PETUNIA.
THIS IS SO STUPID. HELLO? I'M THE WORLD'S SMARTEST GIRL AND DOCTOR DOOM'S GODDAUGHTER.
HE'D TOTALLY LISTEN TO ME.
YEAH! AND I'VE GOT THE POWERS OF A GOD! GALACTUS USED TO BE MY HERALD.
IF THEY'D BROUGHT EITHER OF US, THIS'D BE OVER BY NOW!
HEY, WORLD'S SMARTEST GIRL. MR. POWERS OF A GOD.
HELP AUNT PETUNIA WITH THE DISHES.
UGH. YES, AUNT ALICIA.
"AUNT ALICIA."
PART OF A FAMILY.
OH, BEN, HURRY HOME. AND LET'S DO THIS TOGETHER.

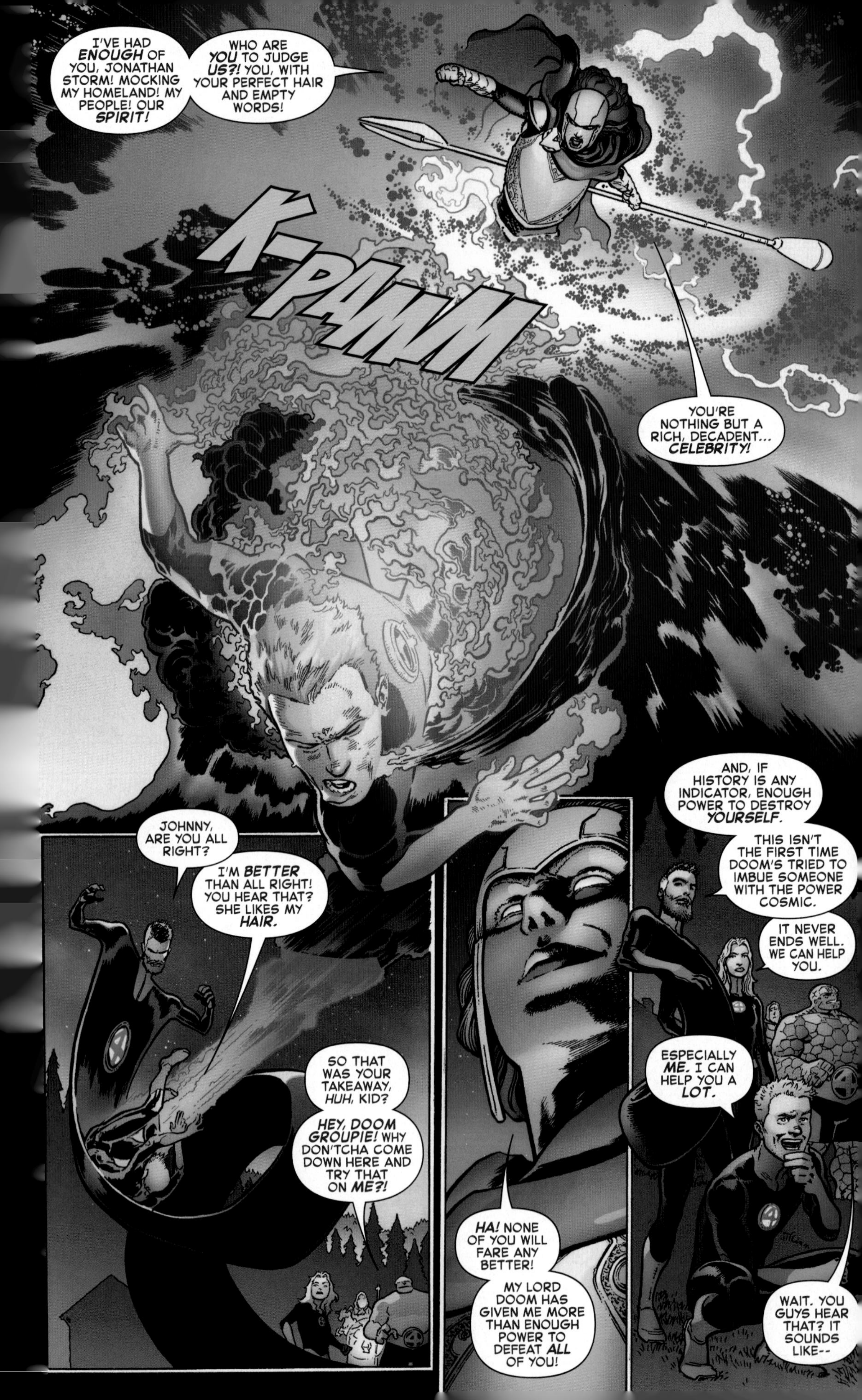
I'VE HAD ENOUGH OF YOU, JONATHAN STORM! MOCKING MY HOMELAND! MY PEOPLE! OUR SPIRIT!
WHO ARE YOU TO JUDGE US?! YOU, WITH YOUR PERFECT HAIR AND EMPTY WORDS!
K-PAMM
YOU'RE NOTHING BUT A RICH, DECADENT... CELEBRITY!
JOHNNY, ARE YOU ALL RIGHT?
I'M BETTER THAN ALL RIGHT! YOU HEAR THAT? SHE LIKES MY HAIR.
SO THAT WAS YOUR TAKEAWAY, HUH, KID?
HEY, DOOM GROUPIE! WHY DON'TCHA COME DOWN HERE AND TRY THAT ON ME?!
HA! NONE OF YOU WILL FARE ANY BETTER!
MY LORD DOOM HAS GIVEN ME MORE THAN ENOUGH POWER TO DEFEAT ALL OF YOU!
AND, IF HISTORY IS ANY INDICATOR, ENOUGH POWER TO DESTROY YOURSELF.
THIS ISN'T THE FIRST TIME DOOM'S TRIED TO IMBUE SOMEONE WITH THE POWER COSMIC.
IT NEVER ENDS WELL. WE CAN HELP YOU.
ESPECIALLY ME. I CAN HELP YOU A LOT.
WAIT. YOU GUYS HEAR THAT? IT SOUNDS LIKE--

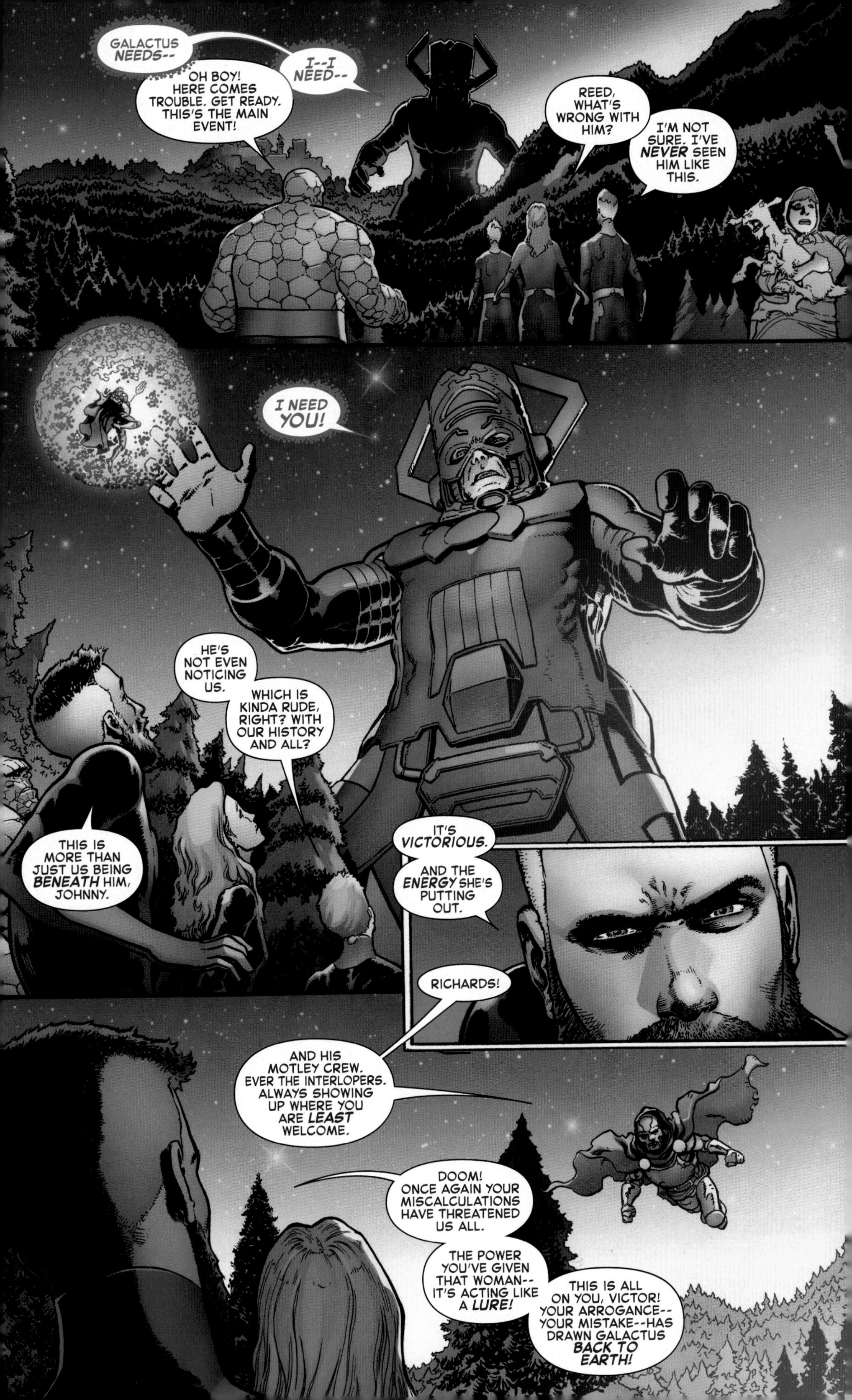
GALACTUS NEEDS--
I--I NEED--
OH BOY! HERE COMES TROUBLE. GET READY. THIS'S THE MAIN EVENT!
REED, WHAT'S WRONG WITH HIM?
I'M NOT SURE. I'VE NEVER SEEN HIM LIKE THIS.
I NEED YOU!
HE'S NOT EVEN NOTICING US.
WHICH IS KINDA RUDE, RIGHT? WITH OUR HISTORY AND ALL?
THIS IS MORE THAN JUST US BEING BENEATH HIM, JOHNNY.
IT'S VICTORIOUS.
AND THE ENERGY SHE'S PUTTING OUT.
RICHARDS!
AND HIS MOTLEY CREW. EVER THE INTERLOPERS. ALWAYS SHOWING UP WHERE YOU ARE LEAST WELCOME.
DOOM! ONCE AGAIN YOUR MISCALCULATIONS HAVE THREATENED US ALL.
THE POWER YOU'VE GIVEN THAT WOMAN-- IT'S ACTING LIKE A LURE!
THIS IS ALL ON YOU, VICTOR! YOUR ARROGANCE-- YOUR MISTAKE--HAS DRAWN GALACTUS BACK TO EARTH!

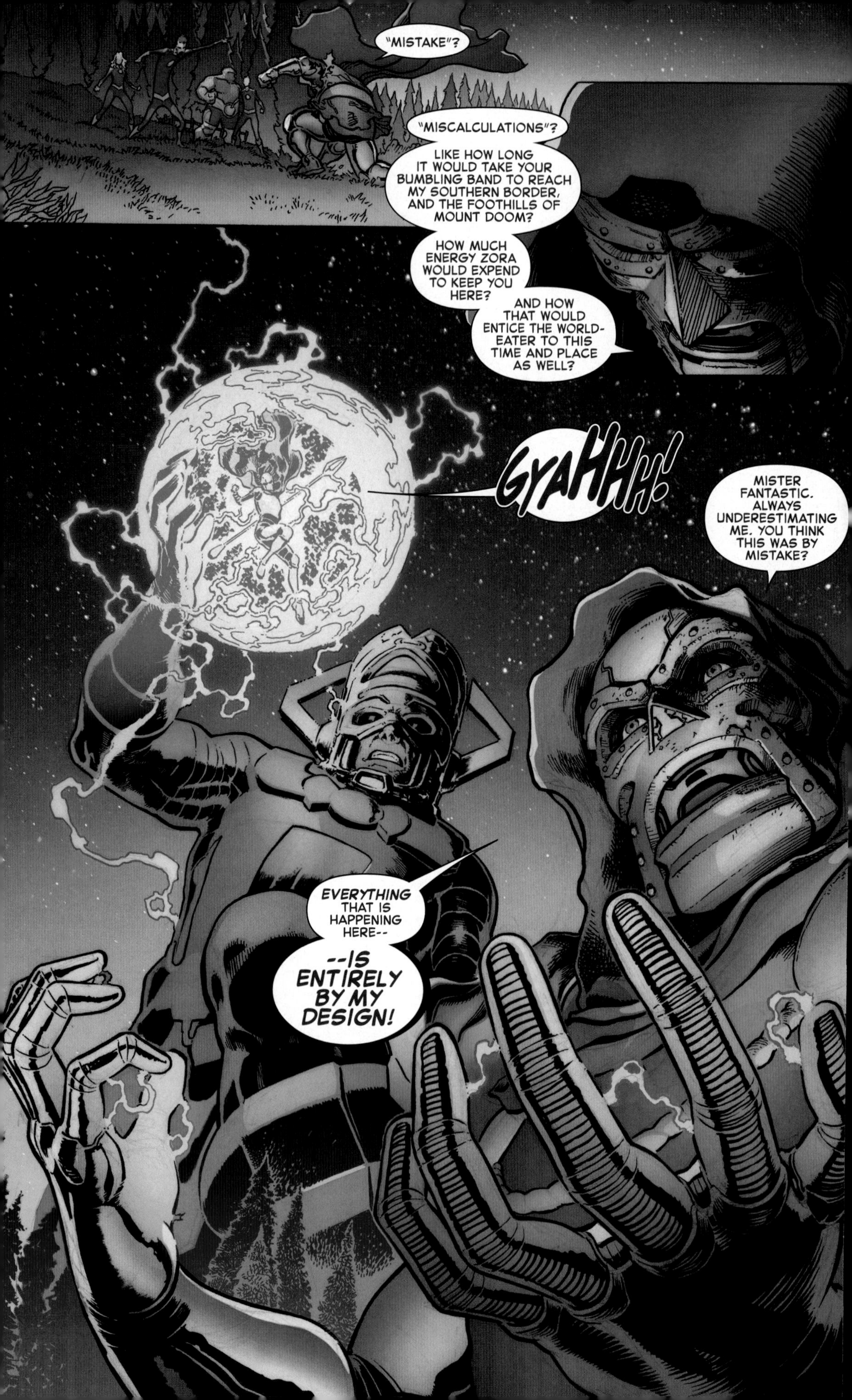
"MISTAKE"?
"MISCALCULATIONS"?
LIKE HOW LONG IT WOULD TAKE YOUR BUMBLING BAND TO REACH MY SOUTHERN BORDER, AND THE FOOTHILLS OF MOUNT DOOM?
HOW MUCH ENERGY ZORA WOULD EXPEND TO KEEP YOU HERE?
AND HOW THAT WOULD ENTICE THE WORLD-EATER TO THIS TIME AND PLACE AS WELL?
GYAHHHH!
MISTER FANTASTIC. ALWAYS UNDERESTIMATING ME. YOU THINK THIS WAS BY MISTAKE?
EVERYTHING THAT IS HAPPENING HERE--
--IS ENTIRELY BY MY DESIGN!

# 7

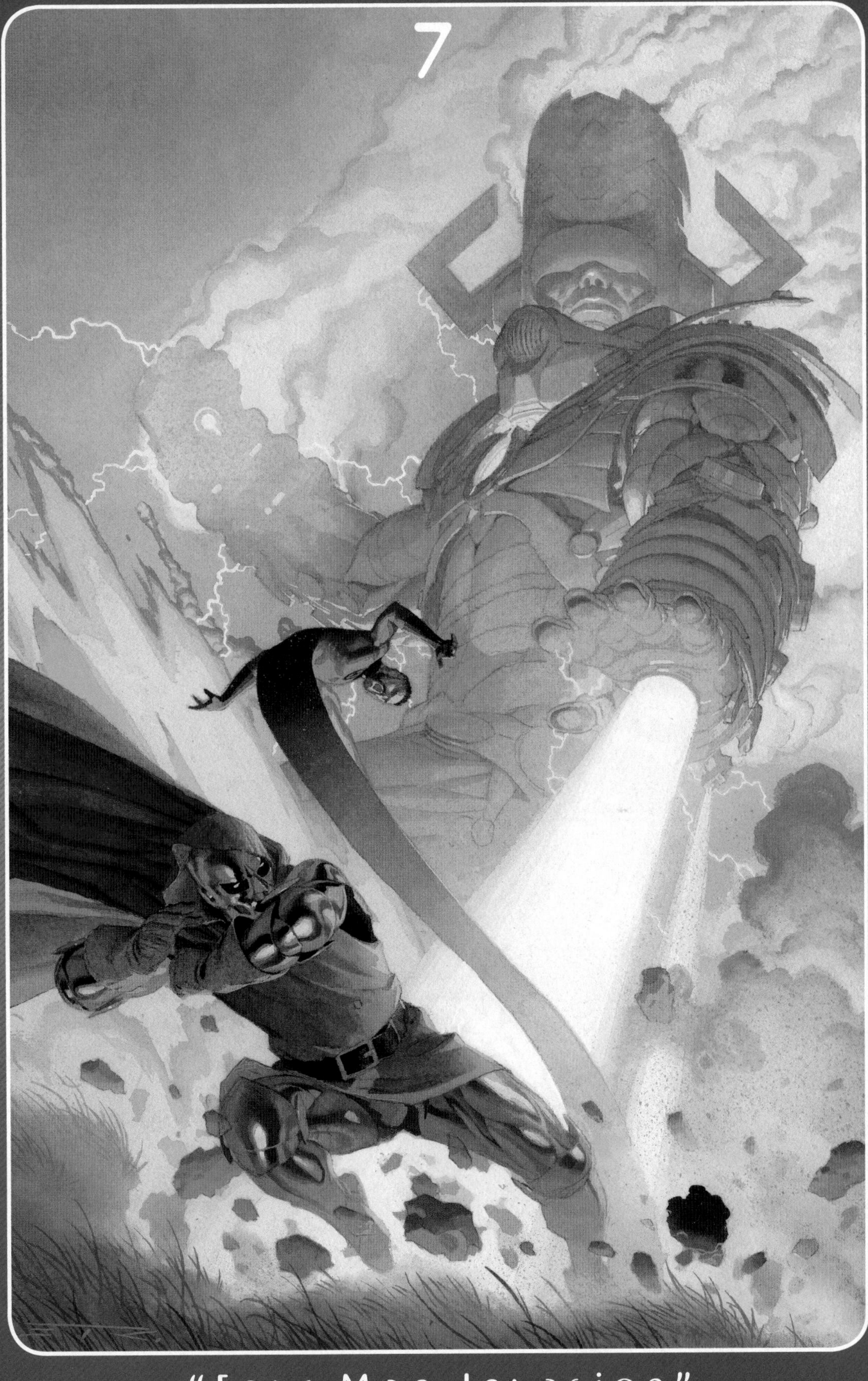

"Four-Man Invasion"

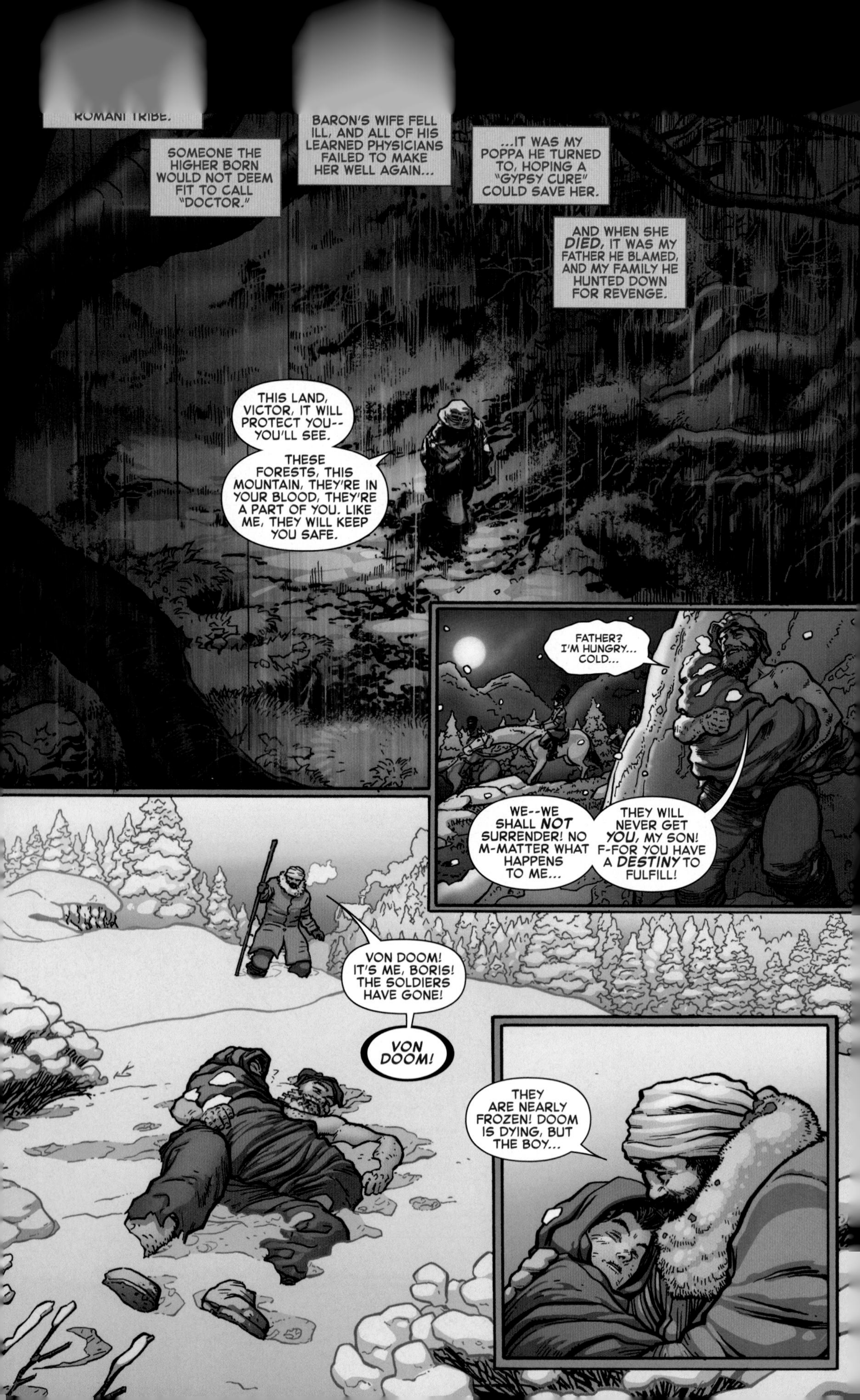
ROMANI TRIBE.
SOMEONE THE HIGHER BORN WOULD NOT DEEM FIT TO CALL "DOCTOR."
BARON'S WIFE FELL ILL, AND ALL OF HIS LEARNED PHYSICIANS FAILED TO MAKE HER WELL AGAIN...
...IT WAS MY POPPA HE TURNED TO, HOPING A "GYPSY CURE" COULD SAVE HER.
AND WHEN SHE DIED, IT WAS MY FATHER HE BLAMED, AND MY FAMILY HE HUNTED DOWN FOR REVENGE.
THIS LAND, VICTOR, IT WILL PROTECT YOU-- YOU'LL SEE.
THESE FORESTS, THIS MOUNTAIN, THEY'RE IN YOUR BLOOD, THEY'RE A PART OF YOU. LIKE ME, THEY WILL KEEP YOU SAFE.
FATHER? I'M HUNGRY... COLD...
THEY WILL NEVER GET YOU, MY SON! F-FOR YOU HAVE A DESTINY TO FULFILL!
WE--WE SHALL NOT SURRENDER! NO M-MATTER WHAT HAPPENS TO ME...
VON DOOM! IT'S ME, BORIS! THE SOLDIERS HAVE GONE!
VON DOOM!
THEY ARE NEARLY FROZEN! DOOM IS DYING, BUT THE BOY...

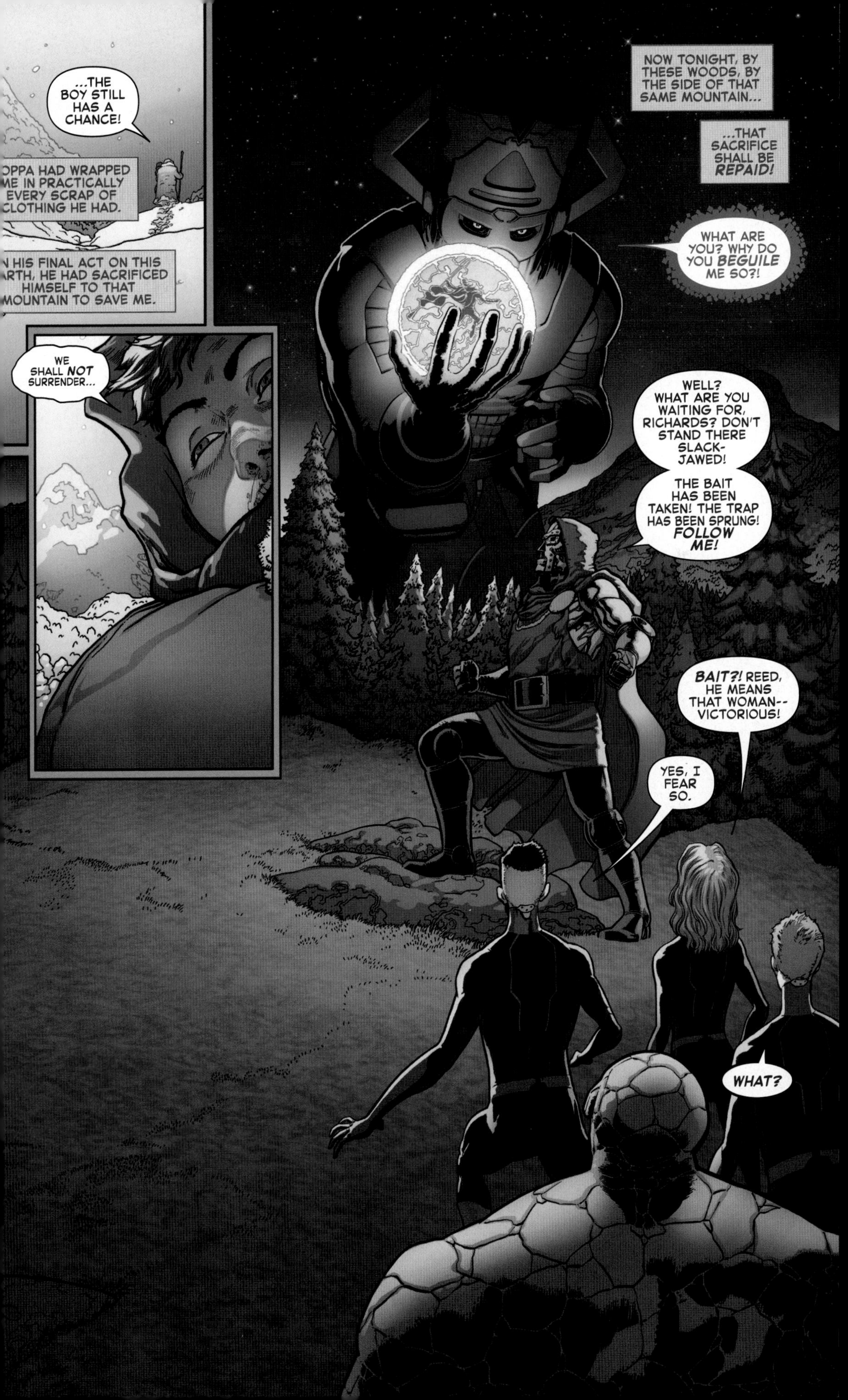
...THE BOY STILL HAS A CHANCE!
OPPA HAD WRAPPED ME IN PRACTICALLY EVERY SCRAP OF CLOTHING HE HAD.
N HIS FINAL ACT ON THIS ARTH, HE HAD SACRIFICED HIMSELF TO THAT MOUNTAIN TO SAVE ME.
WE SHALL NOT SURRENDER...
NOW TONIGHT, BY THESE WOODS, BY THE SIDE OF THAT SAME MOUNTAIN...
...THAT SACRIFICE SHALL BE REPAID!
WHAT ARE YOU? WHY DO YOU BEGUILE ME SO?!
WELL? WHAT ARE YOU WAITING FOR, RICHARDS? DON'T STAND THERE SLACK-JAWED!
THE BAIT HAS BEEN TAKEN! THE TRAP HAS BEEN SPRUNG! FOLLOW ME!
BAIT?! REED, HE MEANS THAT WOMAN--VICTORIOUS!
YES, I FEAR SO.
WHAT?

NEVER HAVE I KNOWN SUCH AN ALL-CONSUMING DESIRE!
THE ENERGIES INSIDE YOU--
--GIVE THEM TO ME!
GYAH!
HE'S KILLING HER! WE HAVE TO DO SOMETHING!
HOLD THAT THOUGHT, KID. REED, YOU SAID THAT GIRL'S POWER MIGHT MAKE HER GO KABOOM, RIGHT?
YOU'RE RIGHT. IT'S TOO CONVENIENT.
BUT IF GALACTUS IS SIPHONING IT OFF...?
NOT CONVENIENT, RICHARDS. ACCORDING TO PLAN.
VICTOR, YOU LURED GALACTUS HERE!
YOU'VE ENDANGERED VICTORIOUS! LATVERIA! THE ENTIRE EARTH!
I'M TELLING YOU, THERE ARE TOO MANY VARIABLES AT PLAY. YOU CAN'T HAVE ACCOUNTED FOR ALL OF THEM!
PERHAPS YOU COULDN'T, MISTER FANTASTIC.

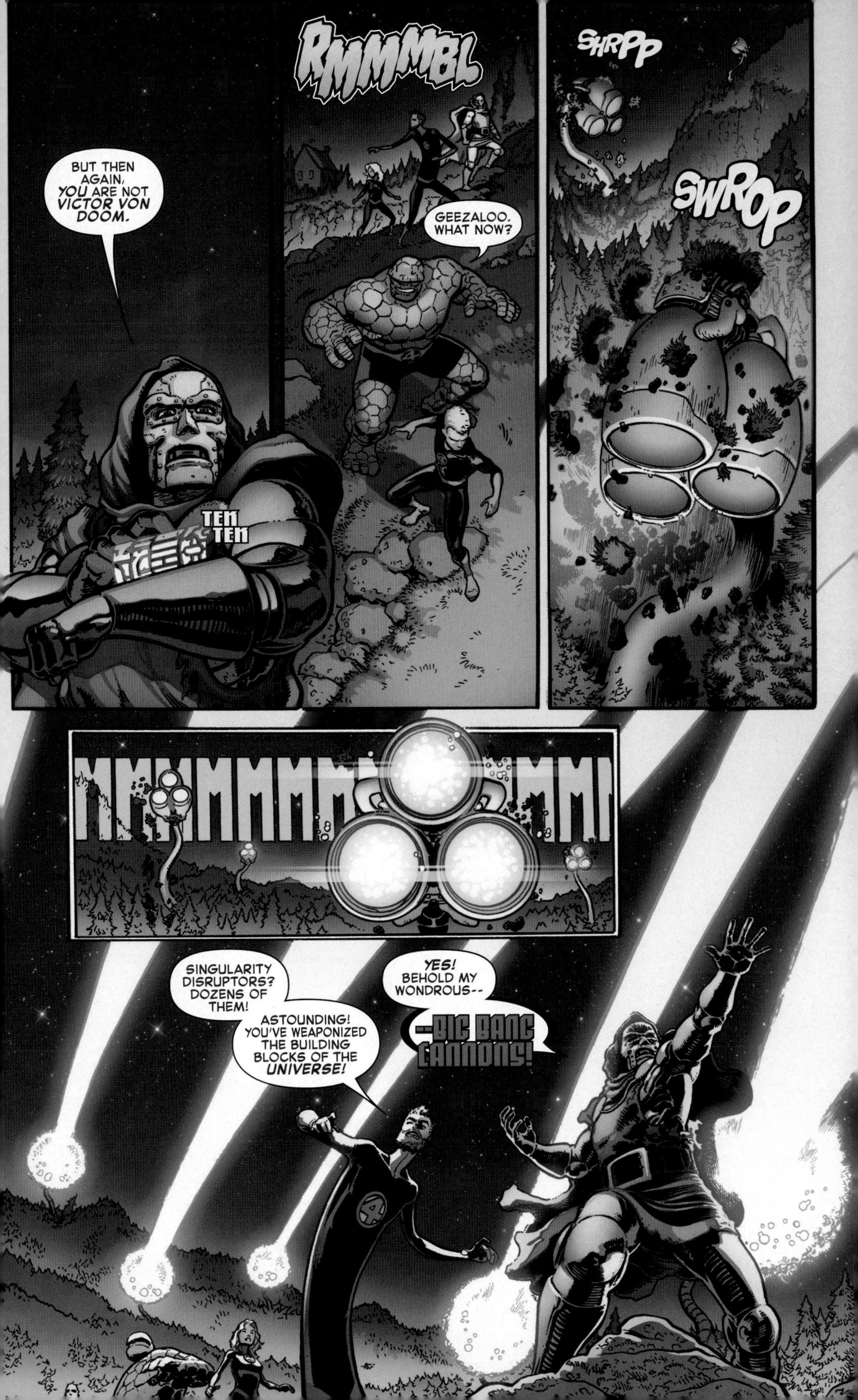
BUT THEN AGAIN, YOU ARE NOT VICTOR VON DOOM.
TEN TEN
RMMMBL
GEEZALOO. WHAT NOW?
SHRPP
SWROP
MMMMMMMMMMMMMMM
SINGULARITY DISRUPTORS? DOZENS OF THEM!
ASTOUNDING! YOU'VE WEAPONIZED THE BUILDING BLOCKS OF THE UNIVERSE!
YES! BEHOLD MY WONDROUS--
--BIG BANG CANNONS!

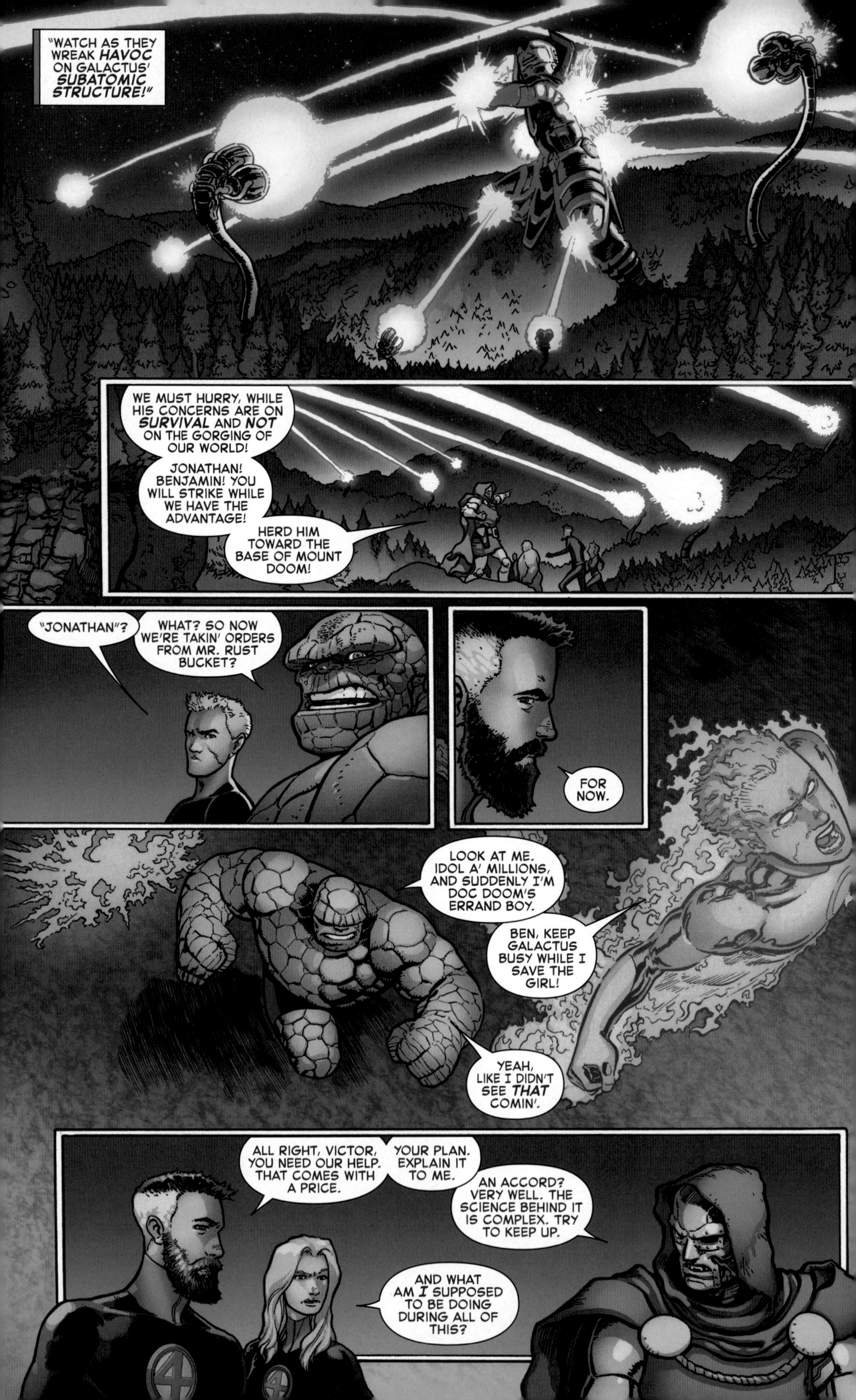
"WATCH AS THEY WREAK HAVOC ON GALACTUS' SUBATOMIC STRUCTURE!"
WE MUST HURRY, WHILE HIS CONCERNS ARE ON SURVIVAL AND NOT ON THE GORGING OF OUR WORLD!
JONATHAN! BENJAMIN! YOU WILL STRIKE WHILE WE HAVE THE ADVANTAGE!
HERD HIM TOWARD THE BASE OF MOUNT DOOM!
"JONATHAN"?
WHAT? SO NOW WE'RE TAKIN' ORDERS FROM MR. RUST BUCKET?
FOR NOW.
LOOK AT ME. IDOL A' MILLIONS, AND SUDDENLY I'M DOC DOOM'S ERRAND BOY.
BEN, KEEP GALACTUS BUSY WHILE I SAVE THE GIRL!
YEAH, LIKE I DIDN'T SEE THAT COMIN'.
ALL RIGHT, VICTOR, YOU NEED OUR HELP. THAT COMES WITH A PRICE.
YOUR PLAN. EXPLAIN IT TO ME.
AN ACCORD? VERY WELL. THE SCIENCE BEHIND IT IS COMPLEX. TRY TO KEEP UP.
AND WHAT AM I SUPPOSED TO BE DOING DURING ALL OF THIS?

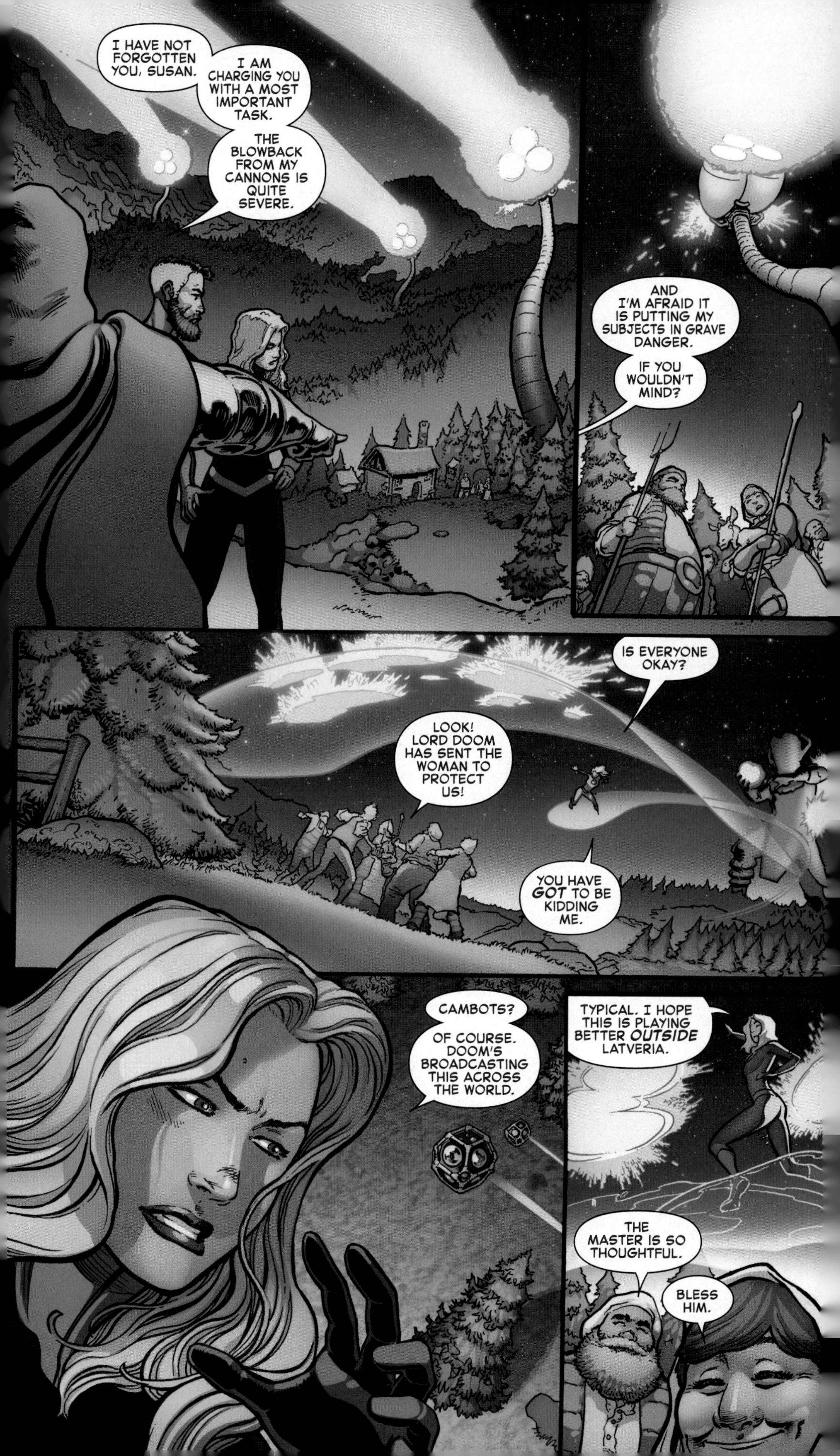
I HAVE NOT FORGOTTEN YOU, SUSAN.
I AM CHARGING YOU WITH A MOST IMPORTANT TASK.
THE BLOWBACK FROM MY CANNONS IS QUITE SEVERE.
AND I'M AFRAID IT IS PUTTING MY SUBJECTS IN GRAVE DANGER.
IF YOU WOULDN'T MIND?
IS EVERYONE OKAY?
LOOK! LORD DOOM HAS SENT THE WOMAN TO PROTECT US!
YOU HAVE GOT TO BE KIDDING ME.
CAMBOTS?
OF COURSE. DOOM'S BROADCASTING THIS ACROSS THE WORLD.
TYPICAL. I HOPE THIS IS PLAYING BETTER OUTSIDE LATVERIA.
THE MASTER IS SO THOUGHTFUL.
BLESS HIM.

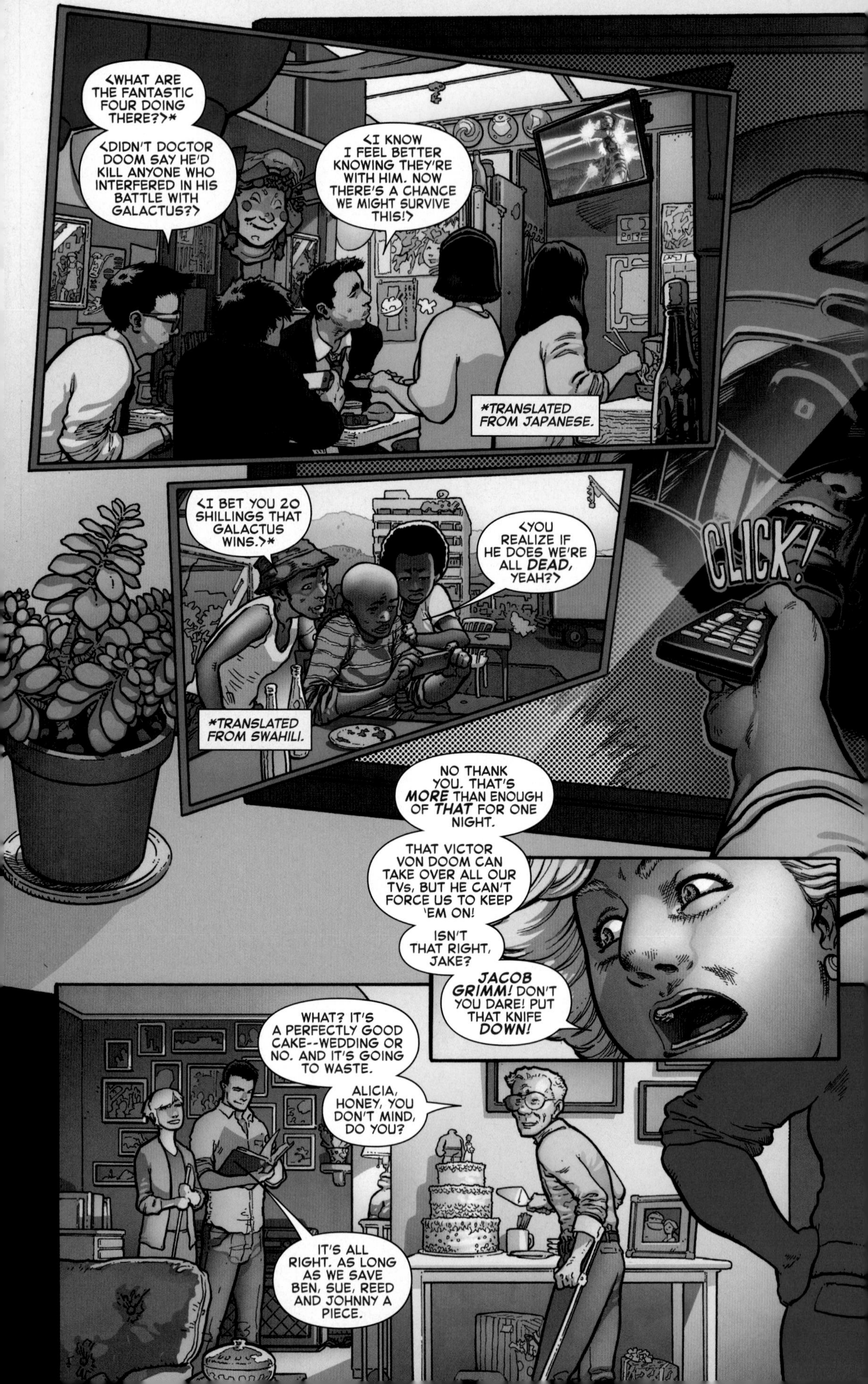
<WHAT ARE THE FANTASTIC FOUR DOING THERE?>*
<DIDN'T DOCTOR DOOM SAY HE'D KILL ANYONE WHO INTERFERED IN HIS BATTLE WITH GALACTUS?>
<I KNOW I FEEL BETTER KNOWING THEY'RE WITH HIM. NOW THERE'S A CHANCE WE MIGHT SURVIVE THIS!>
*TRANSLATED FROM JAPANESE.
<I BET YOU 20 SHILLINGS THAT GALACTUS WINS.>*
<YOU REALIZE IF HE DOES WE'RE ALL DEAD, YEAH?>
*TRANSLATED FROM SWAHILI.
CLICK!
NO THANK YOU. THAT'S MORE THAN ENOUGH OF THAT FOR ONE NIGHT.
THAT VICTOR VON DOOM CAN TAKE OVER ALL OUR TVs, BUT HE CAN'T FORCE US TO KEEP 'EM ON!
ISN'T THAT RIGHT, JAKE?
JACOB GRIMM! DON'T YOU DARE! PUT THAT KNIFE DOWN!
WHAT? IT'S A PERFECTLY GOOD CAKE--WEDDING OR NO. AND IT'S GOING TO WASTE.
ALICIA, HONEY, YOU DON'T MIND, DO YOU?
IT'S ALL RIGHT. AS LONG AS WE SAVE BEN, SUE, REED AND JOHNNY A PIECE.

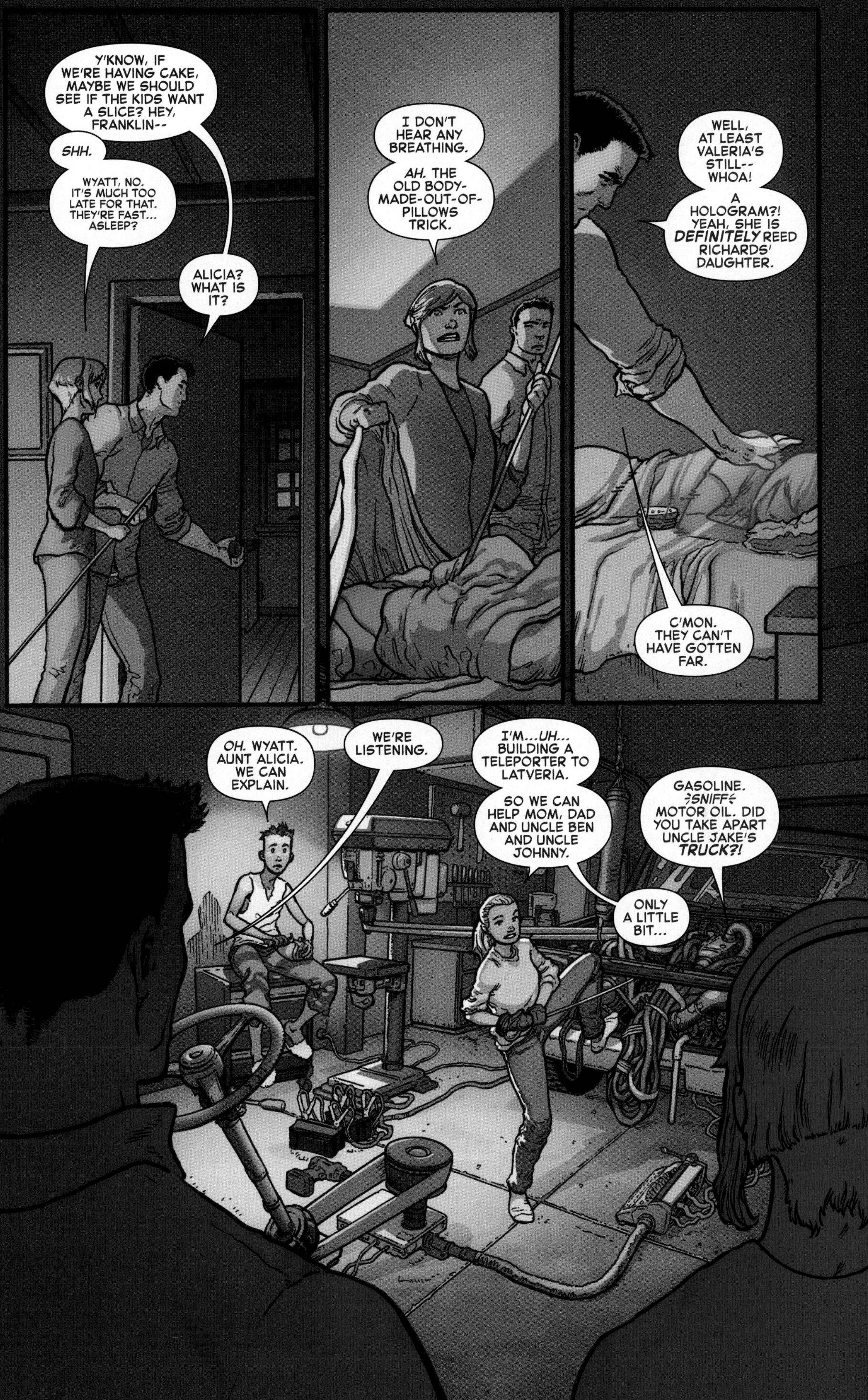

Y'KNOW, IF WE'RE HAVING CAKE, MAYBE WE SHOULD SEE IF THE KIDS WANT A SLICE? HEY, FRANKLIN--
SHH.
WYATT, NO. IT'S MUCH TOO LATE FOR THAT. THEY'RE FAST... ASLEEP?
ALICIA? WHAT IS IT?
I DON'T HEAR ANY BREATHING.
AH. THE OLD BODY-MADE-OUT-OF-PILLOWS TRICK.
WELL, AT LEAST VALERIA'S STILL-- WHOA!
A HOLOGRAM?! YEAH, SHE IS DEFINITELY REED RICHARDS' DAUGHTER.
C'MON. THEY CAN'T HAVE GOTTEN FAR.
OH. WYATT. AUNT ALICIA. WE CAN EXPLAIN.
WE'RE LISTENING.
I'M...UH... BUILDING A TELEPORTER TO LATVERIA.
SO WE CAN HELP MOM, DAD AND UNCLE BEN AND UNCLE JOHNNY.
GASOLINE. SNIFF MOTOR OIL. DID YOU TAKE APART UNCLE JAKE'S TRUCK?!
ONLY A LITTLE BIT...

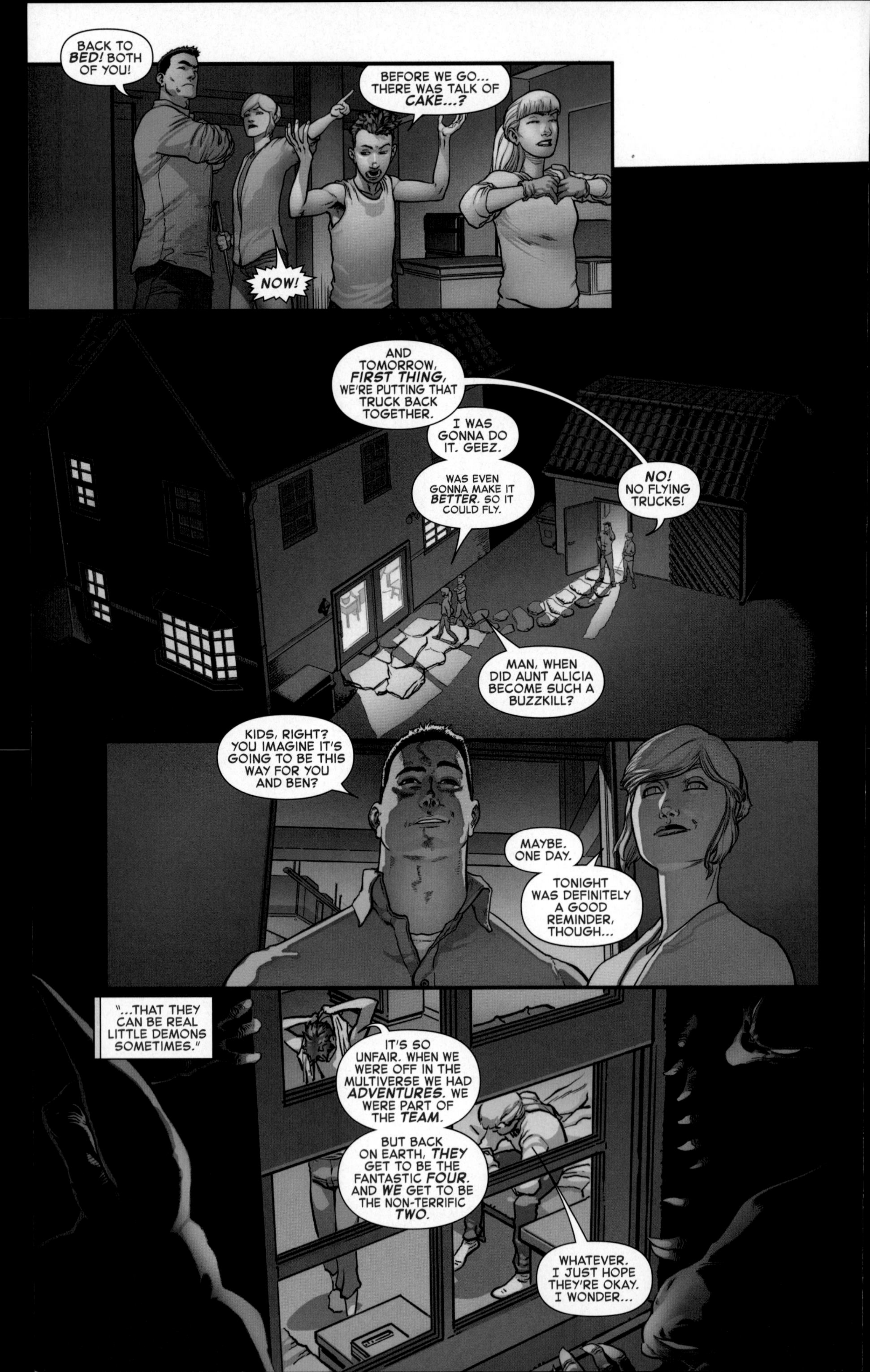
BACK TO BED! BOTH OF YOU!
BEFORE WE GO... THERE WAS TALK OF CAKE...?
NOW!
AND TOMORROW, FIRST THING, WE'RE PUTTING THAT TRUCK BACK TOGETHER.
I WAS GONNA DO IT. GEEZ.
WAS EVEN GONNA MAKE IT BETTER. SO IT COULD FLY.
NO! NO FLYING TRUCKS!
MAN, WHEN DID AUNT ALICIA BECOME SUCH A BUZZKILL?
KIDS, RIGHT? YOU IMAGINE IT'S GOING TO BE THIS WAY FOR YOU AND BEN?
MAYBE. ONE DAY.
TONIGHT WAS DEFINITELY A GOOD REMINDER, THOUGH...
"...THAT THEY CAN BE REAL LITTLE DEMONS SOMETIMES."
IT'S SO UNFAIR. WHEN WE WERE OFF IN THE MULTIVERSE WE HAD ADVENTURES. WE WERE PART OF THE TEAM.
BUT BACK ON EARTH, THEY GET TO BE THE FANTASTIC FOUR. AND WE GET TO BE THE NON-TERRIFIC TWO.
WHATEVER. I JUST HOPE THEY'RE OKAY. I WONDER...

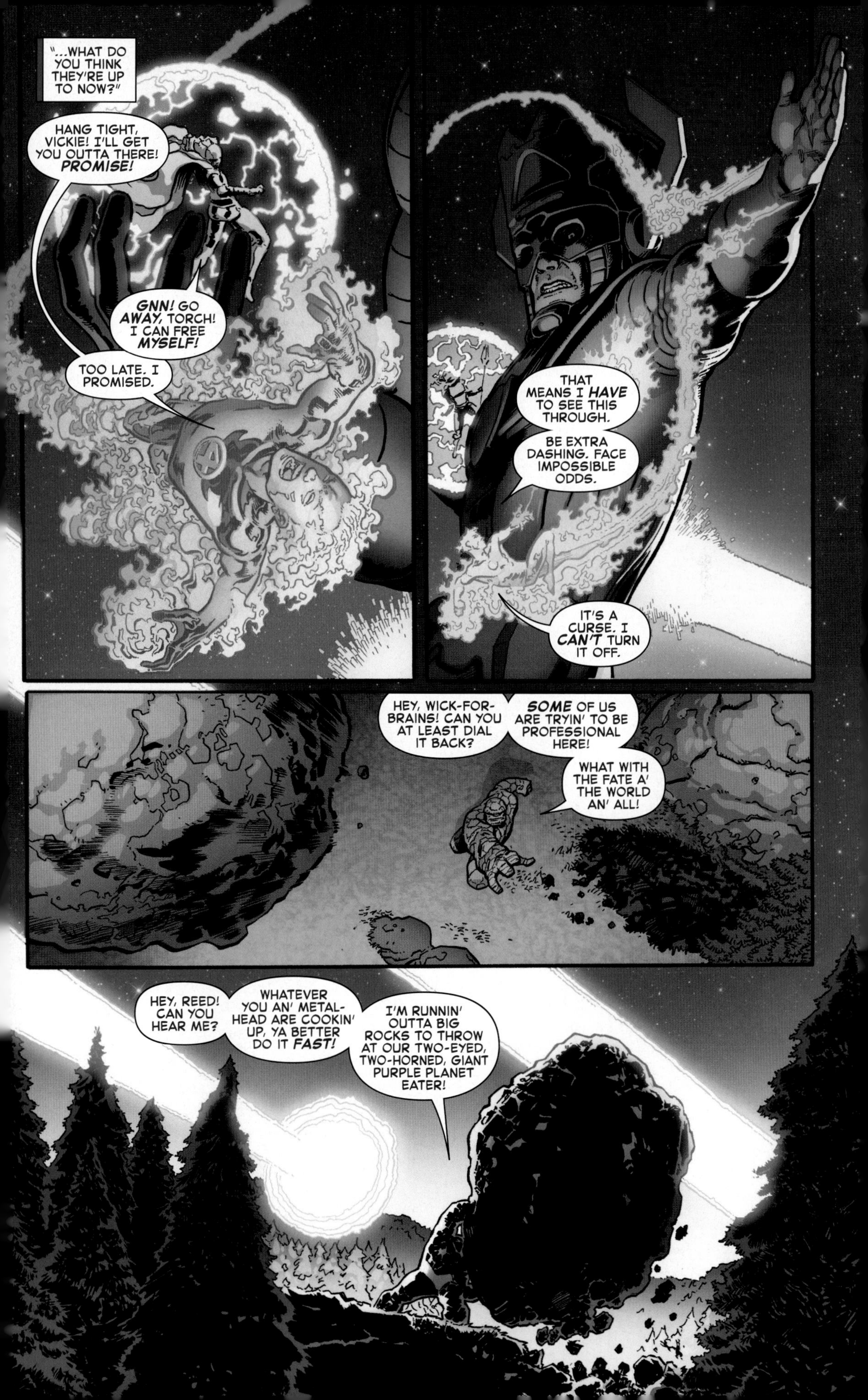
"...WHAT DO YOU THINK THEY'RE UP TO NOW?"
HANG TIGHT, VICKIE! I'LL GET YOU OUTTA THERE! **PROMISE!**
**GNN!** GO **AWAY,** TORCH! I CAN FREE **MYSELF!**
TOO LATE. I PROMISED.
THAT MEANS I **HAVE** TO SEE THIS THROUGH.
BE EXTRA DASHING. FACE IMPOSSIBLE ODDS.
IT'S A CURSE. I **CAN'T** TURN IT OFF.
HEY, WICK-FOR-BRAINS! CAN YOU AT LEAST DIAL IT BACK?
**SOME** OF US ARE TRYIN' TO BE PROFESSIONAL HERE!
WHAT WITH THE FATE A' THE WORLD AN' ALL!
HEY, REED! CAN YOU HEAR ME?
WHATEVER YOU AN' METAL-HEAD ARE COOKIN' UP, YA BETTER DO IT **FAST!**
I'M RUNNIN' OUTTA BIG ROCKS TO THROW AT OUR TWO-EYED, TWO-HORNED, GIANT PURPLE PLANET EATER!

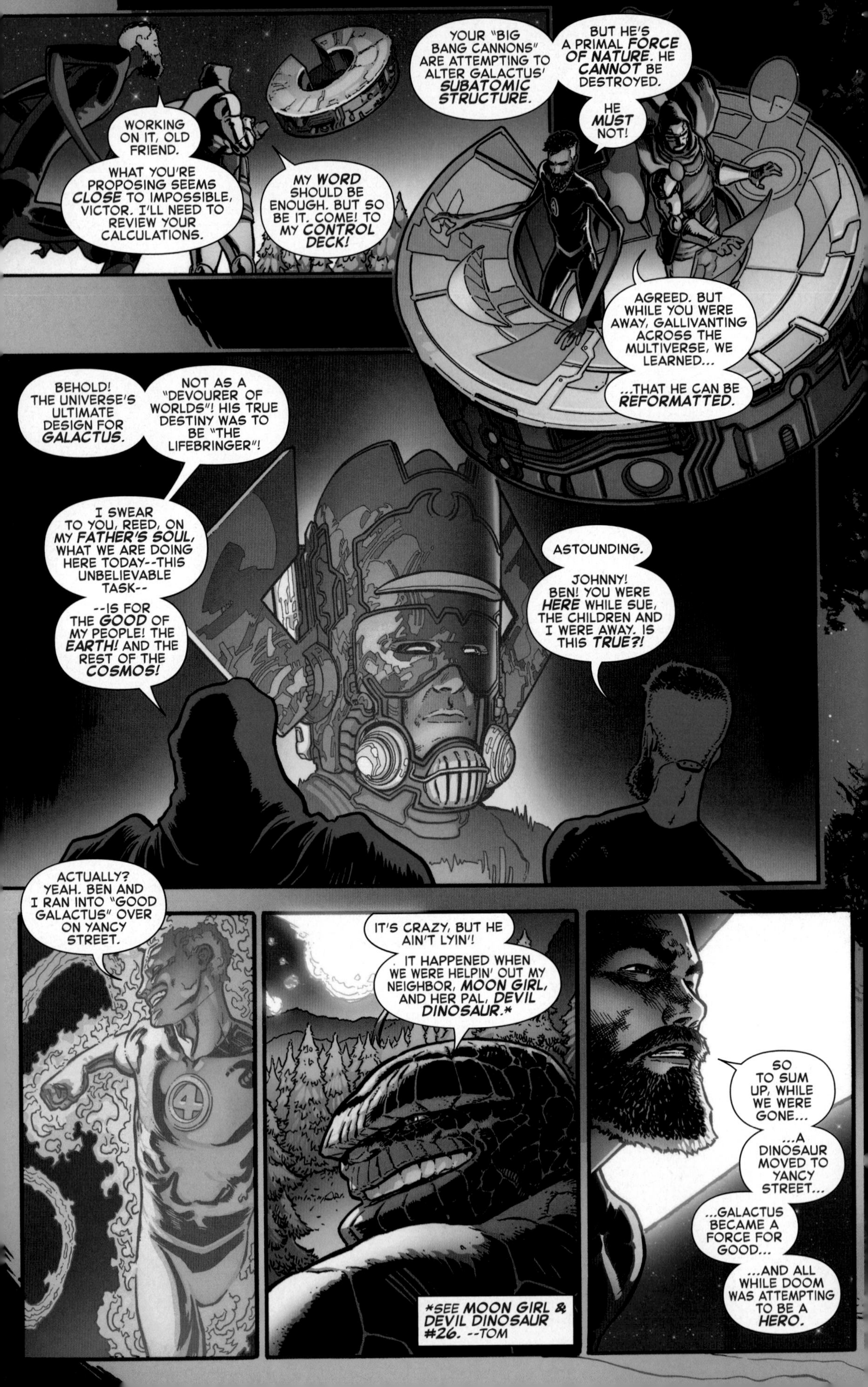
WORKING ON IT, OLD FRIEND.
WHAT YOU'RE PROPOSING SEEMS CLOSE TO IMPOSSIBLE, VICTOR. I'LL NEED TO REVIEW YOUR CALCULATIONS.
MY WORD SHOULD BE ENOUGH. BUT SO BE IT. COME! TO MY CONTROL DECK!
YOUR "BIG BANG CANNONS" ARE ATTEMPTING TO ALTER GALACTUS' SUBATOMIC STRUCTURE.
BUT HE'S A PRIMAL FORCE OF NATURE. HE CANNOT BE DESTROYED.
HE MUST NOT!
AGREED. BUT WHILE YOU WERE AWAY, GALLIVANTING ACROSS THE MULTIVERSE, WE LEARNED...
...THAT HE CAN BE REFORMATTED.
BEHOLD! THE UNIVERSE'S ULTIMATE DESIGN FOR GALACTUS.
NOT AS A "DEVOURER OF WORLDS"! HIS TRUE DESTINY WAS TO BE "THE LIFEBRINGER"!
I SWEAR TO YOU, REED, ON MY FATHER'S SOUL, WHAT WE ARE DOING HERE TODAY--THIS UNBELIEVABLE TASK--
--IS FOR THE GOOD OF MY PEOPLE! THE EARTH! AND THE REST OF THE COSMOS!
ASTOUNDING.
JOHNNY! BEN! YOU WERE HERE WHILE SUE, THE CHILDREN AND I WERE AWAY. IS THIS TRUE?!
ACTUALLY? YEAH. BEN AND I RAN INTO "GOOD GALACTUS" OVER ON YANCY STREET.
IT'S CRAZY, BUT HE AIN'T LYIN'!
IT HAPPENED WHEN WE WERE HELPIN' OUT MY NEIGHBOR, MOON GIRL, AND HER PAL, DEVIL DINOSAUR.*
*SEE MOON GIRL & DEVIL DINOSAUR #26. --TOM
SO TO SUM UP, WHILE WE WERE GONE...
...A DINOSAUR MOVED TO YANCY STREET...
...GALACTUS BECAME A FORCE FOR GOOD...
...AND ALL WHILE DOOM WAS ATTEMPTING TO BE A HERO.

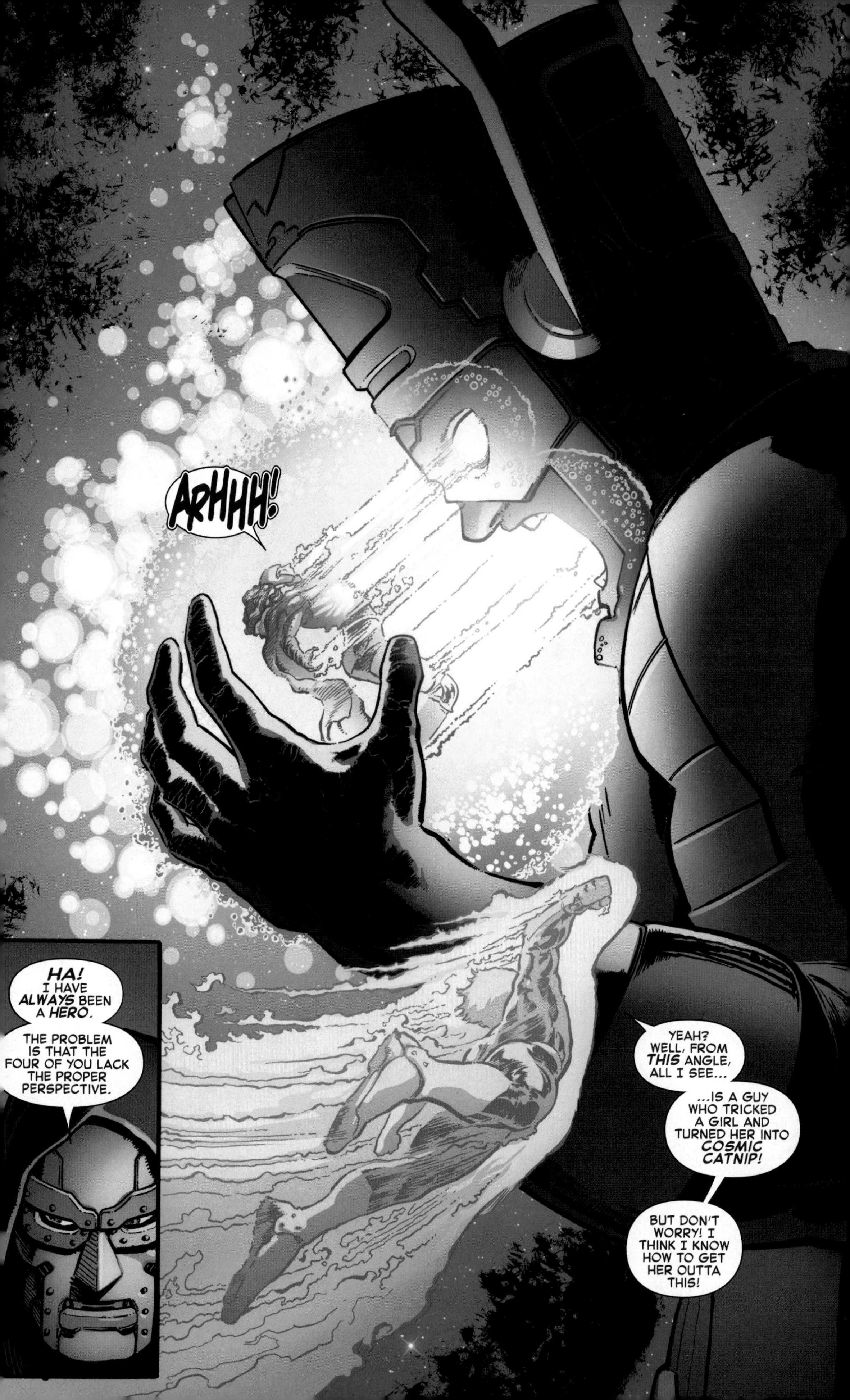
ARHHH!
HA! I HAVE ALWAYS BEEN A HERO.
THE PROBLEM IS THAT THE FOUR OF YOU LACK THE PROPER PERSPECTIVE.
YEAH? WELL, FROM THIS ANGLE, ALL I SEE...
...IS A GUY WHO TRICKED A GIRL AND TURNED HER INTO COSMIC CATNIP!
BUT DON'T WORRY! I THINK I KNOW HOW TO GET HER OUTTA THIS!

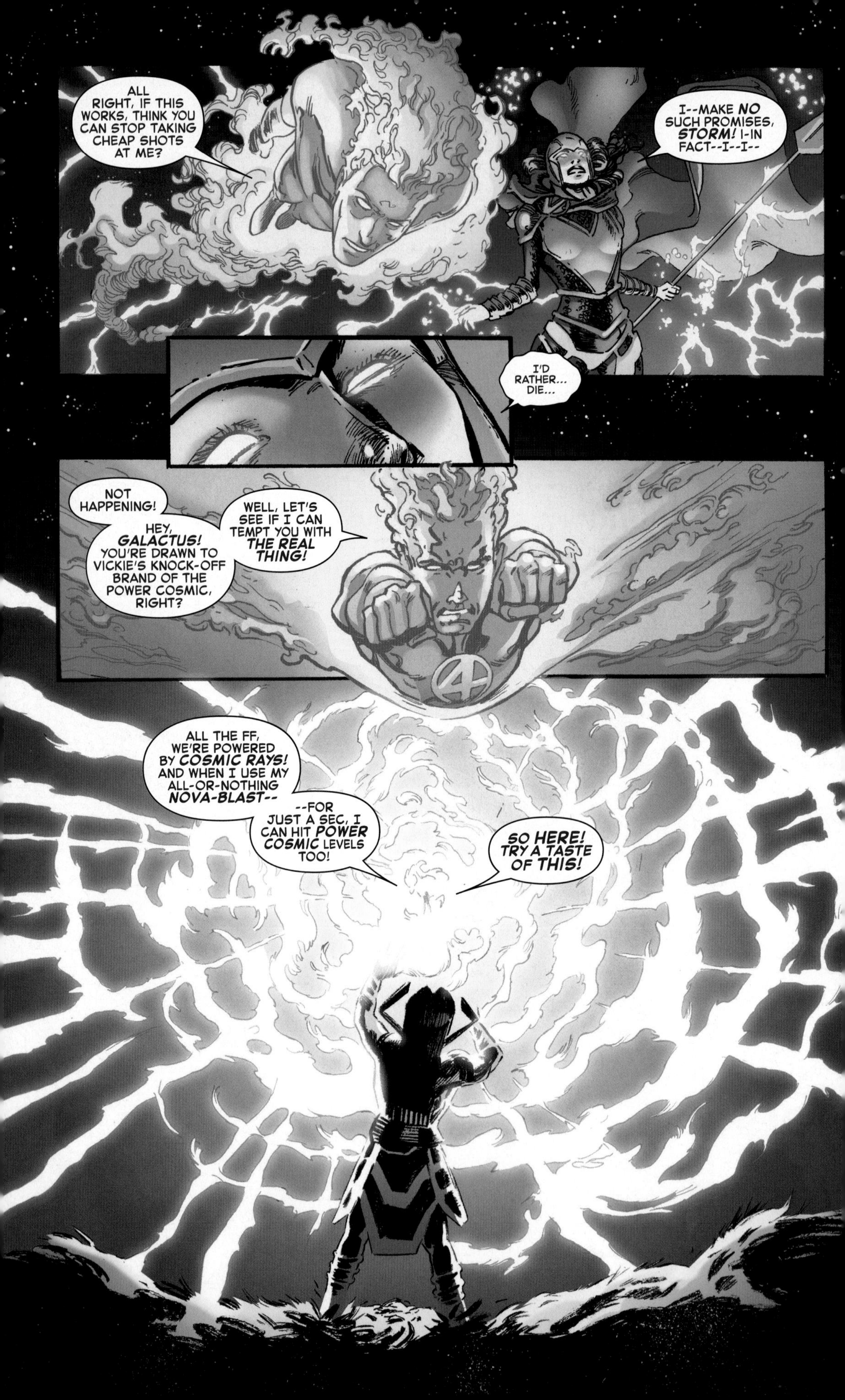
ALL RIGHT, IF THIS WORKS, THINK YOU CAN STOP TAKING CHEAP SHOTS AT ME?
I--MAKE NO SUCH PROMISES, STORM! I-IN FACT--I--I--
I'D RATHER... DIE...
NOT HAPPENING!
HEY, GALACTUS! YOU'RE DRAWN TO VICKIE'S KNOCK-OFF BRAND OF THE POWER COSMIC, RIGHT?
WELL, LET'S SEE IF I CAN TEMPT YOU WITH THE REAL THING!
ALL THE FF, WE'RE POWERED BY COSMIC RAYS! AND WHEN I USE MY ALL-OR-NOTHING NOVA-BLAST--
--FOR JUST A SEC, I CAN HIT POWER COSMIC LEVELS TOO!
SO HERE! TRY A TASTE OF THIS!

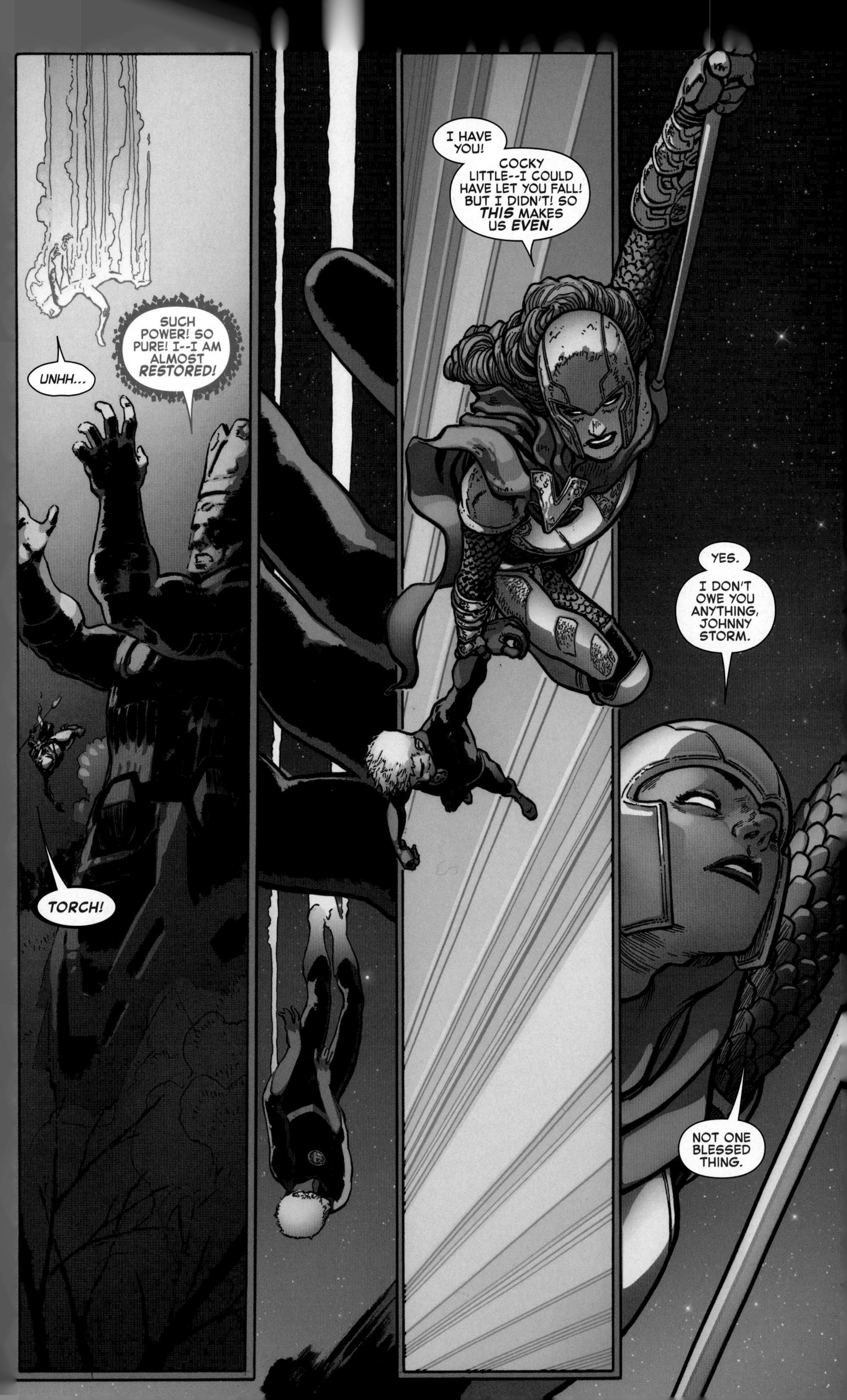
SUCH POWER! SO PURE! I--I AM ALMOST RESTORED!
UNHH...
TORCH!
I HAVE YOU!
COCKY LITTLE--I COULD HAVE LET YOU FALL! BUT I DIDN'T! SO THIS MAKES US EVEN.
YES.
I DON'T OWE YOU ANYTHING, JOHNNY STORM.
NOT ONE BLESSED THING.

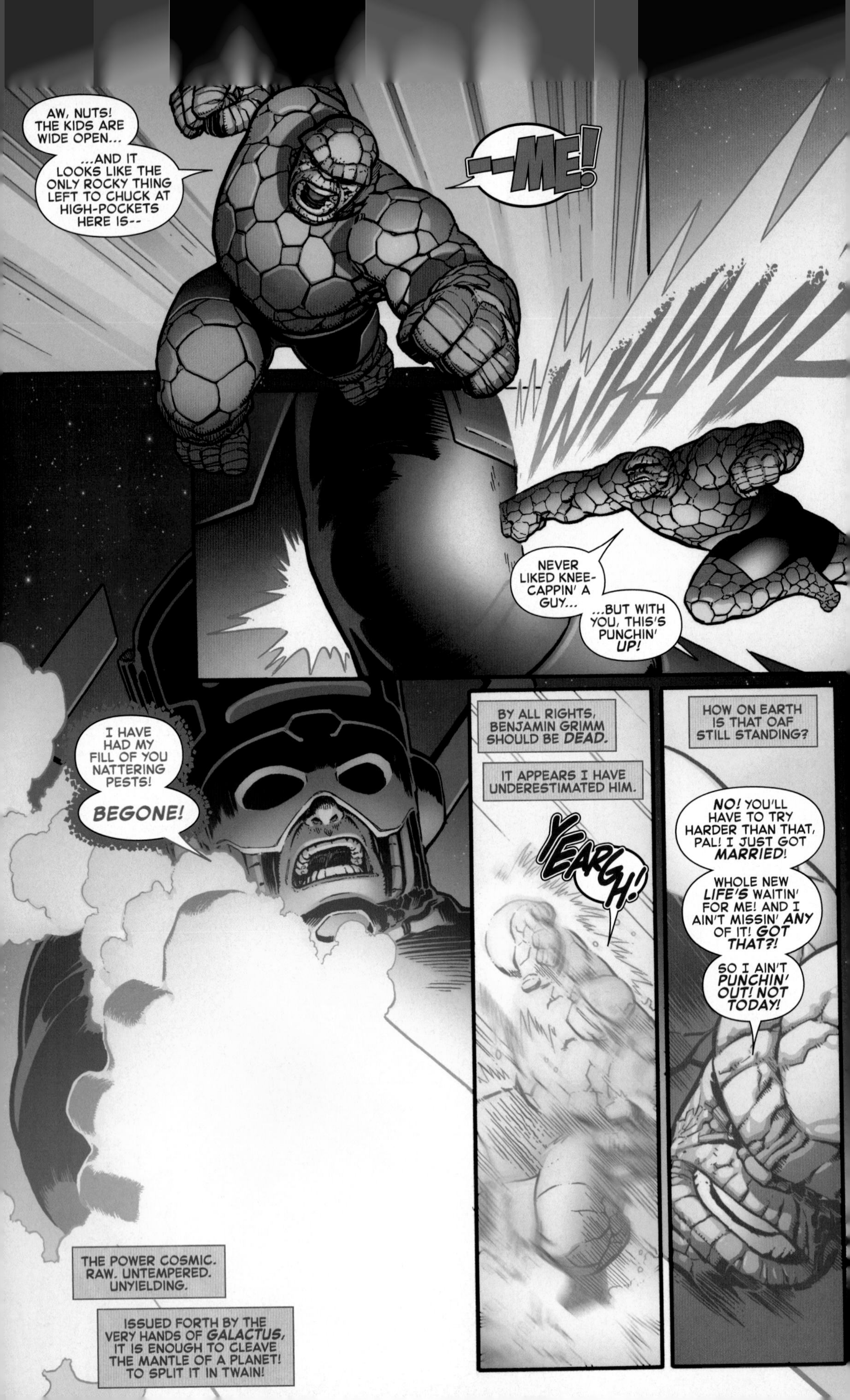
AW, NUTS! THE KIDS ARE WIDE OPEN...
...AND IT LOOKS LIKE THE ONLY ROCKY THING LEFT TO CHUCK AT HIGH-POCKETS HERE IS--
--ME!
WHAM
NEVER LIKED KNEE-CAPPIN' A GUY...
...BUT WITH YOU, THIS'S PUNCHIN' UP!
I HAVE HAD MY FILL OF YOU NATTERING PESTS!
BEGONE!
THE POWER COSMIC. RAW. UNTEMPERED. UNYIELDING.
ISSUED FORTH BY THE VERY HANDS OF GALACTUS, IT IS ENOUGH TO CLEAVE THE MANTLE OF A PLANET! TO SPLIT IT IN TWAIN!
BY ALL RIGHTS, BENJAMIN GRIMM SHOULD BE DEAD.
IT APPEARS I HAVE UNDERESTIMATED HIM.
YEARGH!
HOW ON EARTH IS THAT OAF STILL STANDING?
NO! YOU'LL HAVE TO TRY HARDER THAN THAT, PAL! I JUST GOT MARRIED!
WHOLE NEW LIFE'S WAITIN' FOR ME! AND I AIN'T MISSIN' ANY OF IT! GOT THAT?!
SO I AIN'T PUNCHIN' OUT! NOT TODAY!

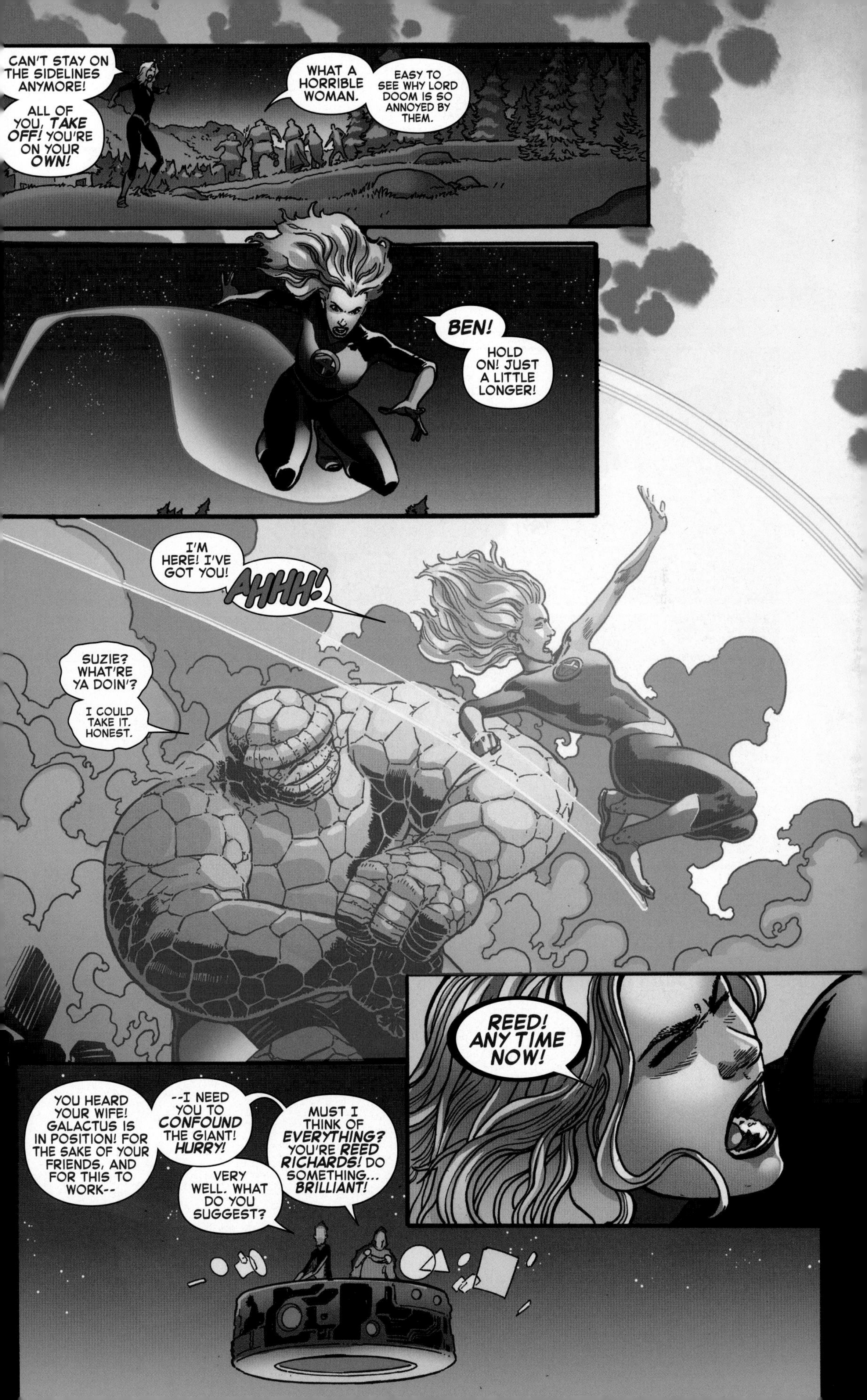

CAN'T STAY ON THE SIDELINES ANYMORE!
ALL OF YOU, TAKE OFF! YOU'RE ON YOUR OWN!
WHAT A HORRIBLE WOMAN.
EASY TO SEE WHY LORD DOOM IS SO ANNOYED BY THEM.
BEN!
HOLD ON! JUST A LITTLE LONGER!
I'M HERE! I'VE GOT YOU!
AHHH!
SUZIE? WHAT'RE YA DOIN'?
I COULD TAKE IT. HONEST.
REED! ANY TIME NOW!
YOU HEARD YOUR WIFE! GALACTUS IS IN POSITION! FOR THE SAKE OF YOUR FRIENDS, AND FOR THIS TO WORK--
--I NEED YOU TO CONFOUND THE GIANT! HURRY!
VERY WELL. WHAT DO YOU SUGGEST?
MUST I THINK OF EVERYTHING? YOU'RE REED RICHARDS! DO SOMETHING... BRILLIANT!

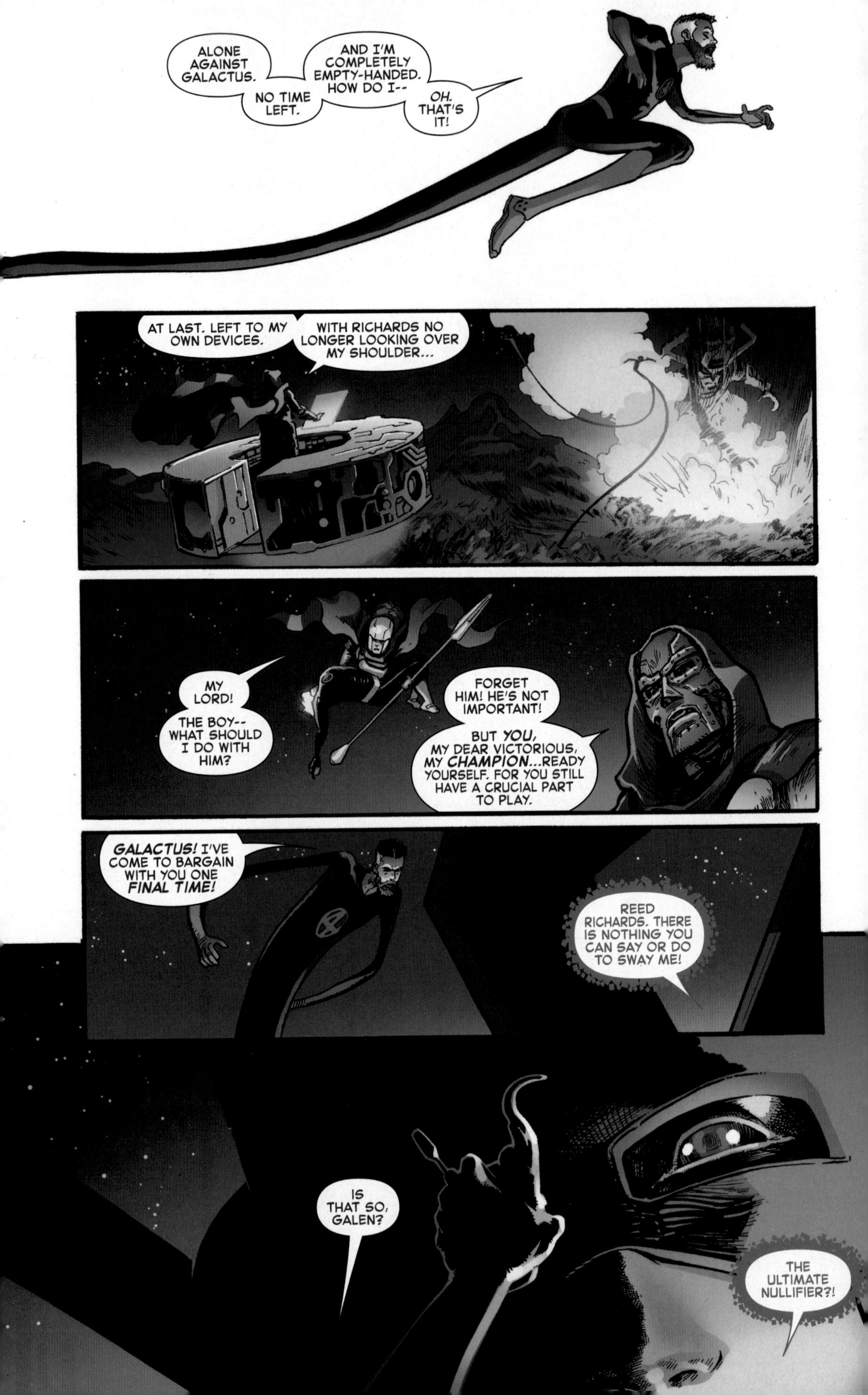
ALONE AGAINST GALACTUS.
NO TIME LEFT.
AND I'M COMPLETELY EMPTY-HANDED. HOW DO I--
OH. THAT'S IT!
AT LAST. LEFT TO MY OWN DEVICES.
WITH RICHARDS NO LONGER LOOKING OVER MY SHOULDER...
MY LORD!
THE BOY-- WHAT SHOULD I DO WITH HIM?
FORGET HIM! HE'S NOT IMPORTANT!
BUT YOU, MY DEAR VICTORIOUS, MY CHAMPION...READY YOURSELF. FOR YOU STILL HAVE A CRUCIAL PART TO PLAY.
GALACTUS! I'VE COME TO BARGAIN WITH YOU ONE FINAL TIME!
REED RICHARDS. THERE IS NOTHING YOU CAN SAY OR DO TO SWAY ME!
IS THAT SO, GALEN?
THE ULTIMATE NULLIFIER?!

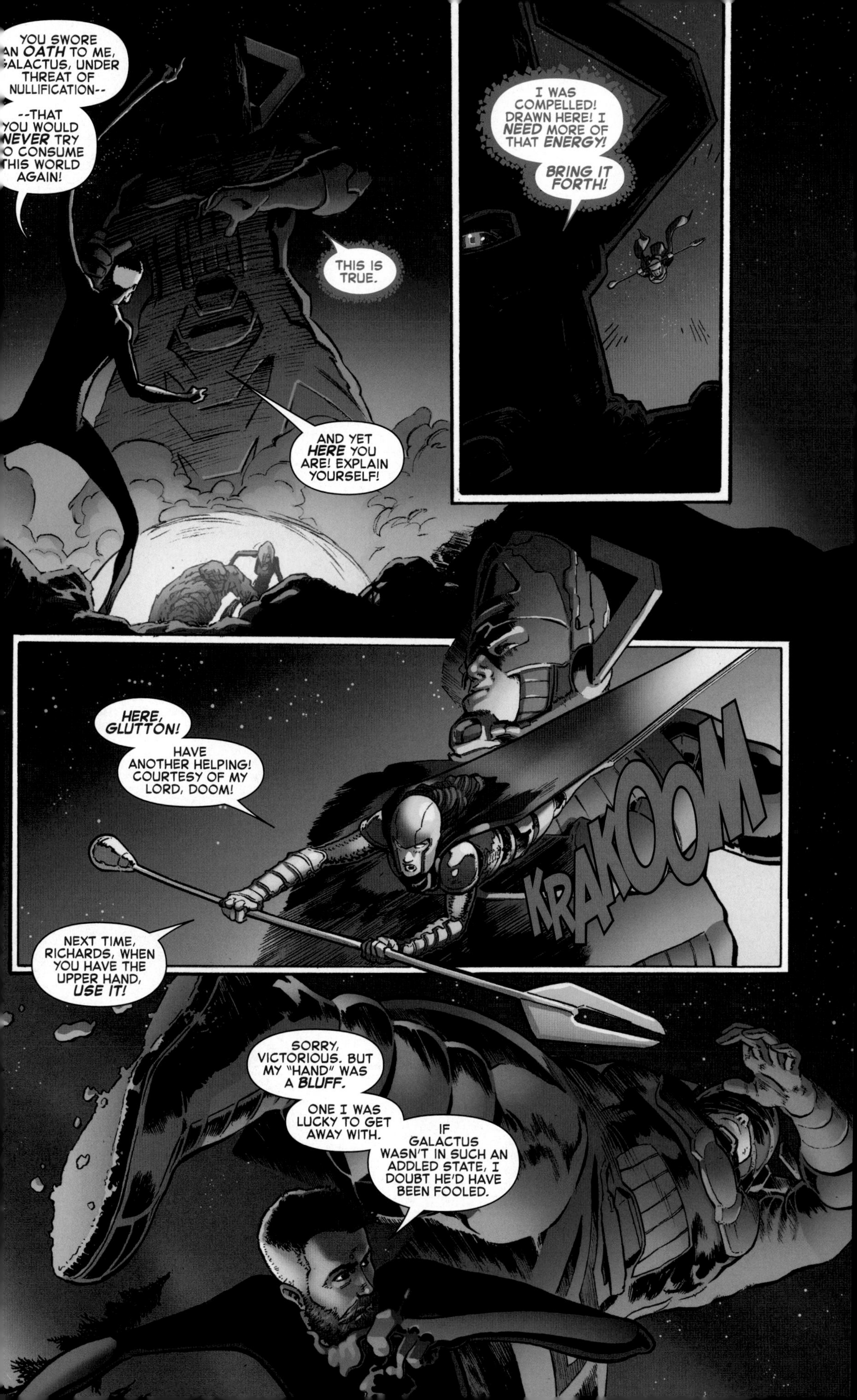
YOU SWORE AN OATH TO ME, GALACTUS, UNDER THREAT OF NULLIFICATION--
--THAT YOU WOULD NEVER TRY TO CONSUME THIS WORLD AGAIN!
THIS IS TRUE.
AND YET HERE YOU ARE! EXPLAIN YOURSELF!
I WAS COMPELLED! DRAWN HERE! I NEED MORE OF THAT ENERGY!
BRING IT FORTH!
HERE, GLUTTON!
HAVE ANOTHER HELPING! COURTESY OF MY LORD, DOOM!
KRAKOOM
NEXT TIME, RICHARDS, WHEN YOU HAVE THE UPPER HAND, USE IT!
SORRY, VICTORIOUS. BUT MY "HAND" WAS A BLUFF.
ONE I WAS LUCKY TO GET AWAY WITH.
IF GALACTUS WASN'T IN SUCH AN ADDLED STATE, I DOUBT HE'D HAVE BEEN FOOLED.

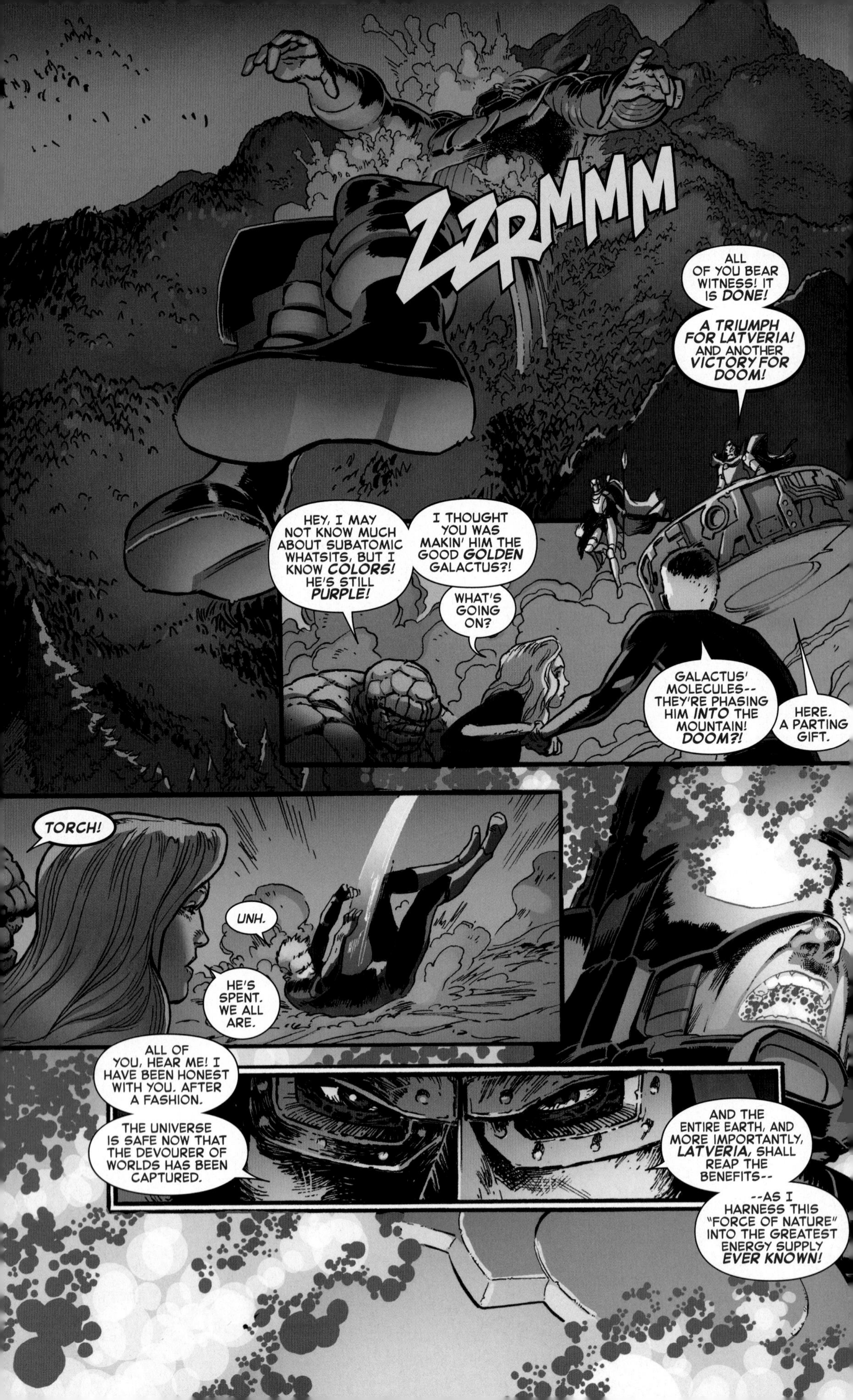
ZZRMMM
ALL OF YOU BEAR WITNESS! IT IS DONE!
A TRIUMPH FOR LATVERIA! AND ANOTHER VICTORY FOR DOOM!
HEY, I MAY NOT KNOW MUCH ABOUT SUBATOMIC WHATSITS, BUT I KNOW COLORS! HE'S STILL PURPLE!
I THOUGHT YOU WAS MAKIN' HIM THE GOOD GOLDEN GALACTUS?!
WHAT'S GOING ON?
GALACTUS' MOLECULES-- THEY'RE PHASING HIM INTO THE MOUNTAIN! DOOM?!
HERE. A PARTING GIFT.
TORCH!
UNH.
HE'S SPENT. WE ALL ARE.
ALL OF YOU, HEAR ME! I HAVE BEEN HONEST WITH YOU. AFTER A FASHION.
THE UNIVERSE IS SAFE NOW THAT THE DEVOURER OF WORLDS HAS BEEN CAPTURED.
AND THE ENTIRE EARTH, AND MORE IMPORTANTLY, LATVERIA, SHALL REAP THE BENEFITS--
--AS I HARNESS THIS "FORCE OF NATURE" INTO THE GREATEST ENERGY SUPPLY EVER KNOWN!

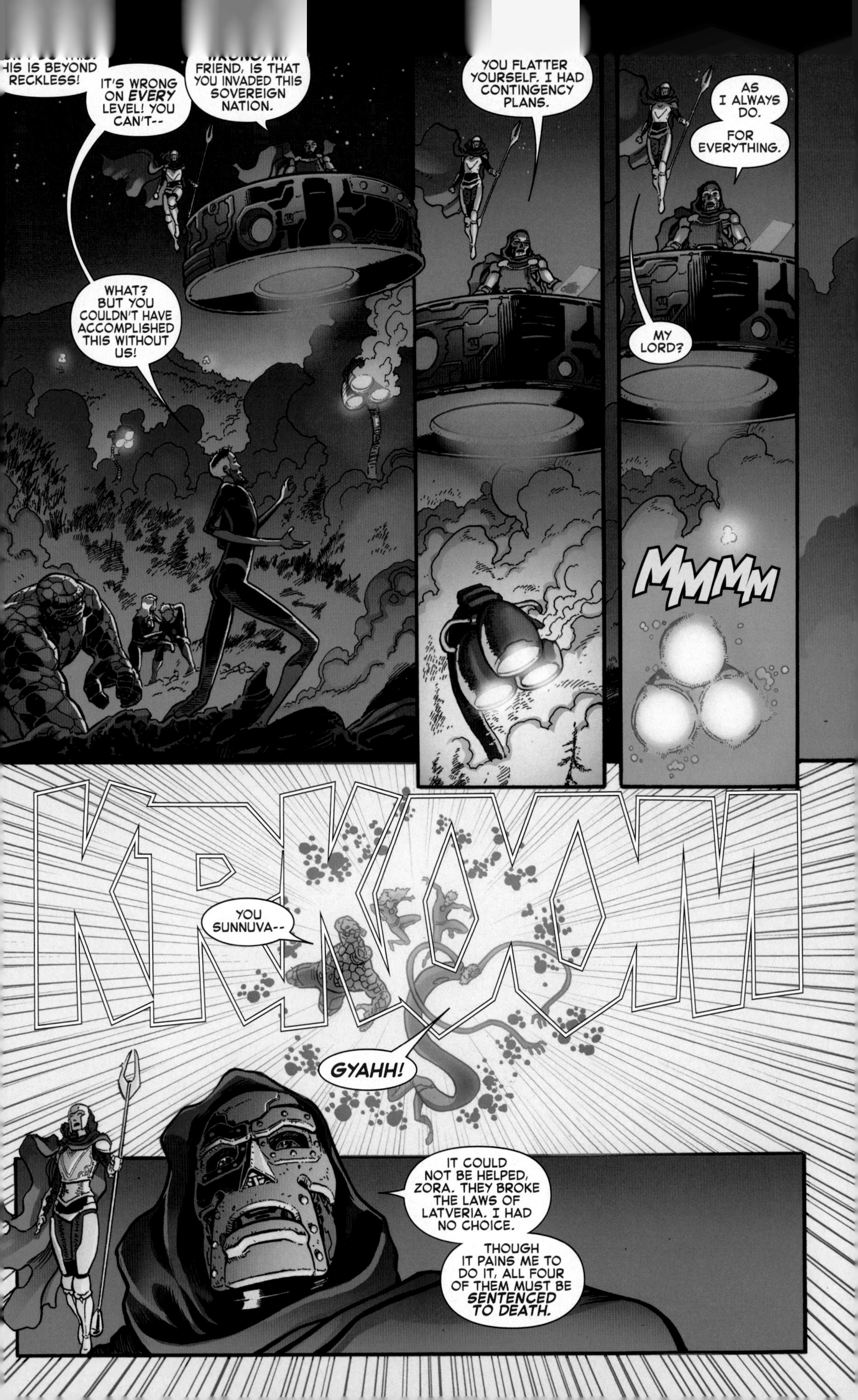

IS BEYOND RECKLESS!
IT'S WRONG ON *EVERY* LEVEL! YOU CAN'T--
FRIEND, IS THAT YOU INVADED THIS SOVEREIGN NATION.
WHAT? BUT YOU COULDN'T HAVE ACCOMPLISHED THIS WITHOUT US!
YOU FLATTER YOURSELF. I HAD CONTINGENCY PLANS.
AS I ALWAYS DO.
FOR EVERYTHING.
MY LORD?
MMMM
KRKOOM
YOU SUNNUVA--
GYAHH!
IT COULD NOT BE HELPED, ZORA. THEY BROKE THE LAWS OF LATVERIA. I HAD NO CHOICE.
THOUGH IT PAINS ME TO DO IT, ALL FOUR OF THEM MUST BE *SENTENCED TO DEATH.*

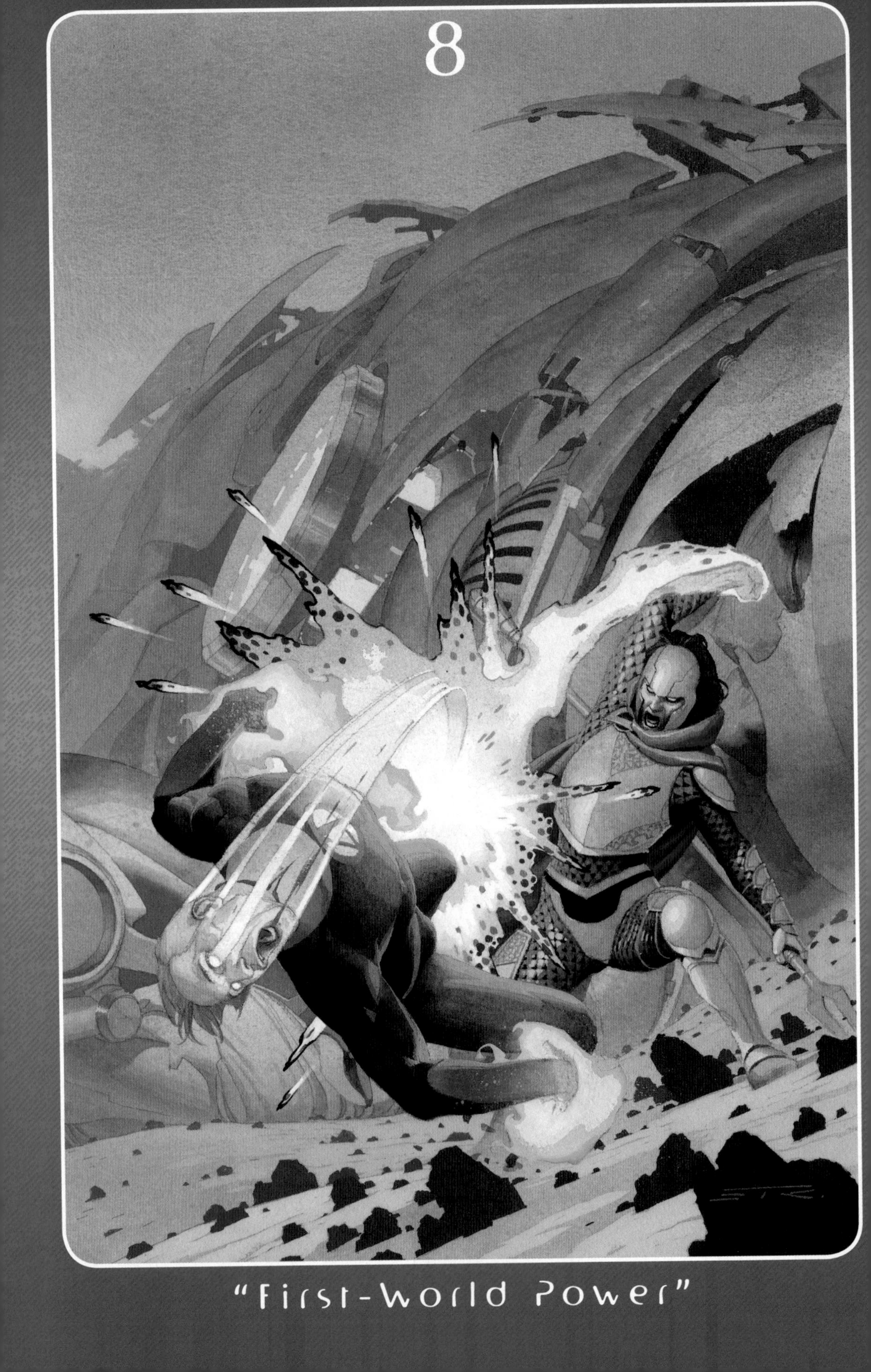
8

"First-World Power"

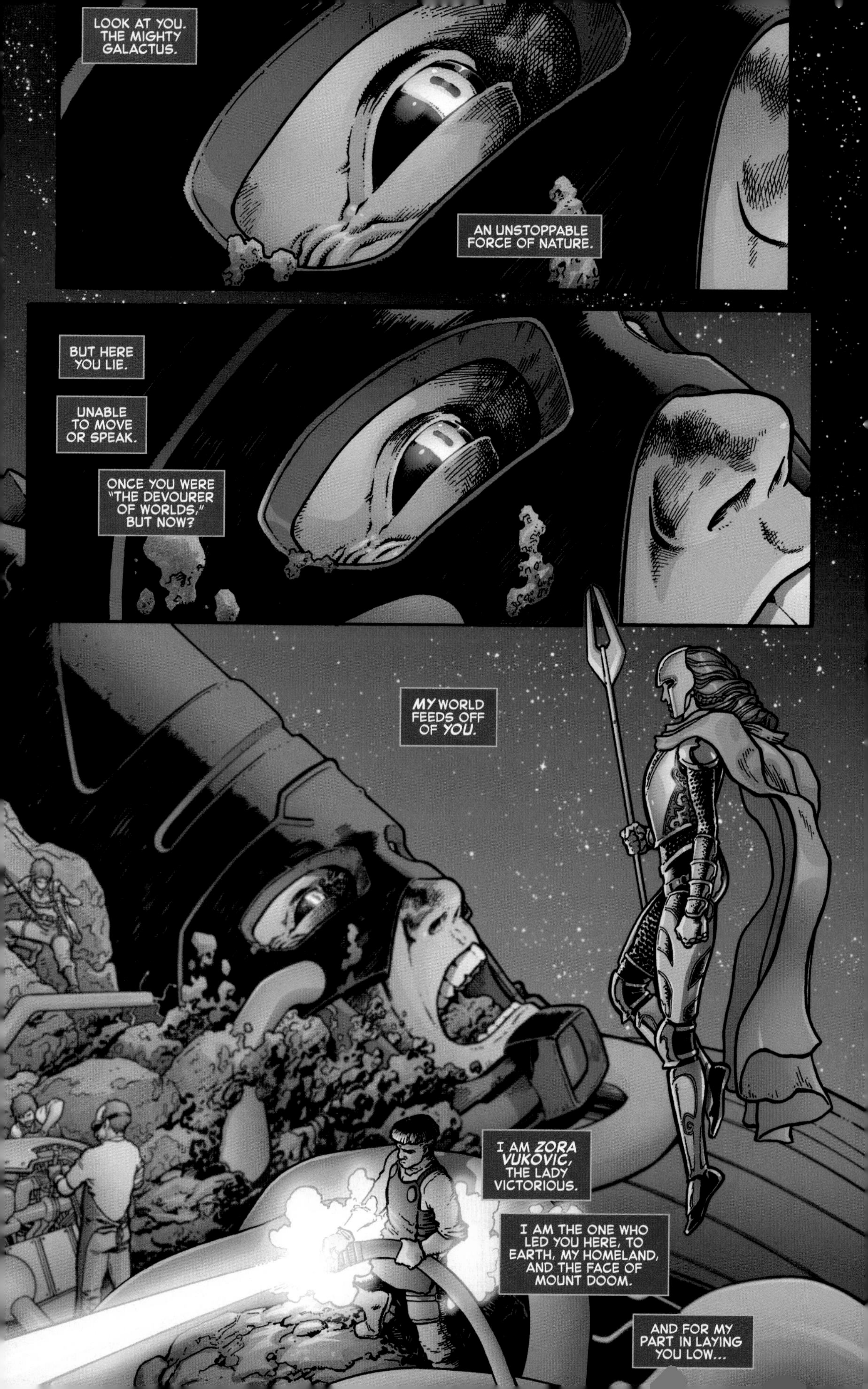
LOOK AT YOU. THE MIGHTY GALACTUS.
AN UNSTOPPABLE FORCE OF NATURE.
BUT HERE YOU LIE.
UNABLE TO MOVE OR SPEAK.
ONCE YOU WERE "THE DEVOURER OF WORLDS," BUT NOW?
MY WORLD FEEDS OFF OF YOU.
I AM ZORA VUKOVIC, THE LADY VICTORIOUS.
I AM THE ONE WHO LED YOU HERE, TO EARTH, MY HOMELAND, AND THE FACE OF MOUNT DOOM.
AND FOR MY PART IN LAYING YOU LOW...

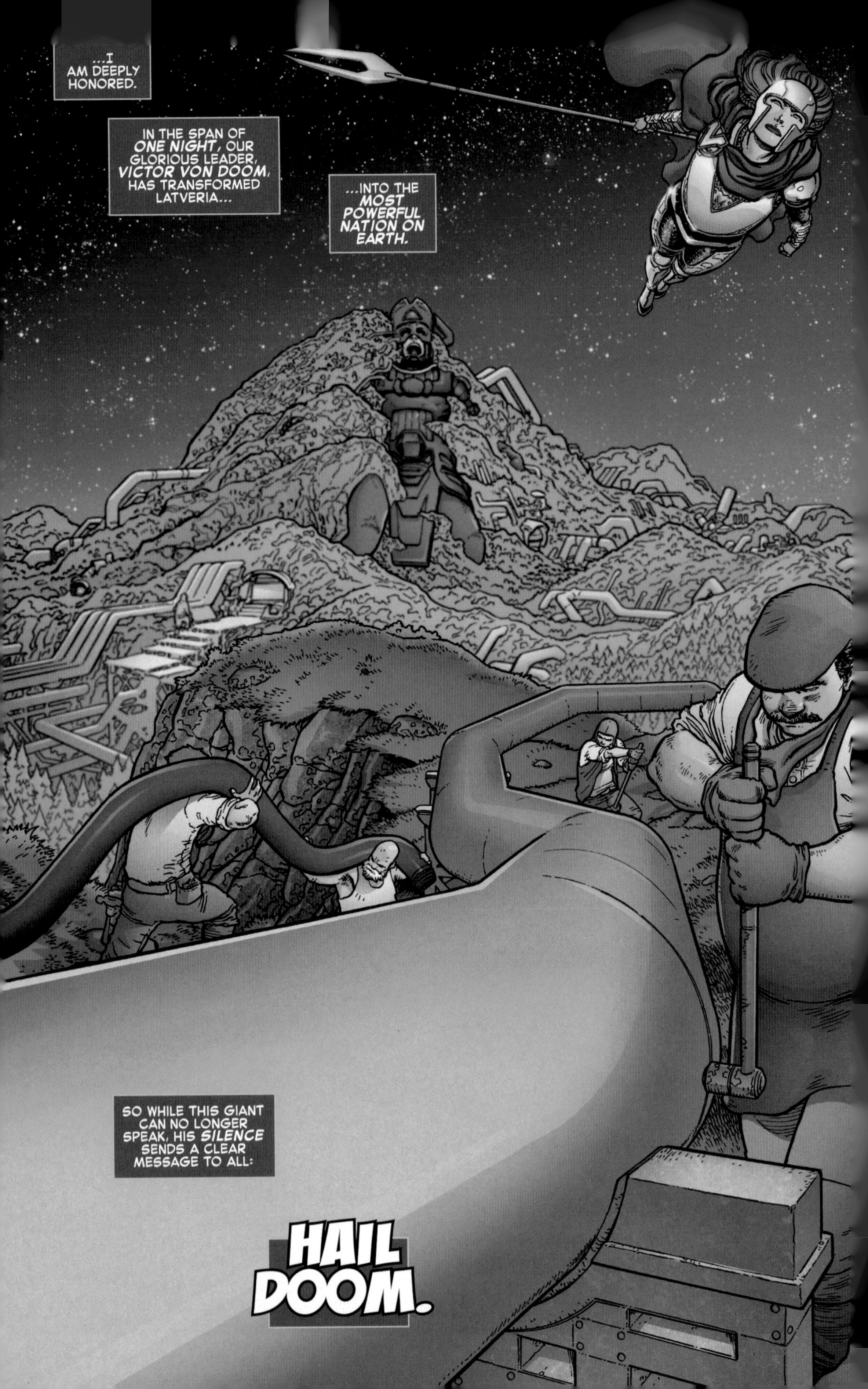
...I AM DEEPLY HONORED.
IN THE SPAN OF ONE NIGHT, OUR GLORIOUS LEADER, VICTOR VON DOOM, HAS TRANSFORMED LATVERIA...
...INTO THE MOST POWERFUL NATION ON EARTH.
SO WHILE THIS GIANT CAN NO LONGER SPEAK, HIS SILENCE SENDS A CLEAR MESSAGE TO ALL:
HAIL DOOM.

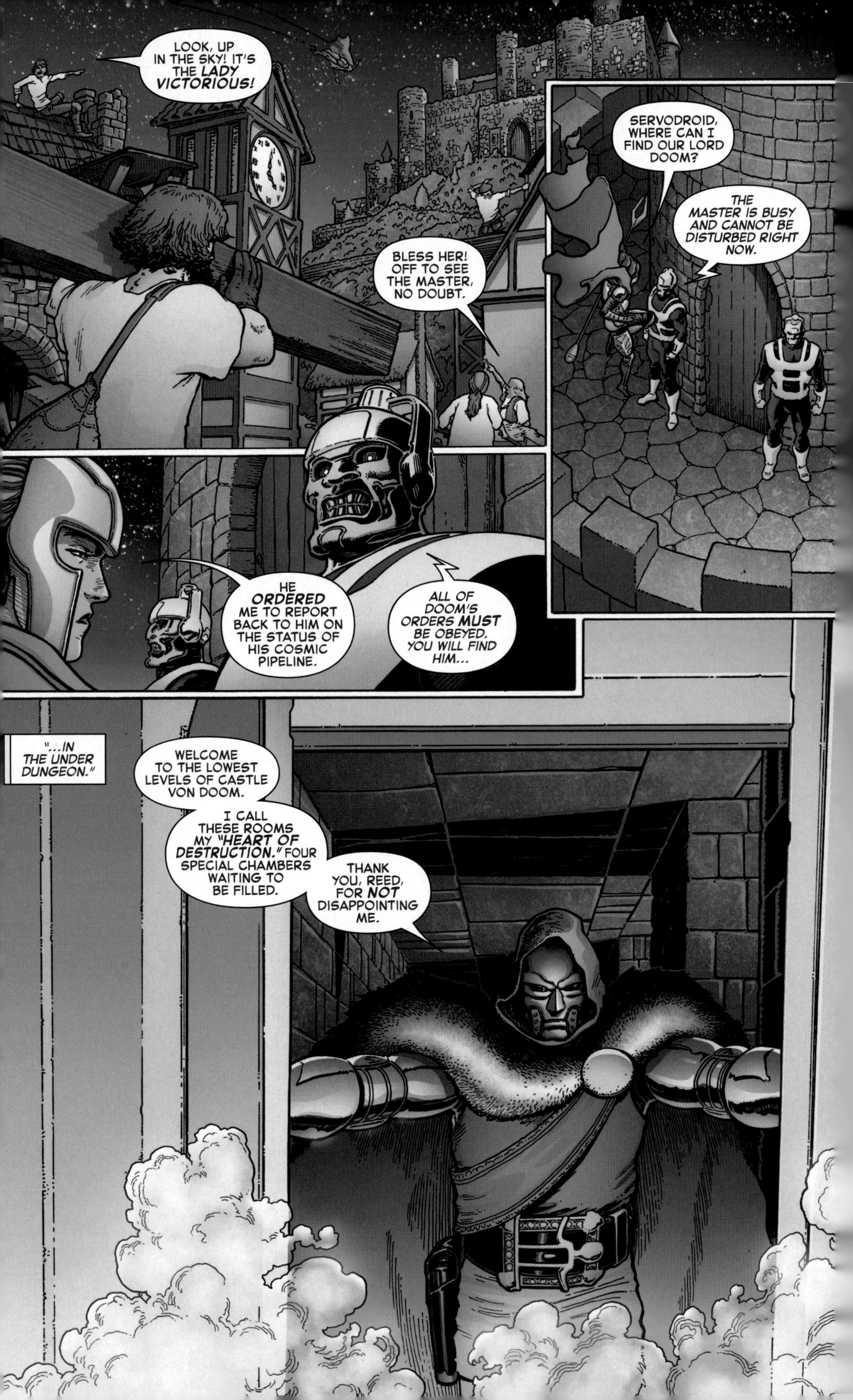
LOOK, UP IN THE SKY! IT'S THE LADY VICTORIOUS!
BLESS HER! OFF TO SEE THE MASTER, NO DOUBT.
SERVODROID, WHERE CAN I FIND OUR LORD DOOM?
THE MASTER IS BUSY AND CANNOT BE DISTURBED RIGHT NOW.
HE ORDERED ME TO REPORT BACK TO HIM ON THE STATUS OF HIS COSMIC PIPELINE.
ALL OF DOOM'S ORDERS MUST BE OBEYED. YOU WILL FIND HIM...
"...IN THE UNDER DUNGEON."
WELCOME TO THE LOWEST LEVELS OF CASTLE VON DOOM.
I CALL THESE ROOMS MY "HEART OF DESTRUCTION." FOUR SPECIAL CHAMBERS WAITING TO BE FILLED.
THANK YOU, REED, FOR NOT DISAPPOINTING ME.

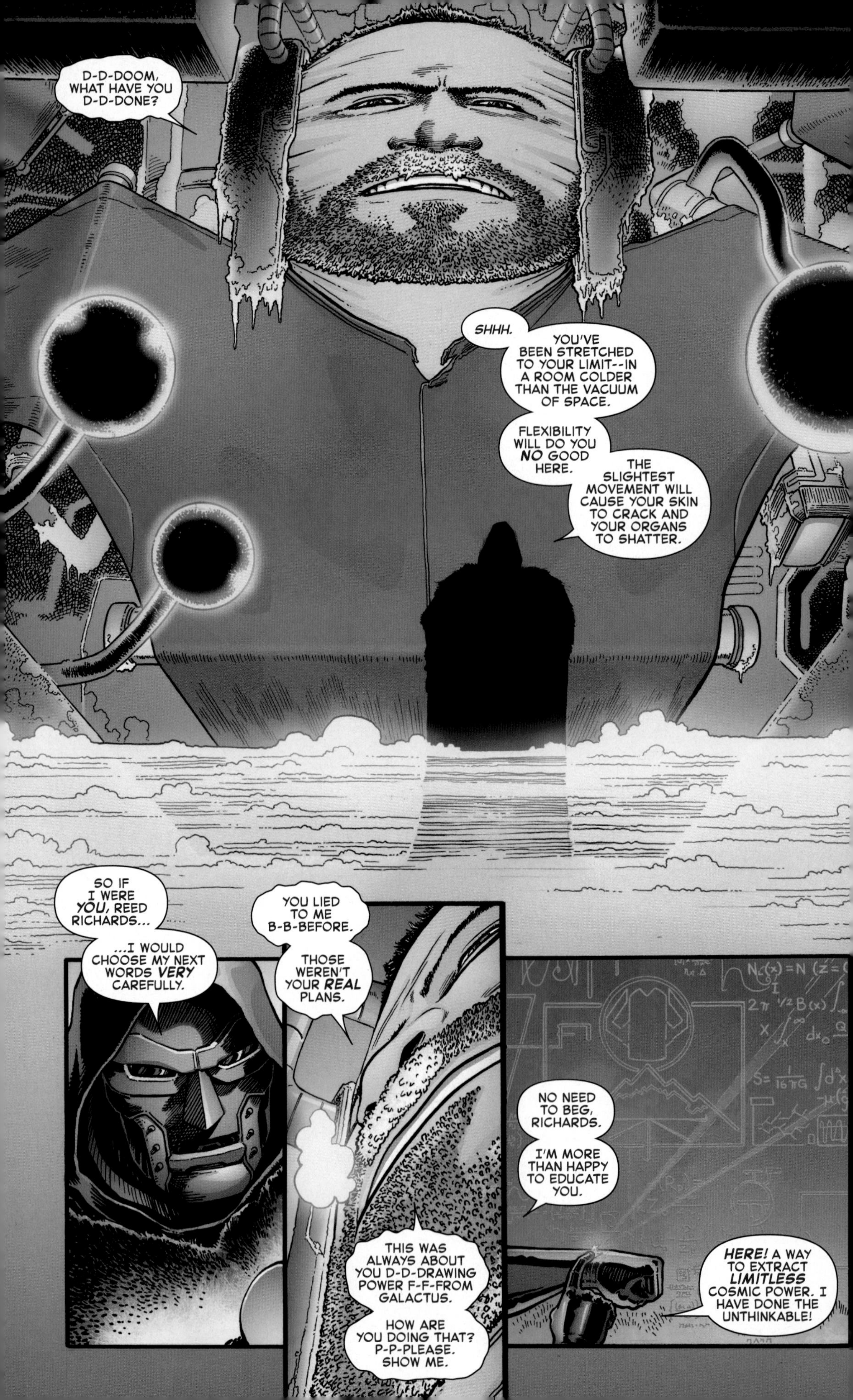
D-D-DOOM, WHAT HAVE YOU D-D-DONE?
SHHH.
YOU'VE BEEN STRETCHED TO YOUR LIMIT--IN A ROOM COLDER THAN THE VACUUM OF SPACE.
FLEXIBILITY WILL DO YOU NO GOOD HERE.
THE SLIGHTEST MOVEMENT WILL CAUSE YOUR SKIN TO CRACK AND YOUR ORGANS TO SHATTER.
SO IF I WERE YOU, REED RICHARDS...
...I WOULD CHOOSE MY NEXT WORDS VERY CAREFULLY.
YOU LIED TO ME B-B-BEFORE.
THOSE WEREN'T YOUR REAL PLANS.
THIS WAS ALWAYS ABOUT YOU D-D-DRAWING POWER F-F-FROM GALACTUS.
HOW ARE YOU DOING THAT? P-P-PLEASE. SHOW ME.
NO NEED TO BEG, RICHARDS.
I'M MORE THAN HAPPY TO EDUCATE YOU.
HERE! A WAY TO EXTRACT LIMITLESS COSMIC POWER. I HAVE DONE THE UNTHINKABLE!

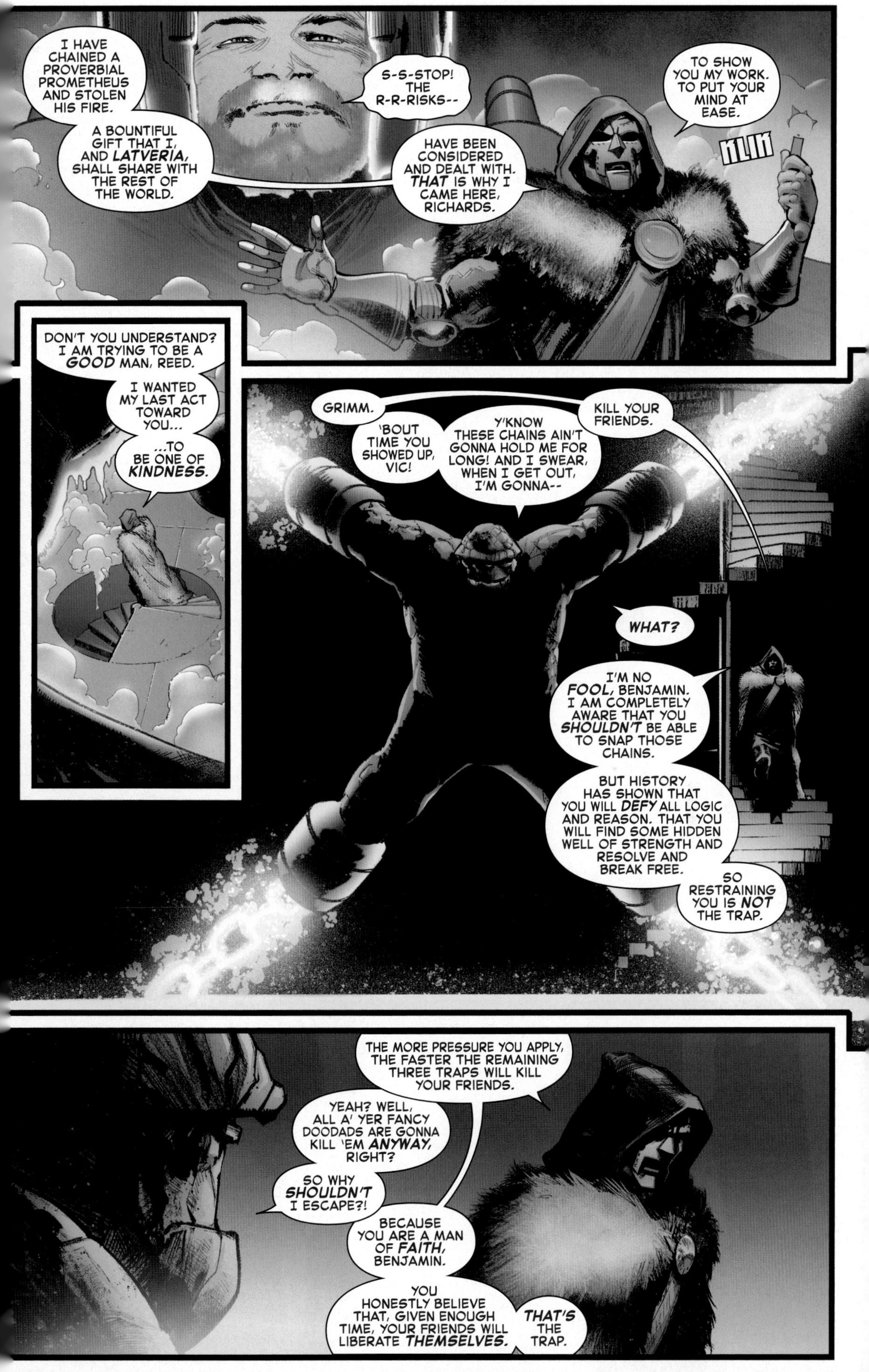
I HAVE CHAINED A PROVERBIAL PROMETHEUS AND STOLEN HIS FIRE.
A BOUNTIFUL GIFT THAT I, AND LATVERIA, SHALL SHARE WITH THE REST OF THE WORLD.
S-S-STOP! THE R-R-RISKS--
HAVE BEEN CONSIDERED AND DEALT WITH. THAT IS WHY I CAME HERE, RICHARDS.
TO SHOW YOU MY WORK. TO PUT YOUR MIND AT EASE.
KLIK
DON'T YOU UNDERSTAND? I AM TRYING TO BE A GOOD MAN, REED.
I WANTED MY LAST ACT TOWARD YOU...
...TO BE ONE OF KINDNESS.
GRIMM.
KILL YOUR FRIENDS.
'BOUT TIME YOU SHOWED UP, VIC!
Y'KNOW THESE CHAINS AIN'T GONNA HOLD ME FOR LONG! AND I SWEAR, WHEN I GET OUT, I'M GONNA--
WHAT?
I'M NO FOOL, BENJAMIN. I AM COMPLETELY AWARE THAT YOU SHOULDN'T BE ABLE TO SNAP THOSE CHAINS.
BUT HISTORY HAS SHOWN THAT YOU WILL DEFY ALL LOGIC AND REASON. THAT YOU WILL FIND SOME HIDDEN WELL OF STRENGTH AND RESOLVE AND BREAK FREE.
SO RESTRAINING YOU IS NOT THE TRAP.
THE MORE PRESSURE YOU APPLY, THE FASTER THE REMAINING THREE TRAPS WILL KILL YOUR FRIENDS.
YEAH? WELL, ALL A' YER FANCY DOODADS ARE GONNA KILL 'EM ANYWAY, RIGHT?
SO WHY SHOULDN'T I ESCAPE?!
BECAUSE YOU ARE A MAN OF FAITH, BENJAMIN.
YOU HONESTLY BELIEVE THAT, GIVEN ENOUGH TIME, YOUR FRIENDS WILL LIBERATE THEMSELVES.
THAT'S THE TRAP.

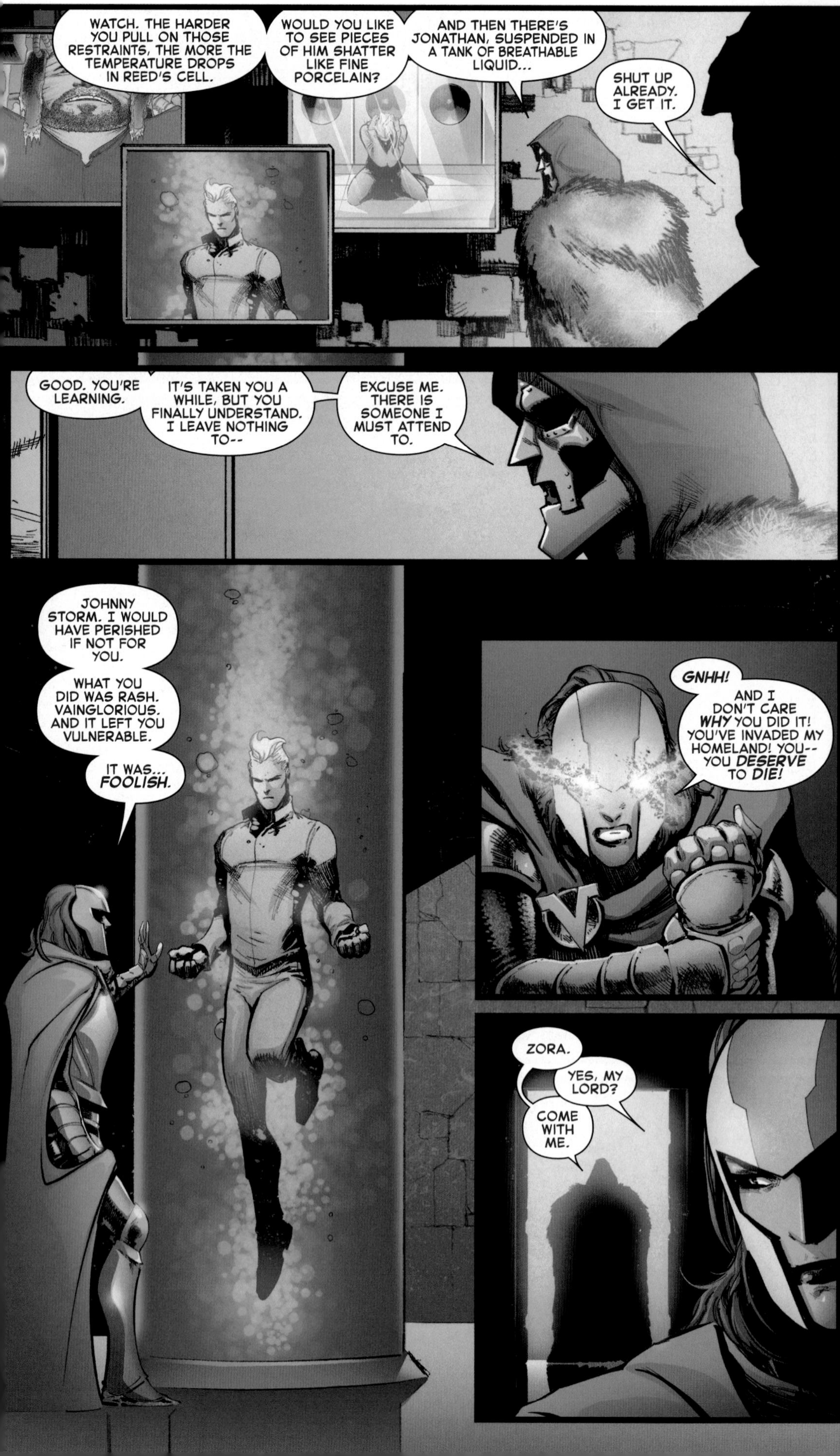
WATCH. THE HARDER YOU PULL ON THOSE RESTRAINTS, THE MORE THE TEMPERATURE DROPS IN REED'S CELL.
WOULD YOU LIKE TO SEE PIECES OF HIM SHATTER LIKE FINE PORCELAIN?
AND THEN THERE'S JONATHAN, SUSPENDED IN A TANK OF BREATHABLE LIQUID...
SHUT UP ALREADY. I GET IT.
GOOD. YOU'RE LEARNING.
IT'S TAKEN YOU A WHILE, BUT YOU FINALLY UNDERSTAND. I LEAVE NOTHING TO--
EXCUSE ME. THERE IS SOMEONE I MUST ATTEND TO.
JOHNNY STORM. I WOULD HAVE PERISHED IF NOT FOR YOU.
WHAT YOU DID WAS RASH. VAINGLORIOUS. AND IT LEFT YOU VULNERABLE.
IT WAS... FOOLISH.
GNHH!
AND I DON'T CARE WHY YOU DID IT! YOU'VE INVADED MY HOMELAND! YOU-- YOU DESERVE TO DIE!
ZORA.
YES, MY LORD?
COME WITH ME.

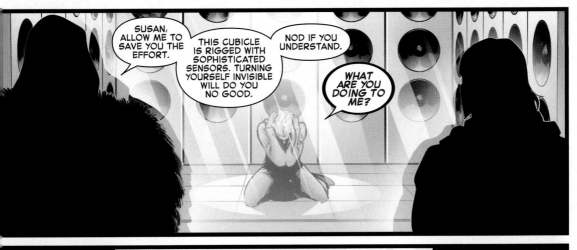

SUSAN, ALLOW ME TO SAVE YOU THE EFFORT.

THIS CUBICLE IS RIGGED WITH SOPHISTICATED SENSORS. TURNING YOURSELF INVISIBLE WILL DO YOU NO GOOD.

NOD IF YOU UNDERSTAND.

WHAT ARE YOU DOING TO ME?

WHAT YOU ARE FEELING ARE SONIC PULSES.

SCRAMBLING THE PORTION OF YOUR BRAIN THAT YOU USE TO GENERATE INVISIBLE FORCE-FIELDS.

WE BOTH KNOW THOSE ARE YOUR ONLY FORMIDABLE WEAPONS.

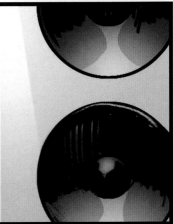

MY APOLOGIES IF THAT CAME ACROSS AS CRUEL OR DISMISSIVE. PLEASE ACCEPT THIS AS A SALVE.

FOR THE SACRIFICE YOU ARE ABOUT TO MAKE, I SWEAR TO YOU...

...THAT BOTH VALERIA AND FRANKLIN SHALL BE WELL LOOKED AFTER.

THAT IS MY PARTING GIFT TO YOU. THAT ONCE YOU ARE GONE...

...YOUR CHILDREN WILL BE UNDER MY PROTECTION. SAFE AND SOUND...

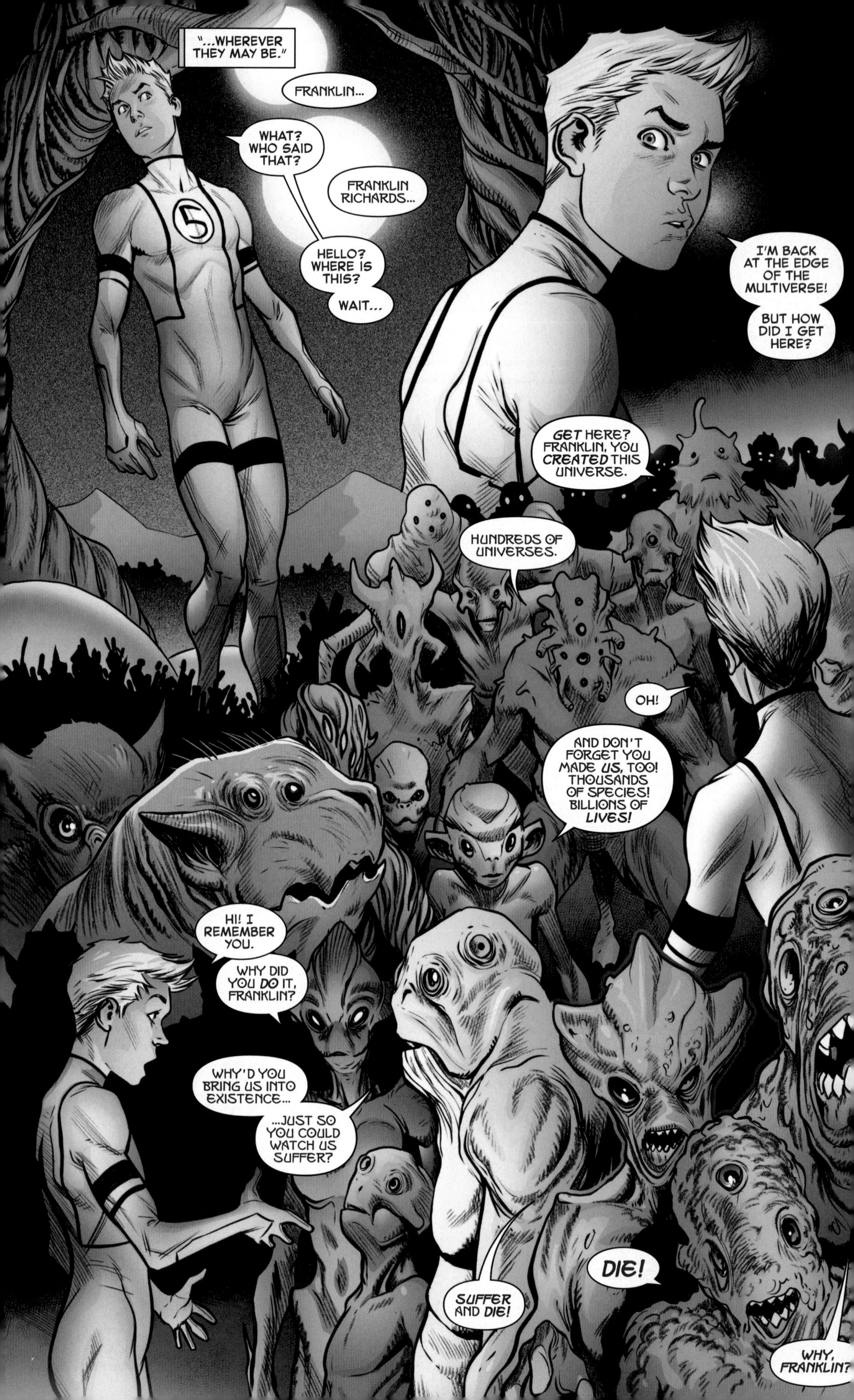
"...WHEREVER THEY MAY BE."
FRANKLIN...
WHAT? WHO SAID THAT?
FRANKLIN RICHARDS...
HELLO? WHERE IS THIS?
WAIT...
I'M BACK AT THE EDGE OF THE MULTIVERSE!
BUT HOW DID I GET HERE?
GET HERE? FRANKLIN, YOU CREATED THIS UNIVERSE.
HUNDREDS OF UNIVERSES.
OH!
AND DON'T FORGET YOU MADE US, TOO! THOUSANDS OF SPECIES! BILLIONS OF LIVES!
HI! I REMEMBER YOU.
WHY DID YOU DO IT, FRANKLIN?
WHY'D YOU BRING US INTO EXISTENCE...
...JUST SO YOU COULD WATCH US SUFFER?
SUFFER AND DIE!
DIE!
WHY, FRANKLIN?

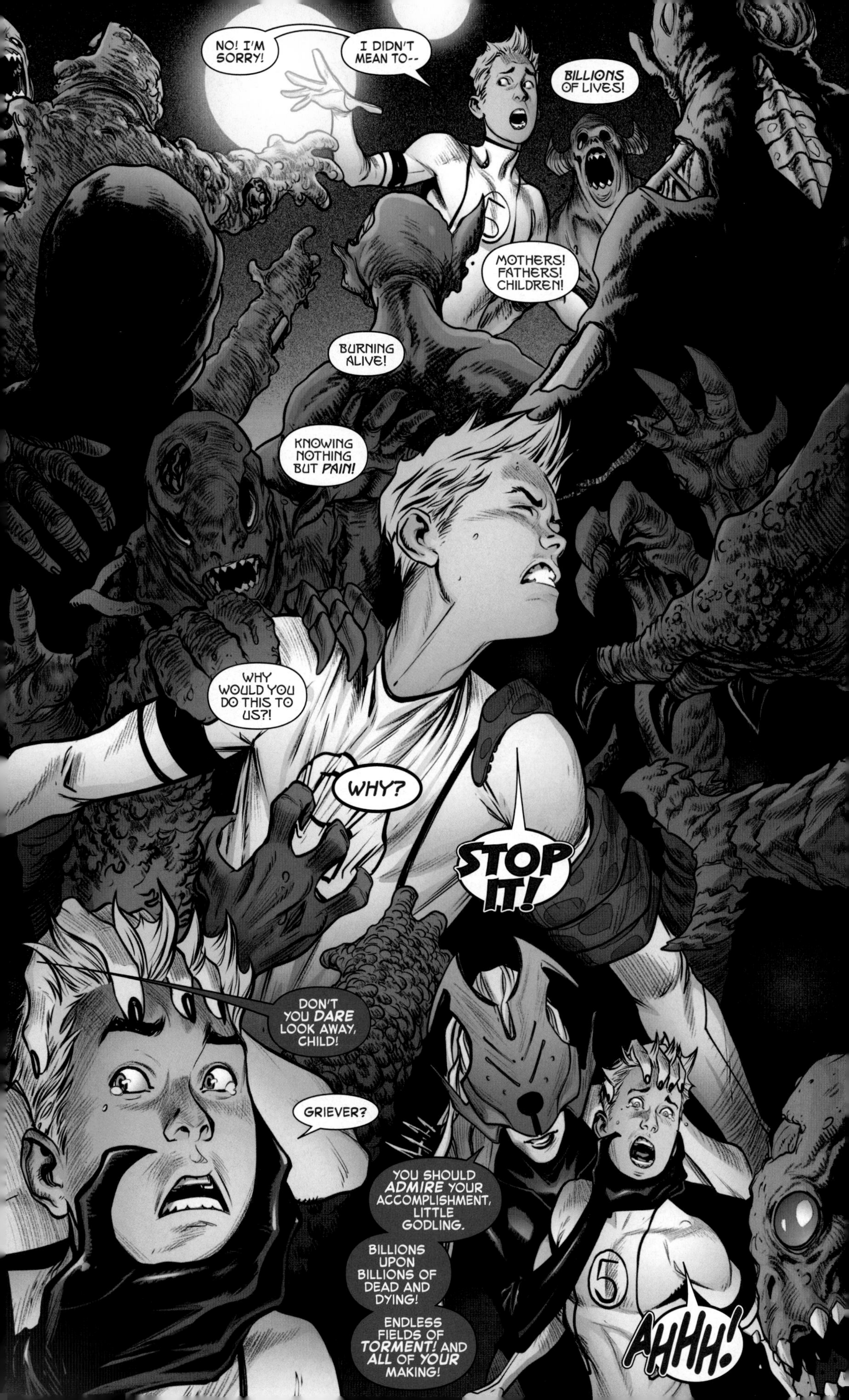
NO! I'M SORRY!
I DIDN'T MEAN TO--
BILLIONS OF LIVES!
MOTHERS! FATHERS! CHILDREN!
BURNING ALIVE!
KNOWING NOTHING BUT PAIN!
WHY WOULD YOU DO THIS TO US?!
WHY?
STOP IT!
DON'T YOU DARE LOOK AWAY, CHILD!
GRIEVER?
YOU SHOULD ADMIRE YOUR ACCOMPLISHMENT, LITTLE GODLING.
BILLIONS UPON BILLIONS OF DEAD AND DYING!
ENDLESS FIELDS OF TORMENT! AND ALL OF YOUR MAKING!
AHHH!

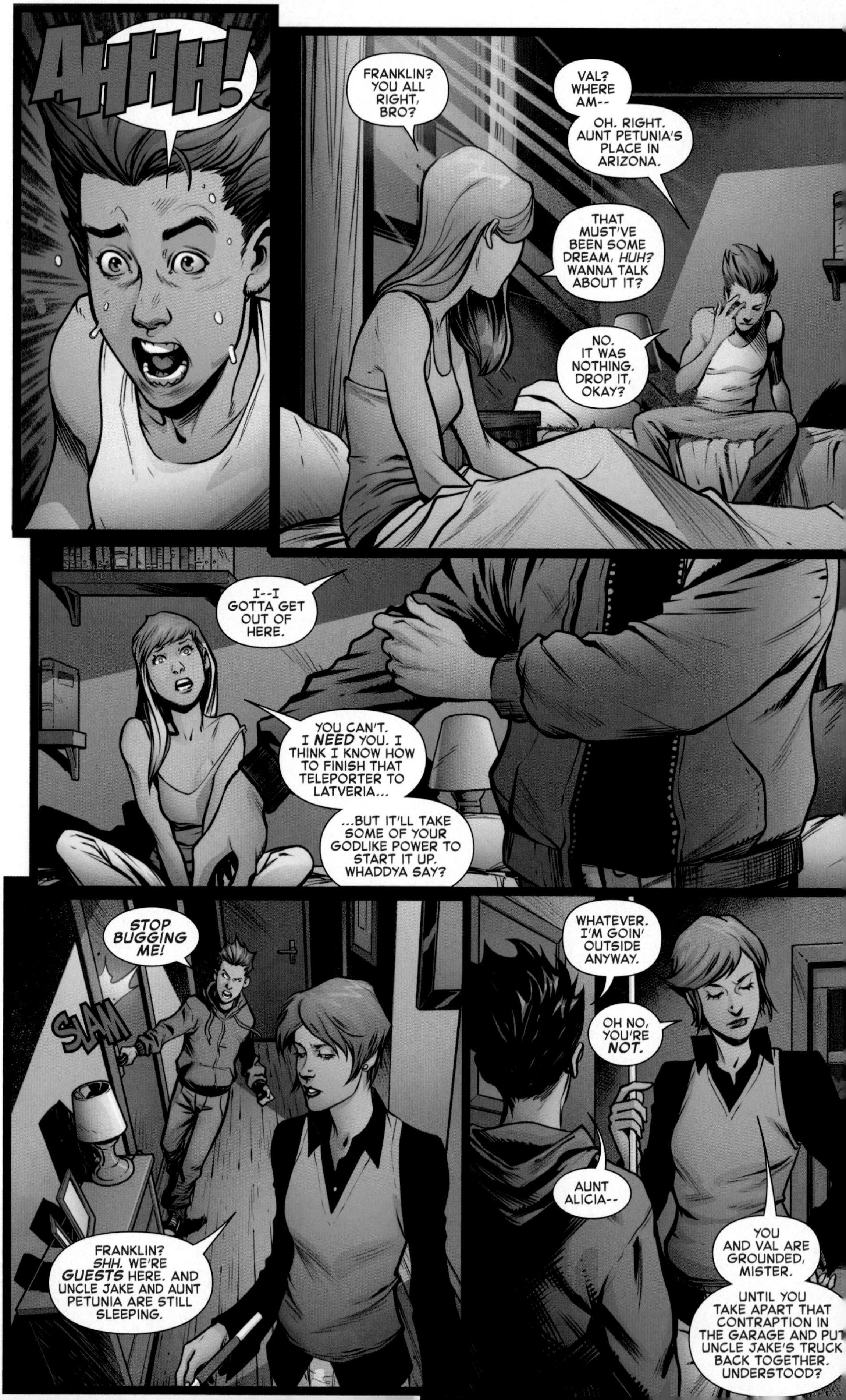
AHHH!
FRANKLIN? YOU ALL RIGHT, BRO?
VAL? WHERE AM--
OH. RIGHT. AUNT PETUNIA'S PLACE IN ARIZONA.
THAT MUST'VE BEEN SOME DREAM, *HUH?* WANNA TALK ABOUT IT?
NO. IT WAS NOTHING. DROP IT, OKAY?
I--I GOTTA GET OUT OF HERE.
YOU CAN'T. I **NEED** YOU. I THINK I KNOW HOW TO FINISH THAT TELEPORTER TO LATVERIA...
...BUT IT'LL TAKE SOME OF YOUR GODLIKE POWER TO START IT UP. WHADDYA SAY?
STOP BUGGING ME!
SLAM
FRANKLIN? *SHH.* WE'RE **GUESTS** HERE. AND UNCLE JAKE AND AUNT PETUNIA ARE STILL SLEEPING.
WHATEVER. I'M GOIN' OUTSIDE ANYWAY.
OH NO, YOU'RE **NOT.**
AUNT ALICIA--
YOU AND VAL ARE GROUNDED, MISTER.
UNTIL YOU TAKE APART THAT CONTRAPTION IN THE GARAGE AND PUT UNCLE JAKE'S TRUCK BACK TOGETHER. UNDERSTOOD?

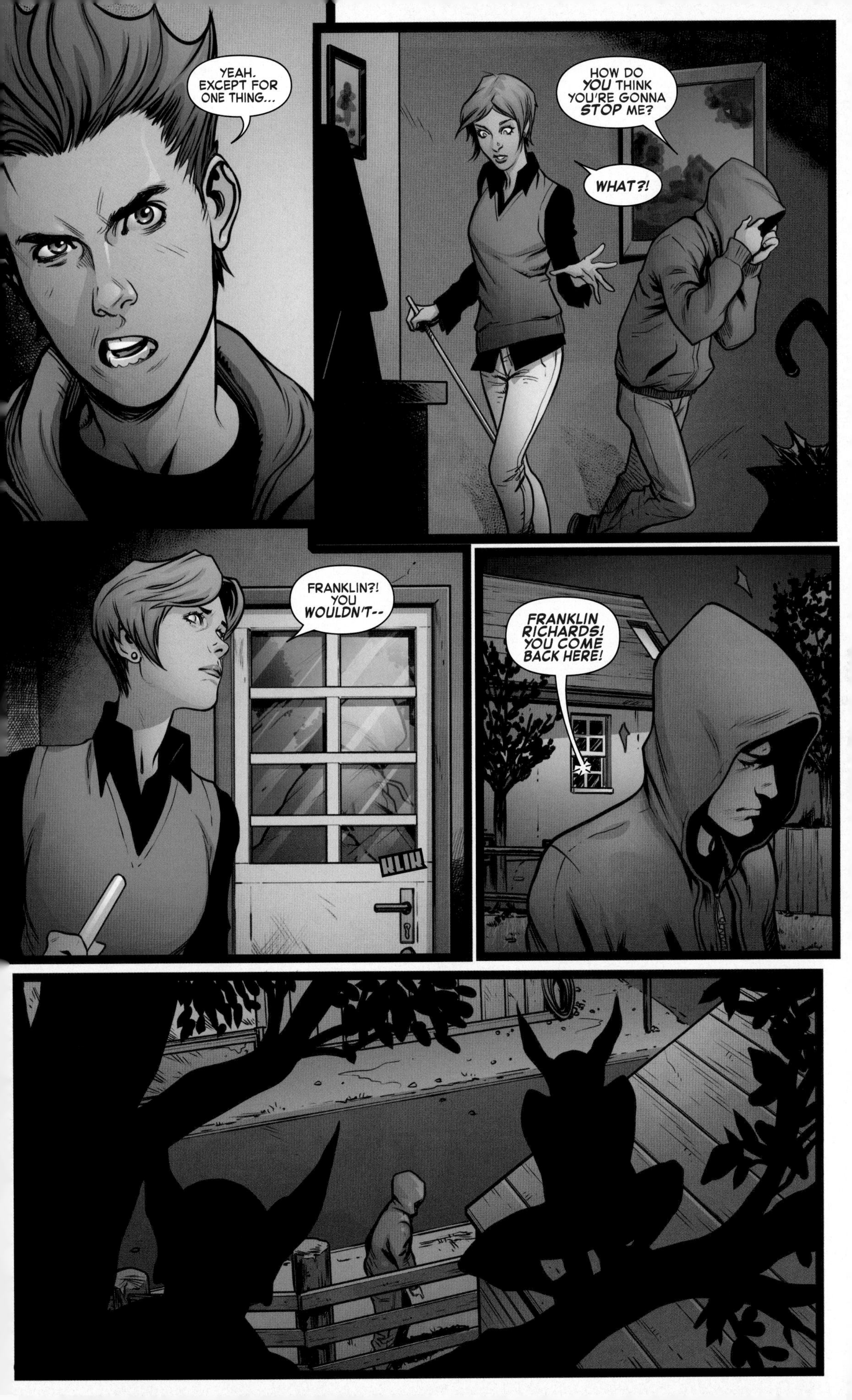
YEAH. EXCEPT FOR ONE THING...
HOW DO YOU THINK YOU'RE GONNA STOP ME?
WHAT?!
FRANKLIN?! YOU WOULDN'T--
KLIK
FRANKLIN RICHARDS! YOU COME BACK HERE!

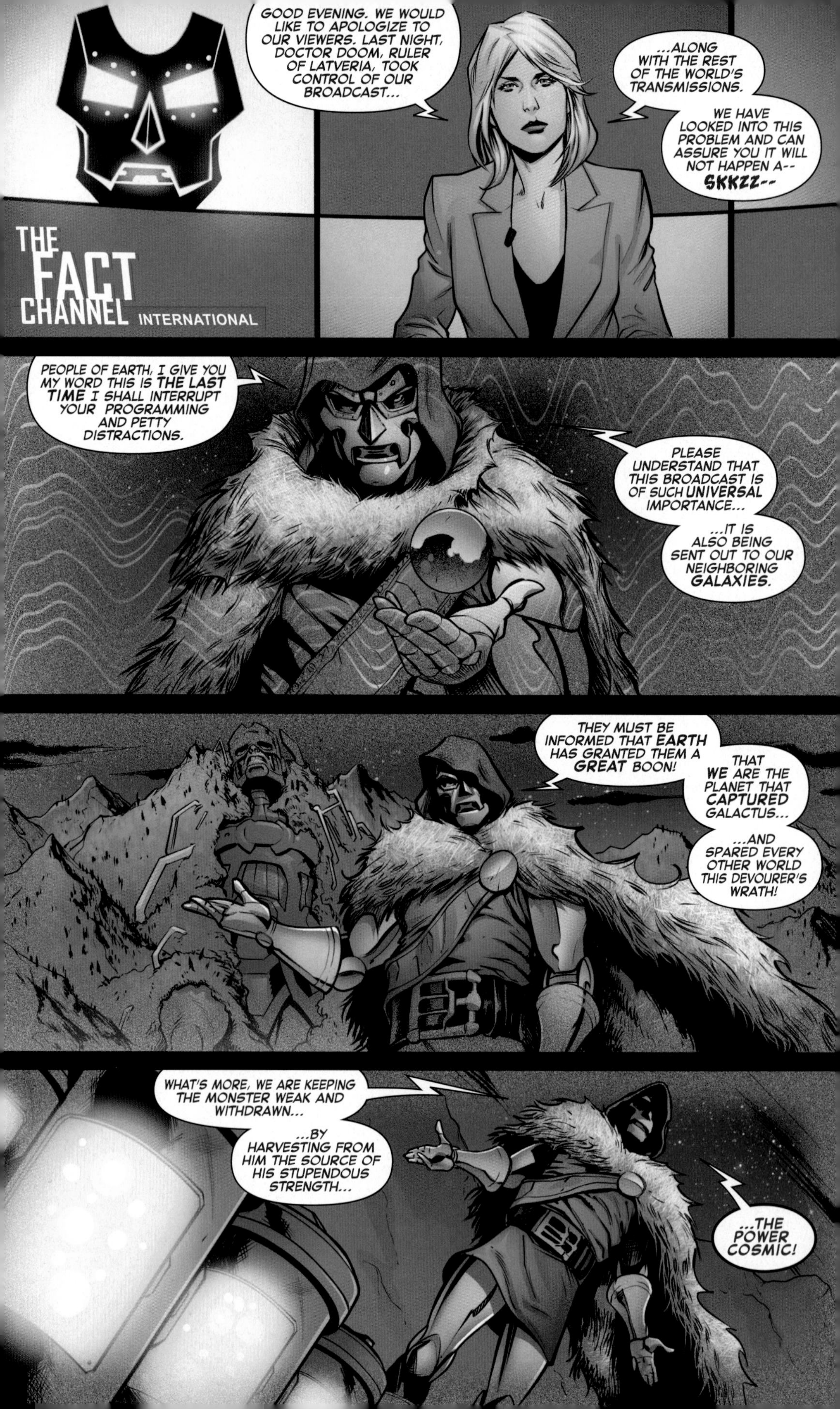
GOOD EVENING. WE WOULD LIKE TO APOLOGIZE TO OUR VIEWERS. LAST NIGHT, DOCTOR DOOM, RULER OF LATVERIA, TOOK CONTROL OF OUR BROADCAST...
...ALONG WITH THE REST OF THE WORLD'S TRANSMISSIONS.
WE HAVE LOOKED INTO THIS PROBLEM AND CAN ASSURE YOU IT WILL NOT HAPPEN A-- SKKZZ--
THE FACT CHANNEL INTERNATIONAL
PEOPLE OF EARTH, I GIVE YOU MY WORD THIS IS THE LAST TIME I SHALL INTERRUPT YOUR PROGRAMMING AND PETTY DISTRACTIONS.
PLEASE UNDERSTAND THAT THIS BROADCAST IS OF SUCH UNIVERSAL IMPORTANCE...
...IT IS ALSO BEING SENT OUT TO OUR NEIGHBORING GALAXIES.
THEY MUST BE INFORMED THAT EARTH HAS GRANTED THEM A GREAT BOON!
THAT WE ARE THE PLANET THAT CAPTURED GALACTUS...
...AND SPARED EVERY OTHER WORLD THIS DEVOURER'S WRATH!
WHAT'S MORE, WE ARE KEEPING THE MONSTER WEAK AND WITHDRAWN...
...BY HARVESTING FROM HIM THE SOURCE OF HIS STUPENDOUS STRENGTH...
...THE POWER COSMIC!

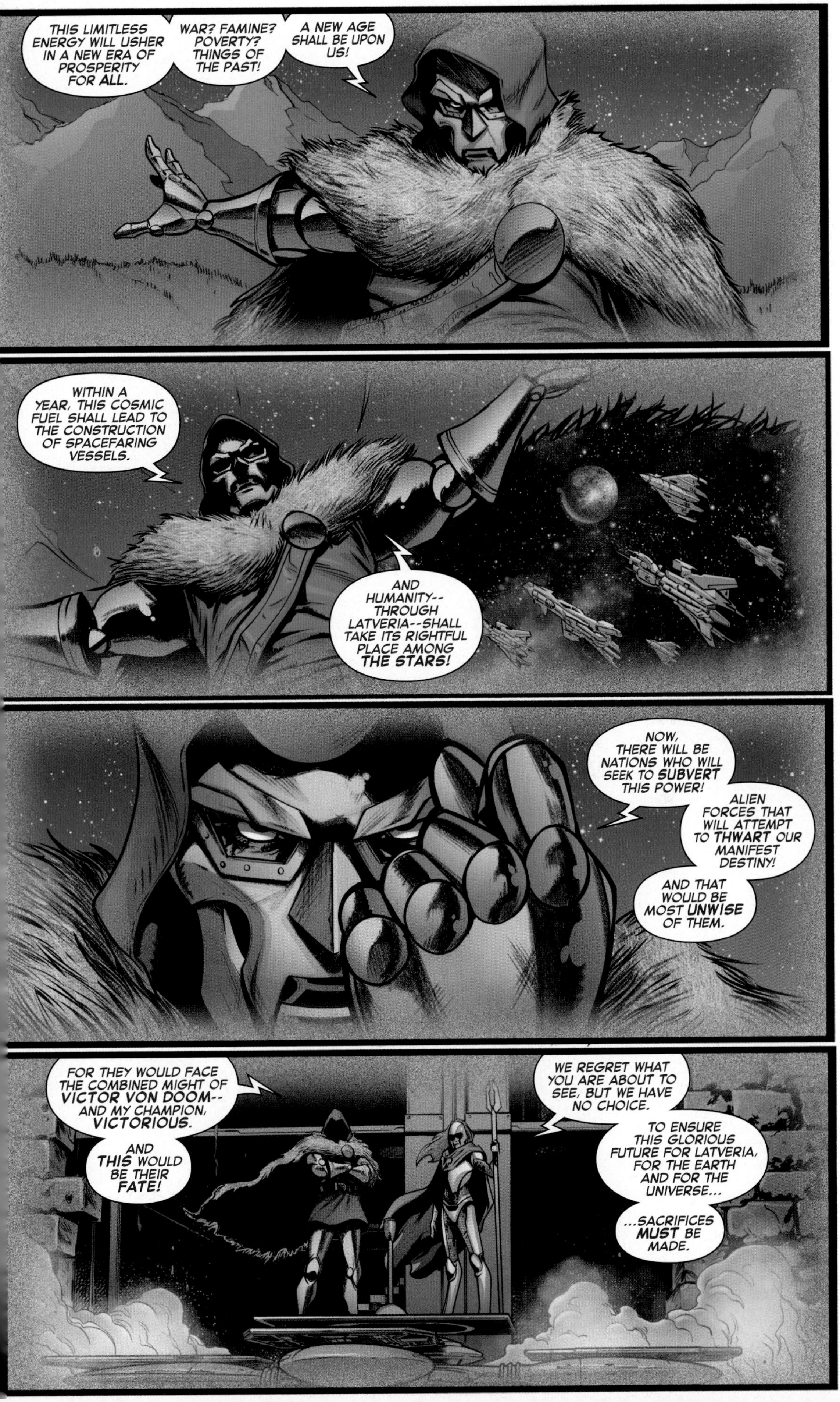
THIS LIMITLESS ENERGY WILL USHER IN A NEW ERA OF PROSPERITY FOR ALL.
WAR? FAMINE? POVERTY? THINGS OF THE PAST!
A NEW AGE SHALL BE UPON US!
WITHIN A YEAR, THIS COSMIC FUEL SHALL LEAD TO THE CONSTRUCTION OF SPACEFARING VESSELS.
AND HUMANITY--THROUGH LATVERIA--SHALL TAKE ITS RIGHTFUL PLACE AMONG THE STARS!
NOW, THERE WILL BE NATIONS WHO WILL SEEK TO SUBVERT THIS POWER!
ALIEN FORCES THAT WILL ATTEMPT TO THWART OUR MANIFEST DESTINY!
AND THAT WOULD BE MOST UNWISE OF THEM.
FOR THEY WOULD FACE THE COMBINED MIGHT OF VICTOR VON DOOM--AND MY CHAMPION, VICTORIOUS.
AND THIS WOULD BE THEIR FATE!
WE REGRET WHAT YOU ARE ABOUT TO SEE, BUT WE HAVE NO CHOICE.
TO ENSURE THIS GLORIOUS FUTURE FOR LATVERIA, FOR THE EARTH AND FOR THE UNIVERSE...
...SACRIFICES MUST BE MADE.

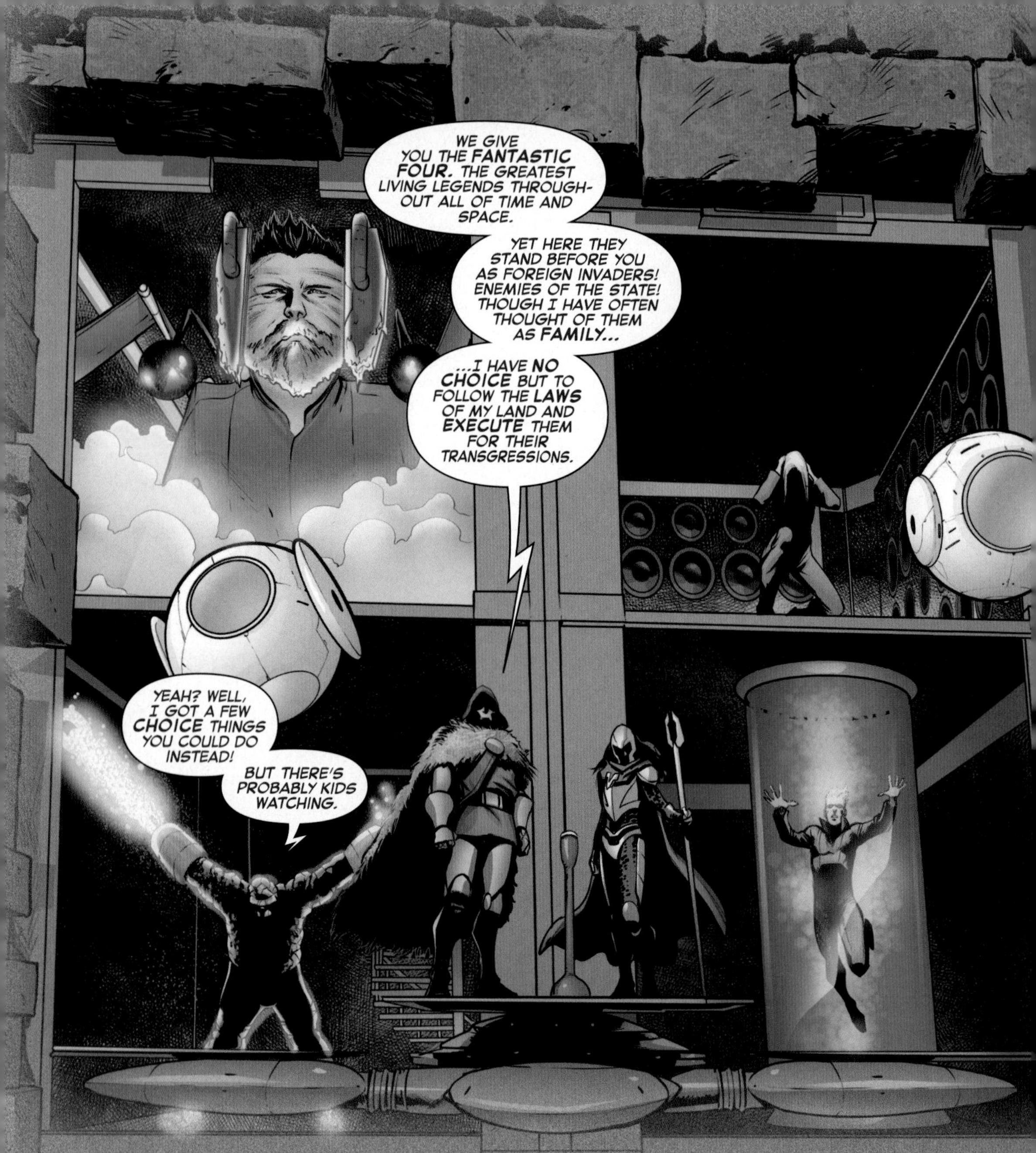
WE GIVE YOU THE FANTASTIC FOUR. THE GREATEST LIVING LEGENDS THROUGH-OUT ALL OF TIME AND SPACE.
YET HERE THEY STAND BEFORE YOU AS FOREIGN INVADERS! ENEMIES OF THE STATE! THOUGH I HAVE OFTEN THOUGHT OF THEM AS FAMILY...
...I HAVE NO CHOICE BUT TO FOLLOW THE LAWS OF MY LAND AND EXECUTE THEM FOR THEIR TRANSGRESSIONS.
YEAH? WELL, I GOT A FEW CHOICE THINGS YOU COULD DO INSTEAD!
BUT THERE'S PROBABLY KIDS WATCHING.

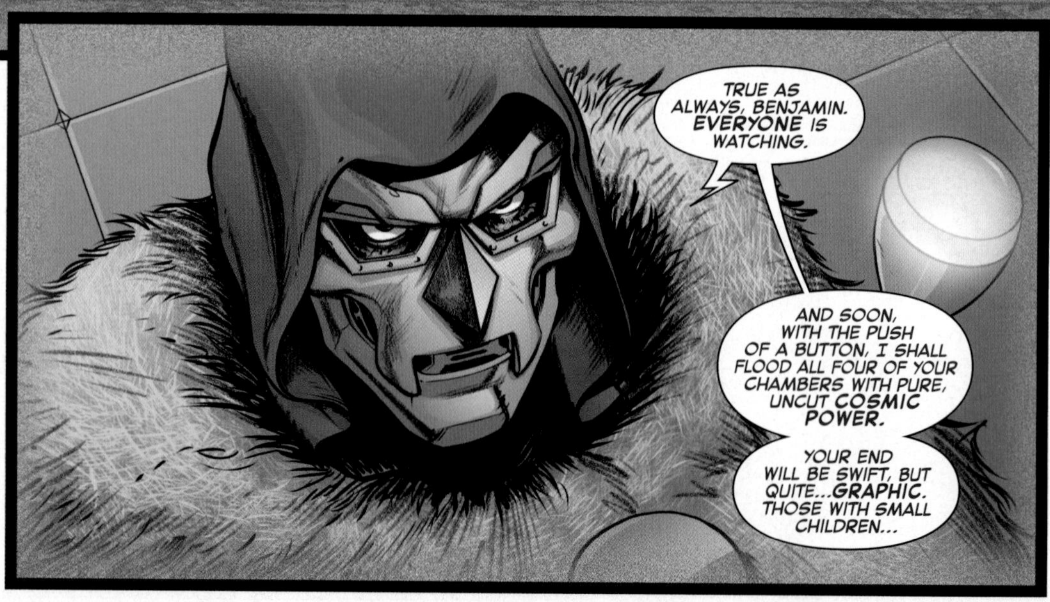
TRUE AS ALWAYS, BENJAMIN. EVERYONE IS WATCHING.
AND SOON, WITH THE PUSH OF A BUTTON, I SHALL FLOOD ALL FOUR OF YOUR CHAMBERS WITH PURE, UNCUT COSMIC POWER.
YOUR END WILL BE SWIFT, BUT QUITE...GRAPHIC. THOSE WITH SMALL CHILDREN...

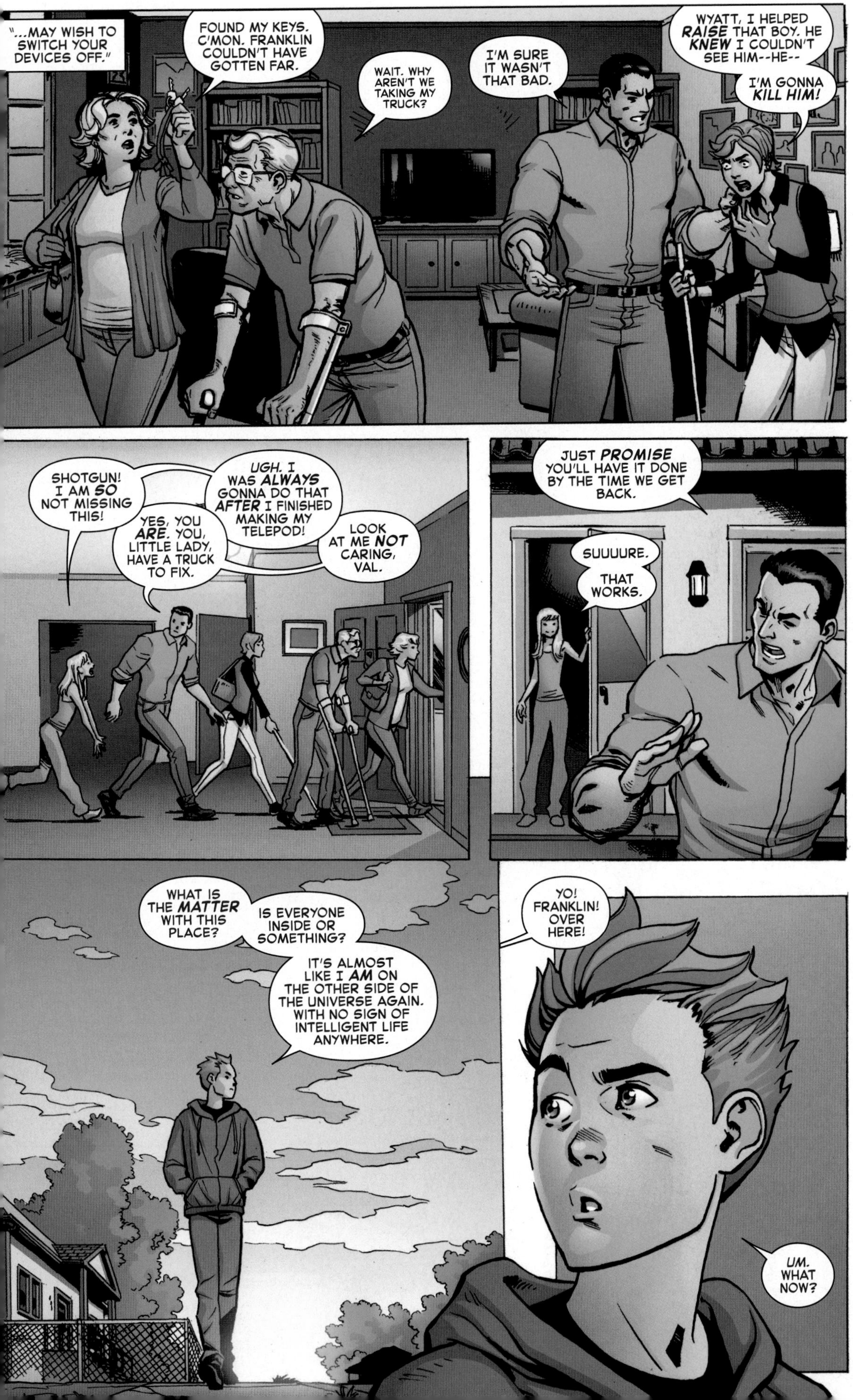
"...MAY WISH TO SWITCH YOUR DEVICES OFF."
FOUND MY KEYS. C'MON. FRANKLIN COULDN'T HAVE GOTTEN FAR.
WAIT. WHY AREN'T WE TAKING MY TRUCK?
I'M SURE IT WASN'T THAT BAD.
WYATT, I HELPED RAISE THAT BOY. HE KNEW I COULDN'T SEE HIM--HE--
I'M GONNA KILL HIM!
SHOTGUN! I AM SO NOT MISSING THIS!
YES, YOU ARE. YOU, LITTLE LADY, HAVE A TRUCK TO FIX.
UGH. I WAS ALWAYS GONNA DO THAT AFTER I FINISHED MAKING MY TELEPOD!
LOOK AT ME NOT CARING, VAL.
JUST PROMISE YOU'LL HAVE IT DONE BY THE TIME WE GET BACK.
SUUUURE.
THAT WORKS.
WHAT IS THE MATTER WITH THIS PLACE?
IS EVERYONE INSIDE OR SOMETHING?
IT'S ALMOST LIKE I AM ON THE OTHER SIDE OF THE UNIVERSE AGAIN. WITH NO SIGN OF INTELLIGENT LIFE ANYWHERE.
YO! FRANKLIN! OVER HERE!
UM. WHAT NOW?

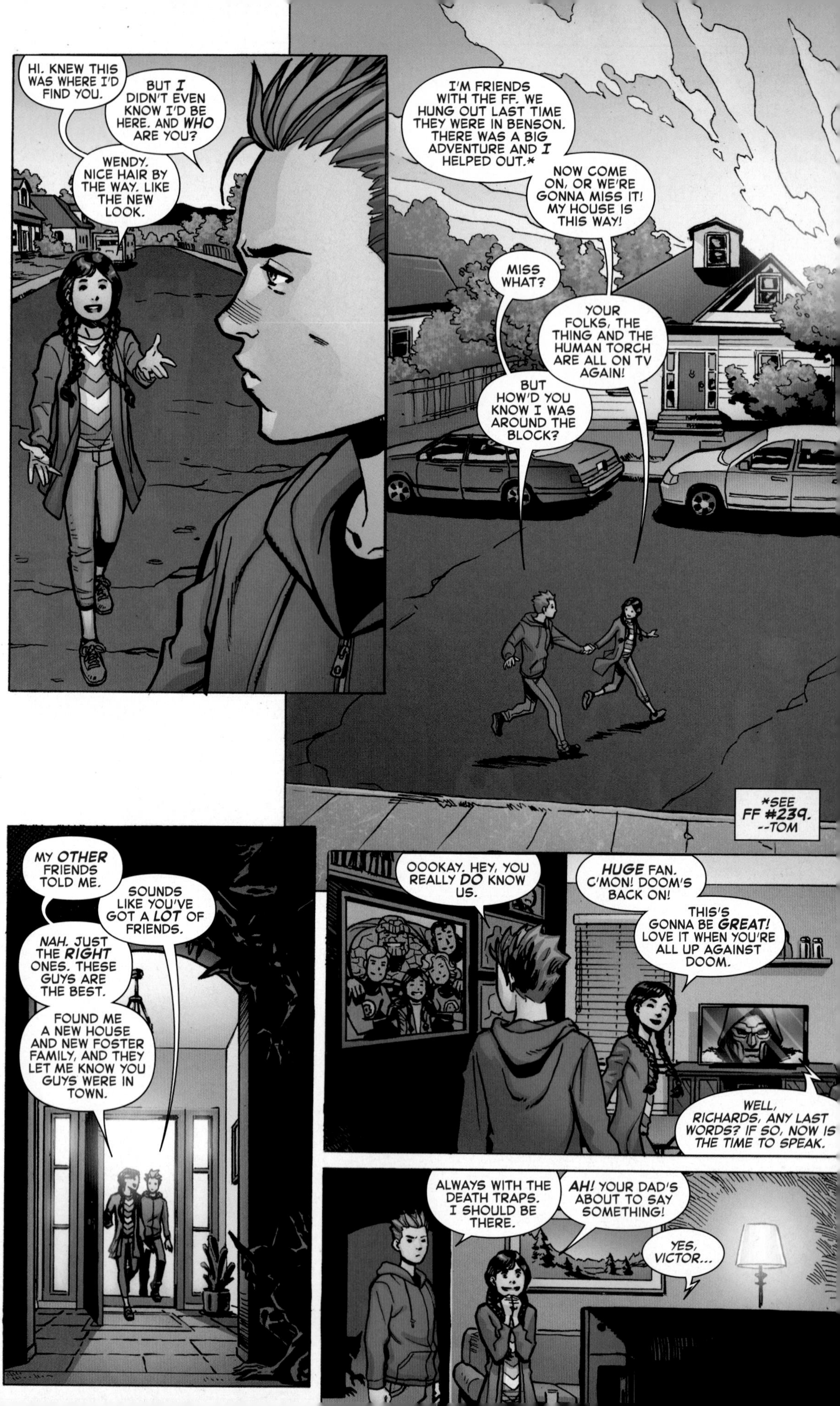
HI. KNEW THIS WAS WHERE I'D FIND YOU.
BUT *I* DIDN'T EVEN KNOW I'D BE HERE. AND *WHO* ARE YOU?
WENDY. NICE HAIR BY THE WAY. LIKE THE NEW LOOK.
I'M FRIENDS WITH THE FF. WE HUNG OUT LAST TIME THEY WERE IN BENSON. THERE WAS A BIG ADVENTURE AND *I* HELPED OUT.*
NOW COME ON, OR WE'RE GONNA MISS IT! MY HOUSE IS THIS WAY!
MISS WHAT?
YOUR FOLKS, THE THING AND THE HUMAN TORCH ARE ALL ON TV AGAIN!
BUT HOW'D YOU KNOW I WAS AROUND THE BLOCK?
*SEE FF #239. --TOM
MY *OTHER* FRIENDS TOLD ME.
SOUNDS LIKE YOU'VE GOT A *LOT* OF FRIENDS.
*NAH.* JUST THE *RIGHT* ONES. THESE GUYS ARE THE BEST.
FOUND ME A NEW HOUSE AND NEW FOSTER FAMILY, AND THEY LET ME KNOW YOU GUYS WERE IN TOWN.
OOOKAY. HEY, YOU REALLY *DO* KNOW US.
*HUGE* FAN. C'MON! DOOM'S BACK ON!
THIS'S GONNA BE *GREAT!* LOVE IT WHEN YOU'RE ALL UP AGAINST DOOM.
WELL, RICHARDS, ANY LAST WORDS? IF SO, NOW IS THE TIME TO SPEAK.
ALWAYS WITH THE DEATH TRAPS. I SHOULD BE THERE.
*AH!* YOUR DAD'S ABOUT TO SAY SOMETHING!
*YES, VICTOR...*

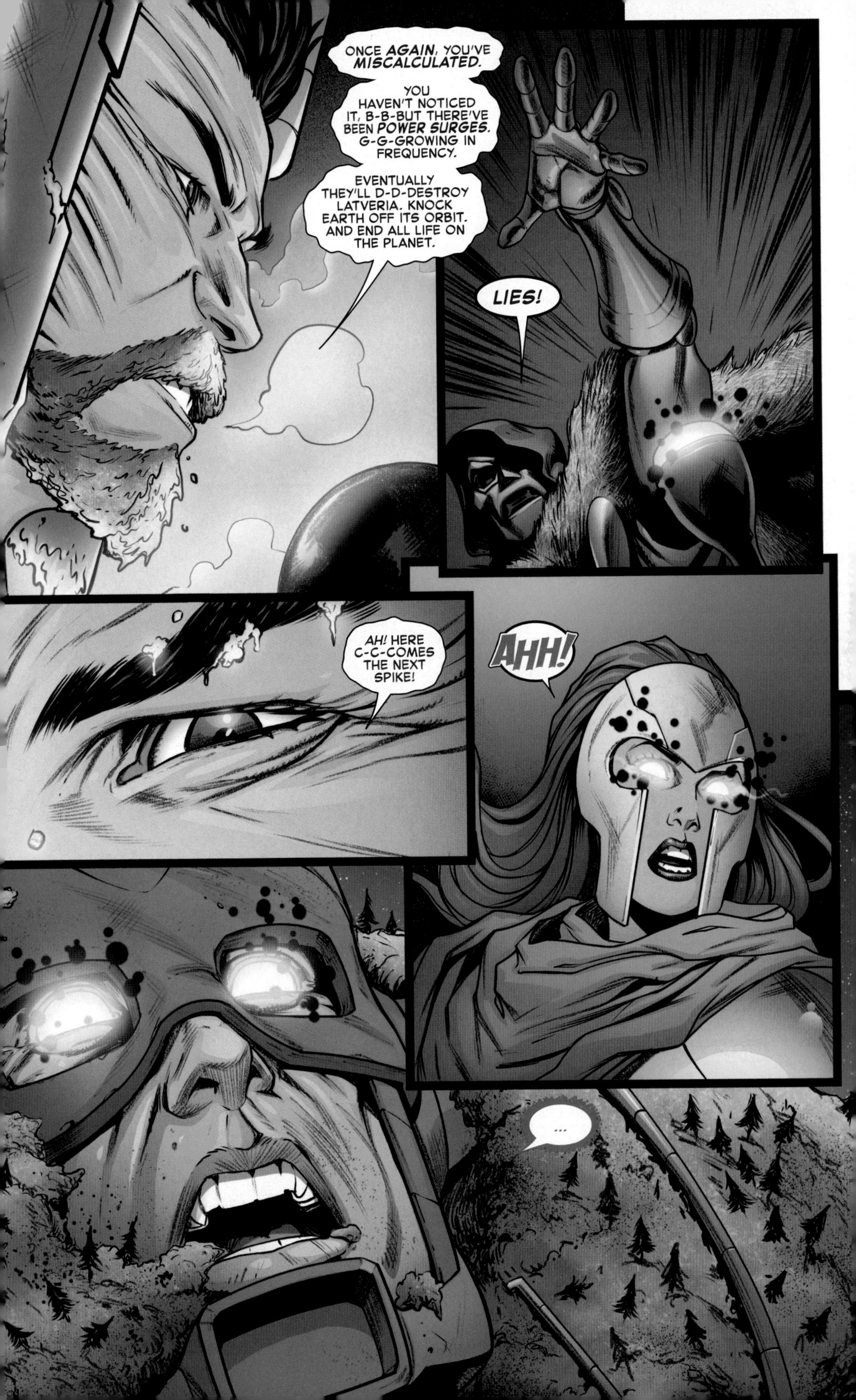
ONCE AGAIN, YOU'VE MISCALCULATED.
YOU HAVEN'T NOTICED IT, B-B-BUT THERE'VE BEEN POWER SURGES. G-G-GROWING IN FREQUENCY.
EVENTUALLY THEY'LL D-D-DESTROY LATVERIA. KNOCK EARTH OFF ITS ORBIT. AND END ALL LIFE ON THE PLANET.
LIES!
AH! HERE C-C-COMES THE NEXT SPIKE!
AHH!
...

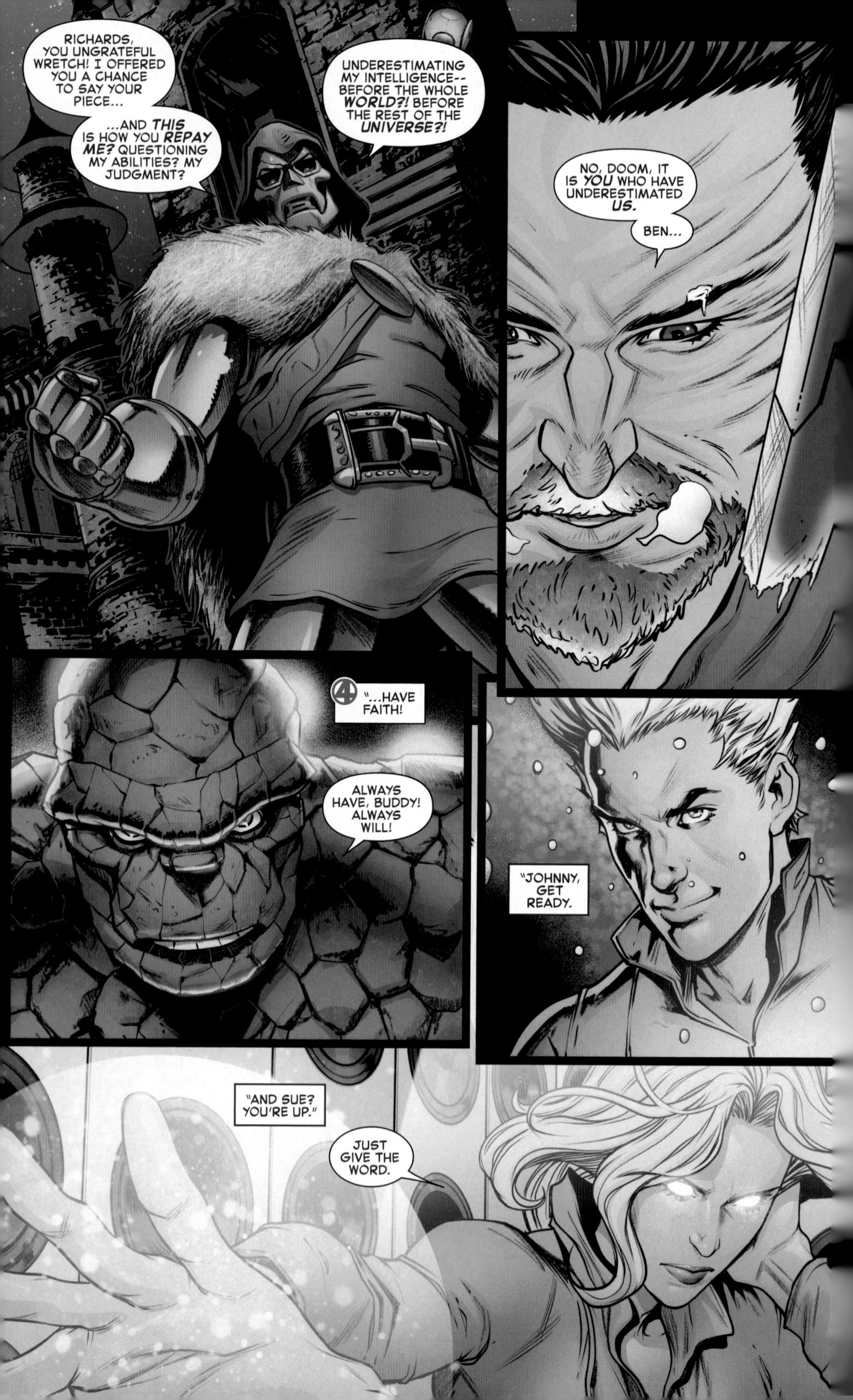
RICHARDS, YOU UNGRATEFUL WRETCH! I OFFERED YOU A CHANCE TO SAY YOUR PIECE...
...AND THIS IS HOW YOU REPAY ME? QUESTIONING MY ABILITIES? MY JUDGMENT?
UNDERESTIMATING MY INTELLIGENCE-- BEFORE THE WHOLE WORLD?! BEFORE THE REST OF THE UNIVERSE?!
NO, DOOM, IT IS YOU WHO HAVE UNDERESTIMATED US.
BEN...
"...HAVE FAITH!
ALWAYS HAVE, BUDDY! ALWAYS WILL!
"JOHNNY, GET READY.
"AND SUE? YOU'RE UP."
JUST GIVE THE WORD.

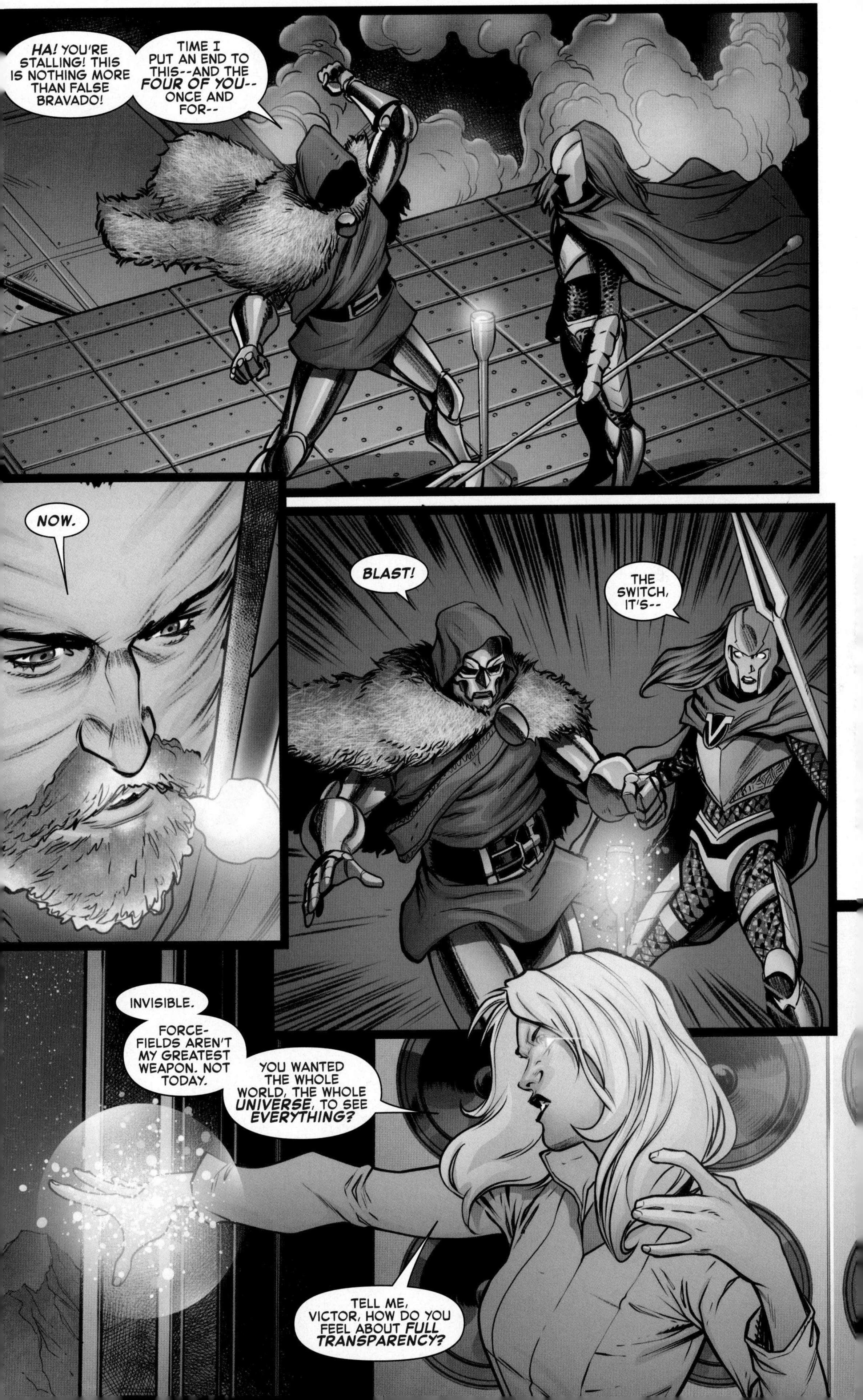
HA! YOU'RE STALLING! THIS IS NOTHING MORE THAN FALSE BRAVADO!
TIME I PUT AN END TO THIS--AND THE FOUR OF YOU-- ONCE AND FOR--
NOW.
BLAST!
THE SWITCH, IT'S--
INVISIBLE.
FORCE-FIELDS AREN'T MY GREATEST WEAPON. NOT TODAY.
YOU WANTED THE WHOLE WORLD, THE WHOLE UNIVERSE, TO SEE EVERYTHING?
TELL ME, VICTOR, HOW DO YOU FEEL ABOUT FULL TRANSPARENCY?

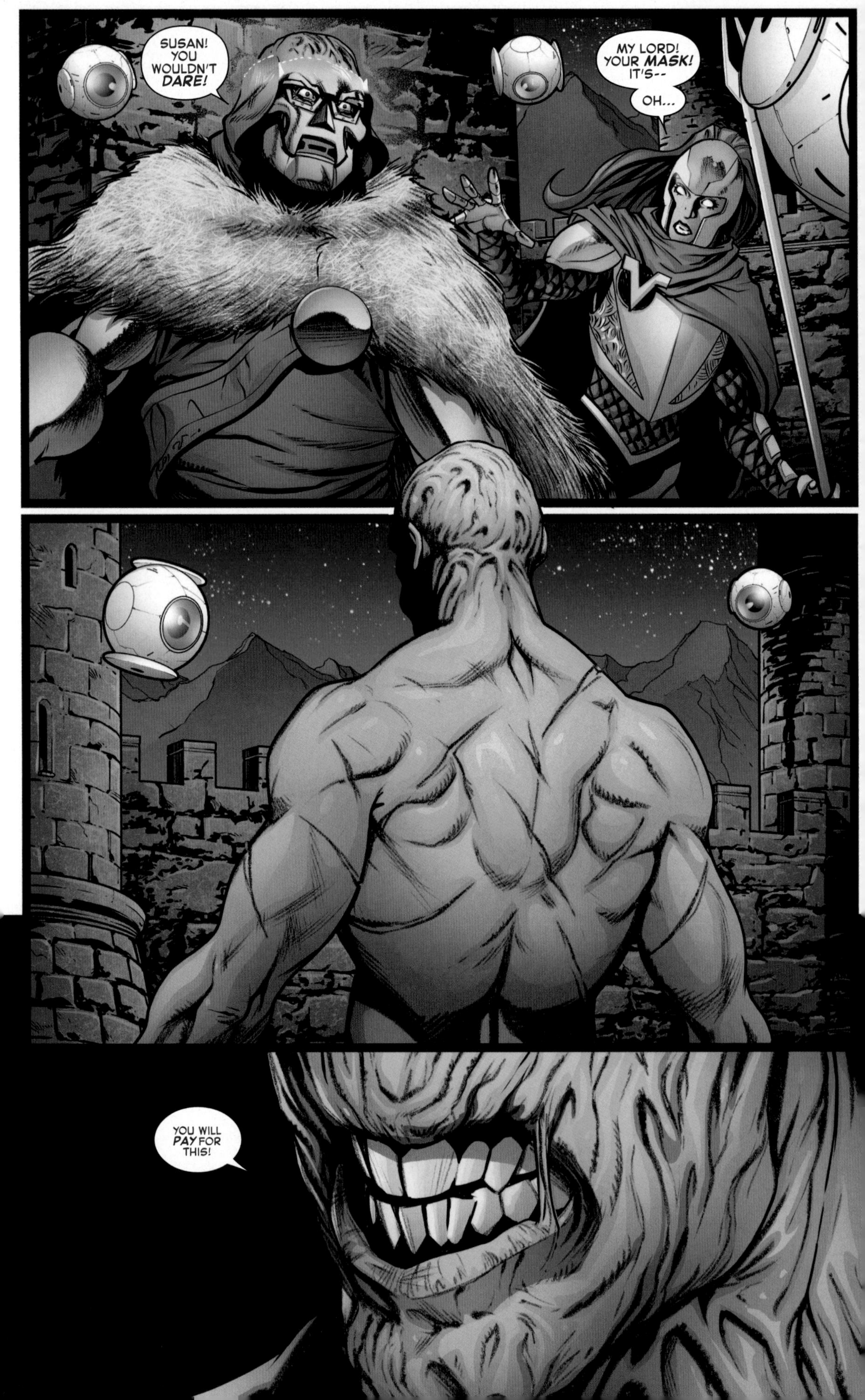
SUSAN! YOU WOULDN'T DARE!
MY LORD! YOUR MASK! IT'S--
OH...
YOU WILL PAY FOR THIS!

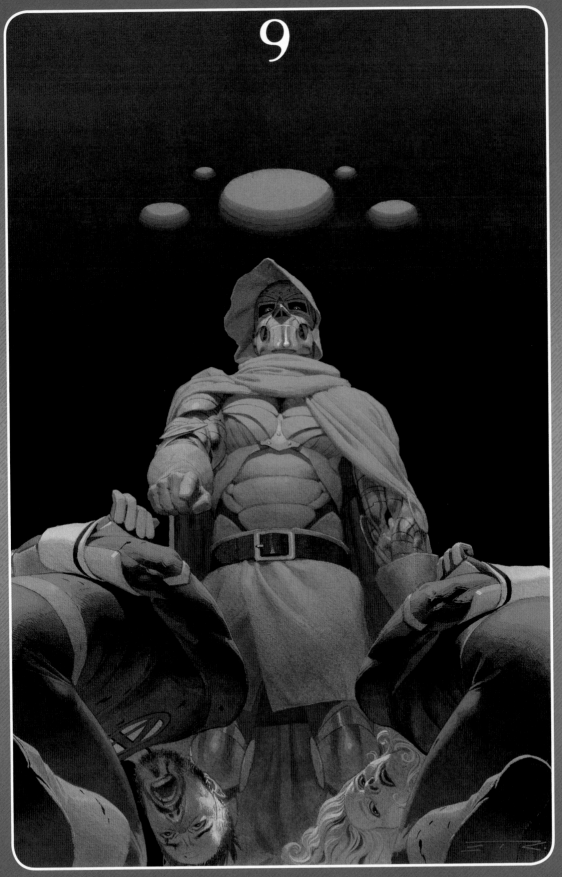

"Outside the Box"

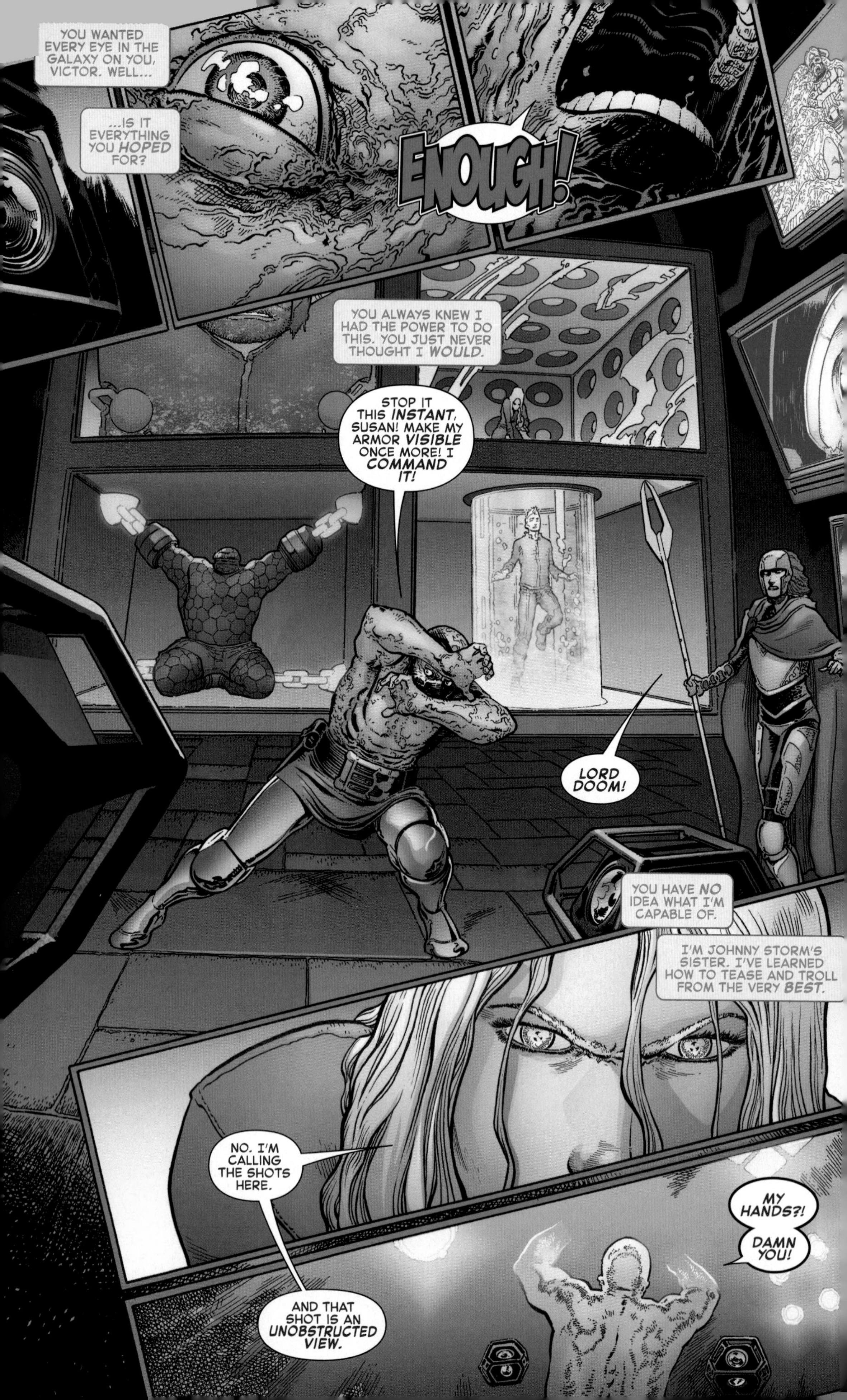
YOU WANTED EVERY EYE IN THE GALAXY ON YOU, VICTOR. WELL...
...IS IT EVERYTHING YOU HOPED FOR?
ENOUGH!
YOU ALWAYS KNEW I HAD THE POWER TO DO THIS. YOU JUST NEVER THOUGHT I WOULD.
STOP IT THIS INSTANT, SUSAN! MAKE MY ARMOR VISIBLE ONCE MORE! I COMMAND IT!
LORD DOOM!
YOU HAVE NO IDEA WHAT I'M CAPABLE OF.
I'M JOHNNY STORM'S SISTER. I'VE LEARNED HOW TO TEASE AND TROLL FROM THE VERY BEST.
NO. I'M CALLING THE SHOTS HERE.
AND THAT SHOT IS AN UNOBSTRUCTED VIEW.
MY HANDS?!
DAMN YOU!

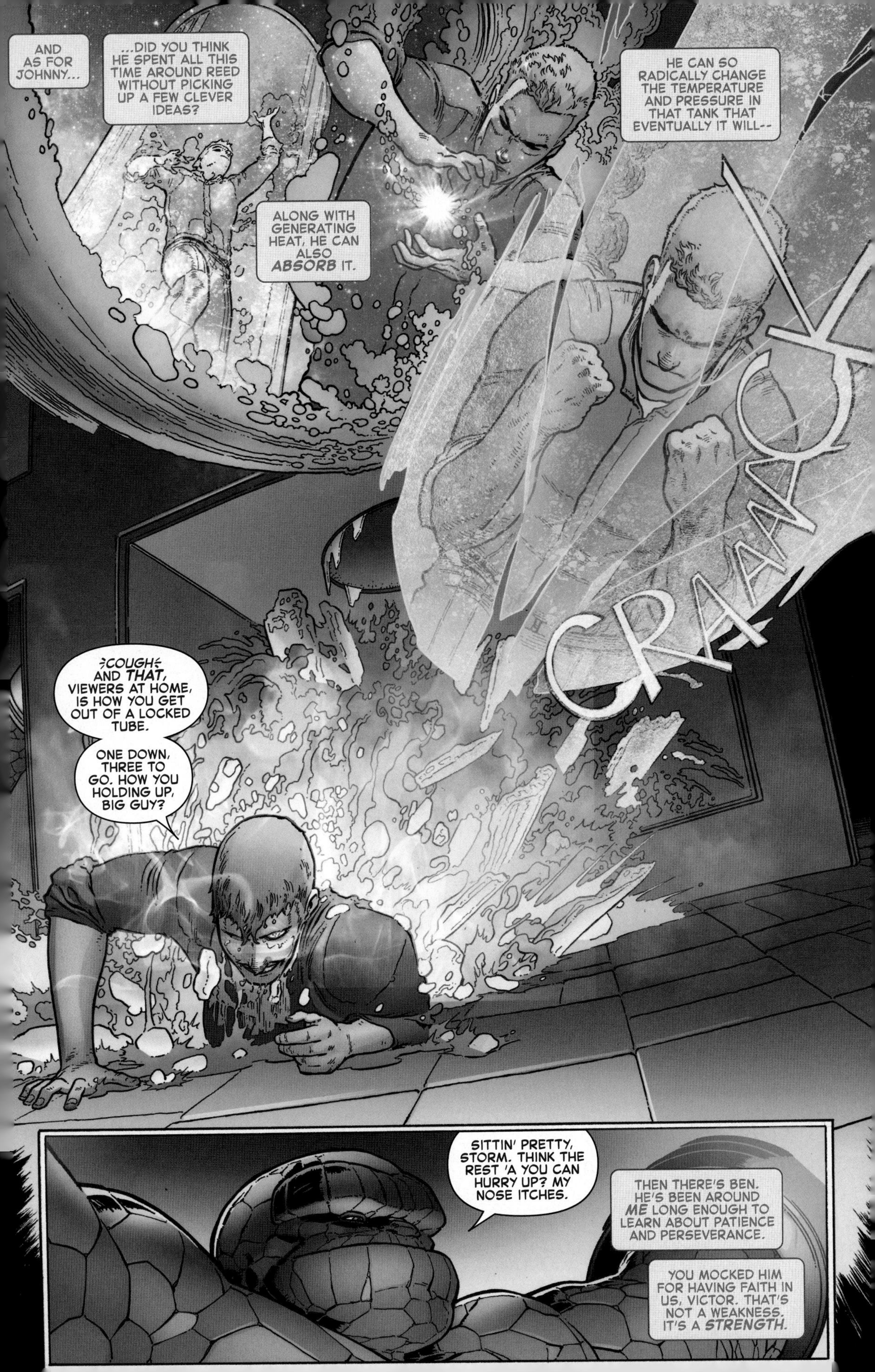
AND AS FOR JOHNNY...
...DID YOU THINK HE SPENT ALL THIS TIME AROUND REED WITHOUT PICKING UP A FEW CLEVER IDEAS?
ALONG WITH GENERATING HEAT, HE CAN ALSO ABSORB IT.
HE CAN SO RADICALLY CHANGE THE TEMPERATURE AND PRESSURE IN THAT TANK THAT EVENTUALLY IT WILL--
CRAAACK
*COUGH* AND THAT, VIEWERS AT HOME, IS HOW YOU GET OUT OF A LOCKED TUBE.
ONE DOWN, THREE TO GO. HOW YOU HOLDING UP, BIG GUY?
SITTIN' PRETTY, STORM. THINK THE REST 'A YOU CAN HURRY UP? MY NOSE ITCHES.
THEN THERE'S BEN. HE'S BEEN AROUND ME LONG ENOUGH TO LEARN ABOUT PATIENCE AND PERSEVERANCE.
YOU MOCKED HIM FOR HAVING FAITH IN US, VICTOR. THAT'S NOT A WEAKNESS. IT'S A STRENGTH.

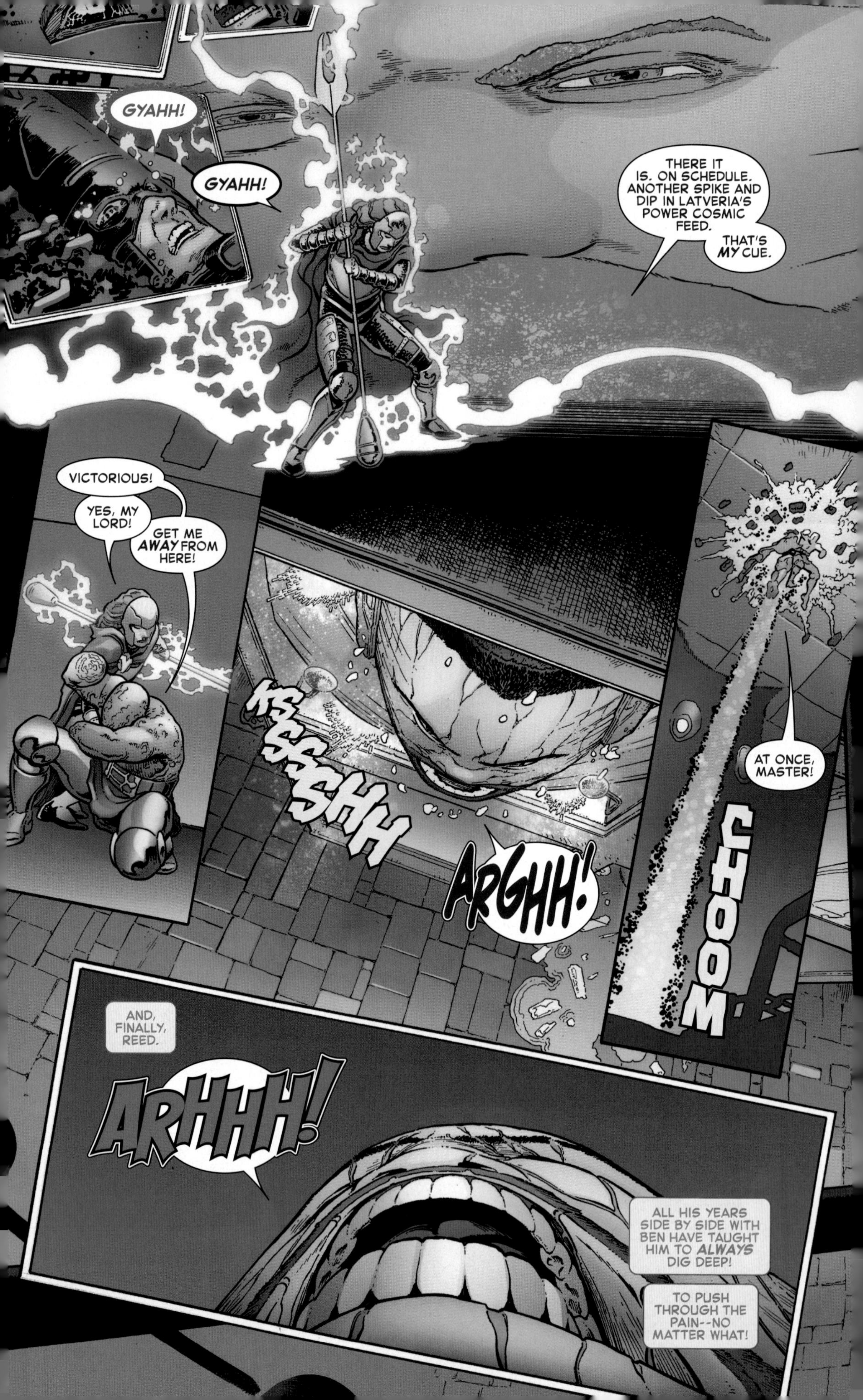
GYAHH!
GYAHH!
THERE IT IS. ON SCHEDULE. ANOTHER SPIKE AND DIP IN LATVERIA'S POWER COSMIC FEED.
THAT'S *MY* CUE.
VICTORIOUS!
YES, MY LORD!
GET ME *AWAY* FROM HERE!
KSSSHH
ARGHH!
AT ONCE, MASTER!
CHOOOM
AND, FINALLY, REED.
ARHHH!
ALL HIS YEARS SIDE BY SIDE WITH BEN HAVE TAUGHT HIM TO *ALWAYS* DIG DEEP!
TO PUSH THROUGH THE PAIN--NO MATTER WHAT!

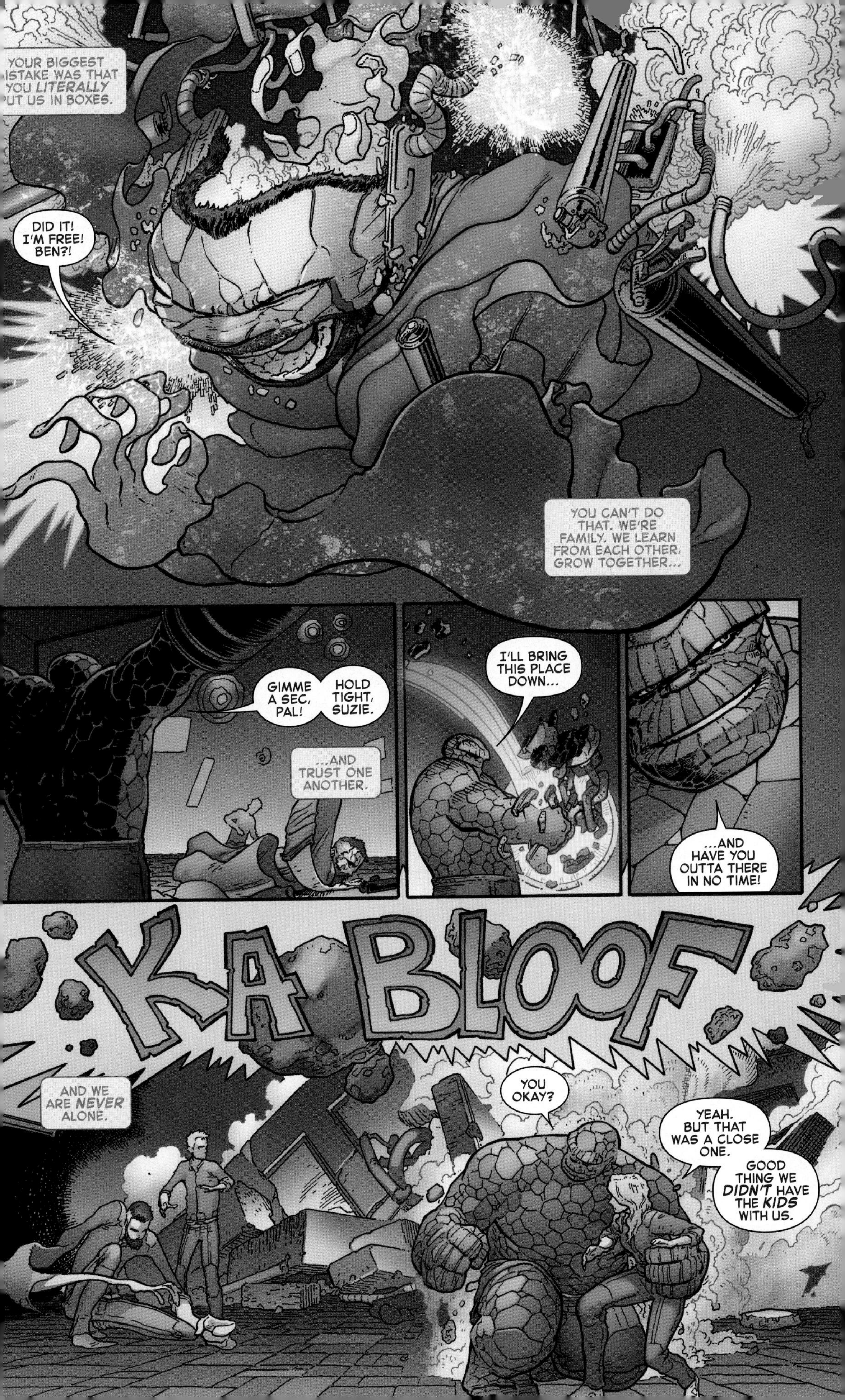
YOUR BIGGEST
ISTAKE WAS THAT
YOU *LITERALLY*
UT US IN BOXES.
DID IT! I'M FREE! BEN?!
YOU CAN'T DO THAT. WE'RE FAMILY. WE LEARN FROM EACH OTHER, GROW TOGETHER...
GIMME A SEC, PAL!
HOLD TIGHT, SUZIE.
...AND TRUST ONE ANOTHER.
I'LL BRING THIS PLACE DOWN...
...AND HAVE YOU OUTTA THERE IN NO TIME!
KA BLOOF
AND WE ARE *NEVER* ALONE.
YOU OKAY?
YEAH. BUT THAT WAS A CLOSE ONE.
GOOD THING WE *DIDN'T* HAVE THE *KIDS* WITH US.

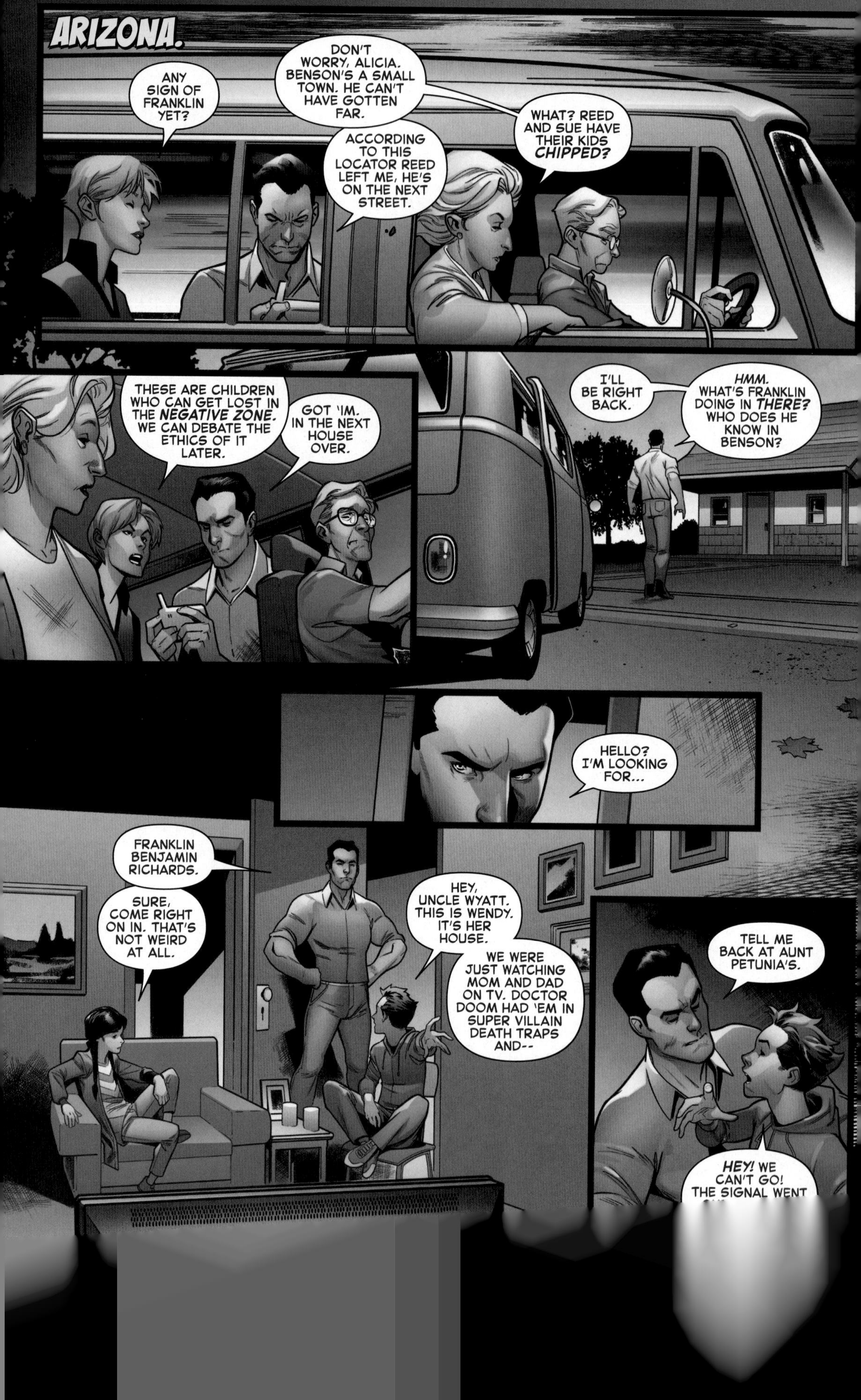
ARIZONA.
ANY SIGN OF FRANKLIN YET?
DON'T WORRY, ALICIA. BENSON'S A SMALL TOWN. HE CAN'T HAVE GOTTEN FAR.
ACCORDING TO THIS LOCATOR REED LEFT ME, HE'S ON THE NEXT STREET.
WHAT? REED AND SUE HAVE THEIR KIDS *CHIPPED?*
THESE ARE CHILDREN WHO CAN GET LOST IN THE *NEGATIVE ZONE*. WE CAN DEBATE THE ETHICS OF IT LATER.
GOT 'IM. IN THE NEXT HOUSE OVER.
I'LL BE RIGHT BACK.
*HMM.* WHAT'S FRANKLIN DOING IN *THERE?* WHO DOES HE KNOW IN BENSON?
HELLO? I'M LOOKING FOR...
FRANKLIN BENJAMIN RICHARDS.
SURE, COME RIGHT ON IN. THAT'S NOT WEIRD AT ALL.
HEY, UNCLE WYATT. THIS IS WENDY. IT'S HER HOUSE.
WE WERE JUST WATCHING MOM AND DAD ON TV. DOCTOR DOOM HAD 'EM IN SUPER VILLAIN DEATH TRAPS AND--
TELL ME BACK AT AUNT PETUNIA'S.
*HEY!* WE CAN'T GO! THE SIGNAL WENT

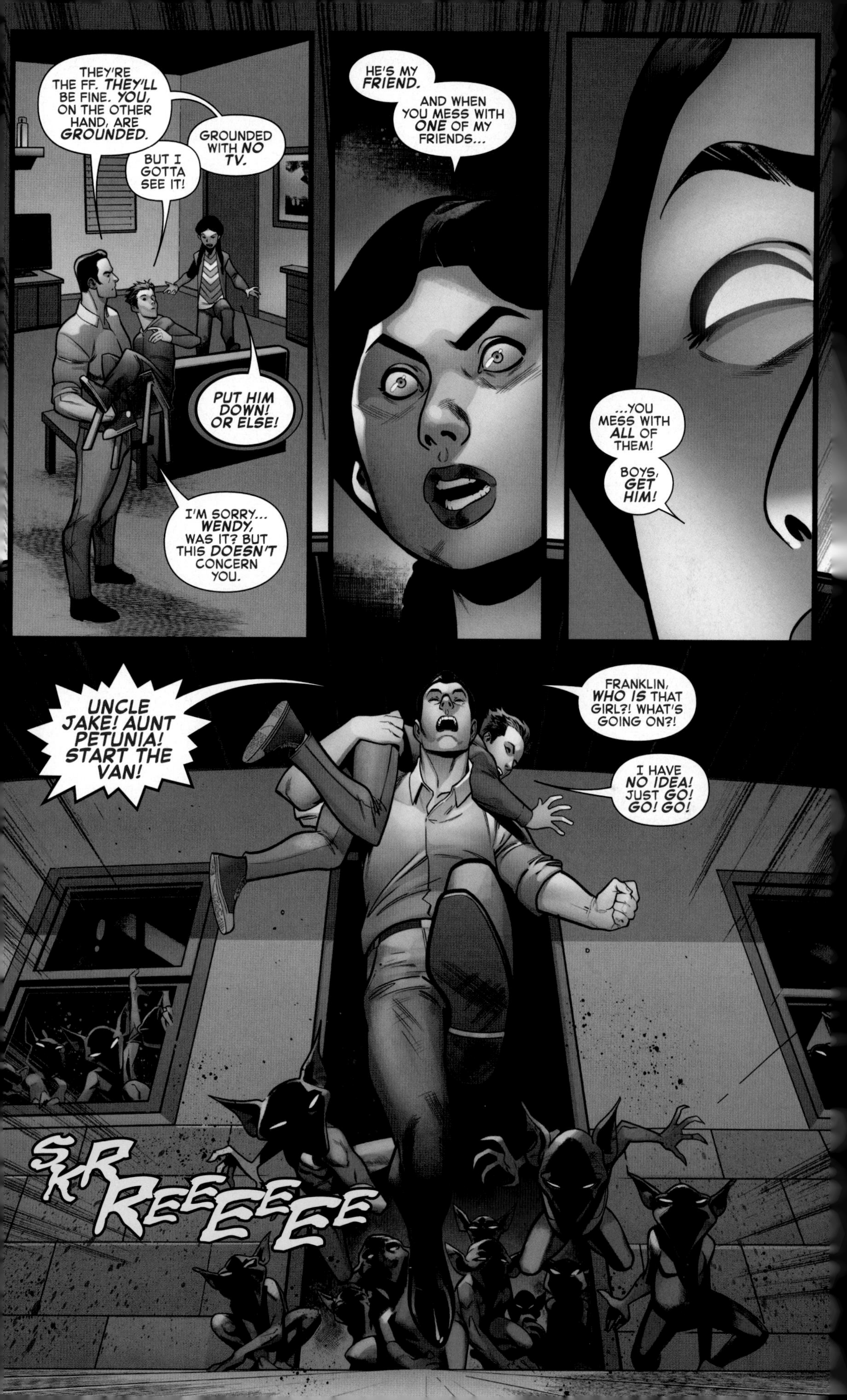
THEY'RE THE FF. THEY'LL BE FINE. YOU, ON THE OTHER HAND, ARE GROUNDED.
GROUNDED WITH NO TV.
BUT I GOTTA SEE IT!
PUT HIM DOWN! OR ELSE!
I'M SORRY... WENDY, WAS IT? BUT THIS DOESN'T CONCERN YOU.
HE'S MY FRIEND.
AND WHEN YOU MESS WITH ONE OF MY FRIENDS...
...YOU MESS WITH ALL OF THEM!
BOYS, GET HIM!
UNCLE JAKE! AUNT PETUNIA! START THE VAN!
FRANKLIN, WHO IS THAT GIRL?! WHAT'S GOING ON?!
I HAVE NO IDEA! JUST GO! GO! GO!
SKREEEEEEE

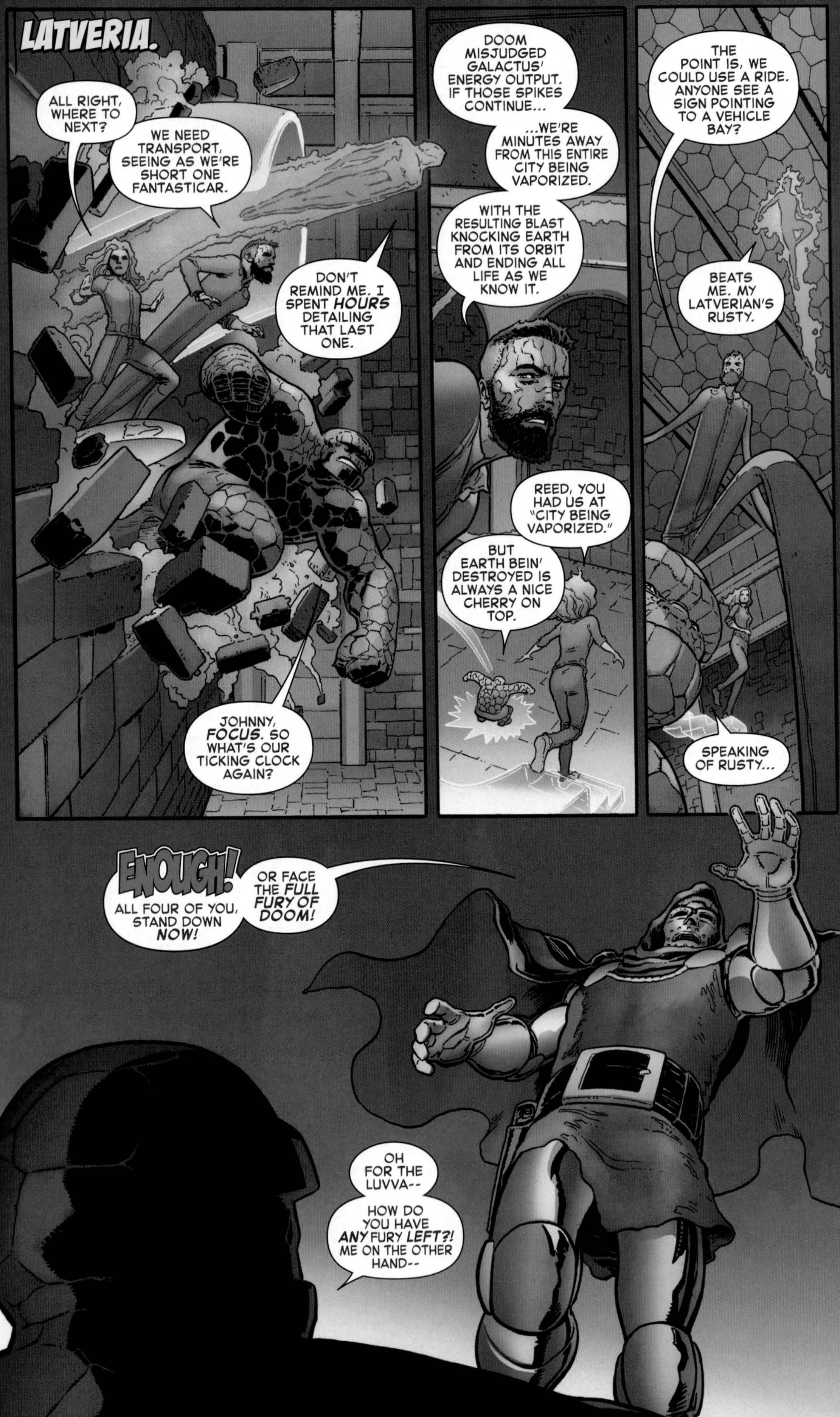

LATVERIA.
ALL RIGHT, WHERE TO NEXT?
WE NEED TRANSPORT, SEEING AS WE'RE SHORT ONE FANTASTICAR.
DON'T REMIND ME. I SPENT HOURS DETAILING THAT LAST ONE.
JOHNNY, FOCUS. SO WHAT'S OUR TICKING CLOCK AGAIN?
DOOM MISJUDGED GALACTUS' ENERGY OUTPUT. IF THOSE SPIKES CONTINUE...
...WE'RE MINUTES AWAY FROM THIS ENTIRE CITY BEING VAPORIZED.
WITH THE RESULTING BLAST KNOCKING EARTH FROM ITS ORBIT AND ENDING ALL LIFE AS WE KNOW IT.
REED, YOU HAD US AT "CITY BEING VAPORIZED."
BUT EARTH BEIN' DESTROYED IS ALWAYS A NICE CHERRY ON TOP.
THE POINT IS, WE COULD USE A RIDE. ANYONE SEE A SIGN POINTING TO A VEHICLE BAY?
BEATS ME. MY LATVERIAN'S RUSTY.
SPEAKING OF RUSTY...
ENOUGH!
ALL FOUR OF YOU, STAND DOWN NOW!
OR FACE THE FULL FURY OF DOOM!
OH FOR THE LUVVA--
HOW DO YOU HAVE ANY FURY LEFT?! ME ON THE OTHER HAND--

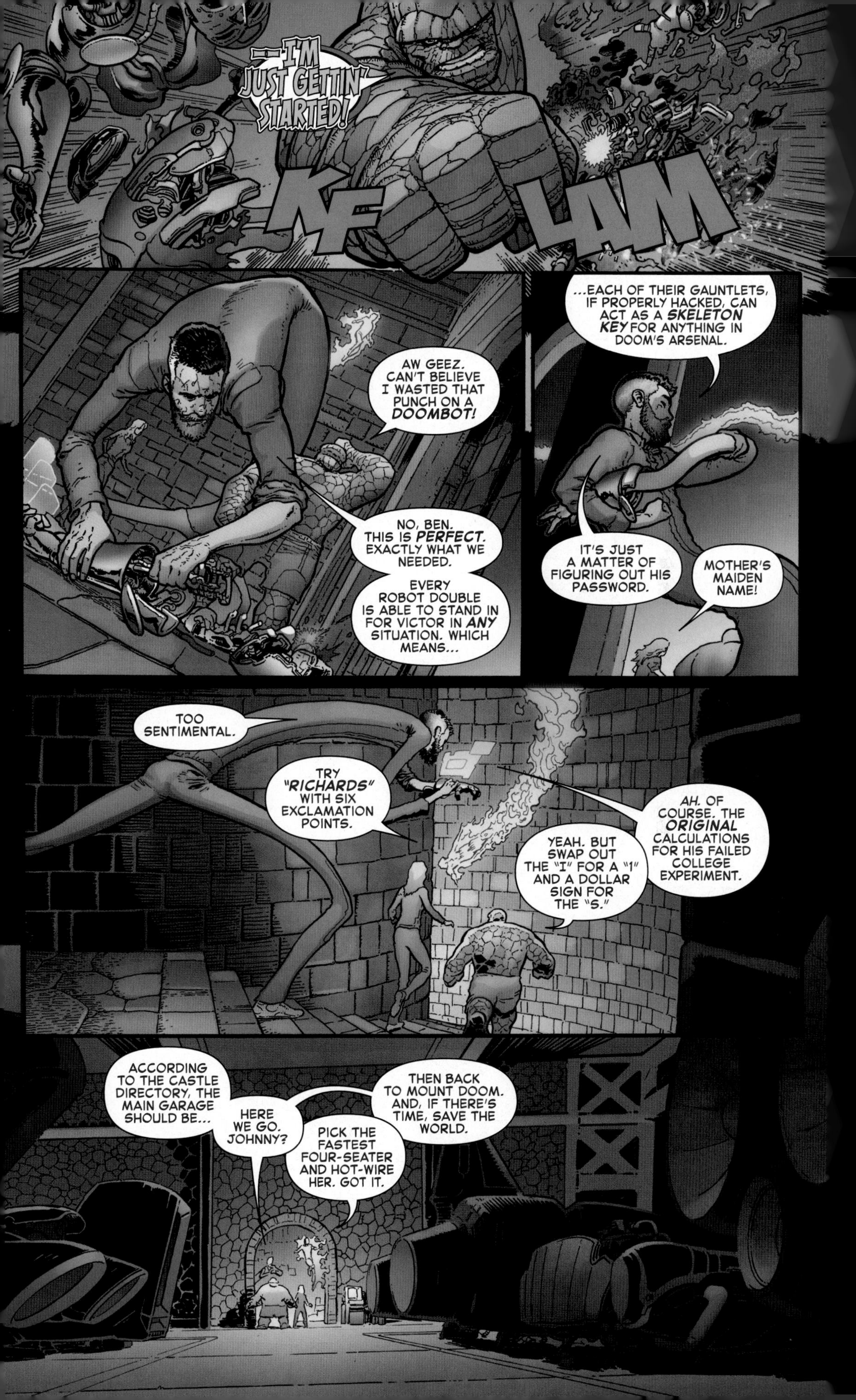

--I'M JUST GETTIN' STARTED!
KF-LAM
AW GEEZ. CAN'T BELIEVE I WASTED THAT PUNCH ON A DOOMBOT!
NO, BEN. THIS IS PERFECT. EXACTLY WHAT WE NEEDED.
EVERY ROBOT DOUBLE IS ABLE TO STAND IN FOR VICTOR IN ANY SITUATION. WHICH MEANS...
...EACH OF THEIR GAUNTLETS, IF PROPERLY HACKED, CAN ACT AS A SKELETON KEY FOR ANYTHING IN DOOM'S ARSENAL.
IT'S JUST A MATTER OF FIGURING OUT HIS PASSWORD.
MOTHER'S MAIDEN NAME!
TOO SENTIMENTAL.
TRY "RICHARDS" WITH SIX EXCLAMATION POINTS.
YEAH. BUT SWAP OUT THE "I" FOR A "1" AND A DOLLAR SIGN FOR THE "S."
AH. OF COURSE. THE ORIGINAL CALCULATIONS FOR HIS FAILED COLLEGE EXPERIMENT.
ACCORDING TO THE CASTLE DIRECTORY, THE MAIN GARAGE SHOULD BE...
HERE WE GO. JOHNNY?
PICK THE FASTEST FOUR-SEATER AND HOT-WIRE HER. GOT IT.
THEN BACK TO MOUNT DOOM. AND, IF THERE'S TIME, SAVE THE WORLD.

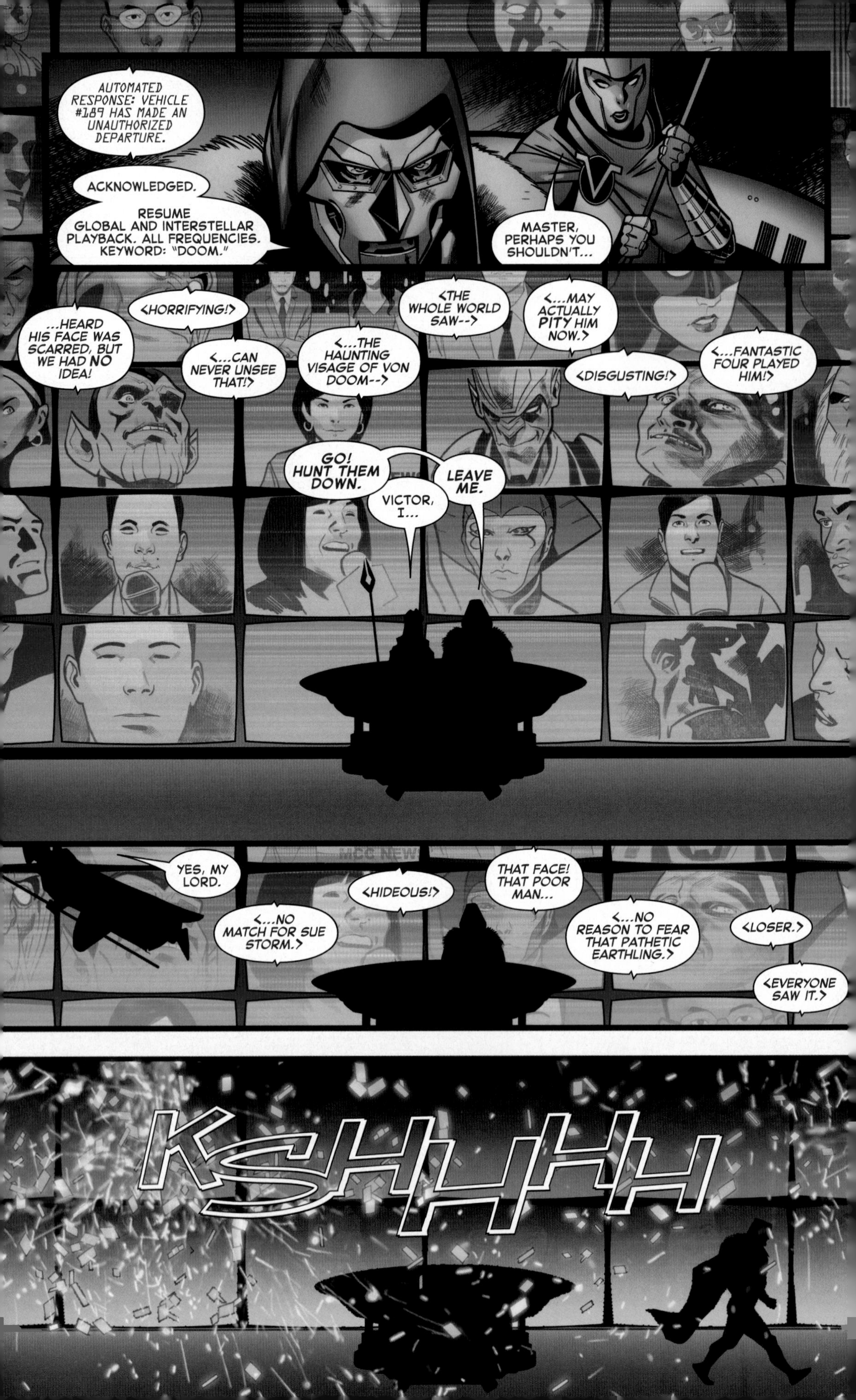
AUTOMATED RESPONSE: VEHICLE #189 HAS MADE AN UNAUTHORIZED DEPARTURE.
ACKNOWLEDGED.
RESUME GLOBAL AND INTERSTELLAR PLAYBACK. ALL FREQUENCIES. KEYWORD: "DOOM."
MASTER, PERHAPS YOU SHOULDN'T...
...HEARD HIS FACE WAS SCARRED, BUT WE HAD NO IDEA!
<HORRIFYING!>
<...CAN NEVER UNSEE THAT!>
<...THE HAUNTING VISAGE OF VON DOOM-->
<THE WHOLE WORLD SAW-->
<...MAY ACTUALLY PITY HIM NOW.>
<DISGUSTING!>
<...FANTASTIC FOUR PLAYED HIM!>
GO! HUNT THEM DOWN.
VICTOR, I...
LEAVE ME.
YES, MY LORD.
<...NO MATCH FOR SUE STORM.>
<HIDEOUS!>
THAT FACE! THAT POOR MAN...
<...NO REASON TO FEAR THAT PATHETIC EARTHLING.>
<LOSER.>
<EVERYONE SAW IT.>
KSHHHH

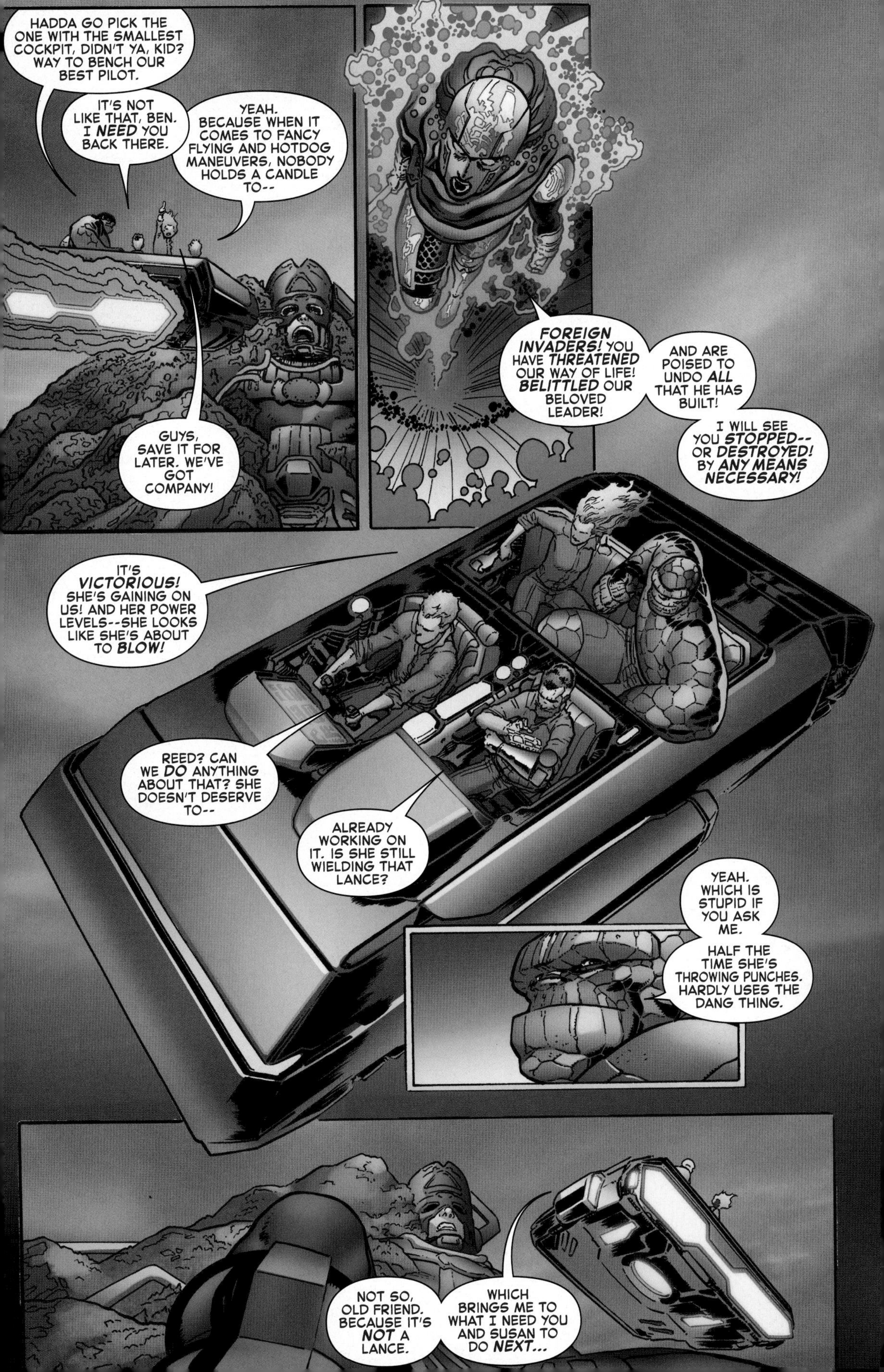
HADDA GO PICK THE ONE WITH THE SMALLEST COCKPIT, DIDN'T YA, KID? WAY TO BENCH OUR BEST PILOT.
IT'S NOT LIKE THAT, BEN. I NEED YOU BACK THERE.
YEAH. BECAUSE WHEN IT COMES TO FANCY FLYING AND HOTDOG MANEUVERS, NOBODY HOLDS A CANDLE TO--
GUYS, SAVE IT FOR LATER. WE'VE GOT COMPANY!
FOREIGN INVADERS! YOU HAVE THREATENED OUR WAY OF LIFE! BELITTLED OUR BELOVED LEADER!
AND ARE POISED TO UNDO ALL THAT HE HAS BUILT!
I WILL SEE YOU STOPPED-- OR DESTROYED! BY ANY MEANS NECESSARY!
IT'S VICTORIOUS! SHE'S GAINING ON US! AND HER POWER LEVELS--SHE LOOKS LIKE SHE'S ABOUT TO BLOW!
REED? CAN WE DO ANYTHING ABOUT THAT? SHE DOESN'T DESERVE TO--
ALREADY WORKING ON IT. IS SHE STILL WIELDING THAT LANCE?
YEAH. WHICH IS STUPID IF YOU ASK ME.
HALF THE TIME SHE'S THROWING PUNCHES. HARDLY USES THE DANG THING.
NOT SO, OLD FRIEND. BECAUSE IT'S NOT A LANCE.
WHICH BRINGS ME TO WHAT I NEED YOU AND SUSAN TO DO NEXT...

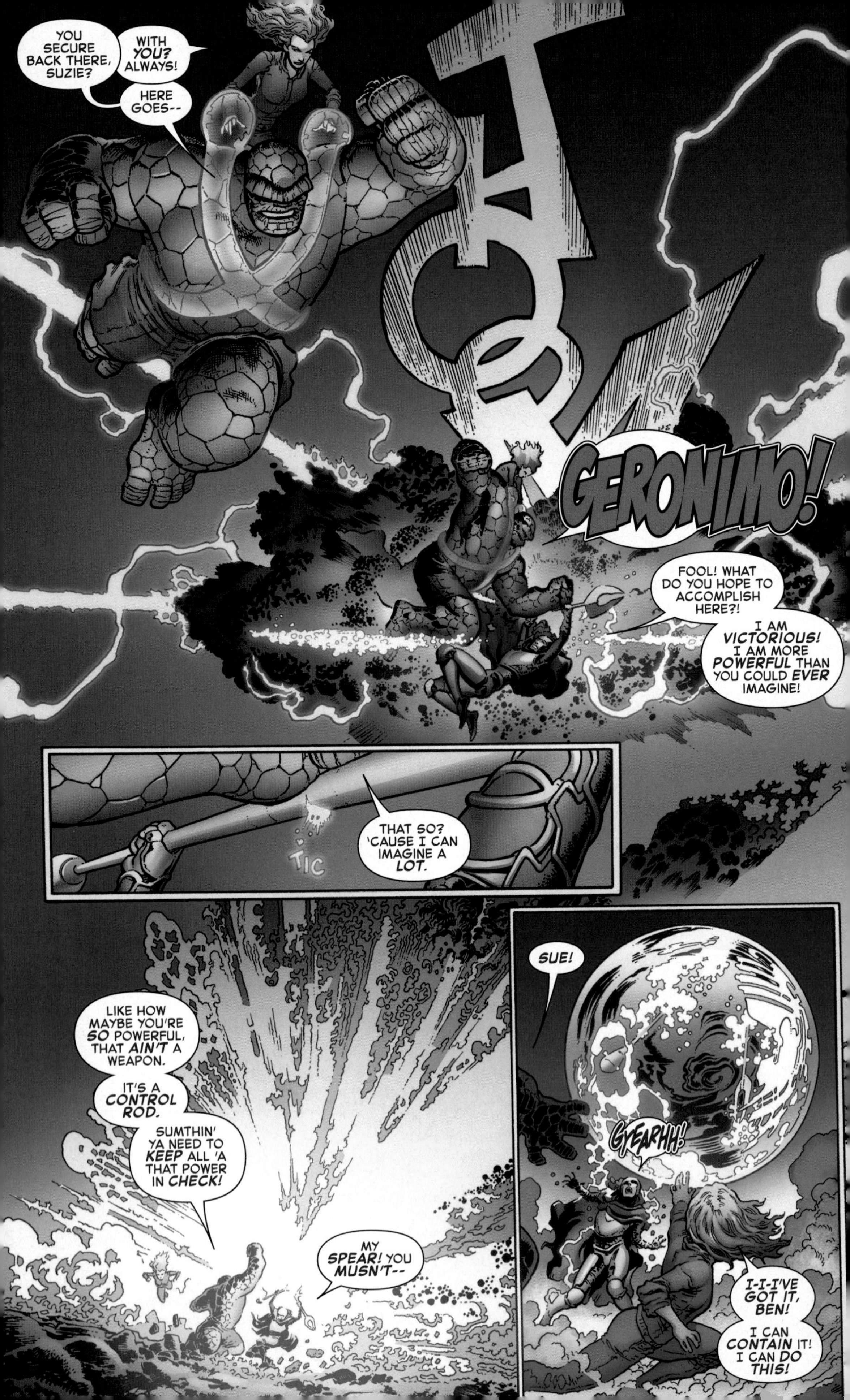

YOU SECURE BACK THERE, SUZIE?
WITH YOU? ALWAYS!
HERE GOES--
TACOW
GERONIMO!
FOOL! WHAT DO YOU HOPE TO ACCOMPLISH HERE?!
I AM VICTORIOUS! I AM MORE POWERFUL THAN YOU COULD EVER IMAGINE!
TIC
THAT SO? 'CAUSE I CAN IMAGINE A LOT.
LIKE HOW MAYBE YOU'RE SO POWERFUL, THAT AIN'T A WEAPON.
IT'S A CONTROL ROD.
SUMTHIN' YA NEED TO KEEP ALL 'A THAT POWER IN CHECK!
MY SPEAR! YOU MUSN'T--
SUE!
GYEARHH!
I-I-I'VE GOT IT, BEN!
I CAN CONTAIN IT! I CAN DO THIS!

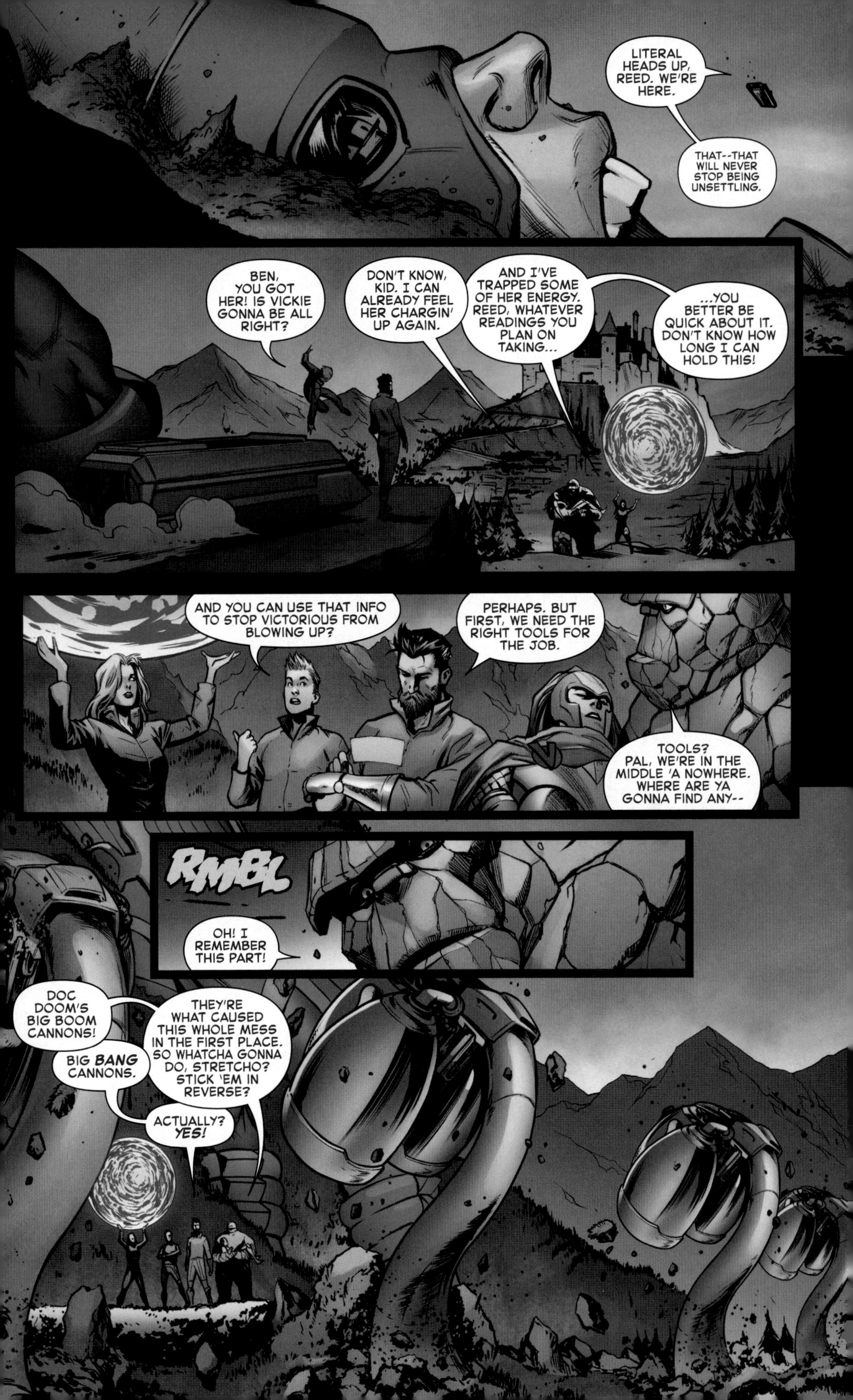
LITERAL HEADS UP, REED. WE'RE HERE.
THAT--THAT WILL NEVER STOP BEING UNSETTLING.
BEN, YOU GOT HER! IS VICKIE GONNA BE ALL RIGHT?
DON'T KNOW, KID. I CAN ALREADY FEEL HER CHARGIN' UP AGAIN.
AND I'VE TRAPPED SOME OF HER ENERGY. REED, WHATEVER READINGS YOU PLAN ON TAKING...
...YOU BETTER BE QUICK ABOUT IT. DON'T KNOW HOW LONG I CAN HOLD THIS!
AND YOU CAN USE THAT INFO TO STOP VICTORIOUS FROM BLOWING UP?
PERHAPS. BUT FIRST, WE NEED THE RIGHT TOOLS FOR THE JOB.
TOOLS? PAL, WE'RE IN THE MIDDLE 'A NOWHERE. WHERE ARE YA GONNA FIND ANY--
RMBL
OH! I REMEMBER THIS PART!
DOC DOOM'S BIG BOOM CANNONS!
BIG BANG CANNONS.
THEY'RE WHAT CAUSED THIS WHOLE MESS IN THE FIRST PLACE. SO WHATCHA GONNA DO, STRETCHO? STICK 'EM IN REVERSE?
ACTUALLY? YES!

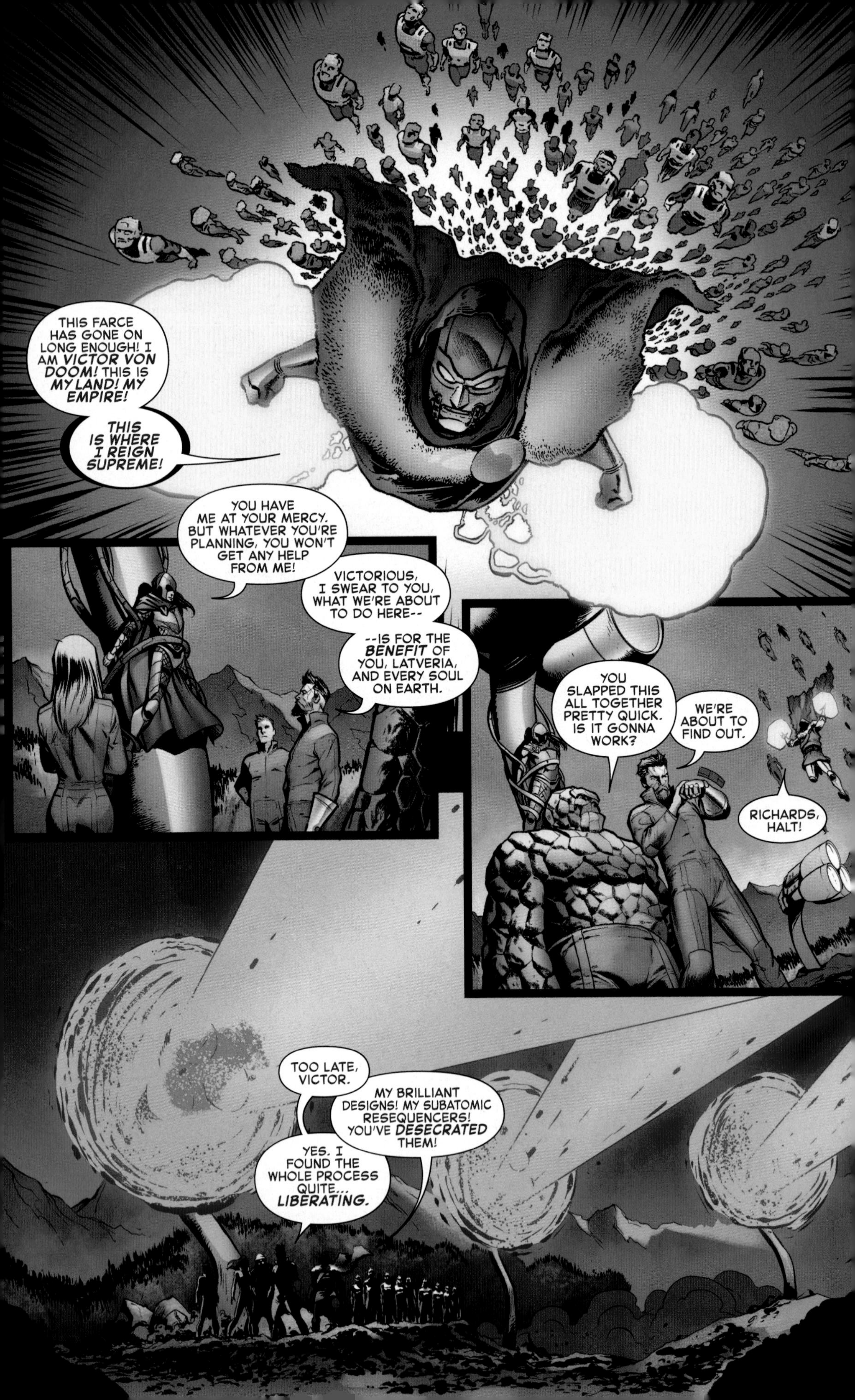
THIS FARCE HAS GONE ON LONG ENOUGH! I AM VICTOR VON DOOM! THIS IS MY LAND! MY EMPIRE!
THIS IS WHERE I REIGN SUPREME!
YOU HAVE ME AT YOUR MERCY. BUT WHATEVER YOU'RE PLANNING, YOU WON'T GET ANY HELP FROM ME!
VICTORIOUS, I SWEAR TO YOU, WHAT WE'RE ABOUT TO DO HERE--
--IS FOR THE BENEFIT OF YOU, LATVERIA, AND EVERY SOUL ON EARTH.
YOU SLAPPED THIS ALL TOGETHER PRETTY QUICK. IS IT GONNA WORK?
WE'RE ABOUT TO FIND OUT.
RICHARDS, HALT!
TOO LATE, VICTOR.
MY BRILLIANT DESIGNS! MY SUBATOMIC RESEQUENCERS! YOU'VE DESECRATED THEM!
YES. I FOUND THE WHOLE PROCESS QUITE... LIBERATING.

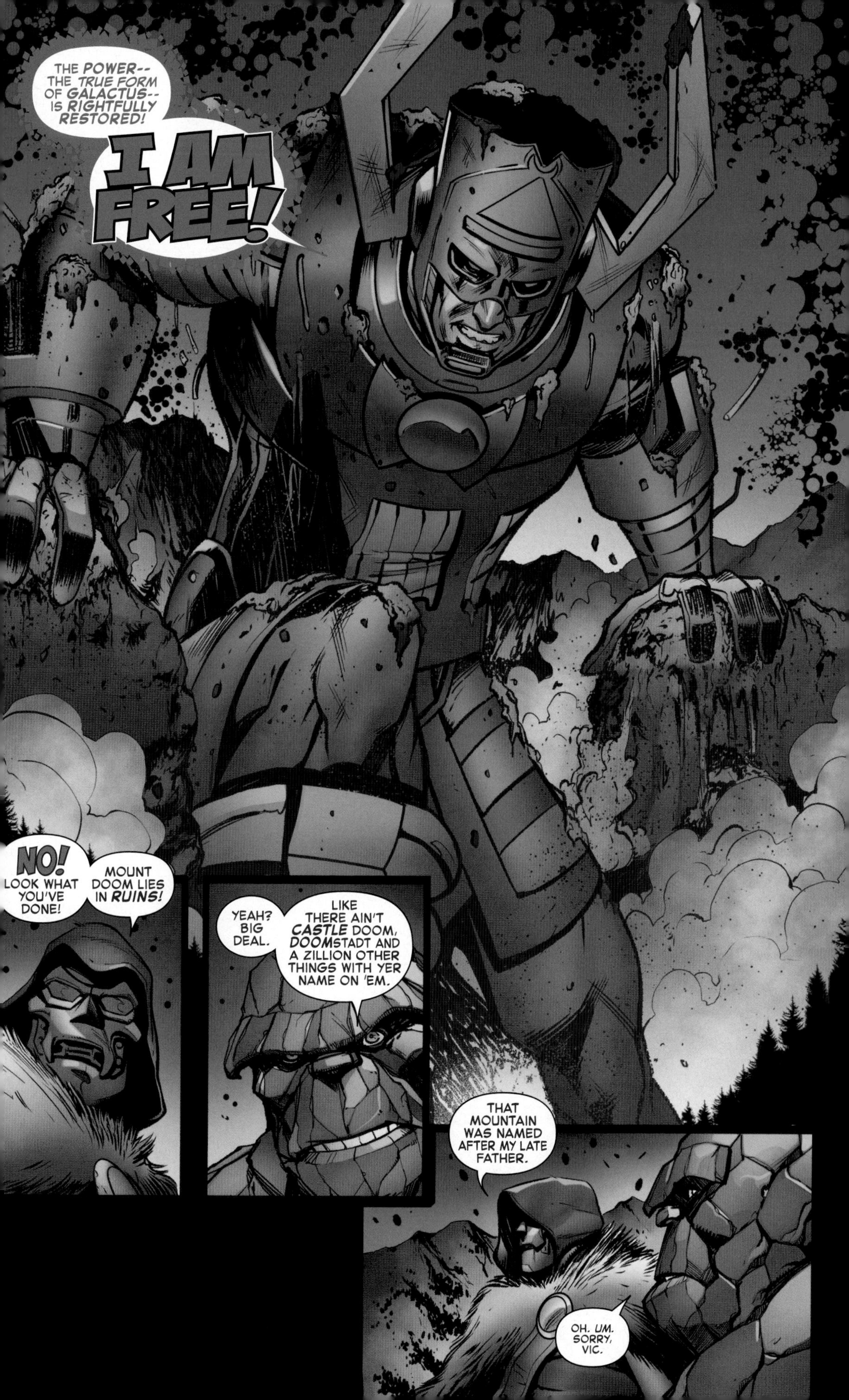
THE POWER-- THE TRUE FORM OF GALACTUS-- IS RIGHTFULLY RESTORED!
I AM FREE!
NO! LOOK WHAT YOU'VE DONE!
MOUNT DOOM LIES IN RUINS!
YEAH? BIG DEAL.
LIKE THERE AIN'T CASTLE DOOM, DOOMSTADT AND A ZILLION OTHER THINGS WITH YER NAME ON 'EM.
THAT MOUNTAIN WAS NAMED AFTER MY LATE FATHER.
OH. UM. SORRY, VIC.

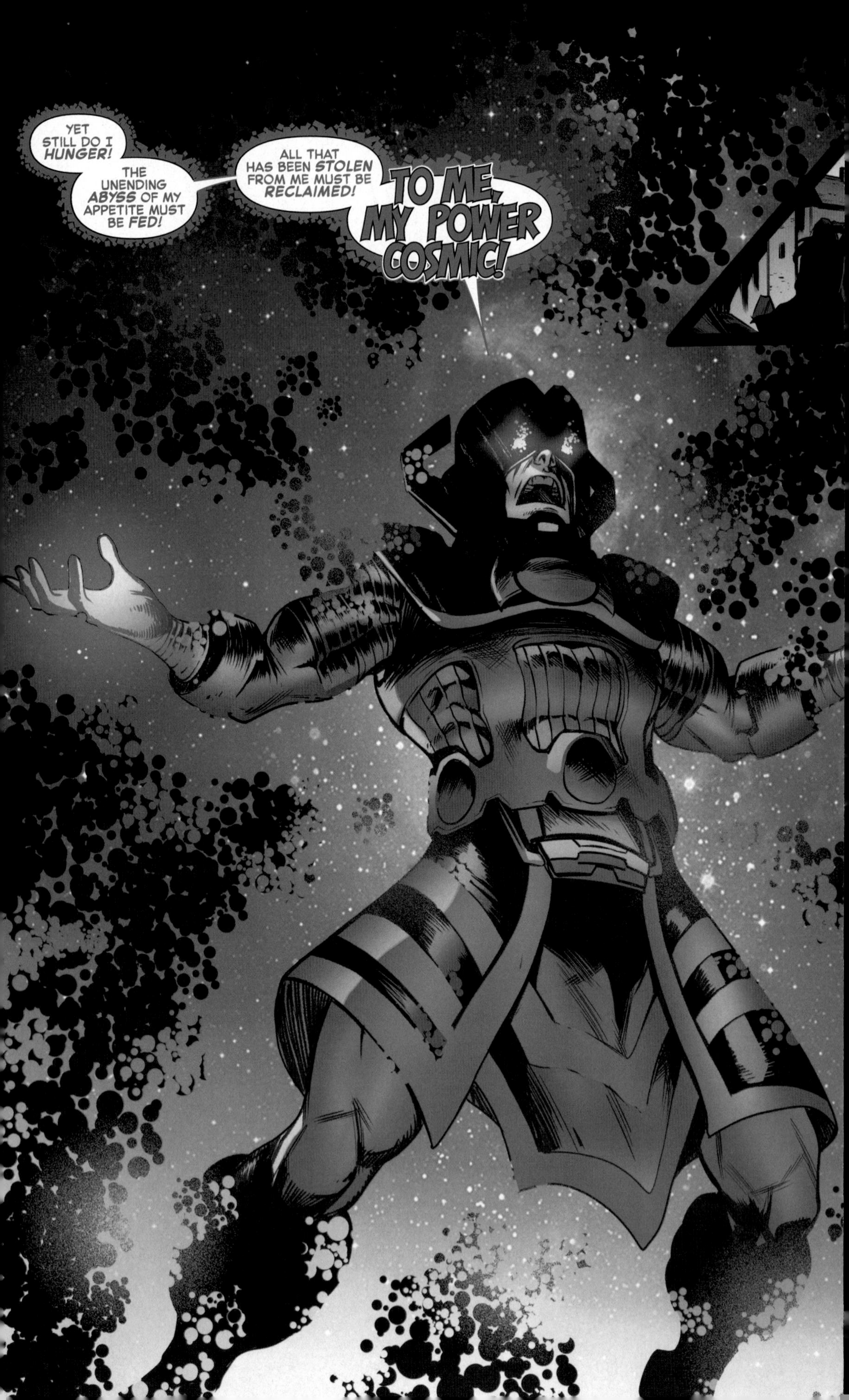
YET STILL DO I HUNGER! THE UNENDING ABYSS OF MY APPETITE MUST BE FED!
ALL THAT HAS BEEN STOLEN FROM ME MUST BE RECLAIMED!
TO ME, MY POWER COSMIC!

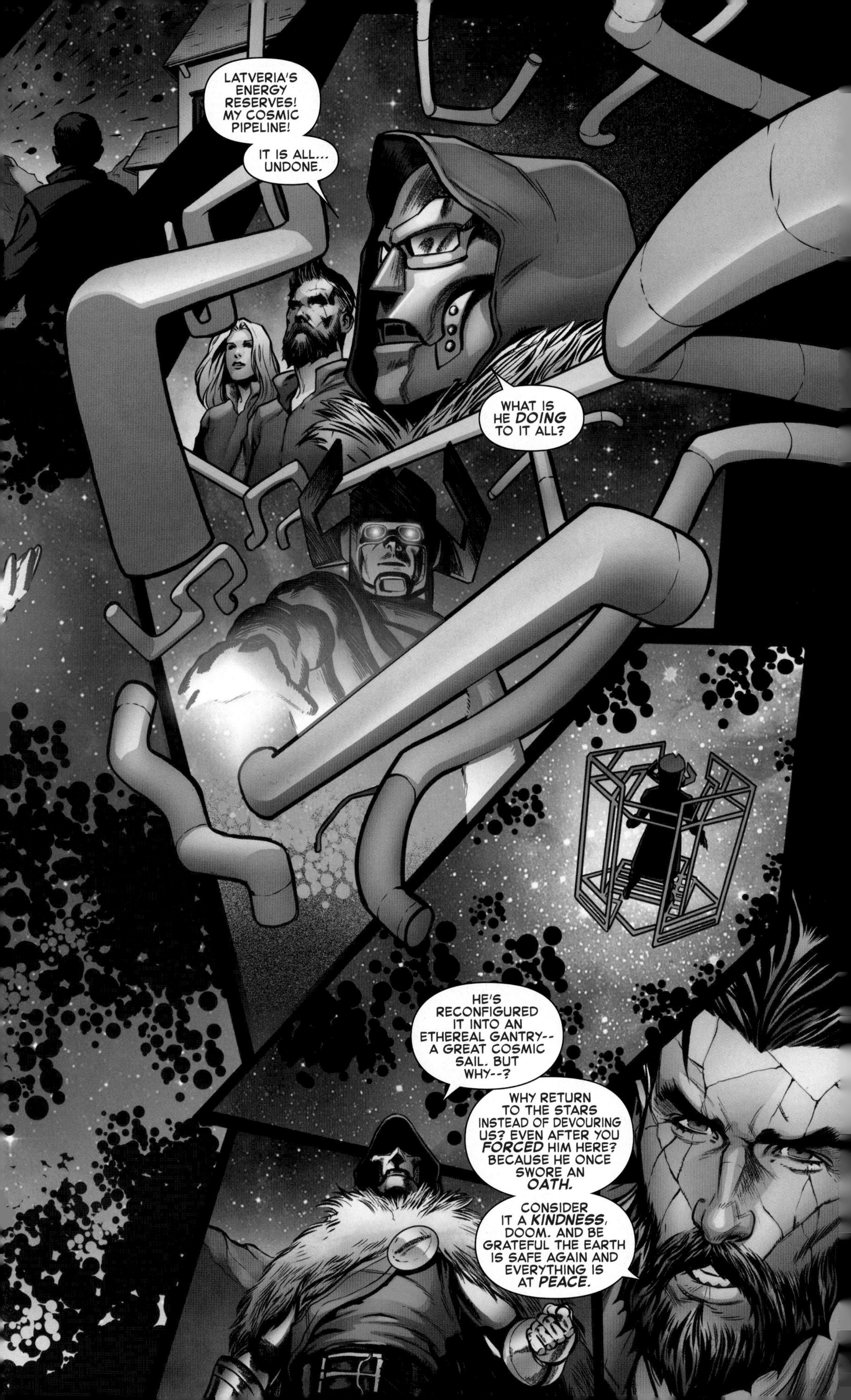
LATVERIA'S ENERGY RESERVES! MY COSMIC PIPELINE!
IT IS ALL... UNDONE.
WHAT IS HE DOING TO IT ALL?
HE'S RECONFIGURED IT INTO AN ETHEREAL GANTRY-- A GREAT COSMIC SAIL. BUT WHY--?
WHY RETURN TO THE STARS INSTEAD OF DEVOURING US? EVEN AFTER YOU FORCED HIM HERE? BECAUSE HE ONCE SWORE AN OATH.
CONSIDER IT A KINDNESS, DOOM. AND BE GRATEFUL THE EARTH IS SAFE AGAIN AND EVERYTHING IS AT PEACE.

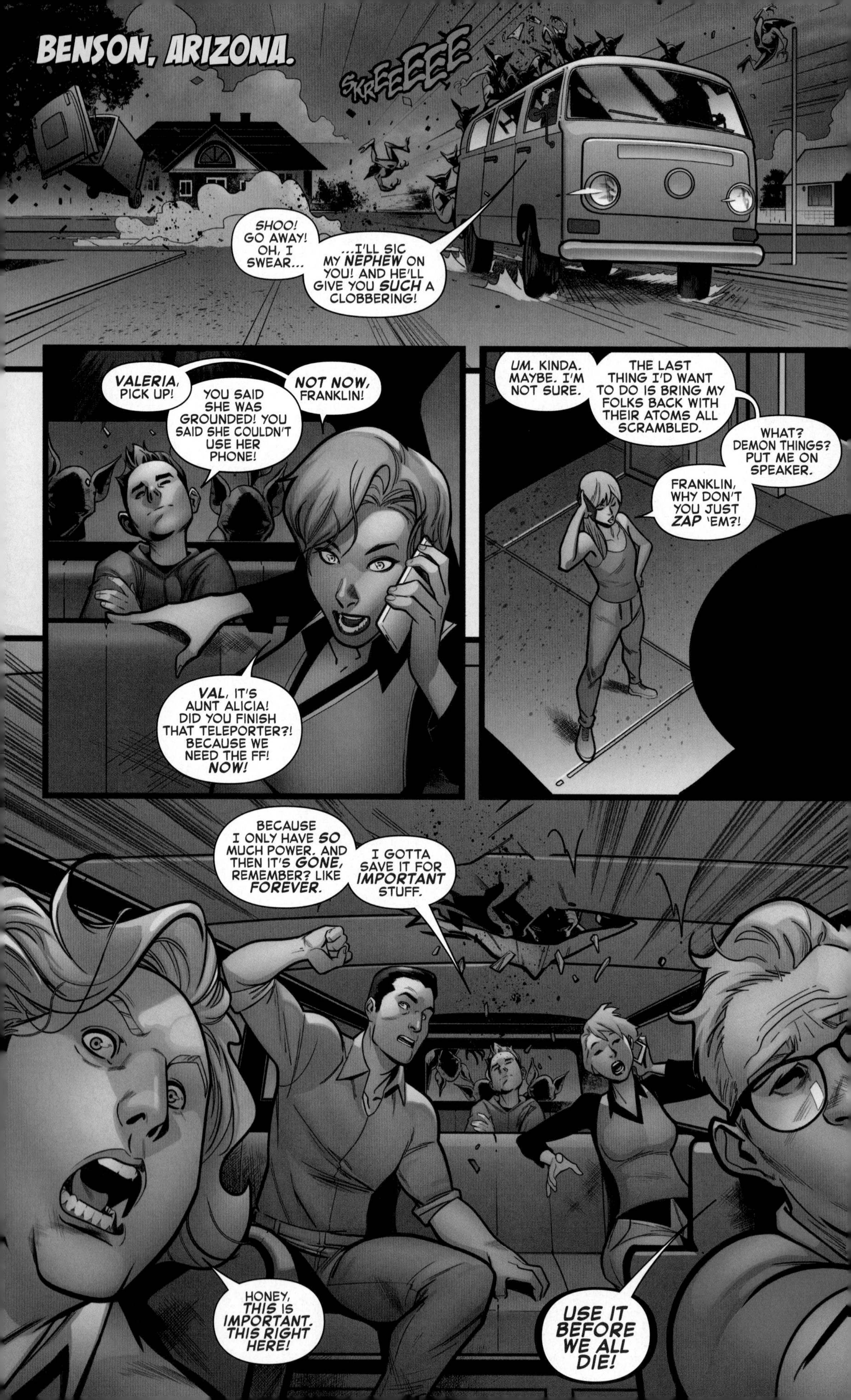

BENSON, ARIZONA.
SKREEEEEE
SHOO! GO AWAY! OH, I SWEAR...
...I'LL SIC MY NEPHEW ON YOU! AND HE'LL GIVE YOU SUCH A CLOBBERING!
VALERIA, PICK UP!
NOT NOW, FRANKLIN!
YOU SAID SHE WAS GROUNDED! YOU SAID SHE COULDN'T USE HER PHONE!
VAL, IT'S AUNT ALICIA! DID YOU FINISH THAT TELEPORTER?! BECAUSE WE NEED THE FF! NOW!
UM. KINDA. MAYBE. I'M NOT SURE.
THE LAST THING I'D WANT TO DO IS BRING MY FOLKS BACK WITH THEIR ATOMS ALL SCRAMBLED.
WHAT? DEMON THINGS? PUT ME ON SPEAKER.
FRANKLIN, WHY DON'T YOU JUST ZAP 'EM?!
BECAUSE I ONLY HAVE SO MUCH POWER. AND THEN IT'S GONE, REMEMBER? LIKE FOREVER.
I GOTTA SAVE IT FOR IMPORTANT STUFF.
HONEY, THIS IS IMPORTANT. THIS RIGHT HERE!
USE IT BEFORE WE ALL DIE!

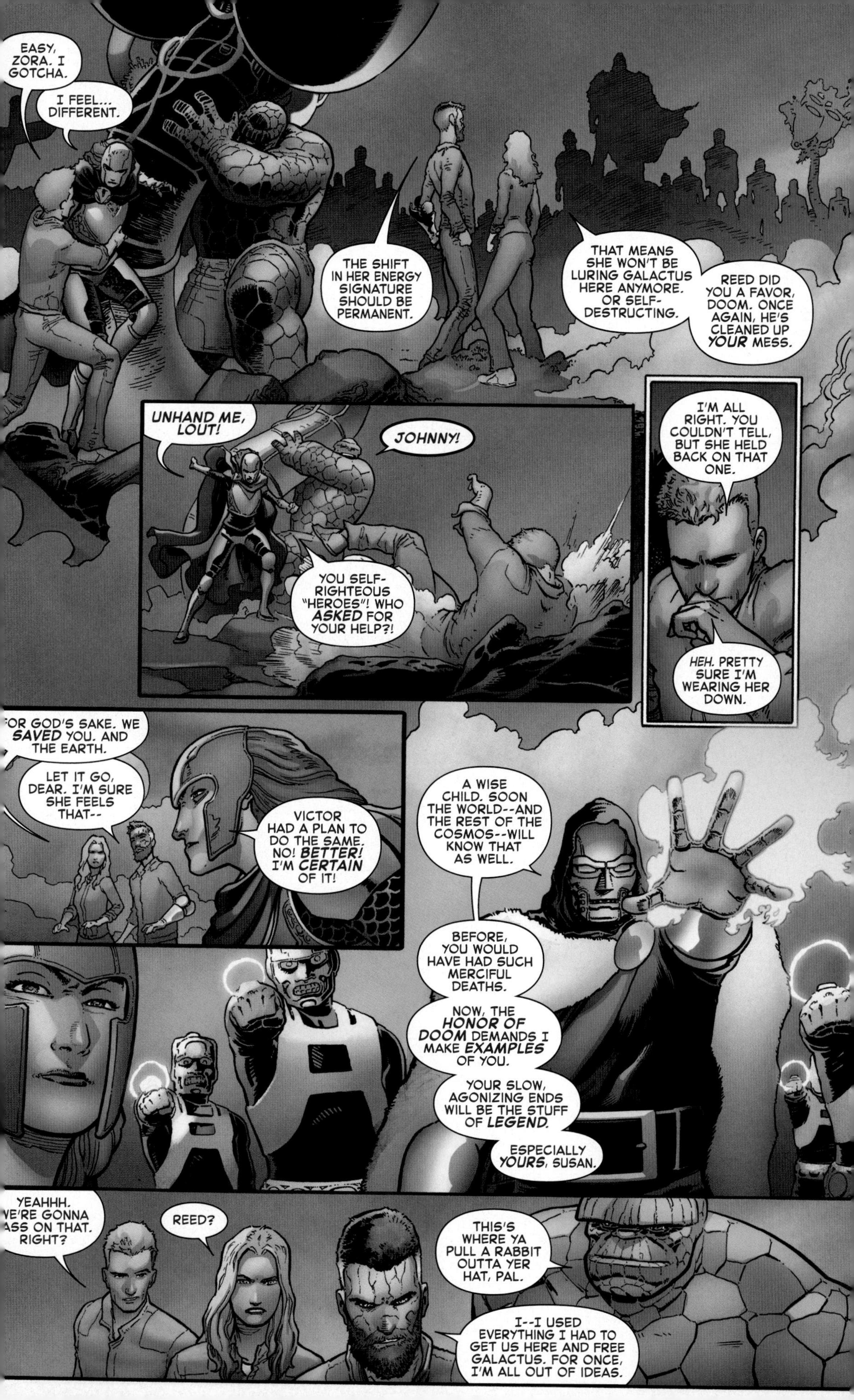
EASY, ZORA. I GOTCHA.
I FEEL... DIFFERENT.
THE SHIFT IN HER ENERGY SIGNATURE SHOULD BE PERMANENT.
THAT MEANS SHE WON'T BE LURING GALACTUS HERE ANYMORE. OR SELF-DESTRUCTING.
REED DID YOU A FAVOR, DOOM. ONCE AGAIN, HE'S CLEANED UP YOUR MESS.
UNHAND ME, LOUT!
JOHNNY!
YOU SELF-RIGHTEOUS "HEROES"! WHO ASKED FOR YOUR HELP?!
I'M ALL RIGHT. YOU COULDN'T TELL, BUT SHE HELD BACK ON THAT ONE.
HEH. PRETTY SURE I'M WEARING HER DOWN.
FOR GOD'S SAKE. WE SAVED YOU. AND THE EARTH.
LET IT GO, DEAR. I'M SURE SHE FEELS THAT--
VICTOR HAD A PLAN TO DO THE SAME. NO! BETTER! I'M CERTAIN OF IT!
A WISE CHILD. SOON THE WORLD--AND THE REST OF THE COSMOS--WILL KNOW THAT AS WELL.
BEFORE, YOU WOULD HAVE HAD SUCH MERCIFUL DEATHS.
NOW, THE HONOR OF DOOM DEMANDS I MAKE EXAMPLES OF YOU.
YOUR SLOW, AGONIZING ENDS WILL BE THE STUFF OF LEGEND.
ESPECIALLY YOURS, SUSAN.
YEAHHH. WE'RE GONNA PASS ON THAT. RIGHT?
REED?
THIS'S WHERE YA PULL A RABBIT OUTTA YER HAT, PAL.
I--I USED EVERYTHING I HAD TO GET US HERE AND FREE GALACTUS. FOR ONCE, I'M ALL OUT OF IDEAS.

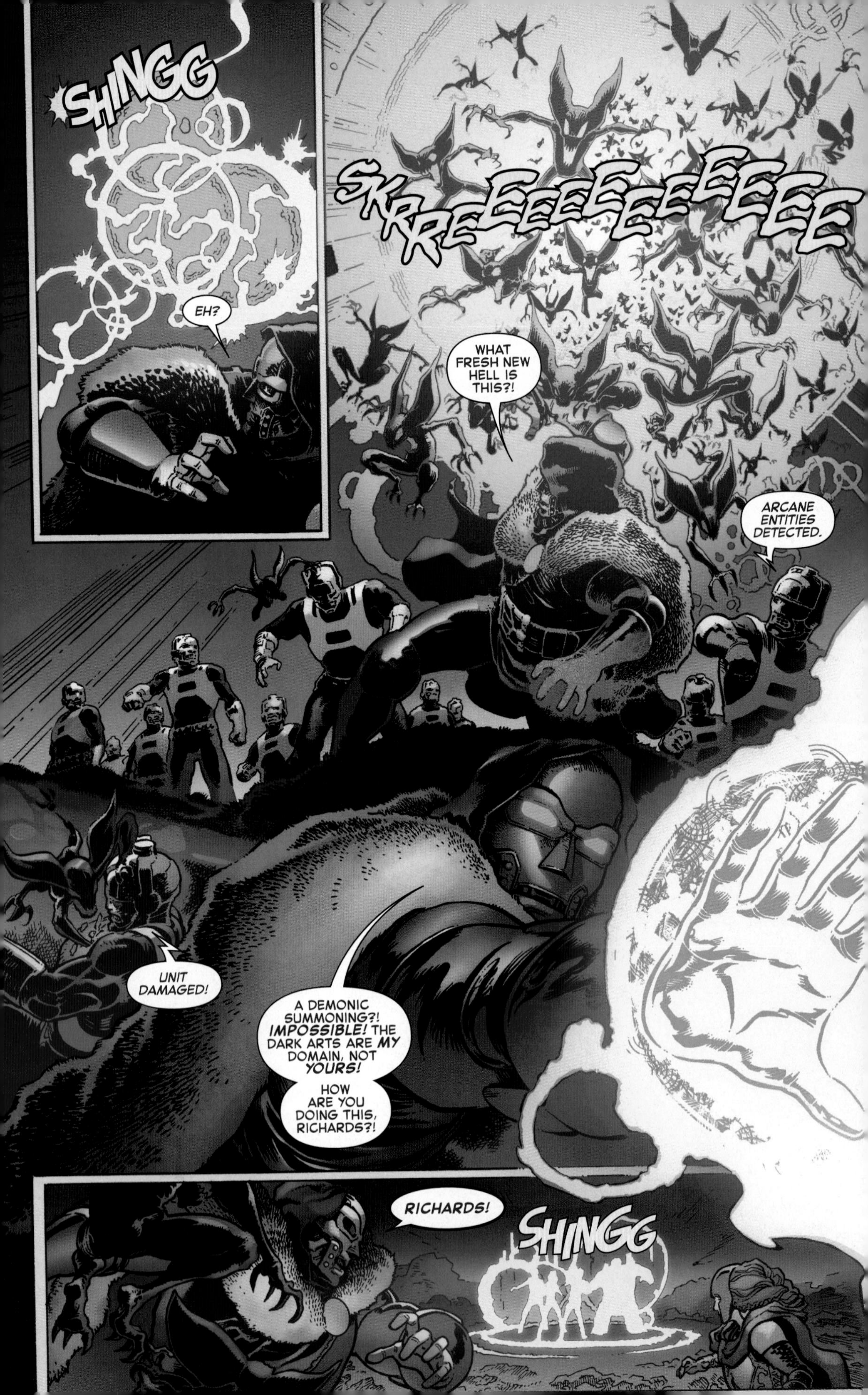
SHINGG
EH?
SKRREEEEEEEEEEEEE
WHAT FRESH NEW HELL IS THIS?!
ARCANE ENTITIES DETECTED.
UNIT DAMAGED!
A DEMONIC SUMMONING?! IMPOSSIBLE! THE DARK ARTS ARE MY DOMAIN, NOT YOURS!
HOW ARE YOU DOING THIS, RICHARDS?!
RICHARDS!
SHINGG

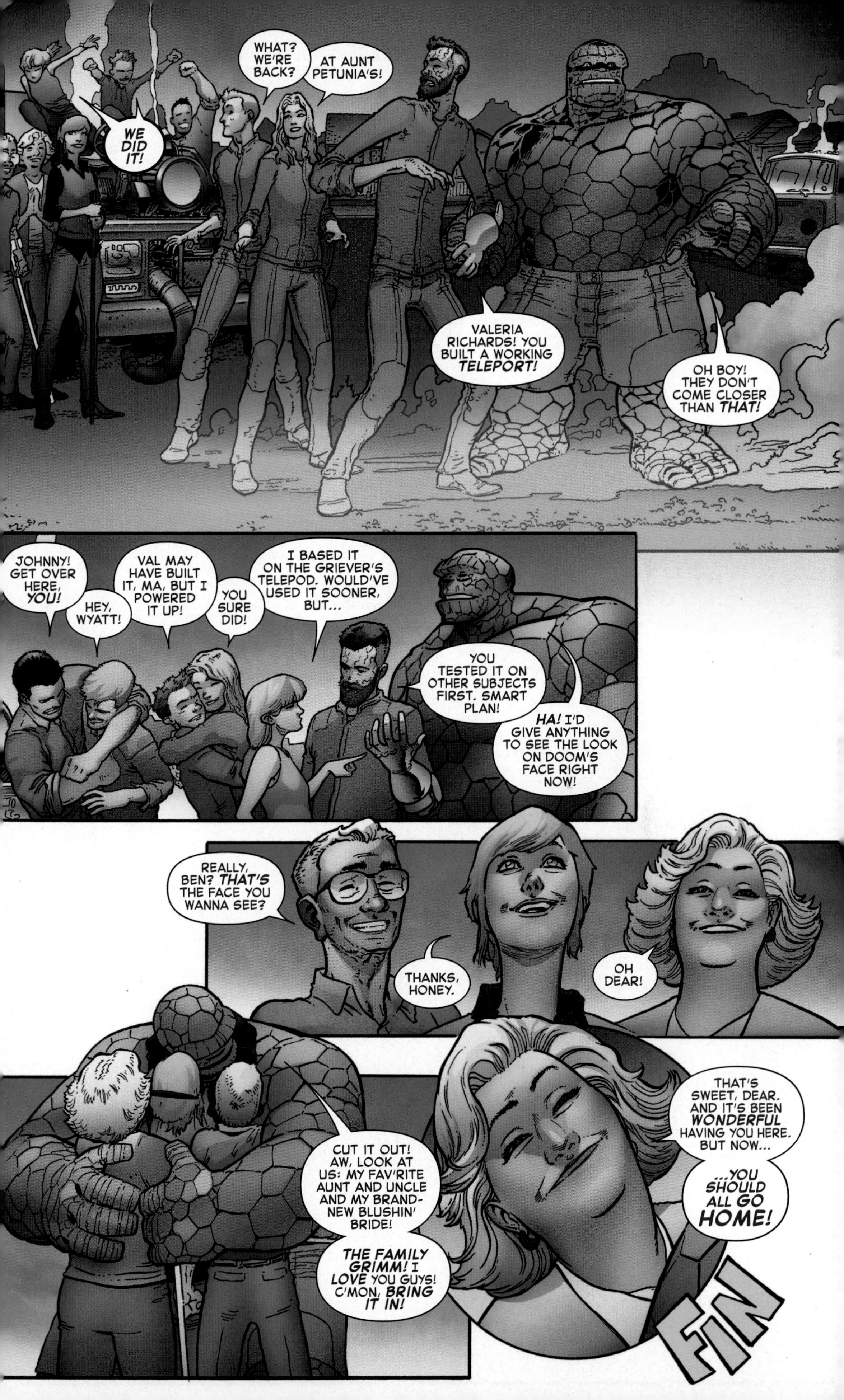
WHAT? WE'RE BACK?
AT AUNT PETUNIA'S!
WE DID IT!
VALERIA RICHARDS! YOU BUILT A WORKING TELEPORT!
OH BOY! THEY DON'T COME CLOSER THAN THAT!
JOHNNY! GET OVER HERE, YOU!
HEY, WYATT!
VAL MAY HAVE BUILT IT, MA, BUT I POWERED IT UP!
YOU SURE DID!
I BASED IT ON THE GRIEVER'S TELEPOD. WOULD'VE USED IT SOONER, BUT...
YOU TESTED IT ON OTHER SUBJECTS FIRST. SMART PLAN!
HA! I'D GIVE ANYTHING TO SEE THE LOOK ON DOOM'S FACE RIGHT NOW!
REALLY, BEN? THAT'S THE FACE YOU WANNA SEE?
THANKS, HONEY.
OH DEAR!
CUT IT OUT! AW, LOOK AT US: MY FAV'RITE AUNT AND UNCLE AND MY BRAND-NEW BLUSHIN' BRIDE!
THE FAMILY GRIMM! I LOVE YOU GUYS! C'MON, BRING IT IN!
THAT'S SWEET, DEAR. AND IT'S BEEN WONDERFUL HAVING YOU HERE. BUT NOW...
...YOU SHOULD ALL GO HOME!
FIN

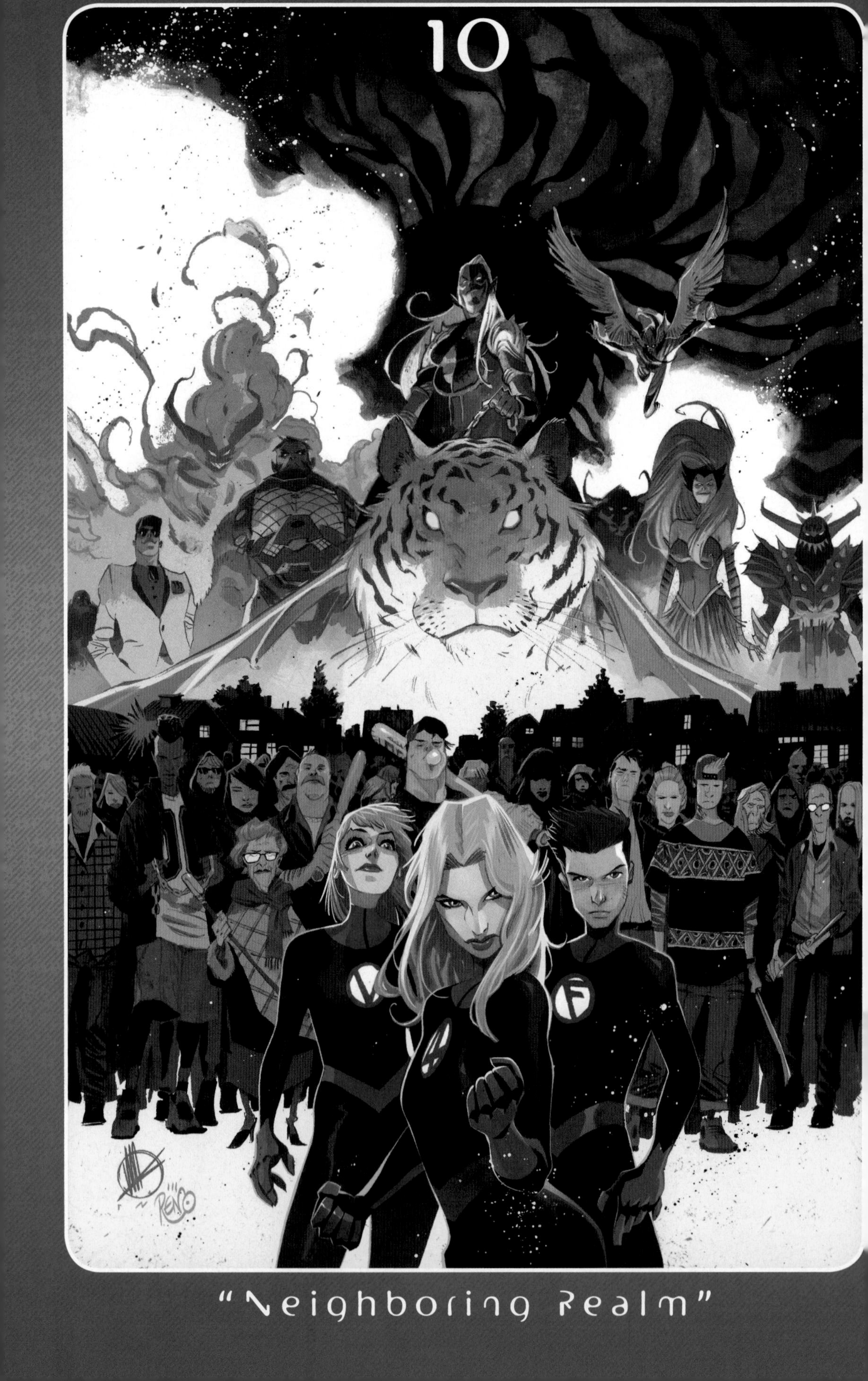
10

"Neighboring Realm"

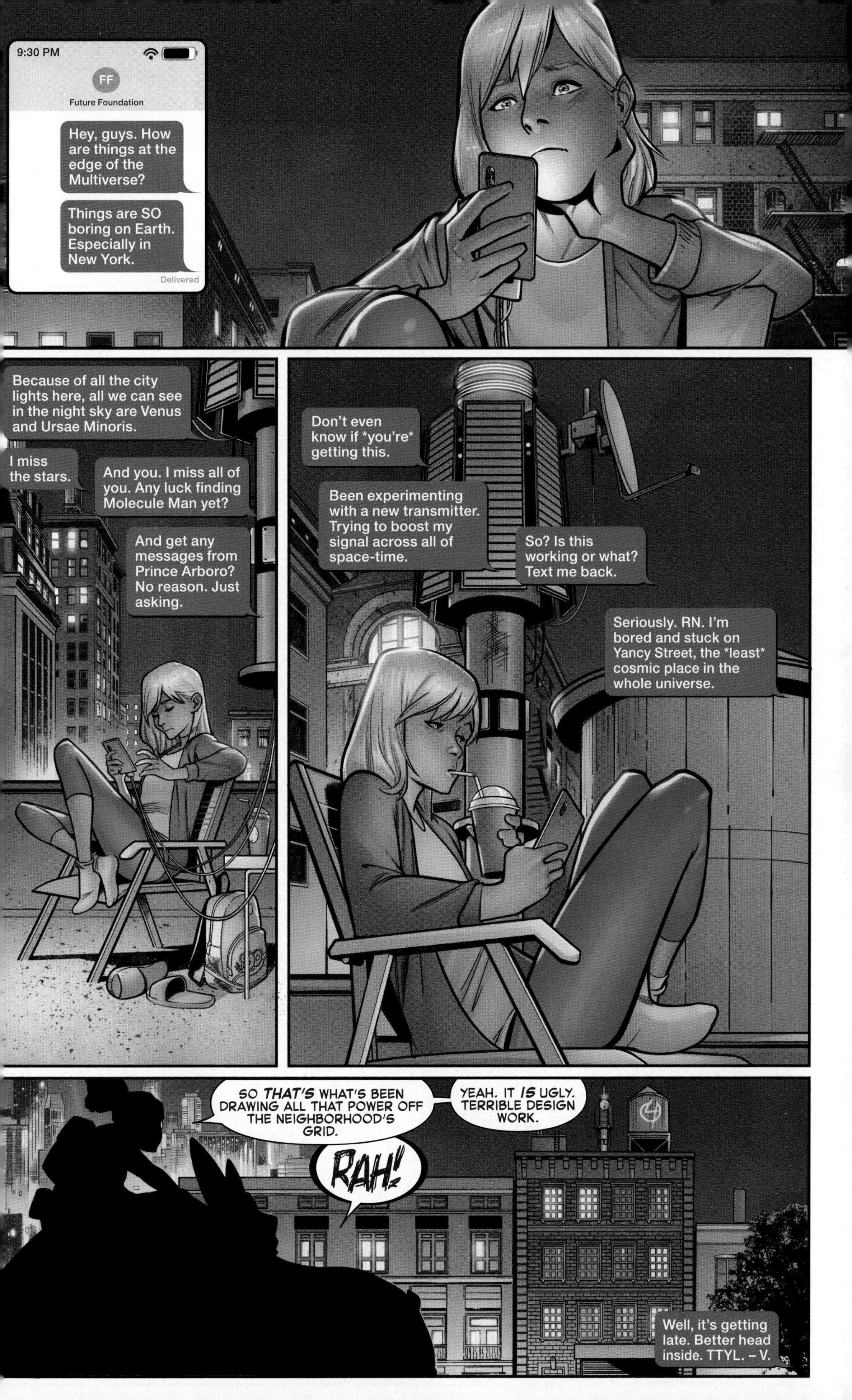
9:30 PM
FF
Future Foundation
Hey, guys. How are things at the edge of the Multiverse?
Things are SO boring on Earth. Especially in New York.
Delivered
Because of all the city lights here, all we can see in the night sky are Venus and Ursae Minoris.
I miss the stars.
And you. I miss all of you. Any luck finding Molecule Man yet?
And get any messages from Prince Arboro? No reason. Just asking.
Don't even know if *you're* getting this.
Been experimenting with a new transmitter. Trying to boost my signal across all of space-time.
So? Is this working or what? Text me back.
Seriously. RN. I'm bored and stuck on Yancy Street, the *least* cosmic place in the whole universe.
SO THAT'S WHAT'S BEEN DRAWING ALL THAT POWER OFF THE NEIGHBORHOOD'S GRID.
YEAH. IT IS UGLY. TERRIBLE DESIGN WORK.
RAH!
Well, it's getting late. Better head inside. TTYL. – V.

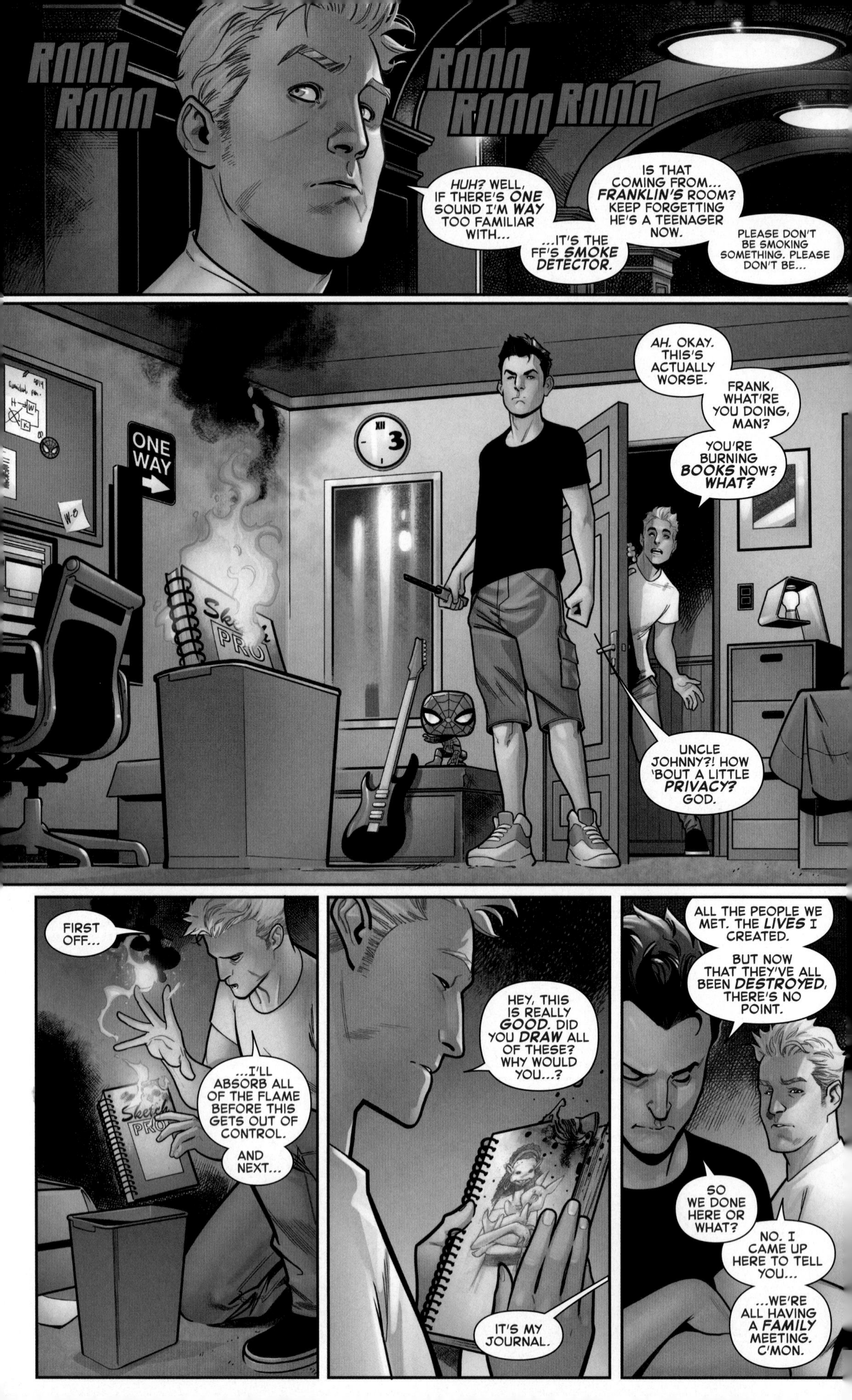
RNNN RNNN
RNNN RNNN RNNN
HUH? WELL, IF THERE'S ONE SOUND I'M WAY TOO FAMILIAR WITH...
...IT'S THE FF'S SMOKE DETECTOR.
IS THAT COMING FROM... FRANKLIN'S ROOM? KEEP FORGETTING HE'S A TEENAGER NOW.
PLEASE DON'T BE SMOKING SOMETHING. PLEASE DON'T BE...
ONE WAY
AH. OKAY. THIS'S ACTUALLY WORSE.
FRANK, WHAT'RE YOU DOING, MAN?
YOU'RE BURNING BOOKS NOW? WHAT?
UNCLE JOHNNY?! HOW 'BOUT A LITTLE PRIVACY? GOD.
FIRST OFF...
...I'LL ABSORB ALL OF THE FLAME BEFORE THIS GETS OUT OF CONTROL.
AND NEXT...
HEY, THIS IS REALLY GOOD. DID YOU DRAW ALL OF THESE? WHY WOULD YOU...?
IT'S MY JOURNAL.
ALL THE PEOPLE WE MET. THE LIVES I CREATED.
BUT NOW THAT THEY'VE ALL BEEN DESTROYED, THERE'S NO POINT.
SO WE DONE HERE OR WHAT?
NO. I CAME UP HERE TO TELL YOU...
...WE'RE ALL HAVING A FAMILY MEETING. C'MON.

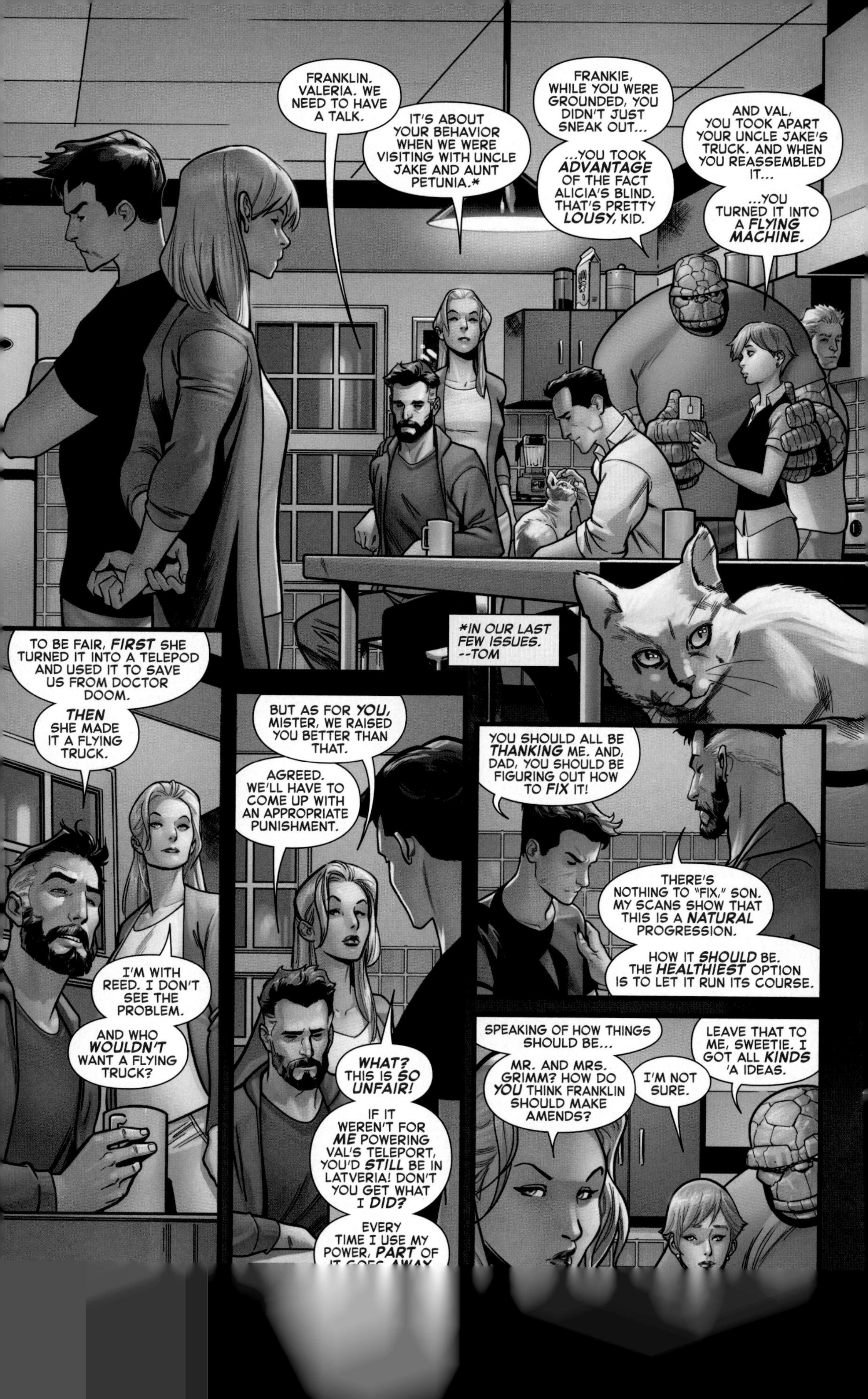
FRANKLIN. VALERIA. WE NEED TO HAVE A TALK.
IT'S ABOUT YOUR BEHAVIOR WHEN WE WERE VISITING WITH UNCLE JAKE AND AUNT PETUNIA.*
FRANKIE, WHILE YOU WERE GROUNDED, YOU DIDN'T JUST SNEAK OUT...
...YOU TOOK ADVANTAGE OF THE FACT ALICIA'S BLIND. THAT'S PRETTY LOUSY, KID.
AND VAL, YOU TOOK APART YOUR UNCLE JAKE'S TRUCK. AND WHEN YOU REASSEMBLED IT...
...YOU TURNED IT INTO A FLYING MACHINE.
*IN OUR LAST FEW ISSUES. --TOM
TO BE FAIR, FIRST SHE TURNED IT INTO A TELEPOD AND USED IT TO SAVE US FROM DOCTOR DOOM.
THEN SHE MADE IT A FLYING TRUCK.
I'M WITH REED. I DON'T SEE THE PROBLEM.
AND WHO WOULDN'T WANT A FLYING TRUCK?
BUT AS FOR YOU, MISTER, WE RAISED YOU BETTER THAN THAT.
AGREED. WE'LL HAVE TO COME UP WITH AN APPROPRIATE PUNISHMENT.
WHAT? THIS IS SO UNFAIR!
IF IT WEREN'T FOR ME POWERING VAL'S TELEPORT, YOU'D STILL BE IN LATVERIA! DON'T YOU GET WHAT I DID?
EVERY TIME I USE MY POWER, PART OF
YOU SHOULD ALL BE THANKING ME. AND, DAD, YOU SHOULD BE FIGURING OUT HOW TO FIX IT!
THERE'S NOTHING TO "FIX," SON. MY SCANS SHOW THAT THIS IS A NATURAL PROGRESSION.
HOW IT SHOULD BE. THE HEALTHIEST OPTION IS TO LET IT RUN ITS COURSE.
SPEAKING OF HOW THINGS SHOULD BE...
MR. AND MRS. GRIMM? HOW DO YOU THINK FRANKLIN SHOULD MAKE AMENDS?
I'M NOT SURE.
LEAVE THAT TO ME, SWEETIE. I GOT ALL KINDS 'A IDEAS.

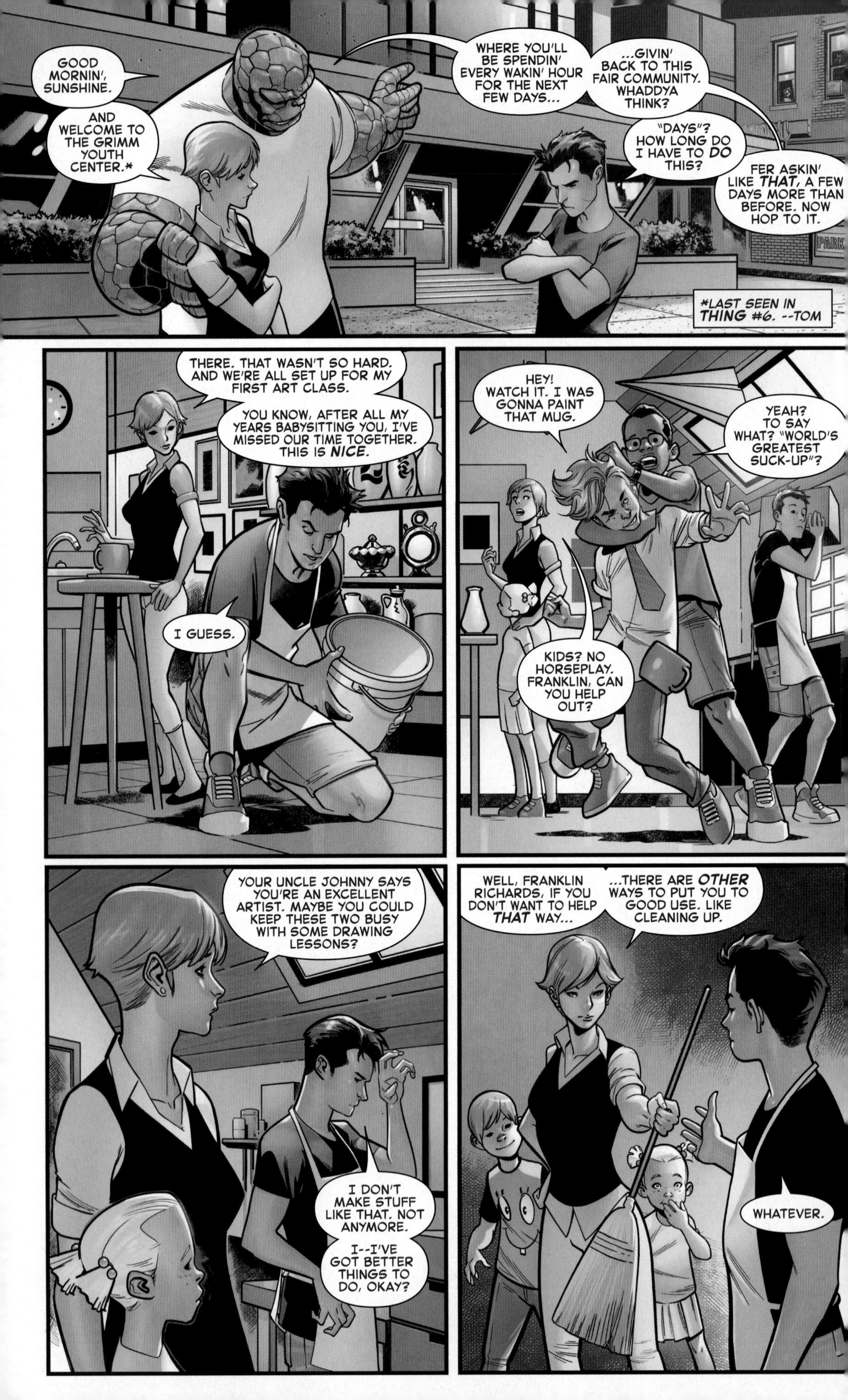
GOOD MORNIN', SUNSHINE.
AND WELCOME TO THE GRIMM YOUTH CENTER.*
WHERE YOU'LL BE SPENDIN' EVERY WAKIN' HOUR FOR THE NEXT FEW DAYS...
...GIVIN' BACK TO THIS FAIR COMMUNITY. WHADDYA THINK?
"DAYS"? HOW LONG DO I HAVE TO DO THIS?
FER ASKIN' LIKE THAT, A FEW DAYS MORE THAN BEFORE. NOW HOP TO IT.
PARK
*LAST SEEN IN THING #6. --TOM
THERE. THAT WASN'T SO HARD. AND WE'RE ALL SET UP FOR MY FIRST ART CLASS.
YOU KNOW, AFTER ALL MY YEARS BABYSITTING YOU, I'VE MISSED OUR TIME TOGETHER. THIS IS NICE.
I GUESS.
HEY! WATCH IT. I WAS GONNA PAINT THAT MUG.
YEAH? TO SAY WHAT? "WORLD'S GREATEST SUCK-UP"?
KIDS? NO HORSEPLAY. FRANKLIN, CAN YOU HELP OUT?
YOUR UNCLE JOHNNY SAYS YOU'RE AN EXCELLENT ARTIST. MAYBE YOU COULD KEEP THESE TWO BUSY WITH SOME DRAWING LESSONS?
I DON'T MAKE STUFF LIKE THAT. NOT ANYMORE.
I--I'VE GOT BETTER THINGS TO DO, OKAY?
WELL, FRANKLIN RICHARDS, IF YOU DON'T WANT TO HELP THAT WAY...
...THERE ARE OTHER WAYS TO PUT YOU TO GOOD USE. LIKE CLEANING UP.
WHATEVER.

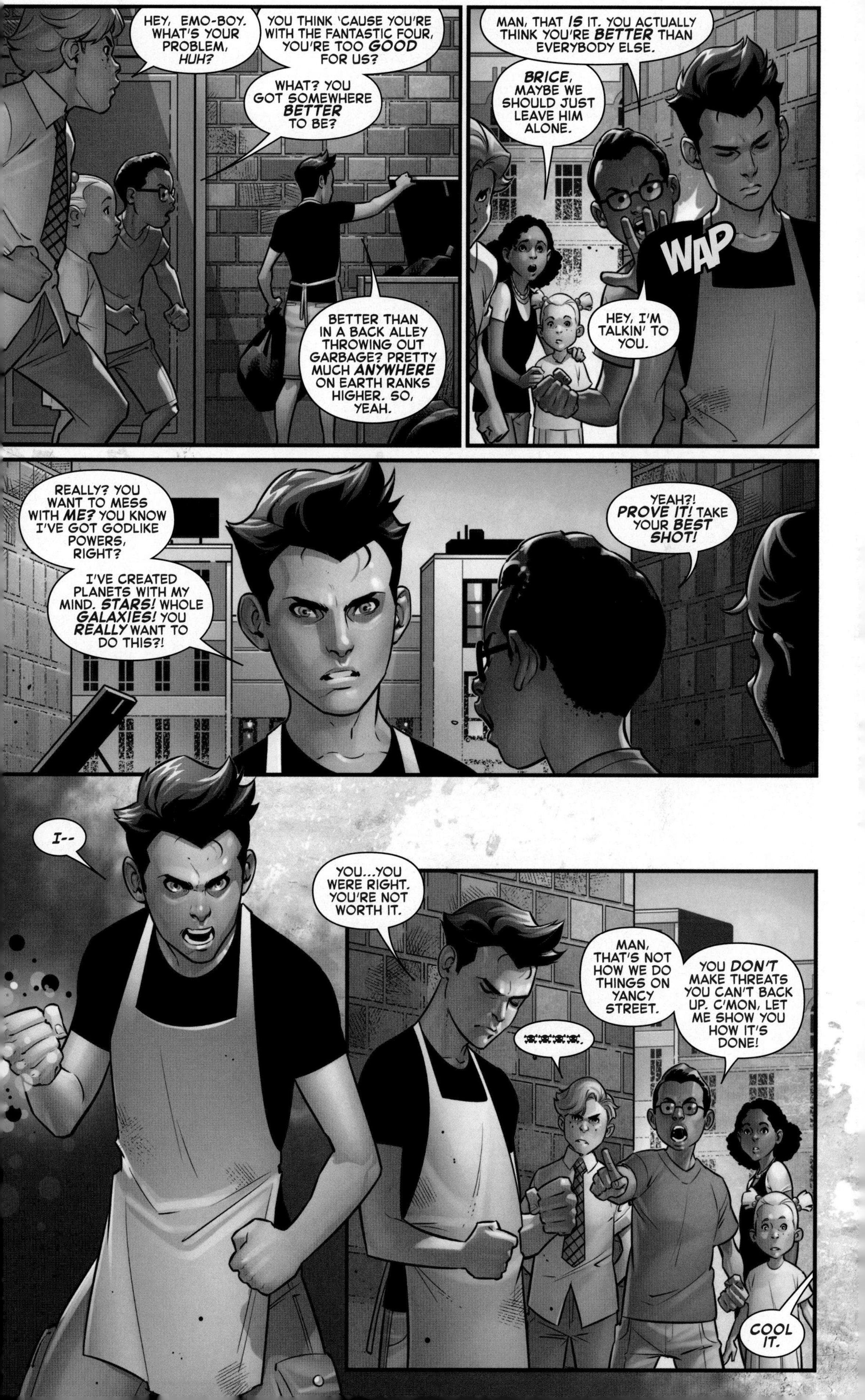
HEY, EMO-BOY. WHAT'S YOUR PROBLEM, HUH?
YOU THINK 'CAUSE YOU'RE WITH THE FANTASTIC FOUR, YOU'RE TOO GOOD FOR US?
WHAT? YOU GOT SOMEWHERE BETTER TO BE?
BETTER THAN IN A BACK ALLEY THROWING OUT GARBAGE? PRETTY MUCH ANYWHERE ON EARTH RANKS HIGHER. SO, YEAH.
MAN, THAT IS IT. YOU ACTUALLY THINK YOU'RE BETTER THAN EVERYBODY ELSE.
BRICE, MAYBE WE SHOULD JUST LEAVE HIM ALONE.
WAP
HEY, I'M TALKIN' TO YOU.
REALLY? YOU WANT TO MESS WITH ME? YOU KNOW I'VE GOT GODLIKE POWERS, RIGHT?
I'VE CREATED PLANETS WITH MY MIND. STARS! WHOLE GALAXIES! YOU REALLY WANT TO DO THIS?!
YEAH?! PROVE IT! TAKE YOUR BEST SHOT!
I--
YOU...YOU WERE RIGHT. YOU'RE NOT WORTH IT.
MAN, THAT'S NOT HOW WE DO THINGS ON YANCY STREET.
YOU DON'T MAKE THREATS YOU CAN'T BACK UP. C'MON, LET ME SHOW YOU HOW IT'S DONE!
COOL IT.

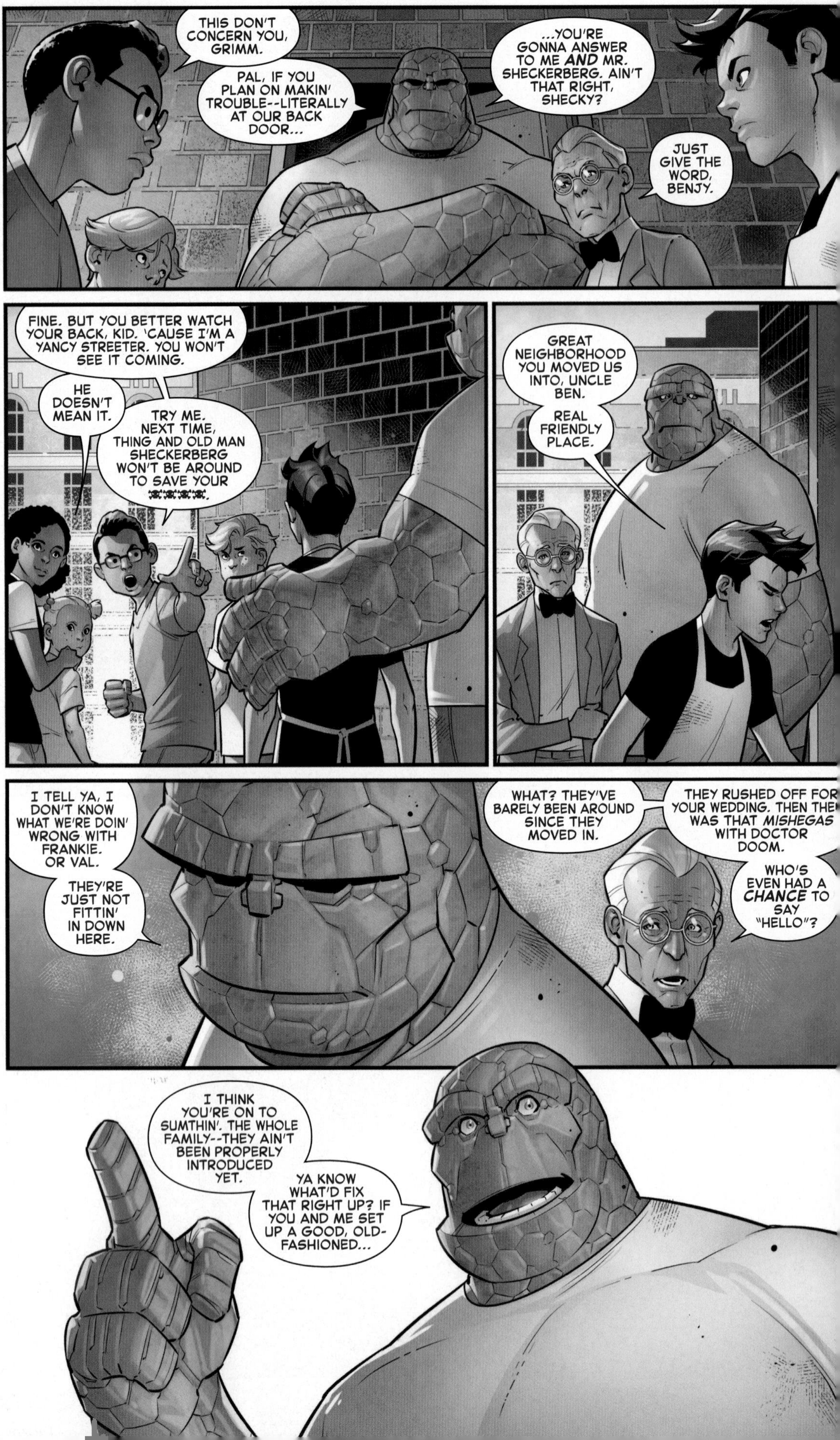

THIS DON'T CONCERN YOU, GRIMM.
PAL, IF YOU PLAN ON MAKIN' TROUBLE--LITERALLY AT OUR BACK DOOR...
...YOU'RE GONNA ANSWER TO ME AND MR. SHECKERBERG. AIN'T THAT RIGHT, SHECKY?
JUST GIVE THE WORD, BENJY.
FINE. BUT YOU BETTER WATCH YOUR BACK, KID. 'CAUSE I'M A YANCY STREETER. YOU WON'T SEE IT COMING.
HE DOESN'T MEAN IT.
TRY ME. NEXT TIME, THING AND OLD MAN SHECKERBERG WON'T BE AROUND TO SAVE YOUR
GREAT NEIGHBORHOOD YOU MOVED US INTO, UNCLE BEN.
REAL FRIENDLY PLACE.
I TELL YA, I DON'T KNOW WHAT WE'RE DOIN' WRONG WITH FRANKIE. OR VAL.
THEY'RE JUST NOT FITTIN' IN DOWN HERE.
WHAT? THEY'VE BARELY BEEN AROUND SINCE THEY MOVED IN.
THEY RUSHED OFF FOR YOUR WEDDING. THEN THE WAS THAT MISHEGAS WITH DOCTOR DOOM.
WHO'S EVEN HAD A CHANCE TO SAY "HELLO"?
I THINK YOU'RE ON TO SUMTHIN'. THE WHOLE FAMILY--THEY AIN'T BEEN PROPERLY INTRODUCED YET.
YA KNOW WHAT'D FIX THAT RIGHT UP? IF YOU AND ME SET UP A GOOD, OLD-FASHIONED...

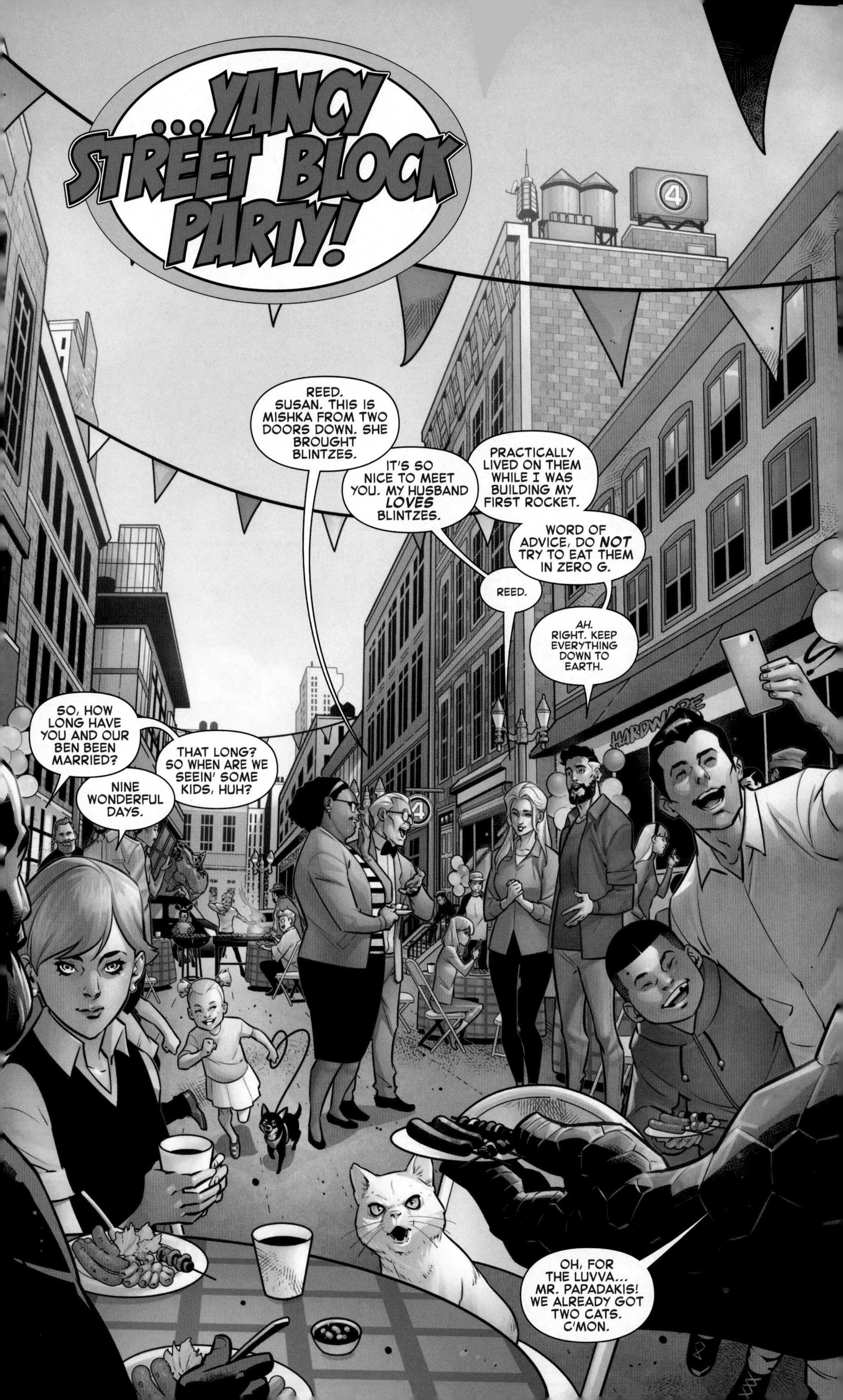
...YANCY STREET BLOCK PARTY!
REED. SUSAN. THIS IS MISHKA FROM TWO DOORS DOWN. SHE BROUGHT BLINTZES.
IT'S SO NICE TO MEET YOU. MY HUSBAND LOVES BLINTZES.
PRACTICALLY LIVED ON THEM WHILE I WAS BUILDING MY FIRST ROCKET.
WORD OF ADVICE, DO NOT TRY TO EAT THEM IN ZERO G.
REED.
AH. RIGHT. KEEP EVERYTHING DOWN TO EARTH.
SO, HOW LONG HAVE YOU AND OUR BEN BEEN MARRIED?
NINE WONDERFUL DAYS.
THAT LONG? SO WHEN ARE WE SEEIN' SOME KIDS, HUH?
HARDWARE
OH, FOR THE LUVVA... MR. PAPADAKIS! WE ALREADY GOT TWO CATS. C'MON.

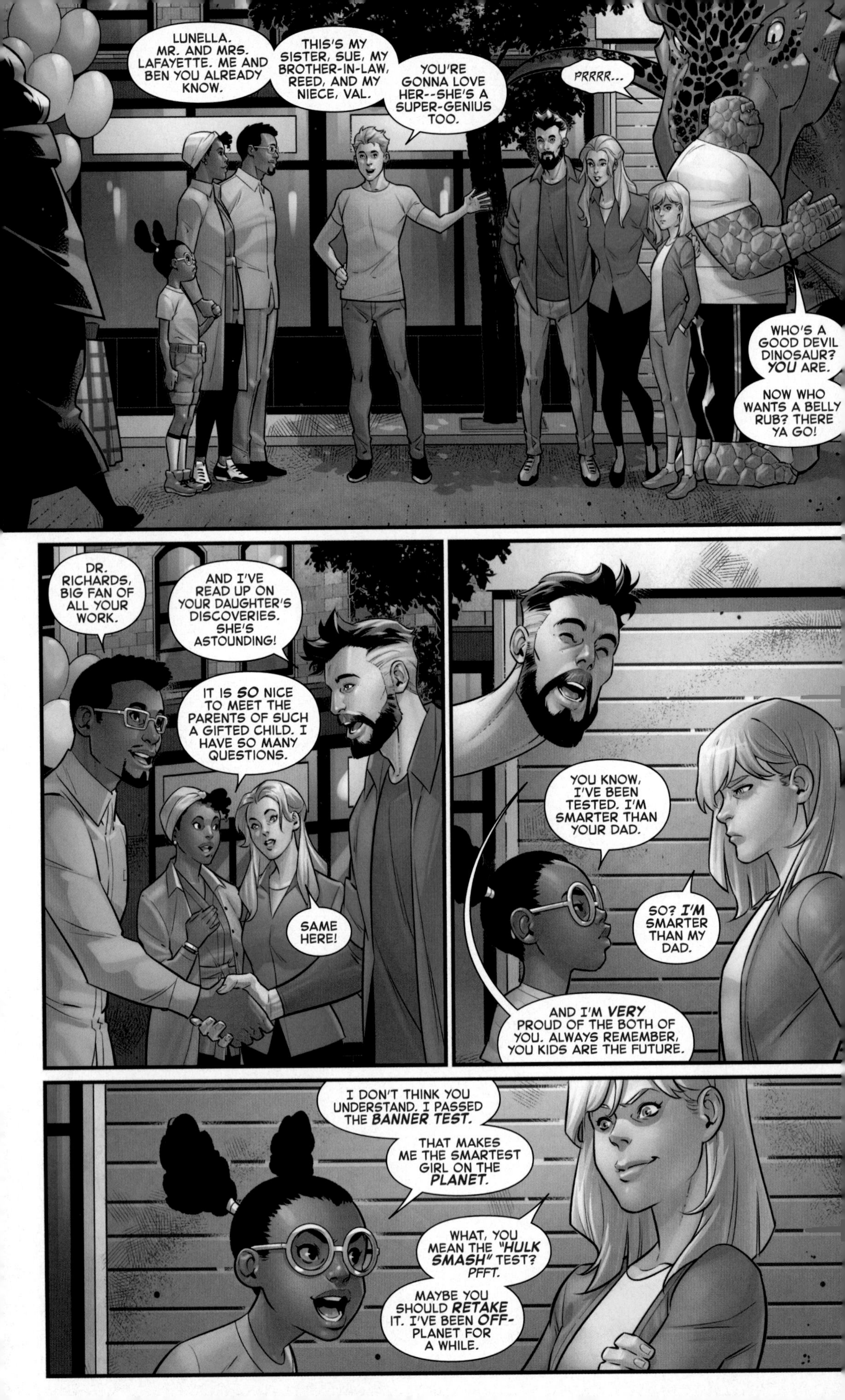

LUNELLA. MR. AND MRS. LAFAYETTE. ME AND BEN YOU ALREADY KNOW.
THIS'S MY SISTER, SUE, MY BROTHER-IN-LAW, REED, AND MY NIECE, VAL.
YOU'RE GONNA LOVE HER--SHE'S A SUPER-GENIUS TOO.
PRRRR...
WHO'S A GOOD DEVIL DINOSAUR? YOU ARE.
NOW WHO WANTS A BELLY RUB? THERE YA GO!
DR. RICHARDS, BIG FAN OF ALL YOUR WORK.
AND I'VE READ UP ON YOUR DAUGHTER'S DISCOVERIES. SHE'S ASTOUNDING!
IT IS SO NICE TO MEET THE PARENTS OF SUCH A GIFTED CHILD. I HAVE SO MANY QUESTIONS.
SAME HERE!
YOU KNOW, I'VE BEEN TESTED. I'M SMARTER THAN YOUR DAD.
SO? I'M SMARTER THAN MY DAD.
AND I'M VERY PROUD OF THE BOTH OF YOU. ALWAYS REMEMBER, YOU KIDS ARE THE FUTURE.
I DON'T THINK YOU UNDERSTAND. I PASSED THE BANNER TEST.
THAT MAKES ME THE SMARTEST GIRL ON THE PLANET.
WHAT, YOU MEAN THE "HULK SMASH" TEST? PFFT.
MAYBE YOU SHOULD RETAKE IT. I'VE BEEN OFF-PLANET FOR A WHILE.

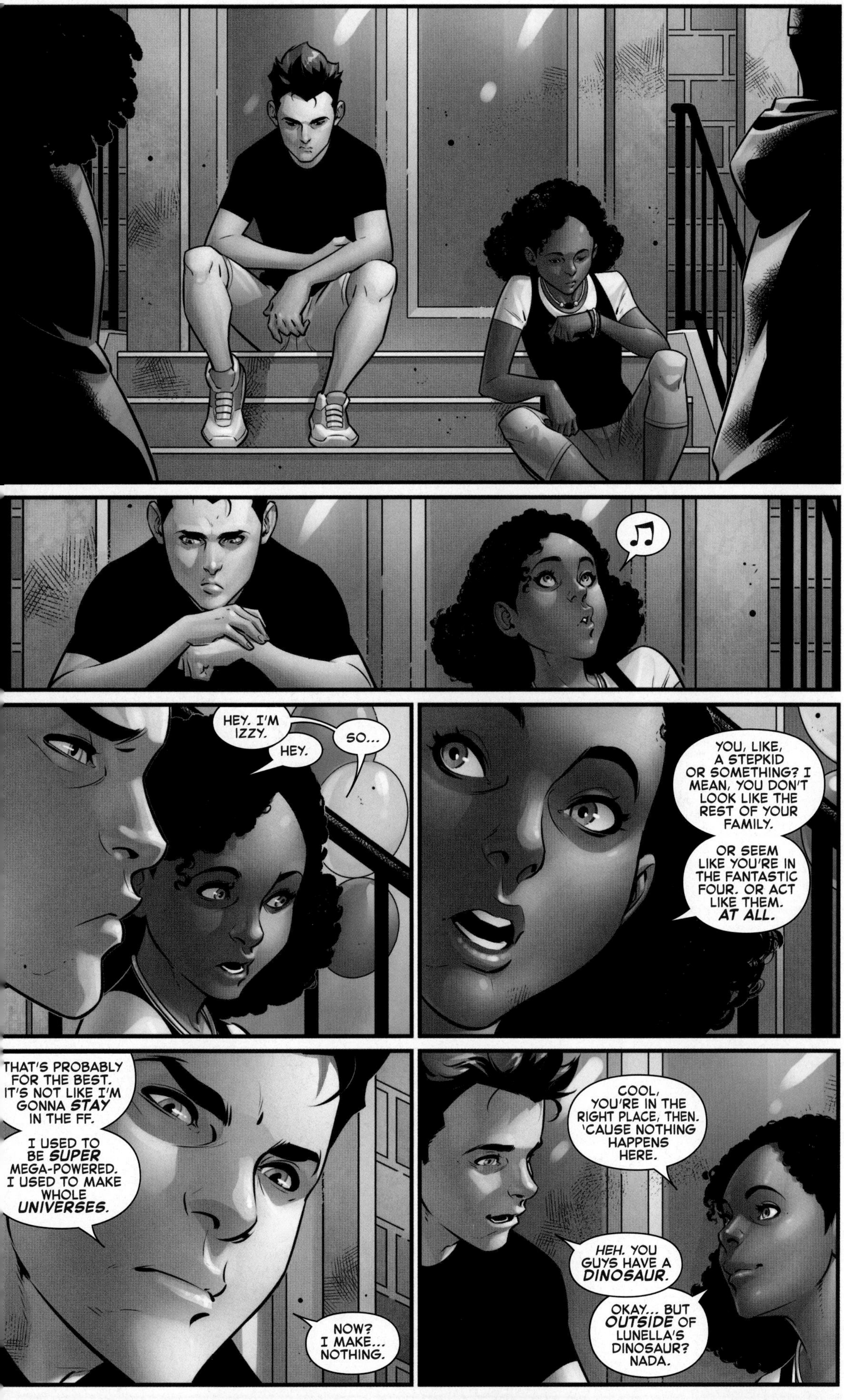
♫
HEY. I'M IZZY.
HEY.
SO...
YOU, LIKE, A STEPKID OR SOMETHING? I MEAN, YOU DON'T LOOK LIKE THE REST OF YOUR FAMILY.
OR SEEM LIKE YOU'RE IN THE FANTASTIC FOUR. OR ACT LIKE THEM. *AT ALL.*
THAT'S PROBABLY FOR THE BEST. IT'S NOT LIKE I'M GONNA *STAY* IN THE FF.
I USED TO BE *SUPER* MEGA-POWERED. I USED TO MAKE WHOLE *UNIVERSES*.
NOW? I MAKE... NOTHING.
COOL, YOU'RE IN THE RIGHT PLACE, THEN. 'CAUSE NOTHING HAPPENS HERE.
*HEH.* YOU GUYS HAVE A *DINOSAUR*.
OKAY... BUT *OUTSIDE* OF LUNELLA'S DINOSAUR? NADA.

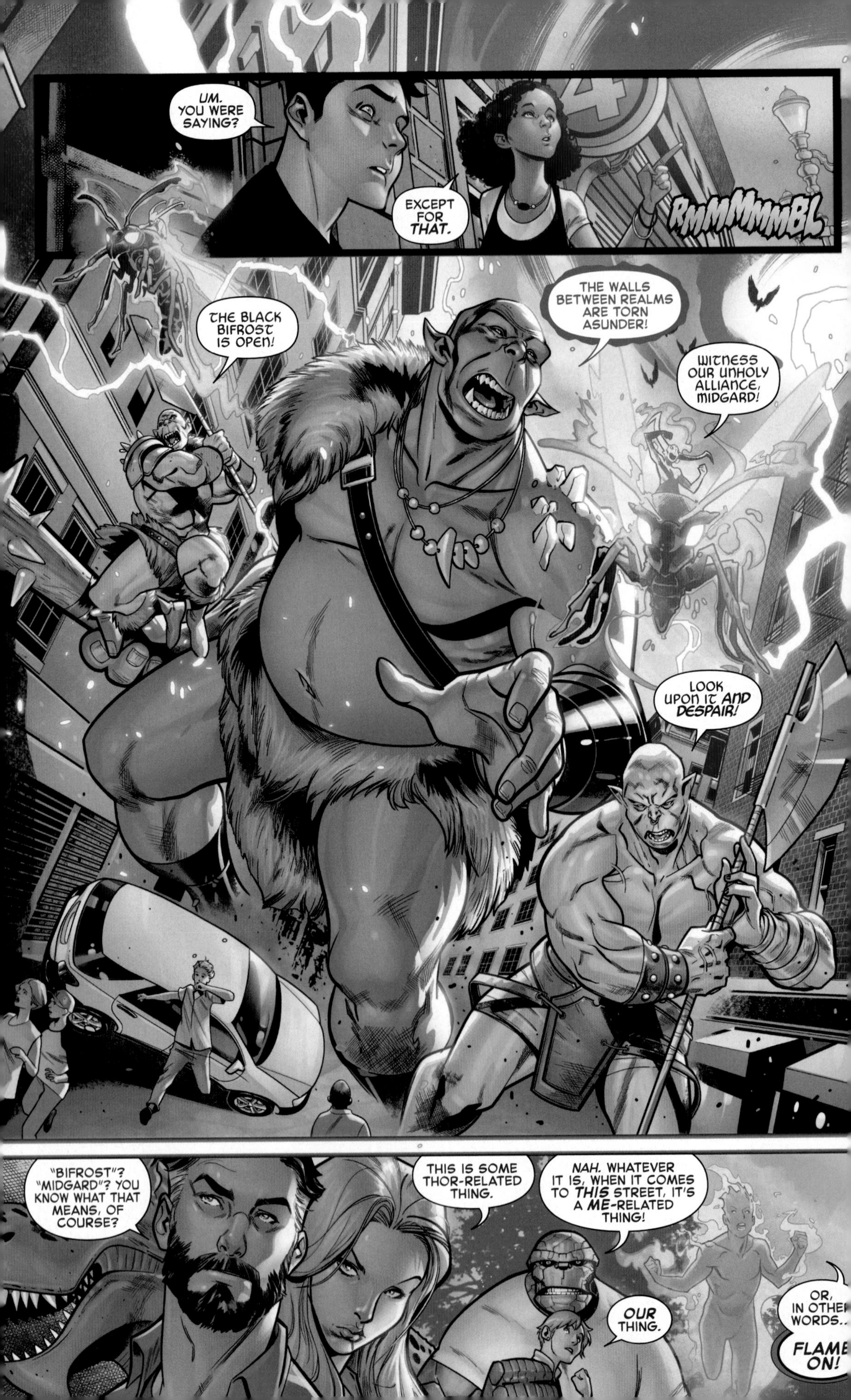
UM. YOU WERE SAYING?
EXCEPT FOR THAT.
RMMMMMMBL
THE BLACK BIFROST IS OPEN!
THE WALLS BETWEEN REALMS ARE TORN ASUNDER!
WITNESS OUR UNHOLY ALLIANCE, MIDGARD!
LOOK UPON IT AND DESPAIR!
"BIFROST"? "MIDGARD"? YOU KNOW WHAT THAT MEANS, OF COURSE?
THIS IS SOME THOR-RELATED THING.
NAH. WHATEVER IT IS, WHEN IT COMES TO THIS STREET, IT'S A ME-RELATED THING!
OUR THING.
OR, IN OTHER WORDS...
FLAME ON!

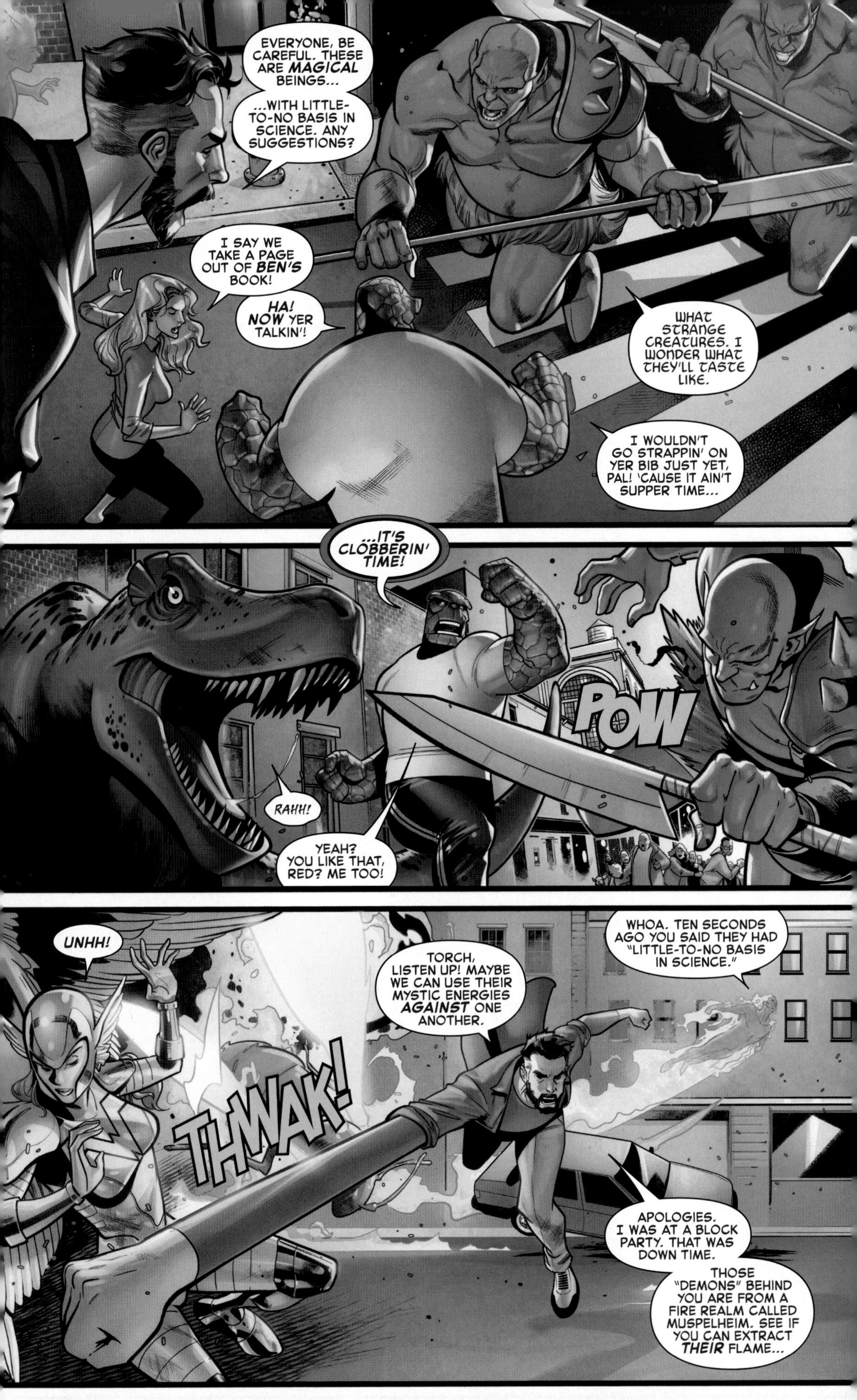

EVERYONE, BE CAREFUL. THESE ARE *MAGICAL* BEINGS...
...WITH LITTLE-TO-NO BASIS IN SCIENCE. ANY SUGGESTIONS?
I SAY WE TAKE A PAGE OUT OF *BEN'S* BOOK!
*HA! NOW* YER TALKIN'!
WHAT STRANGE CREATURES. I WONDER WHAT THEY'LL TASTE LIKE.
I WOULDN'T GO STRAPPIN' ON YER BIB JUST YET, PAL! 'CAUSE IT AIN'T SUPPER TIME...
...IT'S CLOBBERIN' TIME!
POW
RAHH!
YEAH? YOU LIKE THAT, RED? ME TOO!
UNHH!
TORCH, LISTEN UP! MAYBE WE CAN USE THEIR MYSTIC ENERGIES *AGAINST* ONE ANOTHER.
WHOA. TEN SECONDS AGO YOU SAID THEY HAD "LITTLE-TO-NO BASIS IN SCIENCE."
THWAK!
APOLOGIES. I WAS AT A BLOCK PARTY. THAT WAS DOWN TIME.
THOSE "DEMONS" BEHIND YOU ARE FROM A FIRE REALM CALLED MUSPELHEIM. SEE IF YOU CAN EXTRACT *THEIR* FLAME...

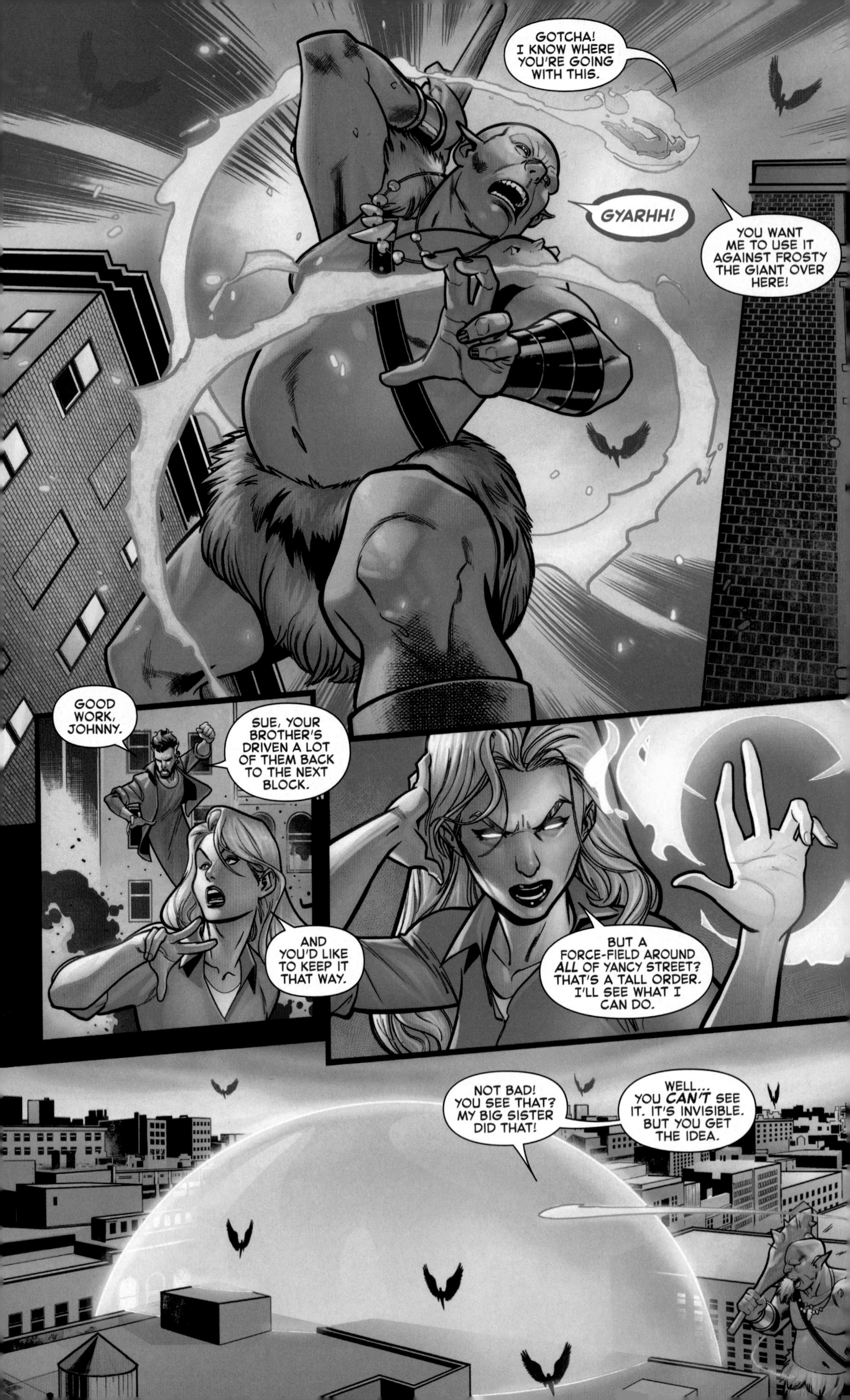
GOTCHA! I KNOW WHERE YOU'RE GOING WITH THIS.
GYARHH!
YOU WANT ME TO USE IT AGAINST FROSTY THE GIANT OVER HERE!
GOOD WORK, JOHNNY.
SUE, YOUR BROTHER'S DRIVEN A LOT OF THEM BACK TO THE NEXT BLOCK.
AND YOU'D LIKE TO KEEP IT THAT WAY.
BUT A FORCE-FIELD AROUND ALL OF YANCY STREET? THAT'S A TALL ORDER. I'LL SEE WHAT I CAN DO.
NOT BAD! YOU SEE THAT? MY BIG SISTER DID THAT!
WELL... YOU CAN'T SEE IT. IT'S INVISIBLE. BUT YOU GET THE IDEA.

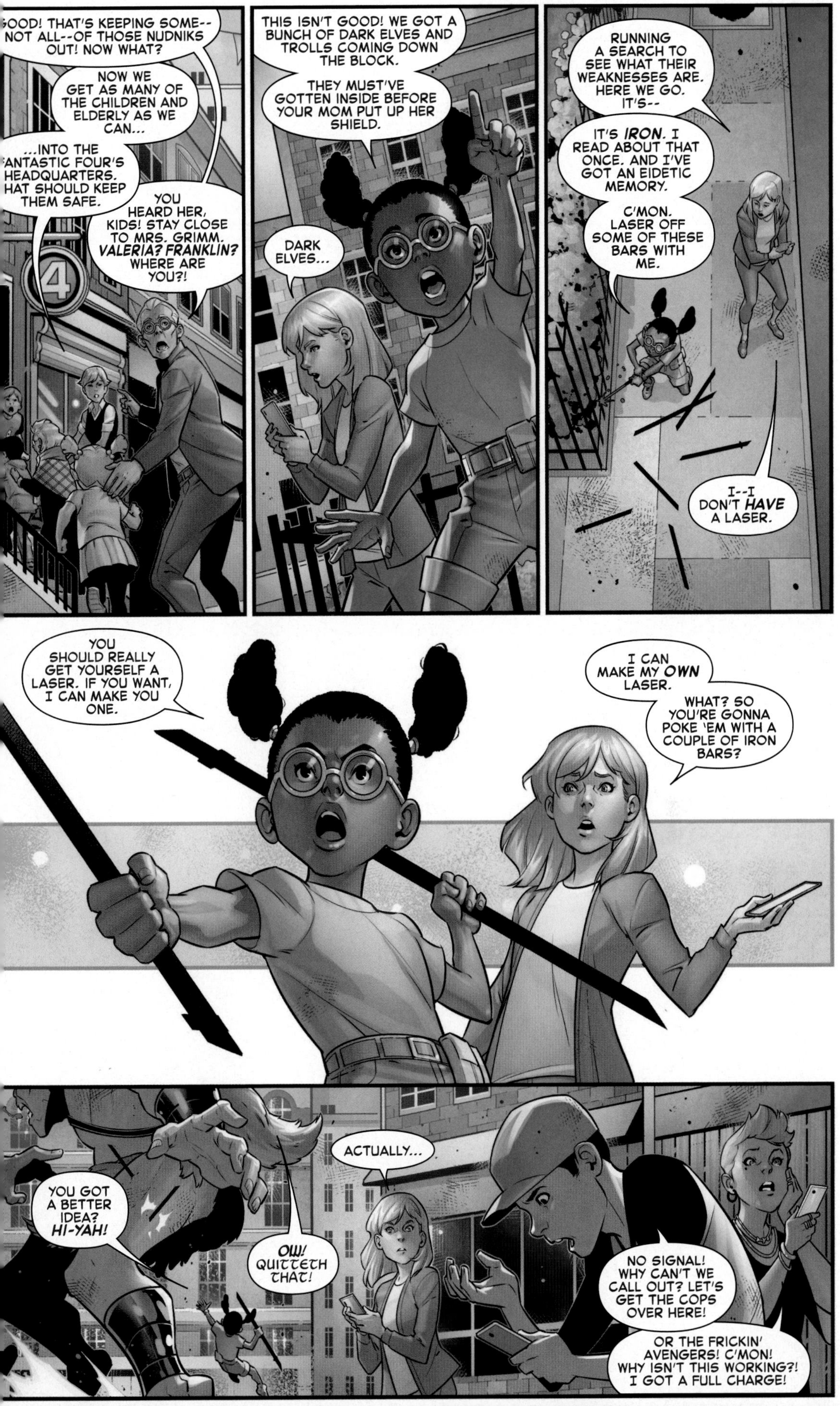
GOOD! THAT'S KEEPING SOME-- NOT ALL--OF THOSE NUDNIKS OUT! NOW WHAT?
NOW WE GET AS MANY OF THE CHILDREN AND ELDERLY AS WE CAN...
...INTO THE FANTASTIC FOUR'S HEADQUARTERS. THAT SHOULD KEEP THEM SAFE.
YOU HEARD HER, KIDS! STAY CLOSE TO MRS. GRIMM. VALERIA? FRANKLIN? WHERE ARE YOU?!
4
THIS ISN'T GOOD! WE GOT A BUNCH OF DARK ELVES AND TROLLS COMING DOWN THE BLOCK.
THEY MUST'VE GOTTEN INSIDE BEFORE YOUR MOM PUT UP HER SHIELD.
DARK ELVES...
RUNNING A SEARCH TO SEE WHAT THEIR WEAKNESSES ARE. HERE WE GO. IT'S--
IT'S IRON. I READ ABOUT THAT ONCE. AND I'VE GOT AN EIDETIC MEMORY.
C'MON. LASER OFF SOME OF THESE BARS WITH ME.
I--I DON'T HAVE A LASER.
YOU SHOULD REALLY GET YOURSELF A LASER. IF YOU WANT, I CAN MAKE YOU ONE.
I CAN MAKE MY OWN LASER.
WHAT? SO YOU'RE GONNA POKE 'EM WITH A COUPLE OF IRON BARS?
YOU GOT A BETTER IDEA? HI-YAH!
OW! QUITTETH THAT!
ACTUALLY...
NO SIGNAL! WHY CAN'T WE CALL OUT? LET'S GET THE COPS OVER HERE!
OR THE FRICKIN' AVENGERS! C'MON! WHY ISN'T THIS WORKING?! I GOT A FULL CHARGE!

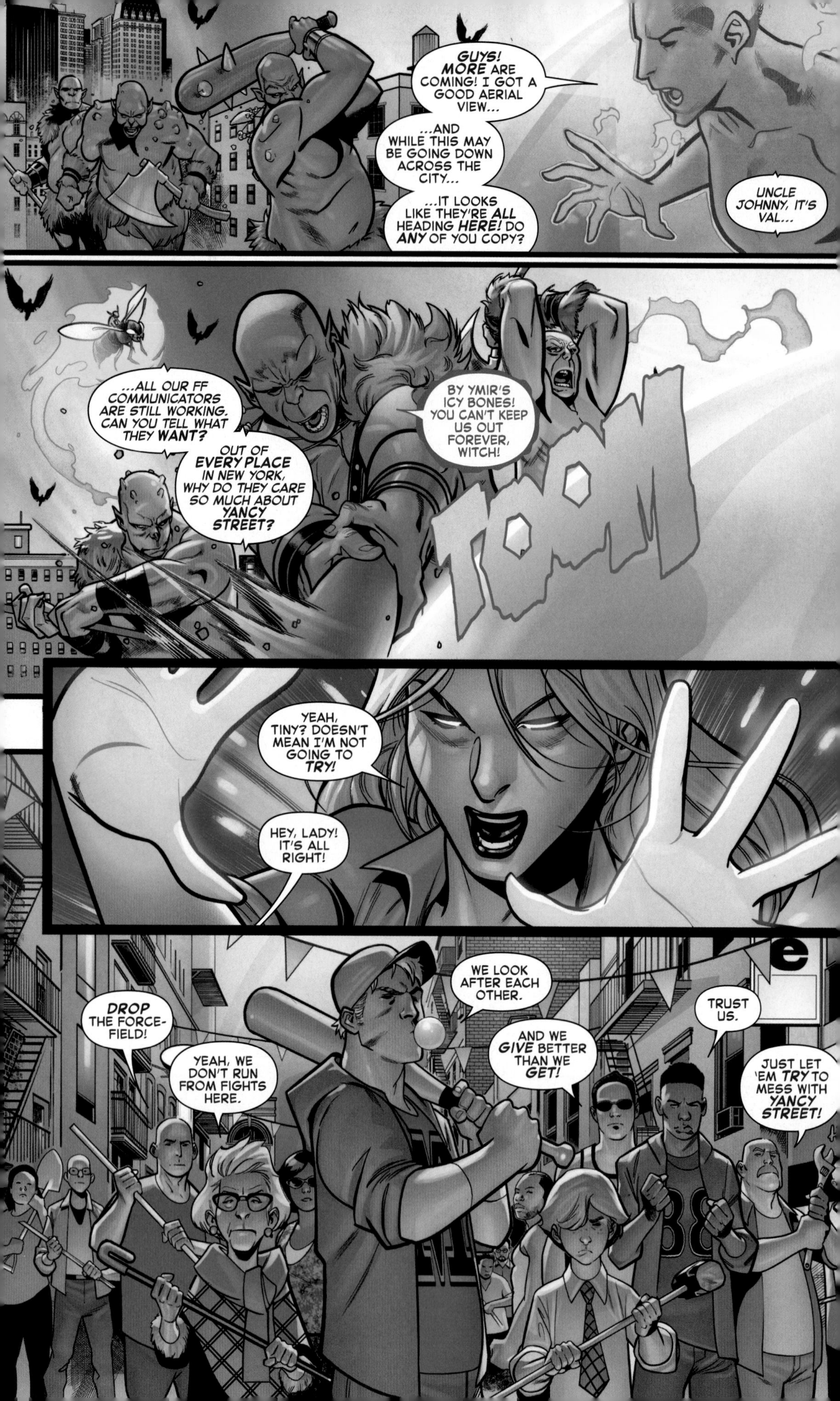
GUYS! MORE ARE COMING! I GOT A GOOD AERIAL VIEW...
...AND WHILE THIS MAY BE GOING DOWN ACROSS THE CITY...
...IT LOOKS LIKE THEY'RE ALL HEADING HERE! DO ANY OF YOU COPY?
UNCLE JOHNNY, IT'S VAL...
...ALL OUR FF COMMUNICATORS ARE STILL WORKING. CAN YOU TELL WHAT THEY WANT?
OUT OF EVERY PLACE IN NEW YORK, WHY DO THEY CARE SO MUCH ABOUT YANCY STREET?
BY YMIR'S ICY BONES! YOU CAN'T KEEP US OUT FOREVER, WITCH!
TOOM
YEAH, TINY? DOESN'T MEAN I'M NOT GOING TO TRY!
HEY, LADY! IT'S ALL RIGHT!
DROP THE FORCE-FIELD!
YEAH, WE DON'T RUN FROM FIGHTS HERE.
WE LOOK AFTER EACH OTHER.
AND WE GIVE BETTER THAN WE GET!
TRUST US.
JUST LET 'EM TRY TO MESS WITH YANCY STREET!

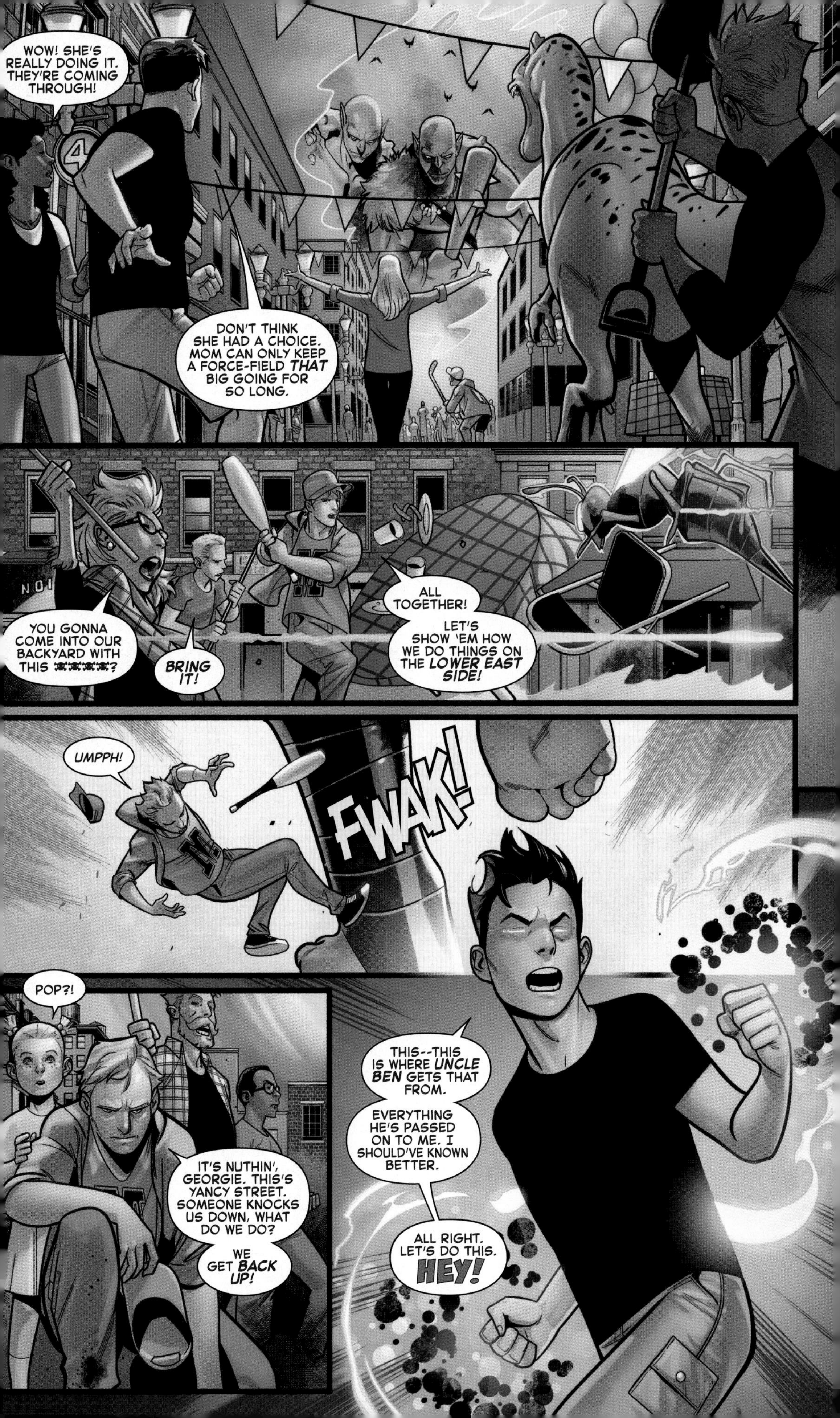
WOW! SHE'S REALLY DOING IT. THEY'RE COMING THROUGH!
DON'T THINK SHE HAD A CHOICE. MOM CAN ONLY KEEP A FORCE-FIELD THAT BIG GOING FOR SO LONG.
NOI
YOU GONNA COME INTO OUR BACKYARD WITH THIS ?
BRING IT!
ALL TOGETHER!
LET'S SHOW 'EM HOW WE DO THINGS ON THE LOWER EAST SIDE!
UMPPH!
FWAK!
POP?!
IT'S NUTHIN', GEORGIE. THIS'S YANCY STREET. SOMEONE KNOCKS US DOWN, WHAT DO WE DO?
WE GET BACK UP!
THIS--THIS IS WHERE UNCLE BEN GETS THAT FROM.
EVERYTHING HE'S PASSED ON TO ME. I SHOULD'VE KNOWN BETTER.
ALL RIGHT. LET'S DO THIS. HEY!

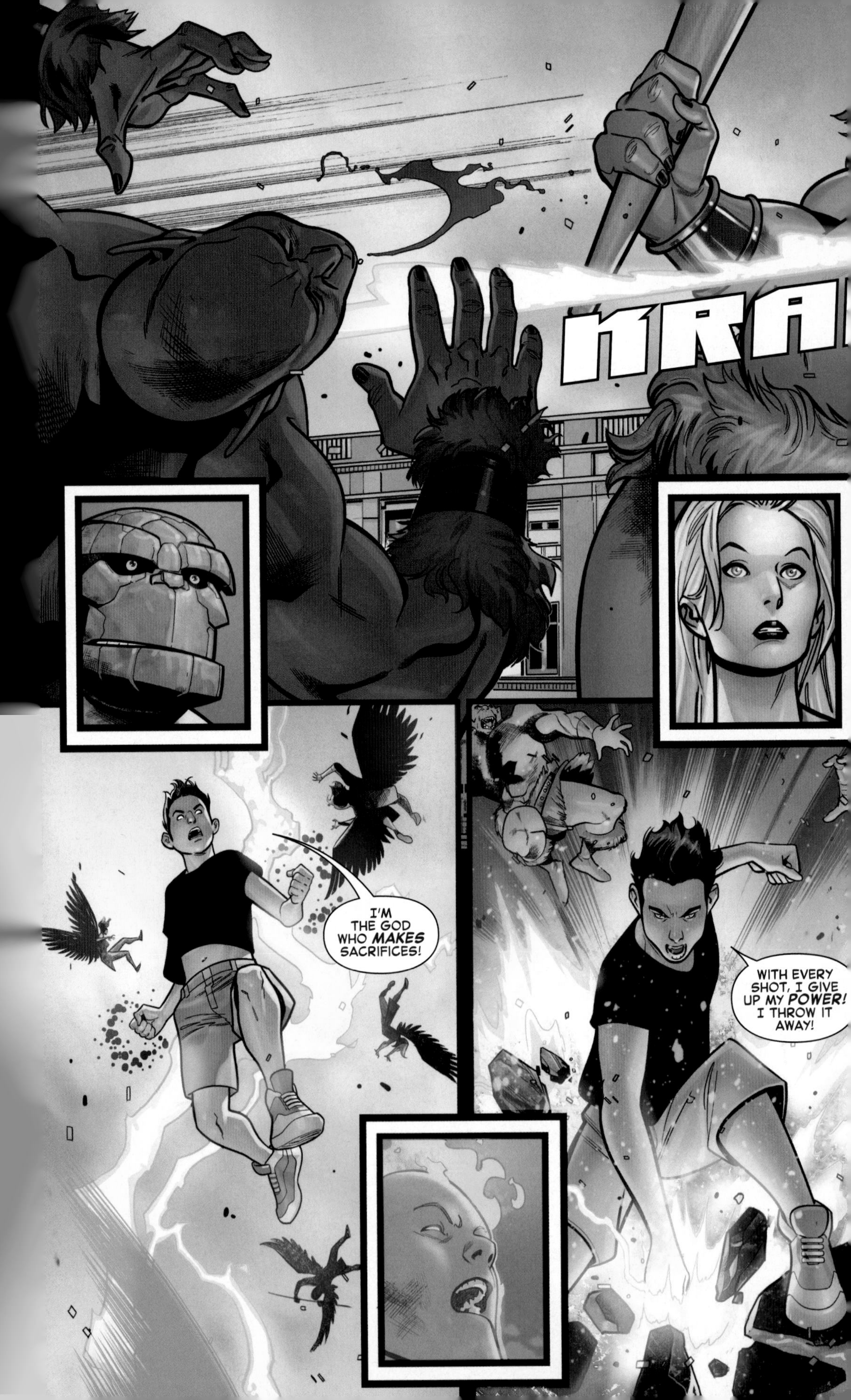
KRA
I'M THE GOD WHO MAKES SACRIFICES!
WITH EVERY SHOT, I GIVE UP MY POWER! I THROW IT AWAY!

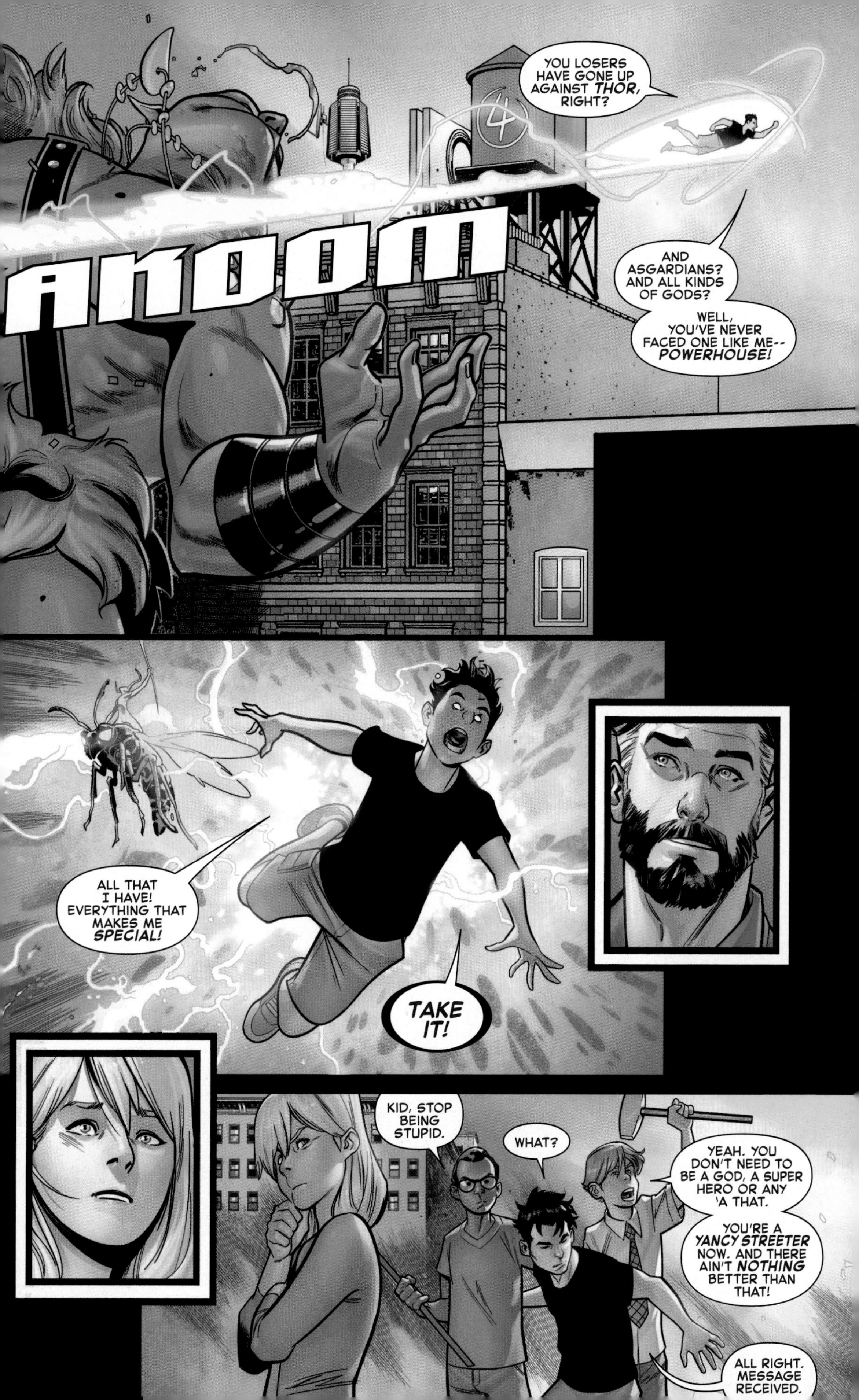
YOU LOSERS HAVE GONE UP AGAINST THOR, RIGHT?
AKOOM
AND ASGARDIANS? AND ALL KINDS OF GODS?
WELL, YOU'VE NEVER FACED ONE LIKE ME-- POWERHOUSE!
ALL THAT I HAVE! EVERYTHING THAT MAKES ME SPECIAL!
TAKE IT!
KID, STOP BEING STUPID.
WHAT?
YEAH. YOU DON'T NEED TO BE A GOD, A SUPER HERO OR ANY 'A THAT.
YOU'RE A YANCY STREETER NOW. AND THERE AIN'T NOTHING BETTER THAN THAT!
ALL RIGHT. MESSAGE RECEIVED.

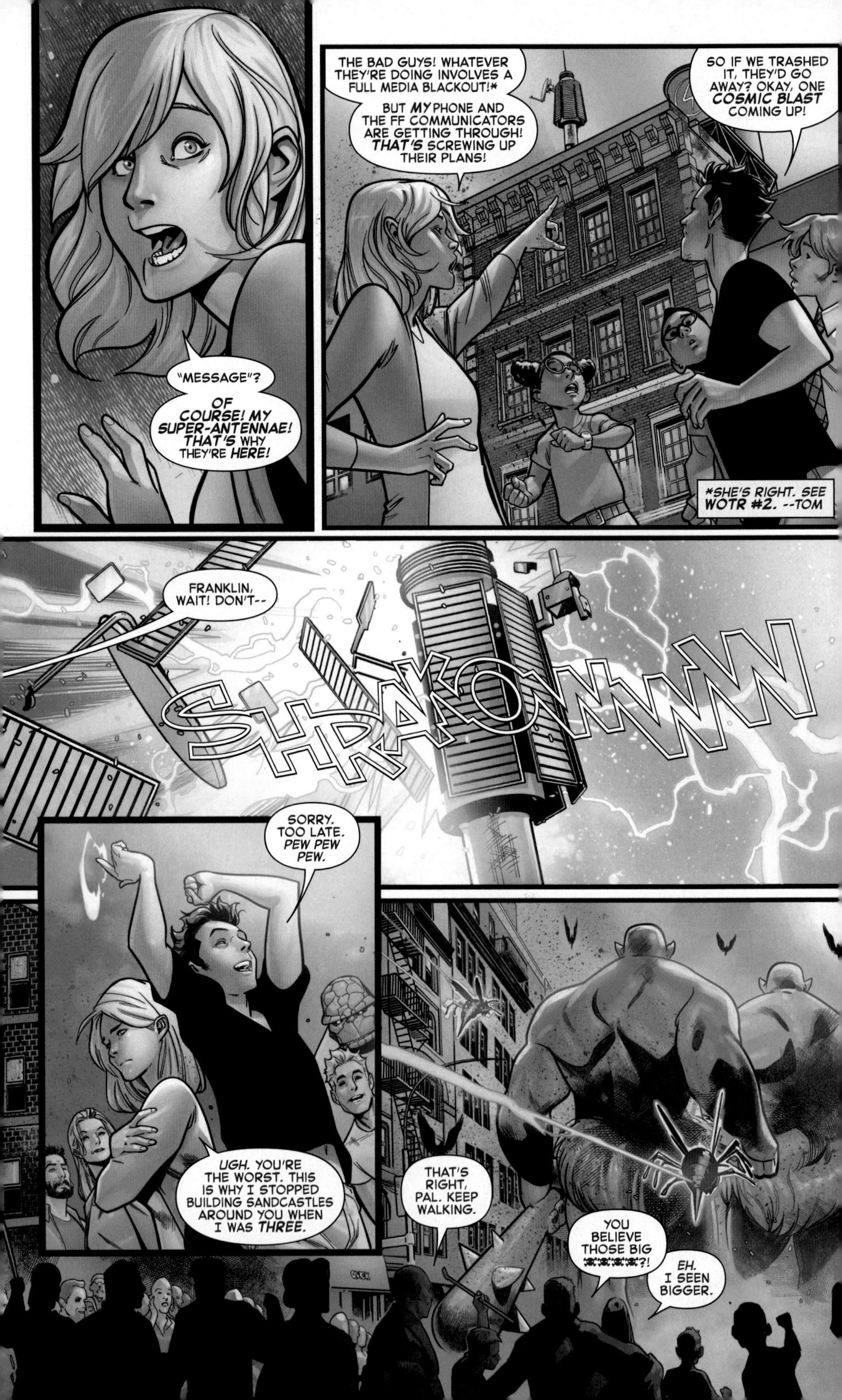
"MESSAGE"?
OF COURSE! MY SUPER-ANTENNAE! THAT'S WHY THEY'RE HERE!
THE BAD GUYS! WHATEVER THEY'RE DOING INVOLVES A FULL MEDIA BLACKOUT!*
BUT MY PHONE AND THE FF COMMUNICATORS ARE GETTING THROUGH! THAT'S SCREWING UP THEIR PLANS!
SO IF WE TRASHED IT, THEY'D GO AWAY? OKAY, ONE COSMIC BLAST COMING UP!
*SHE'S RIGHT. SEE WOTR #2. --TOM
FRANKLIN, WAIT! DON'T--
SHRAKOWWWW
SORRY. TOO LATE. PEW PEW PEW.
UGH. YOU'RE THE WORST. THIS IS WHY I STOPPED BUILDING SANDCASTLES AROUND YOU WHEN I WAS THREE.
THAT'S RIGHT, PAL. KEEP WALKING.
YOU BELIEVE THOSE BIG ☠☠☠☠?!
EH. I SEEN BIGGER.

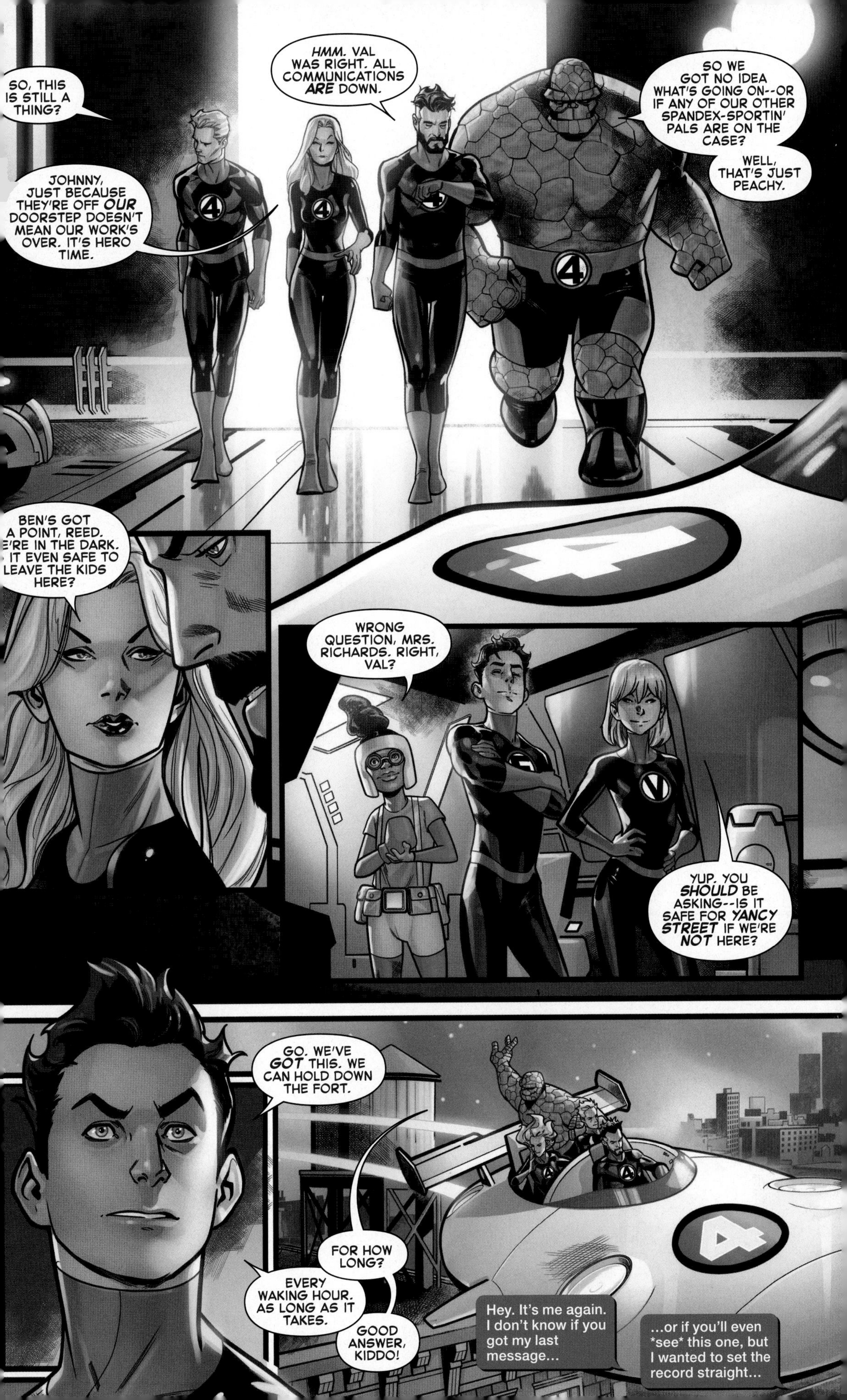
SO, THIS IS STILL A THING?
HMM. VAL WAS RIGHT. ALL COMMUNICATIONS ARE DOWN.
SO WE GOT NO IDEA WHAT'S GOING ON--OR IF ANY OF OUR OTHER SPANDEX-SPORTIN' PALS ARE ON THE CASE?
WELL, THAT'S JUST PEACHY.
JOHNNY, JUST BECAUSE THEY'RE OFF OUR DOORSTEP DOESN'T MEAN OUR WORK'S OVER. IT'S HERO TIME.
BEN'S GOT A POINT, REED. E'RE IN THE DARK. IT EVEN SAFE TO LEAVE THE KIDS HERE?
WRONG QUESTION, MRS. RICHARDS. RIGHT, VAL?
YUP. YOU SHOULD BE ASKING--IS IT SAFE FOR YANCY STREET IF WE'RE NOT HERE?
GO. WE'VE GOT THIS. WE CAN HOLD DOWN THE FORT.
FOR HOW LONG?
EVERY WAKING HOUR. AS LONG AS IT TAKES.
GOOD ANSWER, KIDDO!
Hey. It's me again. I don't know if you got my last message...
...or if you'll even *see* this one, but I wanted to set the record straight...

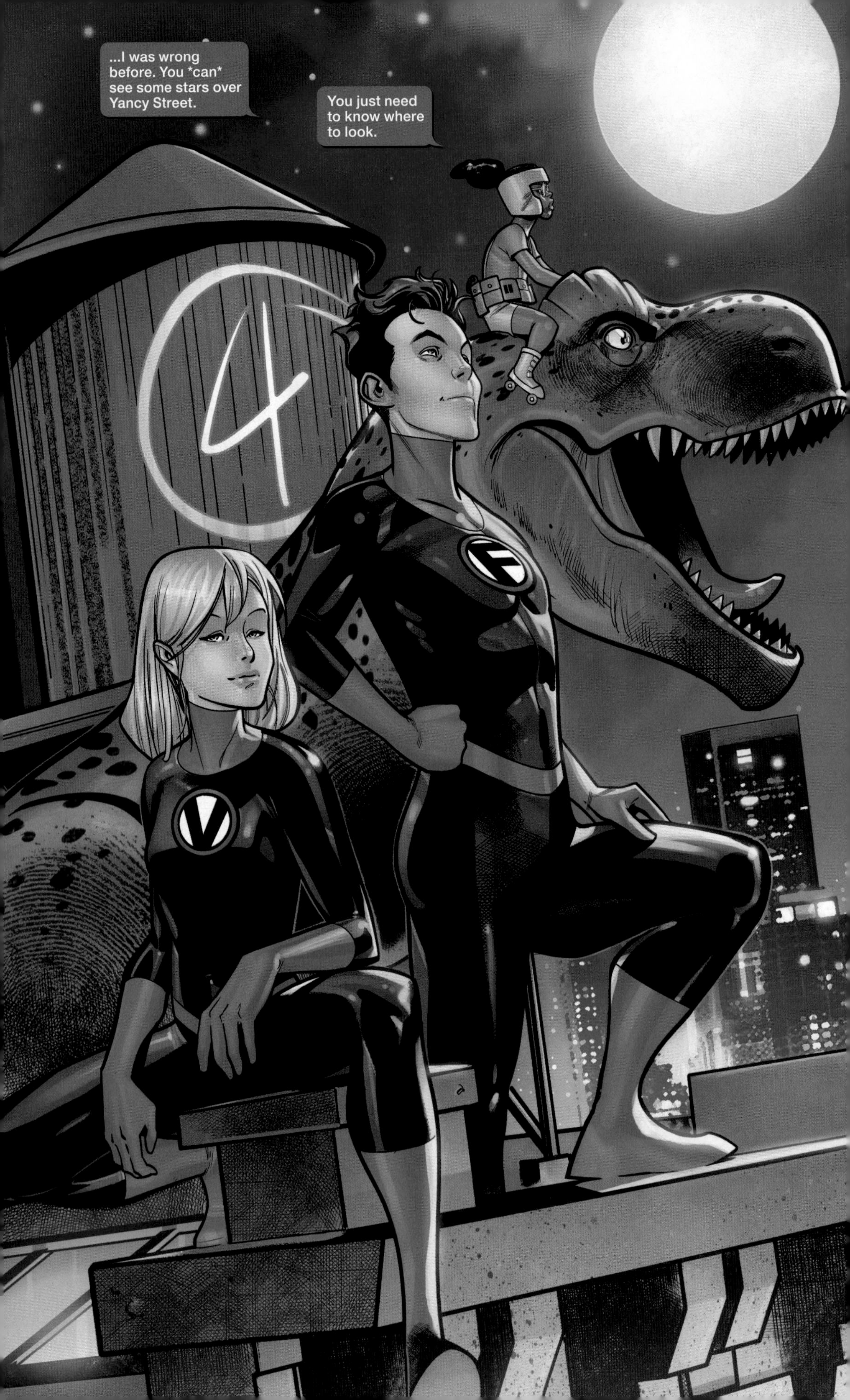
...I was wrong before. You *can* see some stars over Yancy Street.
You just need to know where to look.

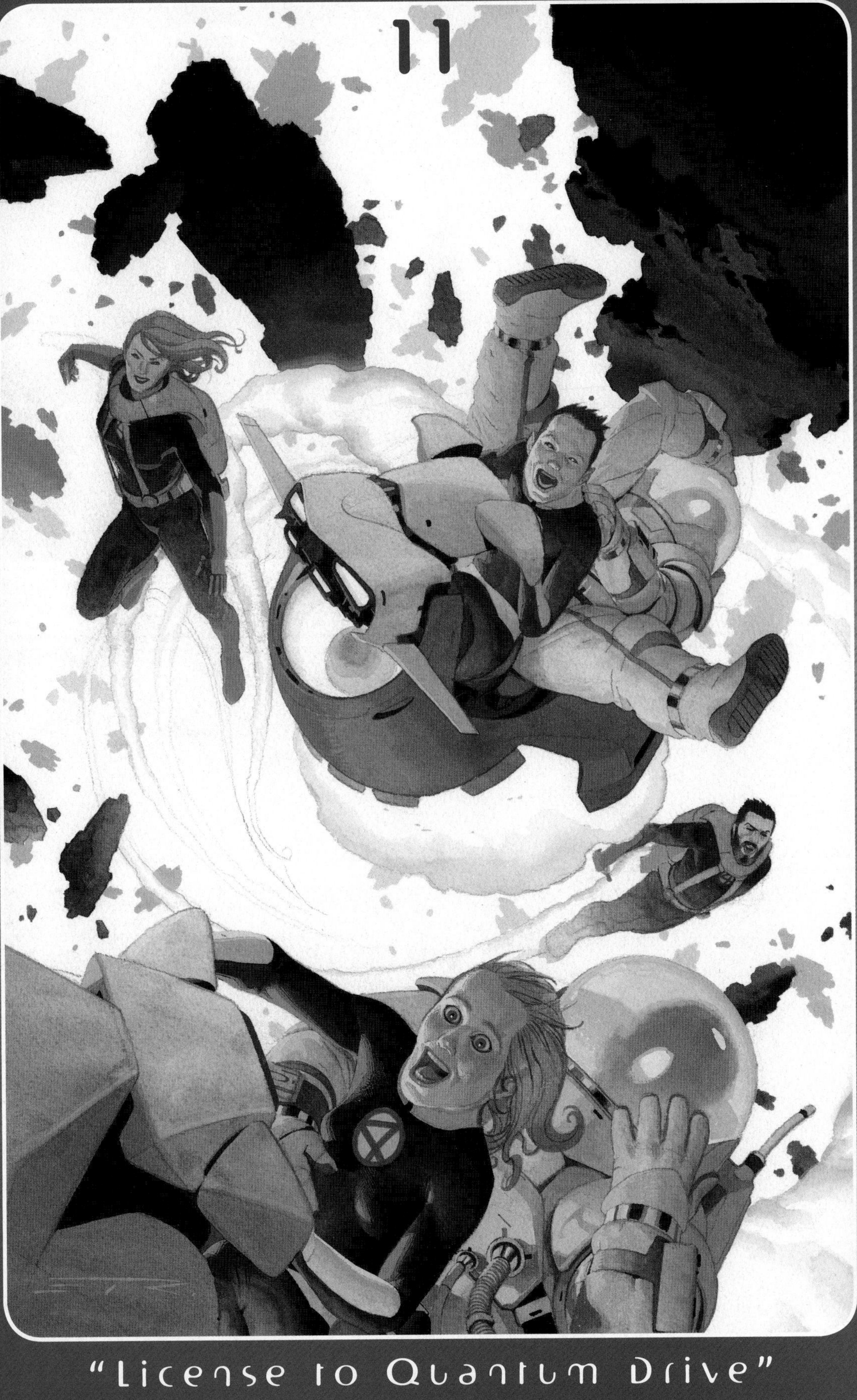

# 11

"License to Quantum Drive"

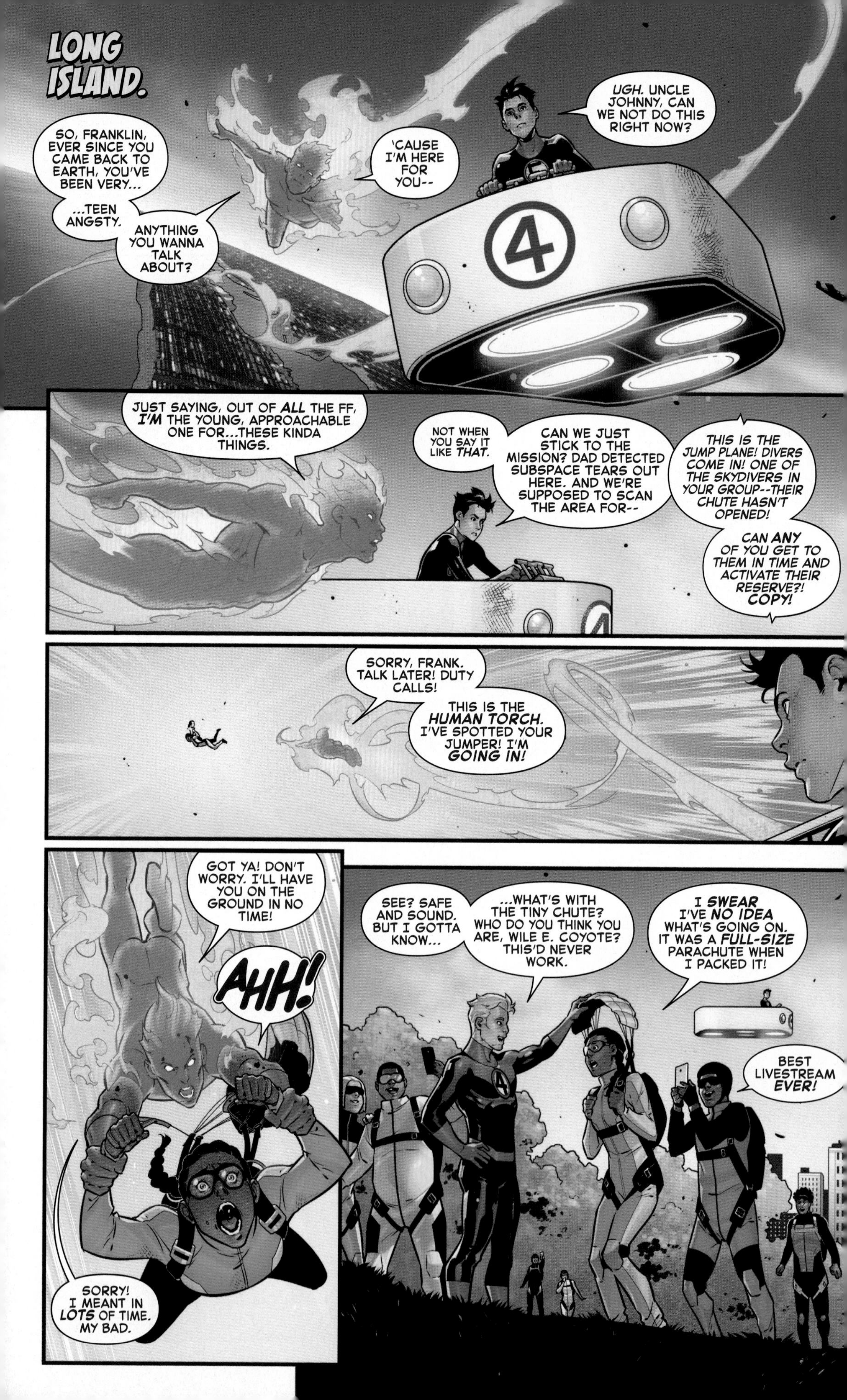
LONG ISLAND.
SO, FRANKLIN, EVER SINCE YOU CAME BACK TO EARTH, YOU'VE BEEN VERY...
...TEEN ANGSTY.
ANYTHING YOU WANNA TALK ABOUT?
'CAUSE I'M HERE FOR YOU--
UGH. UNCLE JOHNNY, CAN WE NOT DO THIS RIGHT NOW?
JUST SAYING, OUT OF ALL THE FF, I'M THE YOUNG, APPROACHABLE ONE FOR...THESE KINDA THINGS.
NOT WHEN YOU SAY IT LIKE THAT.
CAN WE JUST STICK TO THE MISSION? DAD DETECTED SUBSPACE TEARS OUT HERE. AND WE'RE SUPPOSED TO SCAN THE AREA FOR--
THIS IS THE JUMP PLANE! DIVERS COME IN! ONE OF THE SKYDIVERS IN YOUR GROUP--THEIR CHUTE HASN'T OPENED!
CAN ANY OF YOU GET TO THEM IN TIME AND ACTIVATE THEIR RESERVE?! COPY!
SORRY, FRANK. TALK LATER! DUTY CALLS!
THIS IS THE HUMAN TORCH. I'VE SPOTTED YOUR JUMPER! I'M GOING IN!
GOT YA! DON'T WORRY. I'LL HAVE YOU ON THE GROUND IN NO TIME!
AHH!
SORRY! I MEANT IN LOTS OF TIME. MY BAD.
SEE? SAFE AND SOUND. BUT I GOTTA KNOW...
...WHAT'S WITH THE TINY CHUTE? WHO DO YOU THINK YOU ARE, WILE E. COYOTE? THIS'D NEVER WORK.
I SWEAR I'VE NO IDEA WHAT'S GOING ON. IT WAS A FULL-SIZE PARACHUTE WHEN I PACKED IT!
BEST LIVESTREAM EVER!

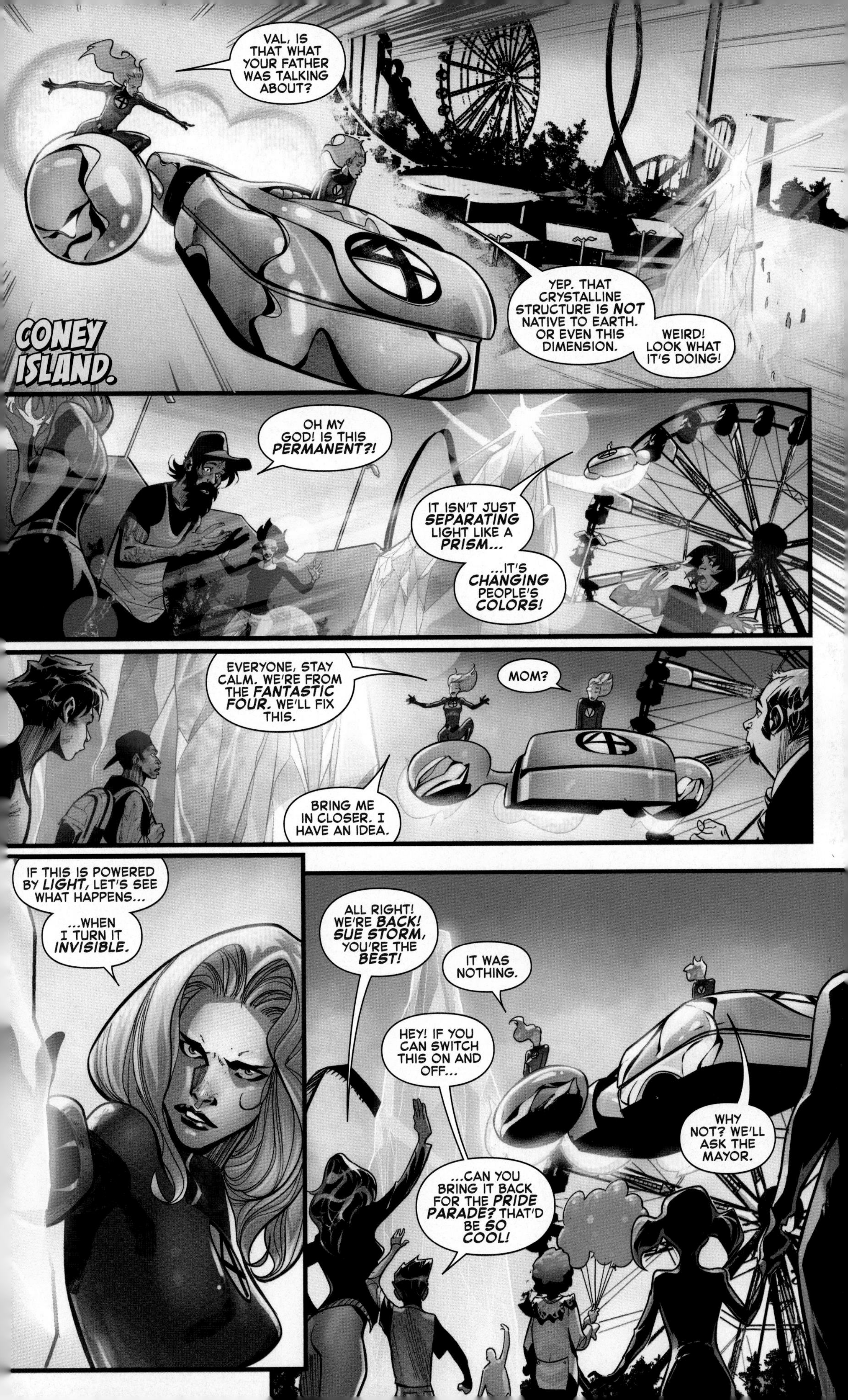
VAL, IS THAT WHAT YOUR FATHER WAS TALKING ABOUT?
YEP. THAT CRYSTALLINE STRUCTURE IS NOT NATIVE TO EARTH. OR EVEN THIS DIMENSION.
WEIRD! LOOK WHAT IT'S DOING!
CONEY ISLAND.
OH MY GOD! IS THIS PERMANENT?!
IT ISN'T JUST SEPARATING LIGHT LIKE A PRISM...
...IT'S CHANGING PEOPLE'S COLORS!
EVERYONE, STAY CALM. WE'RE FROM THE FANTASTIC FOUR. WE'LL FIX THIS.
MOM?
BRING ME IN CLOSER. I HAVE AN IDEA.
IF THIS IS POWERED BY LIGHT, LET'S SEE WHAT HAPPENS...
...WHEN I TURN IT INVISIBLE.
ALL RIGHT! WE'RE BACK! SUE STORM, YOU'RE THE BEST!
IT WAS NOTHING.
HEY! IF YOU CAN SWITCH THIS ON AND OFF...
...CAN YOU BRING IT BACK FOR THE PRIDE PARADE? THAT'D BE SO COOL!
WHY NOT? WE'LL ASK THE MAYOR.

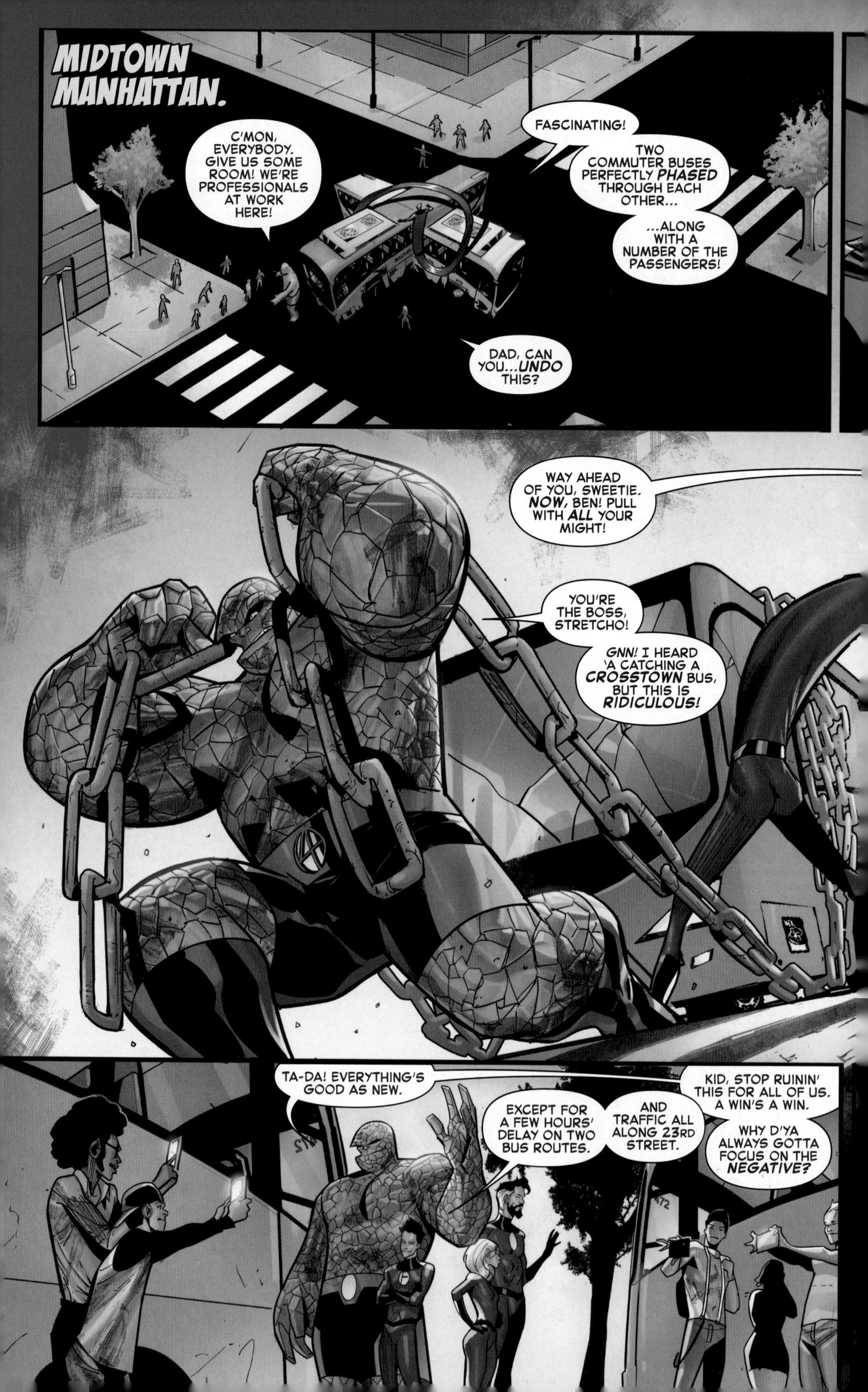
MIDTOWN MANHATTAN.
C'MON, EVERYBODY. GIVE US SOME ROOM! WE'RE PROFESSIONALS AT WORK HERE!
FASCINATING!
TWO COMMUTER BUSES PERFECTLY PHASED THROUGH EACH OTHER...
...ALONG WITH A NUMBER OF THE PASSENGERS!
DAD, CAN YOU...UNDO THIS?
WAY AHEAD OF YOU, SWEETIE. NOW, BEN! PULL WITH ALL YOUR MIGHT!
YOU'RE THE BOSS, STRETCHO!
GNN! I HEARD 'A CATCHING A CROSSTOWN BUS, BUT THIS IS RIDICULOUS!
TA-DA! EVERYTHING'S GOOD AS NEW.
EXCEPT FOR A FEW HOURS' DELAY ON TWO BUS ROUTES.
AND TRAFFIC ALL ALONG 23RD STREET.
KID, STOP RUININ' THIS FOR ALL OF US. A WIN'S A WIN.
WHY D'YA ALWAYS GOTTA FOCUS ON THE NEGATIVE?

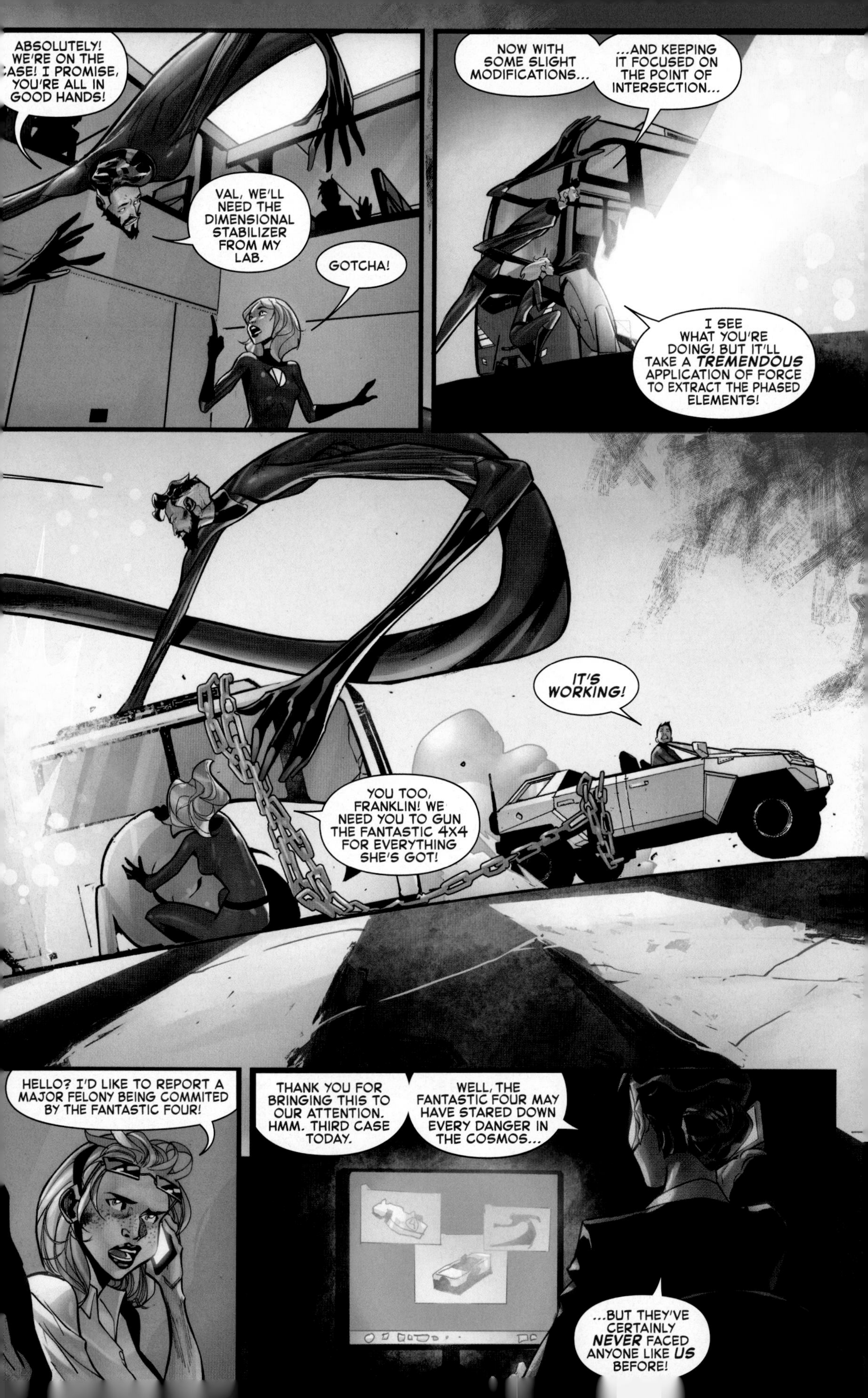
ABSOLUTELY! WE'RE ON THE CASE! I PROMISE, YOU'RE ALL IN GOOD HANDS!
VAL, WE'LL NEED THE DIMENSIONAL STABILIZER FROM MY LAB.
GOTCHA!
NOW WITH SOME SLIGHT MODIFICATIONS...
...AND KEEPING IT FOCUSED ON THE POINT OF INTERSECTION...
I SEE WHAT YOU'RE DOING! BUT IT'LL TAKE A TREMENDOUS APPLICATION OF FORCE TO EXTRACT THE PHASED ELEMENTS!
YOU TOO, FRANKLIN! WE NEED YOU TO GUN THE FANTASTIC 4X4 FOR EVERYTHING SHE'S GOT!
IT'S WORKING!
HELLO? I'D LIKE TO REPORT A MAJOR FELONY BEING COMMITED BY THE FANTASTIC FOUR!
THANK YOU FOR BRINGING THIS TO OUR ATTENTION. HMM. THIRD CASE TODAY.
WELL, THE FANTASTIC FOUR MAY HAVE STARED DOWN EVERY DANGER IN THE COSMOS...
...BUT THEY'VE CERTAINLY NEVER FACED ANYONE LIKE US BEFORE!

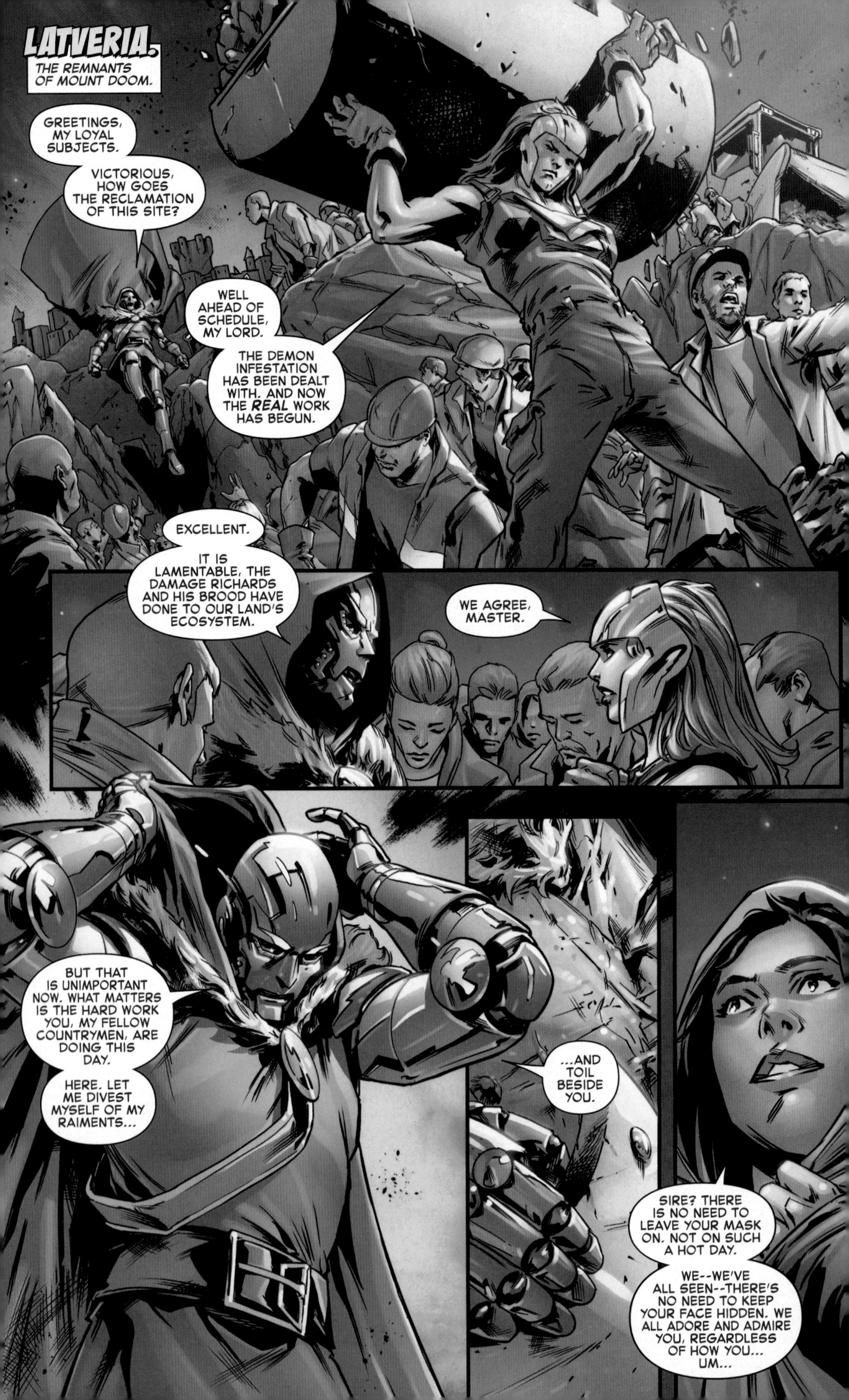
LATVERIA.
THE REMNANTS OF MOUNT DOOM.
GREETINGS, MY LOYAL SUBJECTS.
VICTORIOUS, HOW GOES THE RECLAMATION OF THIS SITE?
WELL AHEAD OF SCHEDULE, MY LORD.
THE DEMON INFESTATION HAS BEEN DEALT WITH. AND NOW THE REAL WORK HAS BEGUN.
EXCELLENT.
IT IS LAMENTABLE, THE DAMAGE RICHARDS AND HIS BROOD HAVE DONE TO OUR LAND'S ECOSYSTEM.
WE AGREE, MASTER.
BUT THAT IS UNIMPORTANT NOW. WHAT MATTERS IS THE HARD WORK YOU, MY FELLOW COUNTRYMEN, ARE DOING THIS DAY.
HERE. LET ME DIVEST MYSELF OF MY RAIMENTS...
...AND TOIL BESIDE YOU.
SIRE? THERE IS NO NEED TO LEAVE YOUR MASK ON. NOT ON SUCH A HOT DAY.
WE--WE'VE ALL SEEN--THERE'S NO NEED TO KEEP YOUR FACE HIDDEN. WE ALL ADORE AND ADMIRE YOU, REGARDLESS OF HOW YOU... UM...

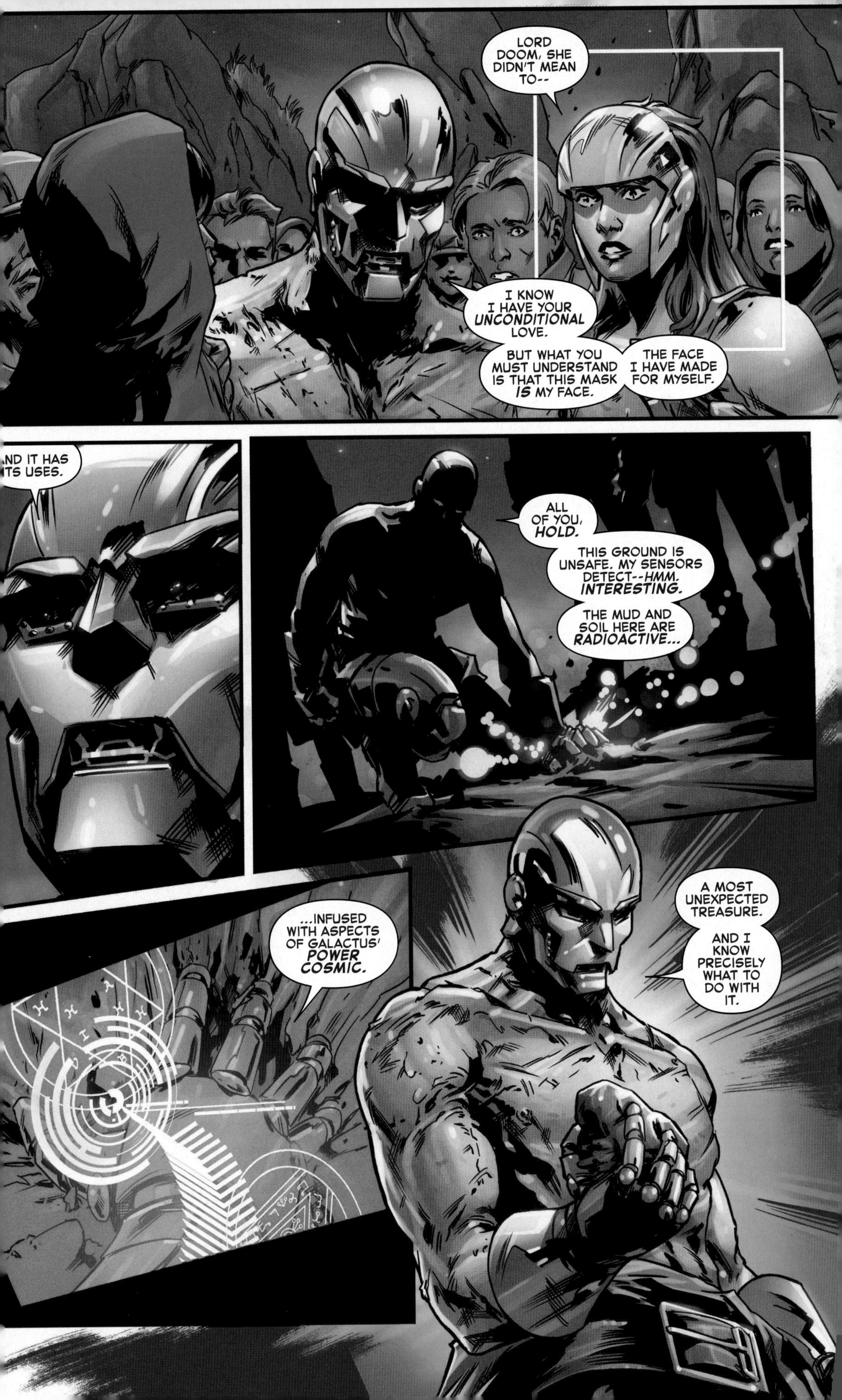
LORD DOOM, SHE DIDN'T MEAN TO--
I KNOW I HAVE YOUR UNCONDITIONAL LOVE.
BUT WHAT YOU MUST UNDERSTAND IS THAT THIS MASK IS MY FACE.
THE FACE I HAVE MADE FOR MYSELF.
ND IT HAS TS USES.
ALL OF YOU, HOLD.
THIS GROUND IS UNSAFE. MY SENSORS DETECT--HMM. INTERESTING.
THE MUD AND SOIL HERE ARE RADIOACTIVE...
...INFUSED WITH ASPECTS OF GALACTUS' POWER COSMIC.
A MOST UNEXPECTED TREASURE.
AND I KNOW PRECISELY WHAT TO DO WITH IT.

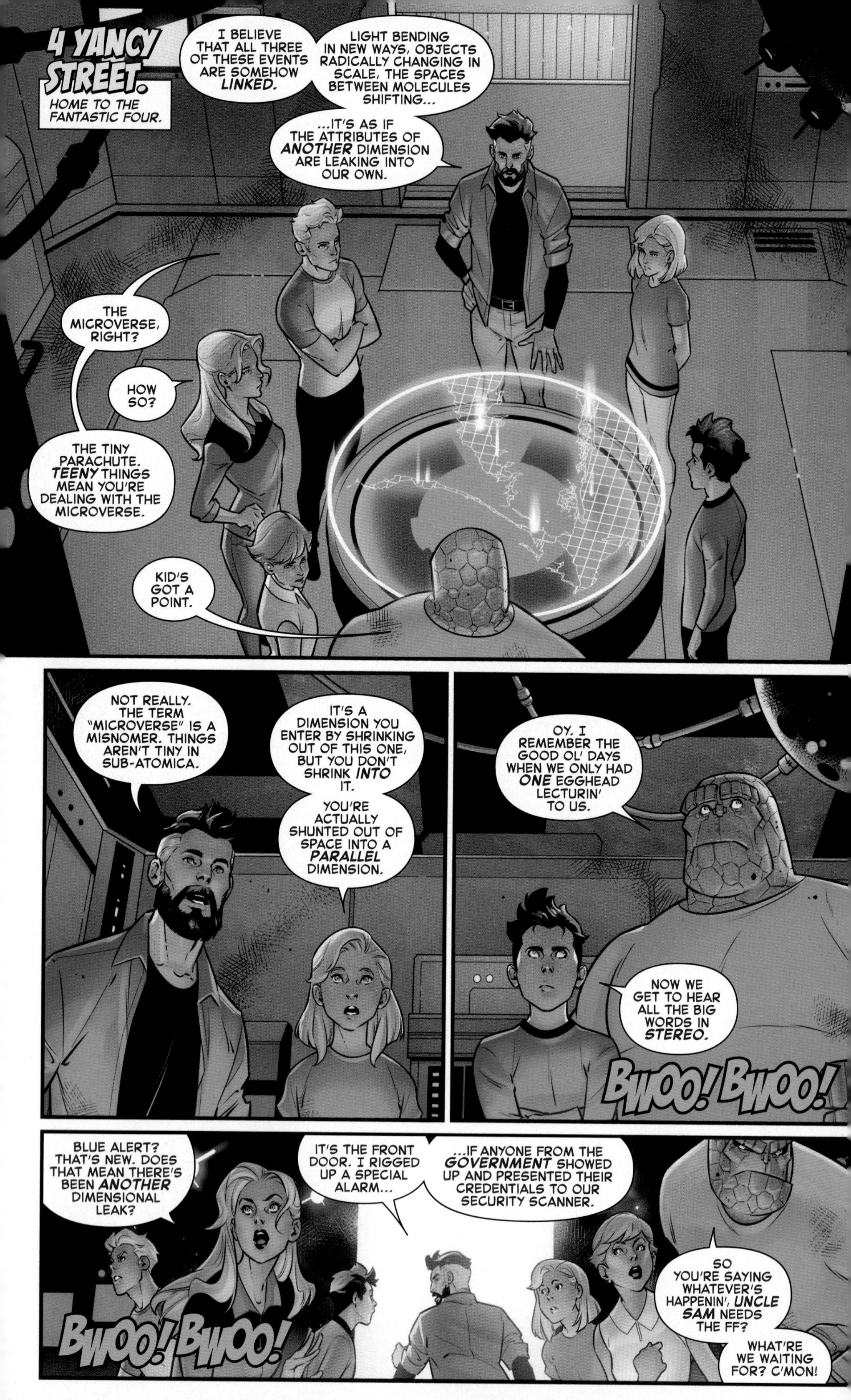

4 YANCY STREET.
HOME TO THE FANTASTIC FOUR.
I BELIEVE THAT ALL THREE OF THESE EVENTS ARE SOMEHOW LINKED.
LIGHT BENDING IN NEW WAYS, OBJECTS RADICALLY CHANGING IN SCALE, THE SPACES BETWEEN MOLECULES SHIFTING...
...IT'S AS IF THE ATTRIBUTES OF ANOTHER DIMENSION ARE LEAKING INTO OUR OWN.
THE MICROVERSE, RIGHT?
HOW SO?
THE TINY PARACHUTE. TEENY THINGS MEAN YOU'RE DEALING WITH THE MICROVERSE.
KID'S GOT A POINT.
NOT REALLY. THE TERM "MICROVERSE" IS A MISNOMER. THINGS AREN'T TINY IN SUB-ATOMICA.
IT'S A DIMENSION YOU ENTER BY SHRINKING OUT OF THIS ONE, BUT YOU DON'T SHRINK INTO IT.
YOU'RE ACTUALLY SHUNTED OUT OF SPACE INTO A PARALLEL DIMENSION.
OY. I REMEMBER THE GOOD OL' DAYS WHEN WE ONLY HAD ONE EGGHEAD LECTURIN' TO US.
NOW WE GET TO HEAR ALL THE BIG WORDS IN STEREO.
BWOO! BWOO!
BLUE ALERT? THAT'S NEW. DOES THAT MEAN THERE'S BEEN ANOTHER DIMENSIONAL LEAK?
IT'S THE FRONT DOOR. I RIGGED UP A SPECIAL ALARM...
...IF ANYONE FROM THE GOVERNMENT SHOWED UP AND PRESENTED THEIR CREDENTIALS TO OUR SECURITY SCANNER.
BWOO! BWOO!
SO YOU'RE SAYING WHATEVER'S HAPPENIN', UNCLE SAM NEEDS THE FF?
WHAT'RE WE WAITING FOR? C'MON!

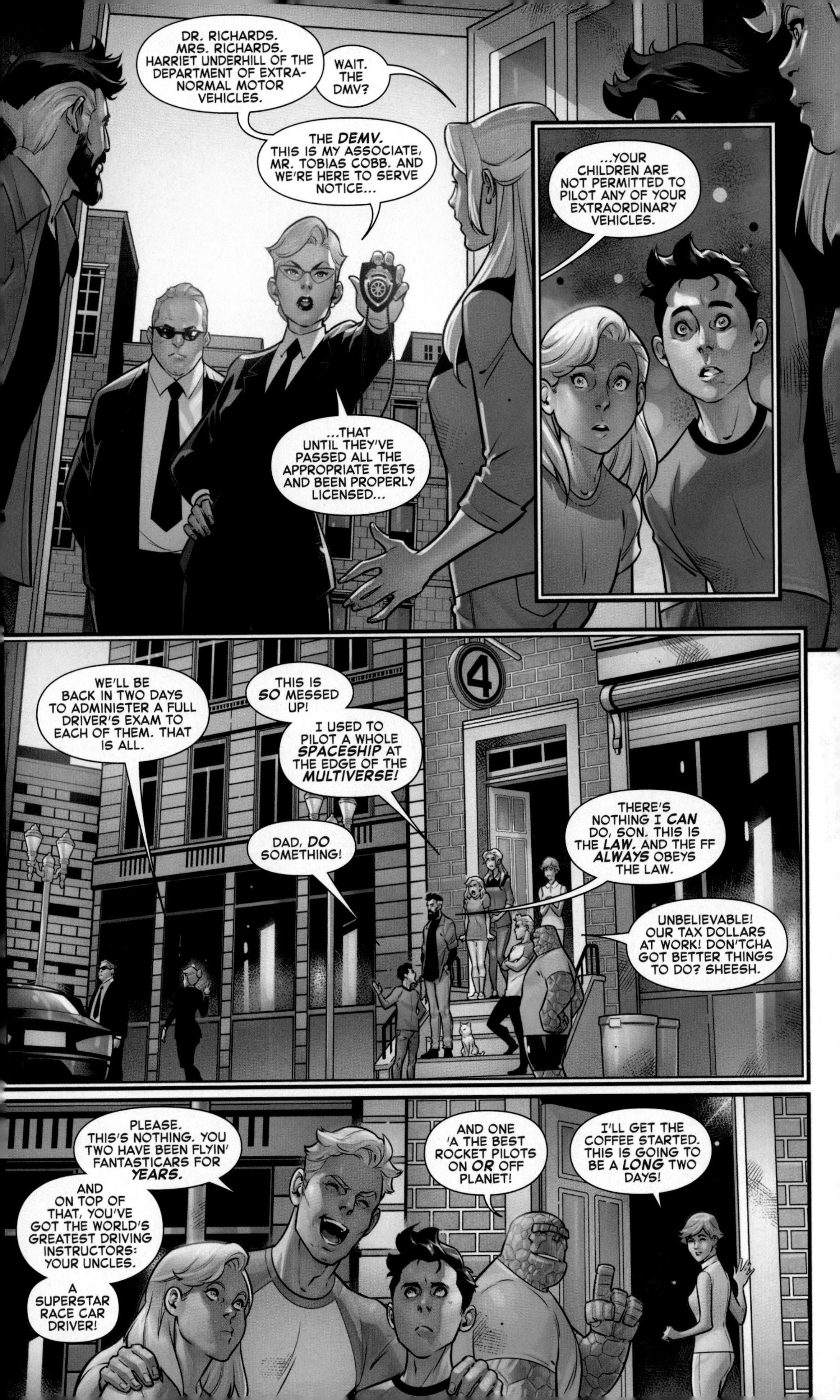

DR. RICHARDS. MRS. RICHARDS. HARRIET UNDERHILL OF THE DEPARTMENT OF EXTRA-NORMAL MOTOR VEHICLES.
WAIT. THE DMV?
THE DEMV. THIS IS MY ASSOCIATE, MR. TOBIAS COBB. AND WE'RE HERE TO SERVE NOTICE...
...THAT UNTIL THEY'VE PASSED ALL THE APPROPRIATE TESTS AND BEEN PROPERLY LICENSED...
...YOUR CHILDREN ARE NOT PERMITTED TO PILOT ANY OF YOUR EXTRAORDINARY VEHICLES.
WE'LL BE BACK IN TWO DAYS TO ADMINISTER A FULL DRIVER'S EXAM TO EACH OF THEM. THAT IS ALL.
THIS IS SO MESSED UP!
I USED TO PILOT A WHOLE SPACESHIP AT THE EDGE OF THE MULTIVERSE!
DAD, DO SOMETHING!
THERE'S NOTHING I CAN DO, SON. THIS IS THE LAW. AND THE FF ALWAYS OBEYS THE LAW.
UNBELIEVABLE! OUR TAX DOLLARS AT WORK! DON'TCHA GOT BETTER THINGS TO DO? SHEESH.
PLEASE. THIS'S NOTHING. YOU TWO HAVE BEEN FLYIN' FANTASTICARS FOR YEARS.
AND ON TOP OF THAT, YOU'VE GOT THE WORLD'S GREATEST DRIVING INSTRUCTORS: YOUR UNCLES.
A SUPERSTAR RACE CAR DRIVER!
AND ONE 'A THE BEST ROCKET PILOTS ON OR OFF PLANET!
I'LL GET THE COFFEE STARTED. THIS IS GOING TO BE A LONG TWO DAYS!

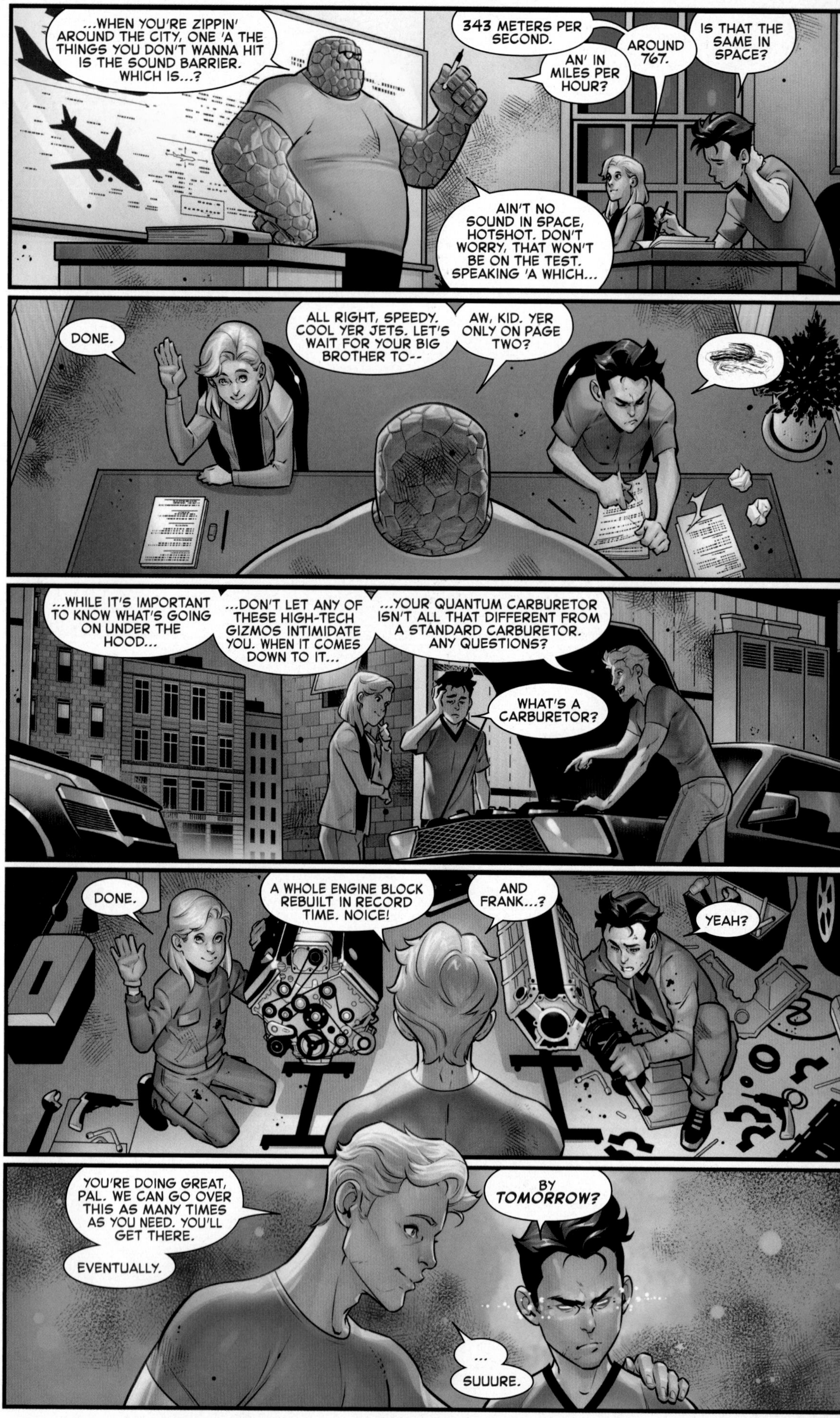
...WHEN YOU'RE ZIPPIN' AROUND THE CITY, ONE 'A THE THINGS YOU DON'T WANNA HIT IS THE SOUND BARRIER. WHICH IS...?
343 METERS PER SECOND.
AN' IN MILES PER HOUR?
AROUND 767.
IS THAT THE SAME IN SPACE?
AIN'T NO SOUND IN SPACE, HOTSHOT. DON'T WORRY, THAT WON'T BE ON THE TEST. SPEAKING 'A WHICH...
DONE.
ALL RIGHT, SPEEDY. COOL YER JETS. LET'S WAIT FOR YOUR BIG BROTHER TO--
AW, KID. YER ONLY ON PAGE TWO?
...WHILE IT'S IMPORTANT TO KNOW WHAT'S GOING ON UNDER THE HOOD...
...DON'T LET ANY OF THESE HIGH-TECH GIZMOS INTIMIDATE YOU. WHEN IT COMES DOWN TO IT...
...YOUR QUANTUM CARBURETOR ISN'T ALL THAT DIFFERENT FROM A STANDARD CARBURETOR. ANY QUESTIONS?
WHAT'S A CARBURETOR?
DONE.
A WHOLE ENGINE BLOCK REBUILT IN RECORD TIME. NOICE!
AND FRANK...?
YEAH?
YOU'RE DOING GREAT, PAL. WE CAN GO OVER THIS AS MANY TIMES AS YOU NEED. YOU'LL GET THERE.
EVENTUALLY.
BY *TOMORROW?*
...
SUUURE.

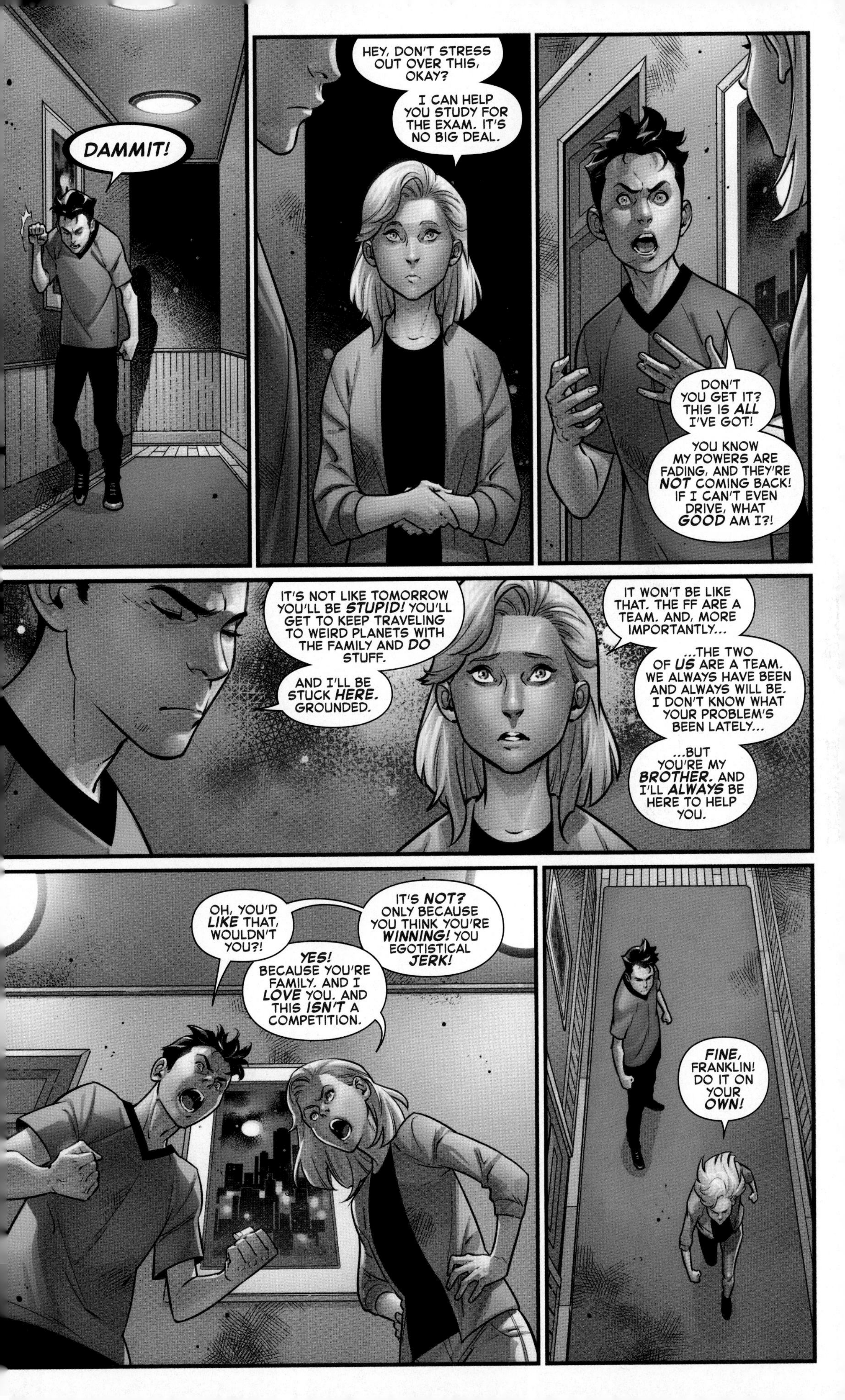
DAMMIT!
HEY, DON'T STRESS OUT OVER THIS, OKAY?
I CAN HELP YOU STUDY FOR THE EXAM. IT'S NO BIG DEAL.
DON'T YOU GET IT? THIS IS ALL I'VE GOT!
YOU KNOW MY POWERS ARE FADING, AND THEY'RE NOT COMING BACK! IF I CAN'T EVEN DRIVE, WHAT GOOD AM I?!
IT'S NOT LIKE TOMORROW YOU'LL BE STUPID! YOU'LL GET TO KEEP TRAVELING TO WEIRD PLANETS WITH THE FAMILY AND DO STUFF.
AND I'LL BE STUCK HERE. GROUNDED.
IT WON'T BE LIKE THAT. THE FF ARE A TEAM. AND, MORE IMPORTANTLY...
...THE TWO OF US ARE A TEAM. WE ALWAYS HAVE BEEN AND ALWAYS WILL BE. I DON'T KNOW WHAT YOUR PROBLEM'S BEEN LATELY...
...BUT YOU'RE MY BROTHER. AND I'LL ALWAYS BE HERE TO HELP YOU.
OH, YOU'D LIKE THAT, WOULDN'T YOU?!
YES! BECAUSE YOU'RE FAMILY. AND I LOVE YOU. AND THIS ISN'T A COMPETITION.
IT'S NOT? ONLY BECAUSE YOU THINK YOU'RE WINNING! YOU EGOTISTICAL JERK!
FINE, FRANKLIN! DO IT ON YOUR OWN!

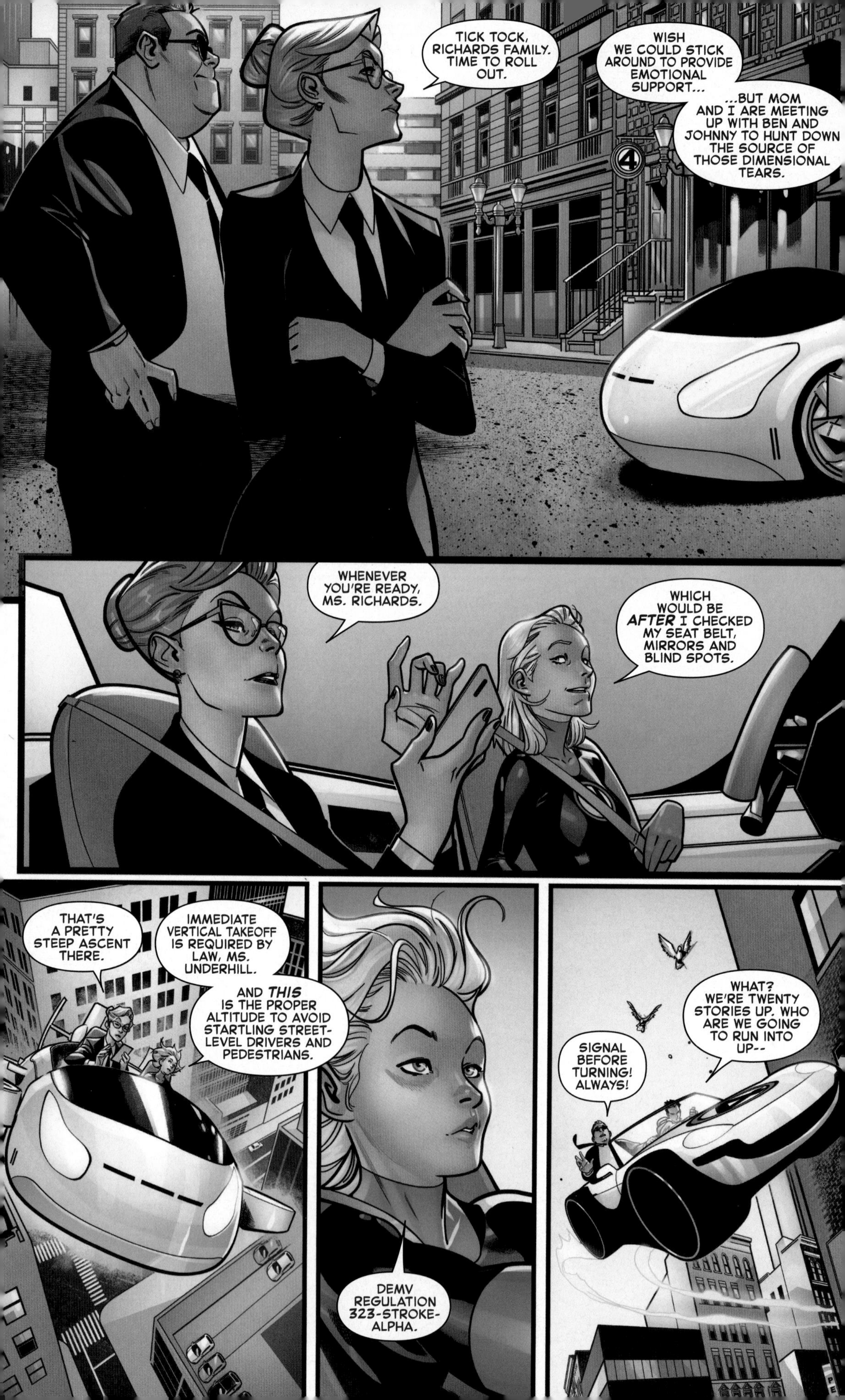

TICK TOCK, RICHARDS FAMILY. TIME TO ROLL OUT.
WISH WE COULD STICK AROUND TO PROVIDE EMOTIONAL SUPPORT...
...BUT MOM AND I ARE MEETING UP WITH BEN AND JOHNNY TO HUNT DOWN THE SOURCE OF THOSE DIMENSIONAL TEARS.
WHENEVER YOU'RE READY, MS. RICHARDS.
WHICH WOULD BE AFTER I CHECKED MY SEAT BELT, MIRRORS AND BLIND SPOTS.
THAT'S A PRETTY STEEP ASCENT THERE.
IMMEDIATE VERTICAL TAKEOFF IS REQUIRED BY LAW, MS. UNDERHILL.
AND THIS IS THE PROPER ALTITUDE TO AVOID STARTLING STREET-LEVEL DRIVERS AND PEDESTRIANS.
DEMV REGULATION 323-STROKE-ALPHA.
SIGNAL BEFORE TURNING! ALWAYS!
WHAT? WE'RE TWENTY STORIES UP. WHO ARE WE GOING TO RUN INTO UP--

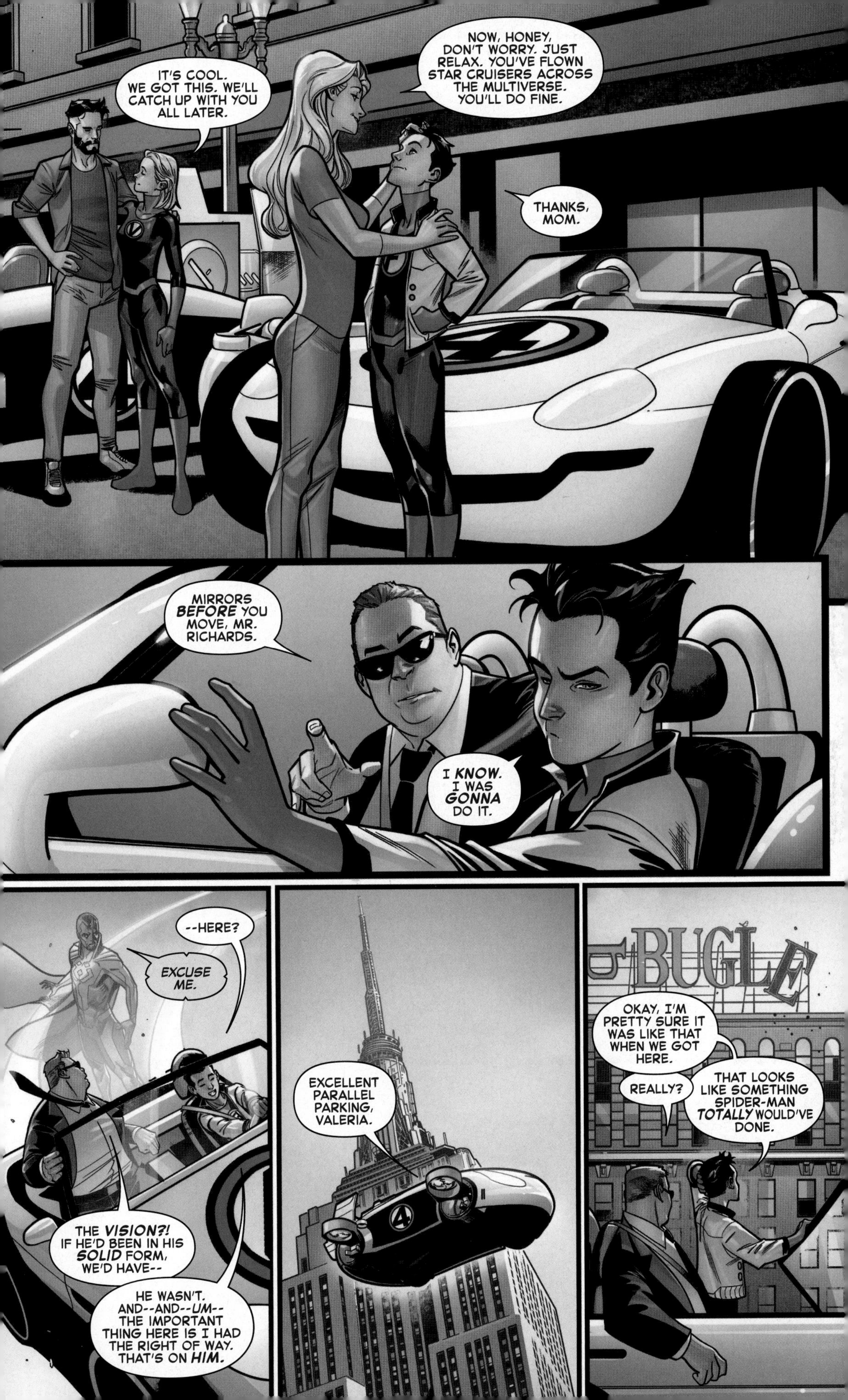
IT'S COOL. WE GOT THIS. WE'LL CATCH UP WITH YOU ALL LATER.
NOW, HONEY, DON'T WORRY. JUST RELAX. YOU'VE FLOWN STAR CRUISERS ACROSS THE MULTIVERSE. YOU'LL DO FINE.
THANKS, MOM.
MIRRORS BEFORE YOU MOVE, MR. RICHARDS.
I KNOW. I WAS GONNA DO IT.
EXCUSE ME.
--HERE?
THE VISION?! IF HE'D BEEN IN HIS SOLID FORM, WE'D HAVE--
HE WASN'T. AND--AND--UM-- THE IMPORTANT THING HERE IS I HAD THE RIGHT OF WAY. THAT'S ON HIM.
EXCELLENT PARALLEL PARKING, VALERIA.
BUGLE
OKAY, I'M PRETTY SURE IT WAS LIKE THAT WHEN WE GOT HERE.
REALLY?
THAT LOOKS LIKE SOMETHING SPIDER-MAN TOTALLY WOULD'VE DONE.

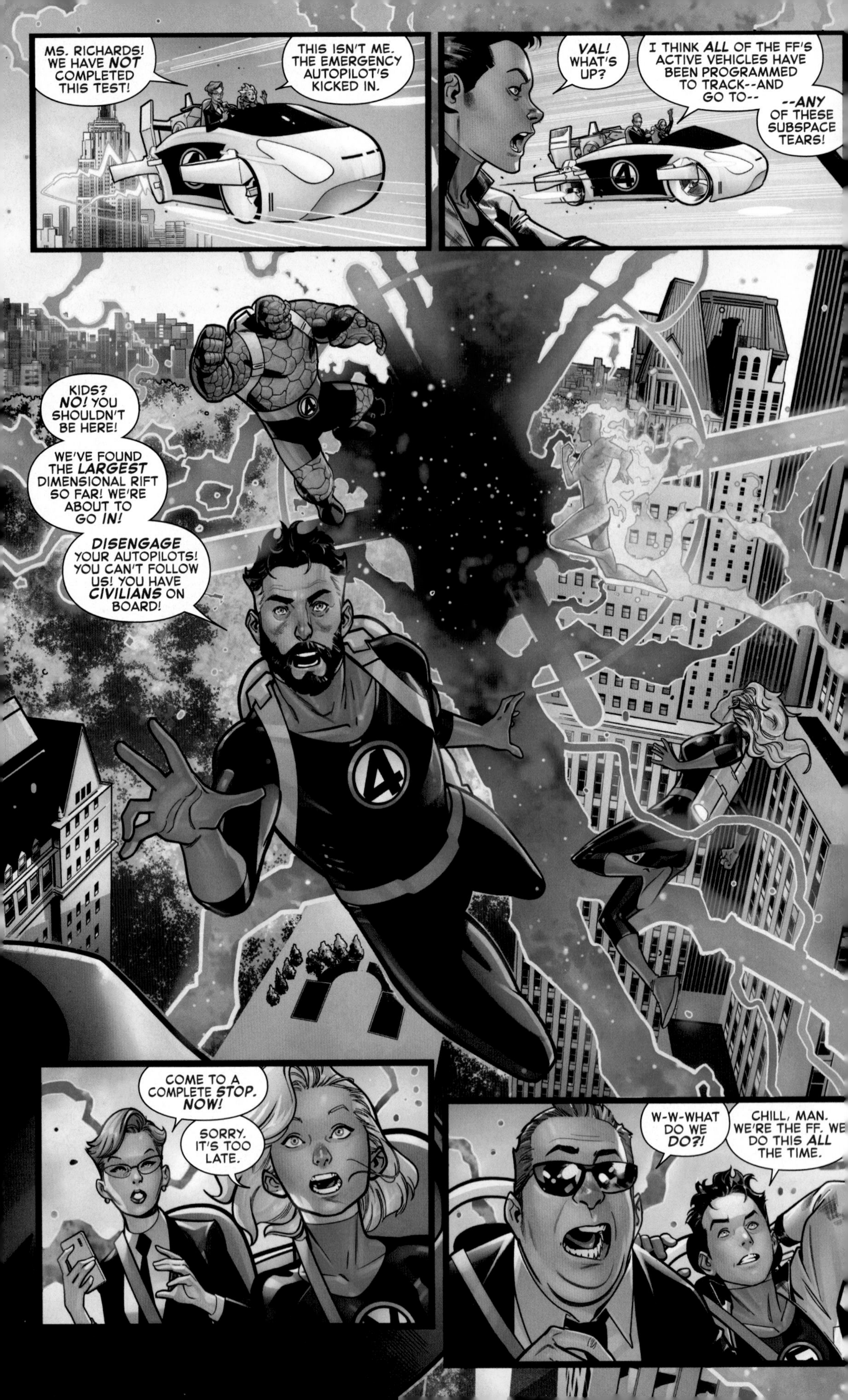
MS. RICHARDS! WE HAVE NOT COMPLETED THIS TEST!
THIS ISN'T ME. THE EMERGENCY AUTOPILOT'S KICKED IN.
VAL! WHAT'S UP?
I THINK ALL OF THE FF'S ACTIVE VEHICLES HAVE BEEN PROGRAMMED TO TRACK--AND GO TO--
--ANY OF THESE SUBSPACE TEARS!
KIDS? NO! YOU SHOULDN'T BE HERE!
WE'VE FOUND THE LARGEST DIMENSIONAL RIFT SO FAR! WE'RE ABOUT TO GO IN!
DISENGAGE YOUR AUTOPILOTS! YOU CAN'T FOLLOW US! YOU HAVE CIVILIANS ON BOARD!
COME TO A COMPLETE STOP. NOW!
SORRY. IT'S TOO LATE.
W-W-WHAT DO WE DO?!
CHILL, MAN. WE'RE THE FF. WE DO THIS ALL THE TIME.

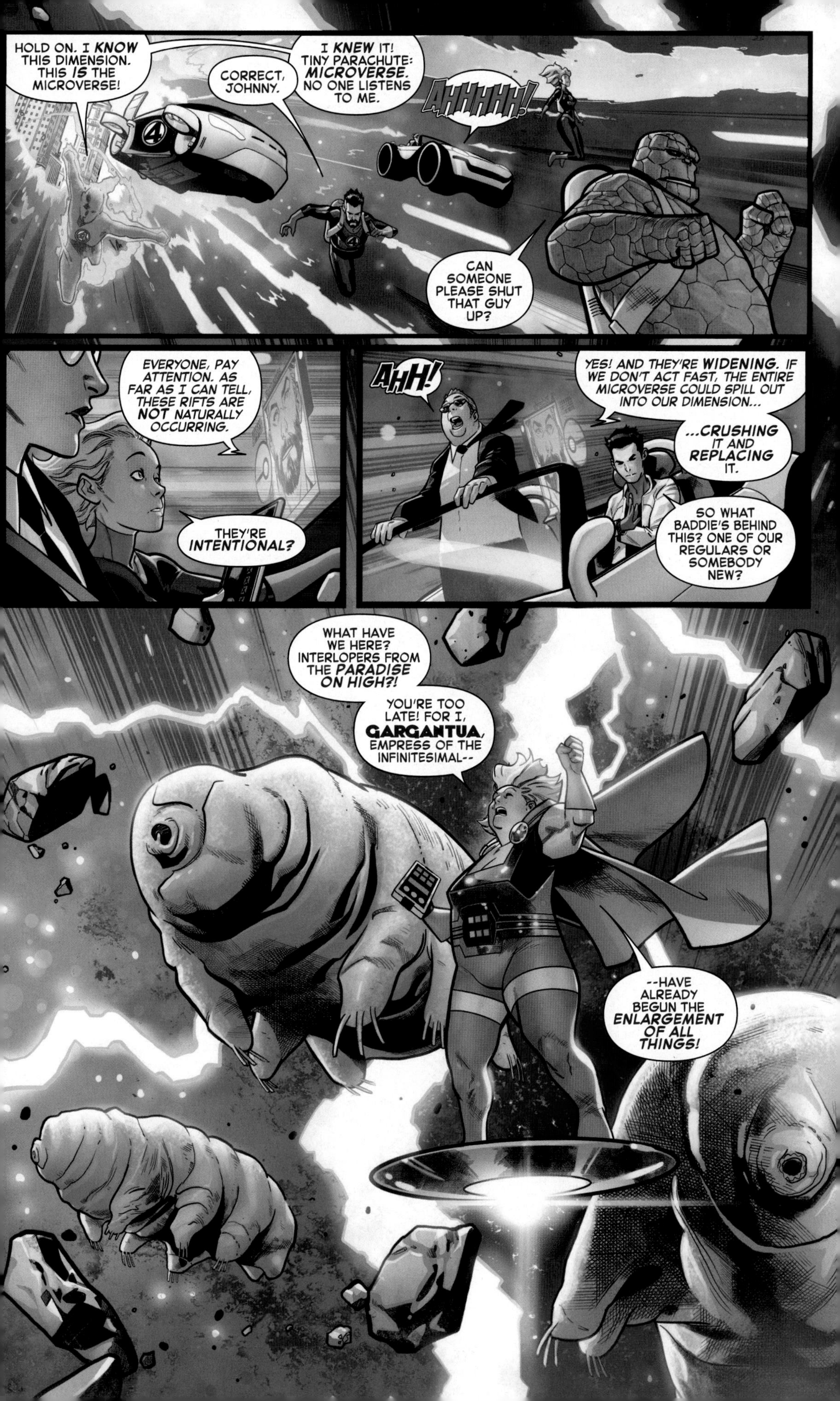

HOLD ON. I KNOW THIS DIMENSION. THIS IS THE MICROVERSE!
CORRECT, JOHNNY.
I KNEW IT! TINY PARACHUTE: MICROVERSE. NO ONE LISTENS TO ME.
AHHHHH!
CAN SOMEONE PLEASE SHUT THAT GUY UP?
EVERYONE, PAY ATTENTION. AS FAR AS I CAN TELL, THESE RIFTS ARE NOT NATURALLY OCCURRING.
THEY'RE INTENTIONAL?
AHH!
YES! AND THEY'RE WIDENING. IF WE DON'T ACT FAST, THE ENTIRE MICROVERSE COULD SPILL OUT INTO OUR DIMENSION...
...CRUSHING IT AND REPLACING IT.
SO WHAT BADDIE'S BEHIND THIS? ONE OF OUR REGULARS OR SOMEBODY NEW?
WHAT HAVE WE HERE? INTERLOPERS FROM THE PARADISE ON HIGH?!
YOU'RE TOO LATE! FOR I, GARGANTUA, EMPRESS OF THE INFINITESIMAL--
--HAVE ALREADY BEGUN THE ENLARGEMENT OF ALL THINGS!

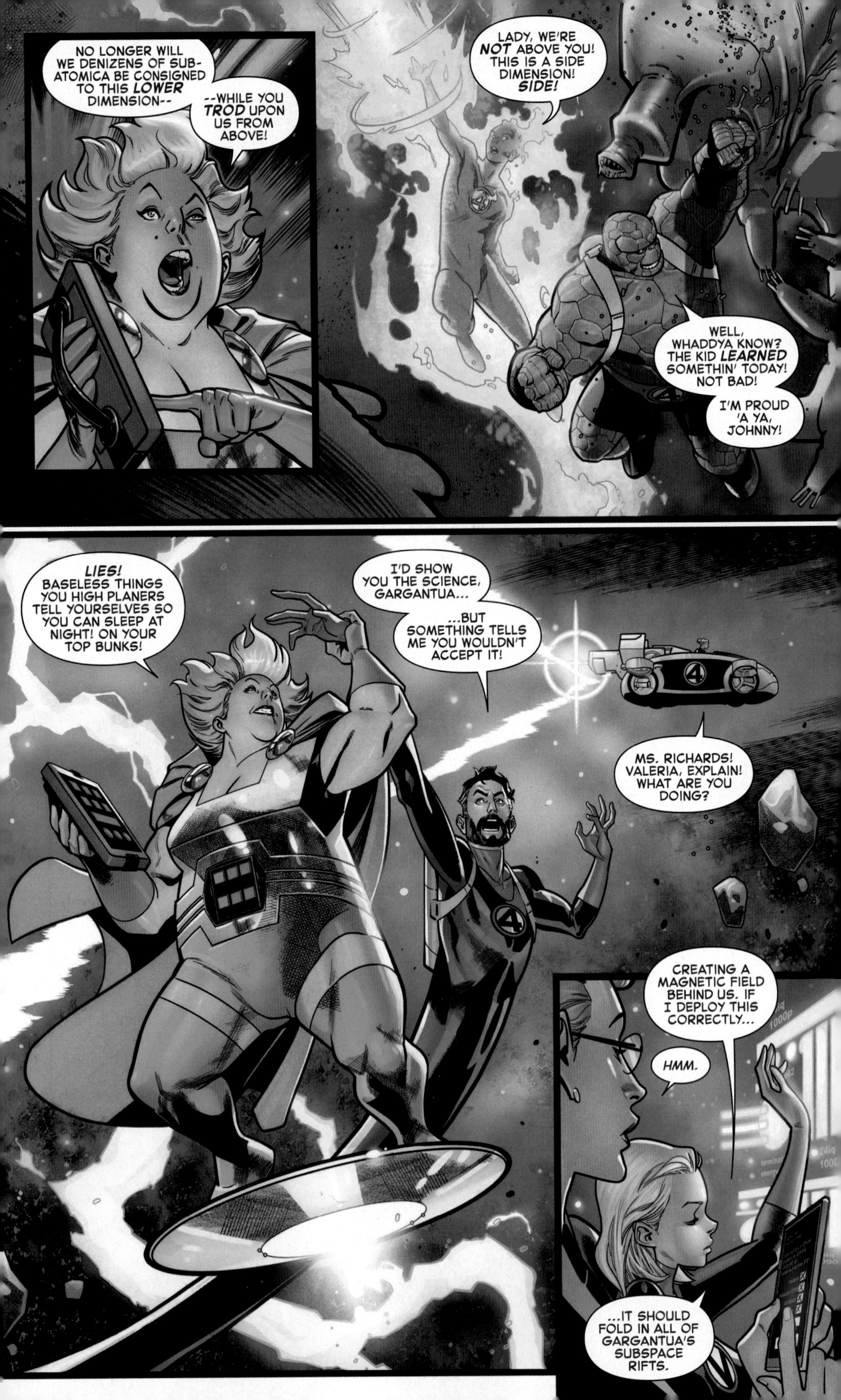
NO LONGER WILL WE DENIZENS OF SUB-ATOMICA BE CONSIGNED TO THIS LOWER DIMENSION--
--WHILE YOU TROD UPON US FROM ABOVE!
LADY, WE'RE NOT ABOVE YOU! THIS IS A SIDE DIMENSION! SIDE!
WELL, WHADDYA KNOW? THE KID LEARNED SOMETHIN' TODAY! NOT BAD!
I'M PROUD 'A YA, JOHNNY!
LIES! BASELESS THINGS YOU HIGH PLANERS TELL YOURSELVES SO YOU CAN SLEEP AT NIGHT! ON YOUR TOP BUNKS!
I'D SHOW YOU THE SCIENCE, GARGANTUA...
...BUT SOMETHING TELLS ME YOU WOULDN'T ACCEPT IT!
MS. RICHARDS! VALERIA, EXPLAIN! WHAT ARE YOU DOING?
CREATING A MAGNETIC FIELD BEHIND US. IF I DEPLOY THIS CORRECTLY...
HMM.
...IT SHOULD FOLD IN ALL OF GARGANTUA'S SUBSPACE RIFTS.

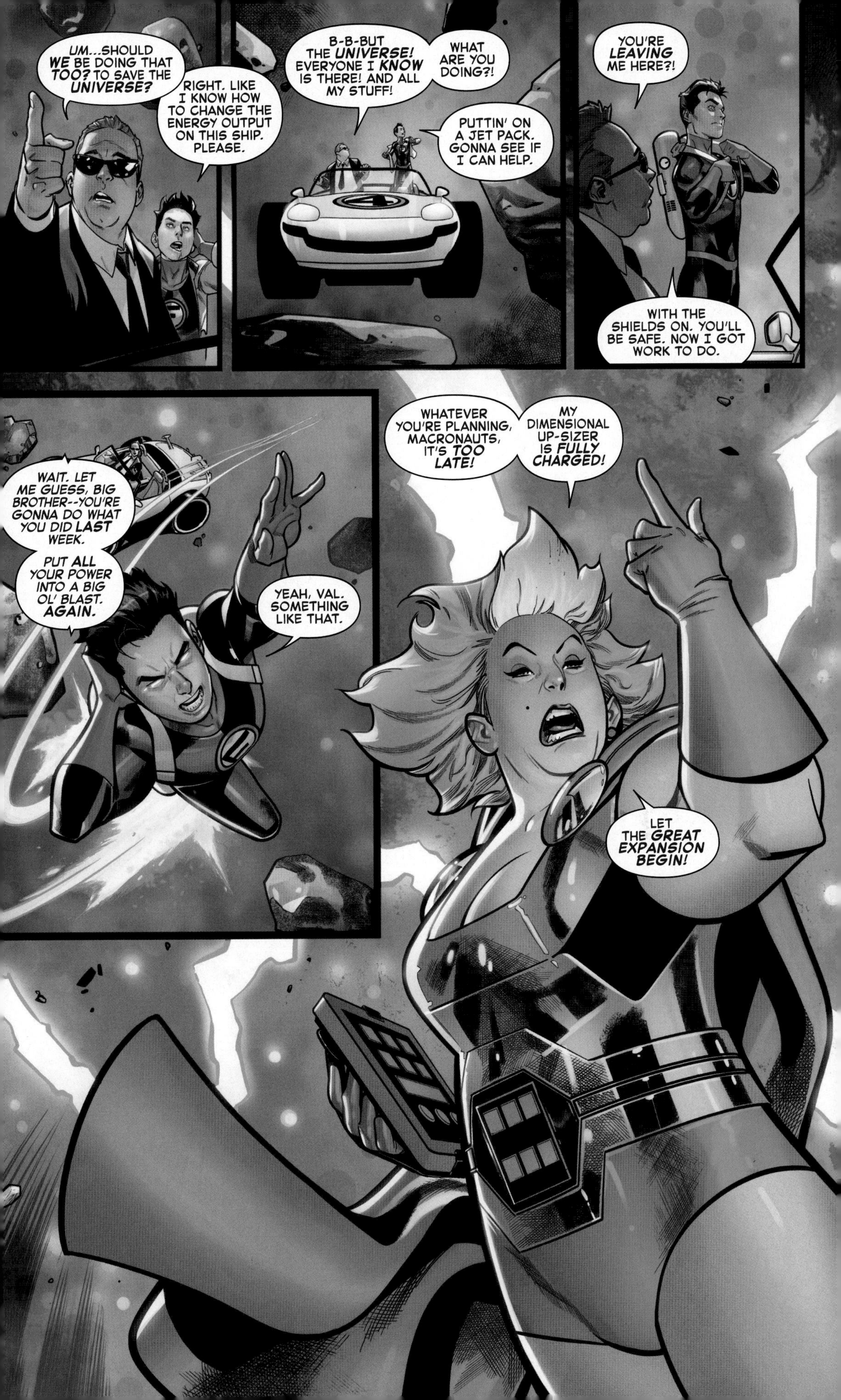
UM...SHOULD WE BE DOING THAT TOO? TO SAVE THE UNIVERSE?
RIGHT. LIKE I KNOW HOW TO CHANGE THE ENERGY OUTPUT ON THIS SHIP. PLEASE.
B-B-BUT THE UNIVERSE! EVERYONE I KNOW IS THERE! AND ALL MY STUFF!
WHAT ARE YOU DOING?!
PUTTIN' ON A JET PACK. GONNA SEE IF I CAN HELP.
YOU'RE LEAVING ME HERE?!
WITH THE SHIELDS ON. YOU'LL BE SAFE. NOW I GOT WORK TO DO.
WAIT. LET ME GUESS, BIG BROTHER--YOU'RE GONNA DO WHAT YOU DID LAST WEEK.
PUT ALL YOUR POWER INTO A BIG OL' BLAST. AGAIN.
YEAH, VAL. SOMETHING LIKE THAT.
WHATEVER YOU'RE PLANNING, MACRONAUTS, IT'S TOO LATE!
MY DIMENSIONAL UP-SIZER IS FULLY CHARGED!
LET THE GREAT EXPANSION BEGIN!

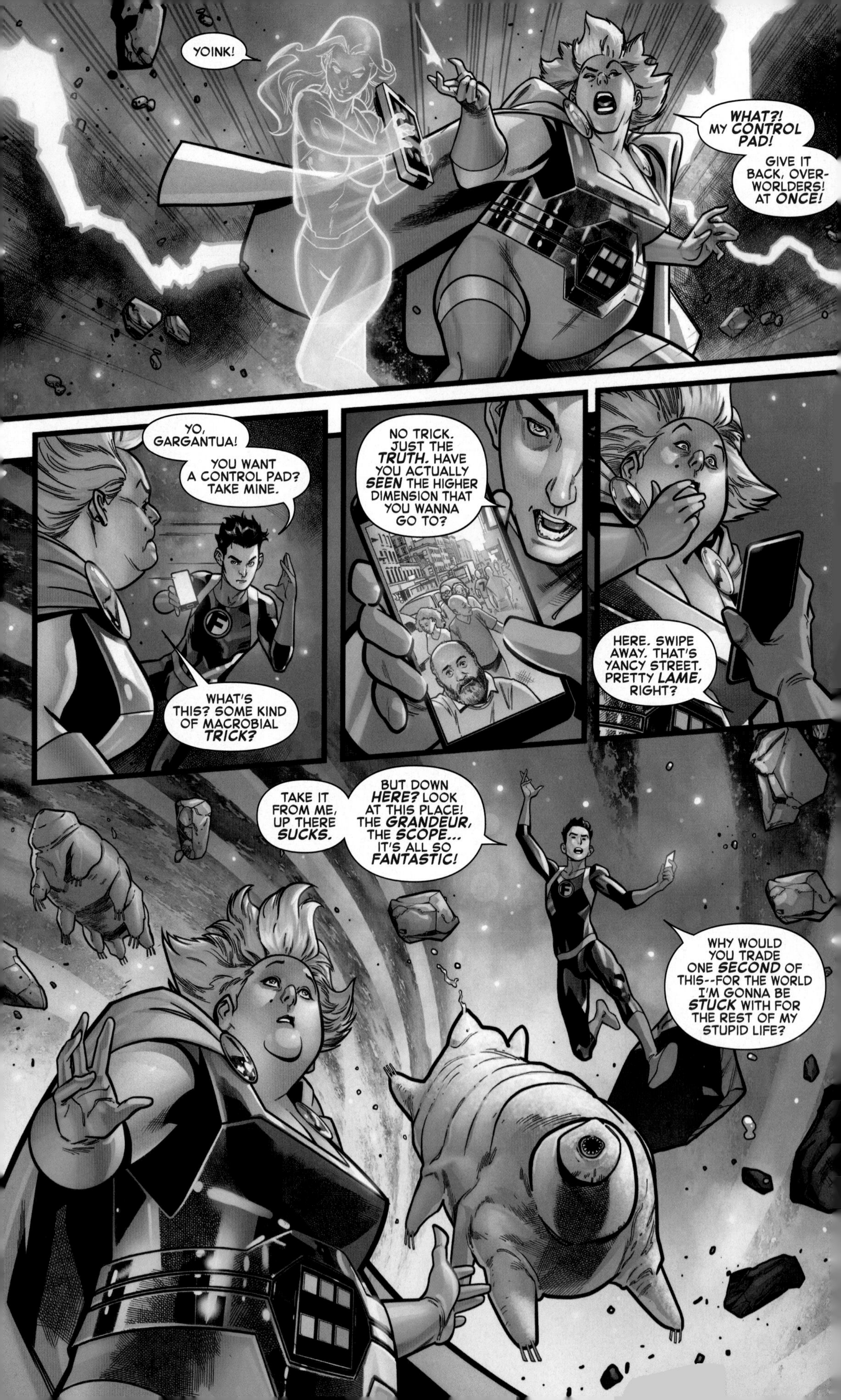
YOINK!
WHAT?! MY CONTROL PAD!
GIVE IT BACK, OVER-WORLDERS! AT ONCE!
YO, GARGANTUA!
YOU WANT A CONTROL PAD? TAKE MINE.
WHAT'S THIS? SOME KIND OF MACROBIAL TRICK?
NO TRICK. JUST THE TRUTH. HAVE YOU ACTUALLY SEEN THE HIGHER DIMENSION THAT YOU WANNA GO TO?
HERE. SWIPE AWAY. THAT'S YANCY STREET. PRETTY LAME, RIGHT?
TAKE IT FROM ME, UP THERE SUCKS.
BUT DOWN HERE? LOOK AT THIS PLACE! THE GRANDEUR, THE SCOPE... IT'S ALL SO FANTASTIC!
WHY WOULD YOU TRADE ONE SECOND OF THIS--FOR THE WORLD I'M GONNA BE STUCK WITH FOR THE REST OF MY STUPID LIFE?

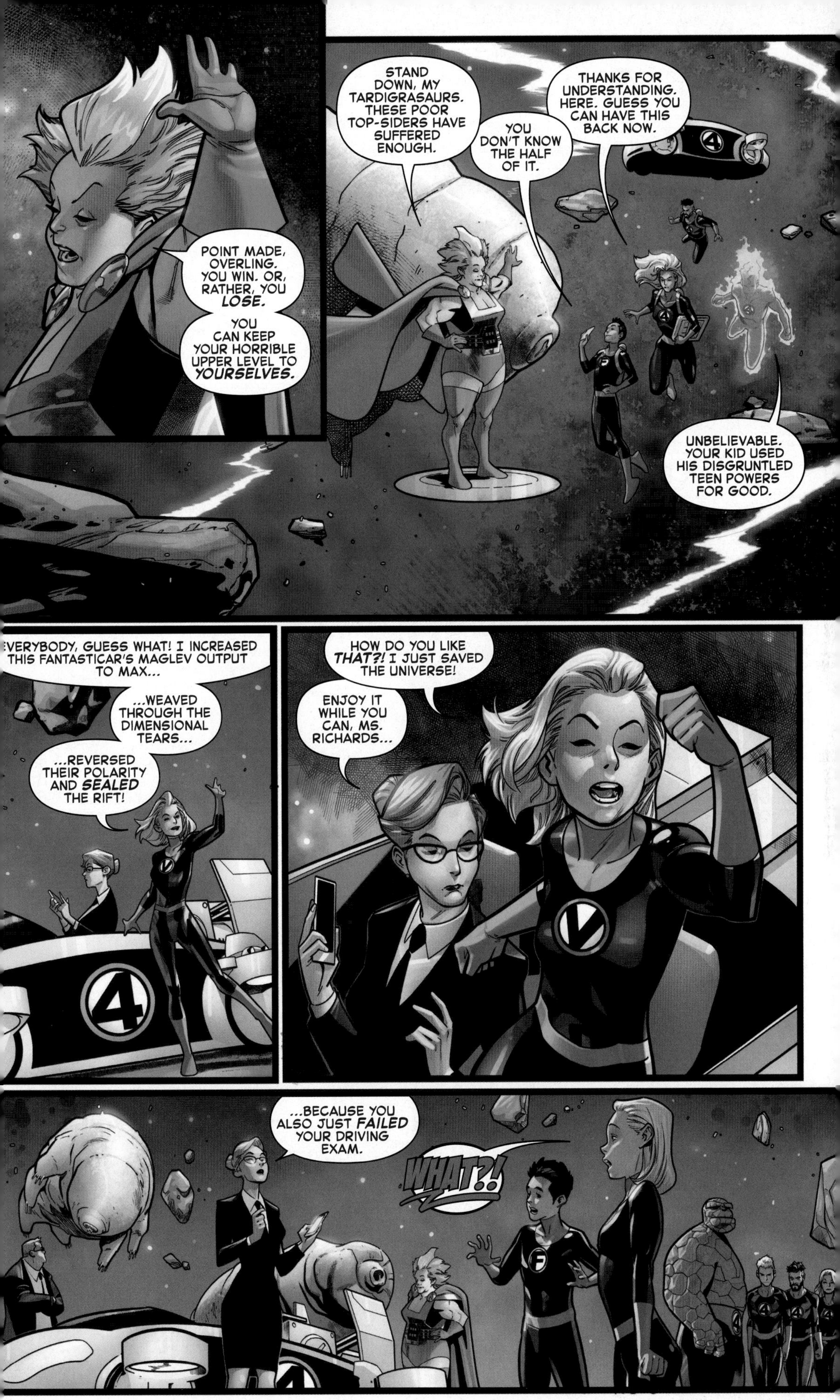
POINT MADE, OVERLING. YOU WIN. OR, RATHER, YOU LOSE.
YOU CAN KEEP YOUR HORRIBLE UPPER LEVEL TO YOURSELVES.
STAND DOWN, MY TARDIGRASAURS. THESE POOR TOP-SIDERS HAVE SUFFERED ENOUGH.
YOU DON'T KNOW THE HALF OF IT.
THANKS FOR UNDERSTANDING. HERE. GUESS YOU CAN HAVE THIS BACK NOW.
UNBELIEVABLE. YOUR KID USED HIS DISGRUNTLED TEEN POWERS FOR GOOD.
EVERYBODY, GUESS WHAT! I INCREASED THIS FANTASTICAR'S MAGLEV OUTPUT TO MAX...
...WEAVED THROUGH THE DIMENSIONAL TEARS...
...REVERSED THEIR POLARITY AND SEALED THE RIFT!
HOW DO YOU LIKE THAT?! I JUST SAVED THE UNIVERSE!
ENJOY IT WHILE YOU CAN, MS. RICHARDS...
...BECAUSE YOU ALSO JUST FAILED YOUR DRIVING EXAM.
WHAT?!

...TALKING ON A COMMUNICATOR, *OPERATING* COMPLEX APPS AND *PERFORMING* SCIENTIFIC EXPERIMENTS...

...*WHILE* PILOTING A VEHICLE?

WHY, THAT'S *WORSE* THAN DRIVING WHILE TEXTING!

MEANWHILE, AT THE FIRST SIGN OF TROUBLE, YOUR BROTHER PULLED HIS VEHICLE OVER...

...AND LOOKED TO THE SAFETY OF HIS PASSENGER. WELL DONE, FRANK. YOU *PASSED.*

AS FOR VAL, SHE CAN RETAKE THE TEST IN A *YEAR.*

A *YEAR?!*

DON'T TAKE IT SO HARD. YOUR DAD FAILED *FOUR* TIMES.

IT'S TRUE. ABSENTMINDED SCIENTISTS MAKE THE WORST DRIVERS.

HEY.

I GET IT. YOU *WON.* NO NEED TO RUB IT IN.

IT'S NOT THAT...

YOU'RE RIGHT. WE WORK BEST AS A *TEAM.* AND *THIS* IS SOMETHING I CAN DO. SO...

...WHERE DO YOU WANNA GO?

WELL, AT LEAST WE AVERTED *ONE* CRISIS TODAY.

YEAH. I'M GLAD IT ALL WORKED OUT.

WHAT? NO. WE SAVED THE WORLD, BUT FRANKLIN'S *FULLY* LICENSED NOW.

CAN YOU IMAGINE WHAT *I'D* HAVE GOTTEN UP TO IF I WAS STREET *AND* SKY LEGAL AT THAT AGE?

WE--WE DID *NOT* THINK THIS THROUGH AT ALL, DID WE?

NOPE.

DON'T WORRY, T BELIEVER. THA' THE LEAST OF FF'S PROBLEM:

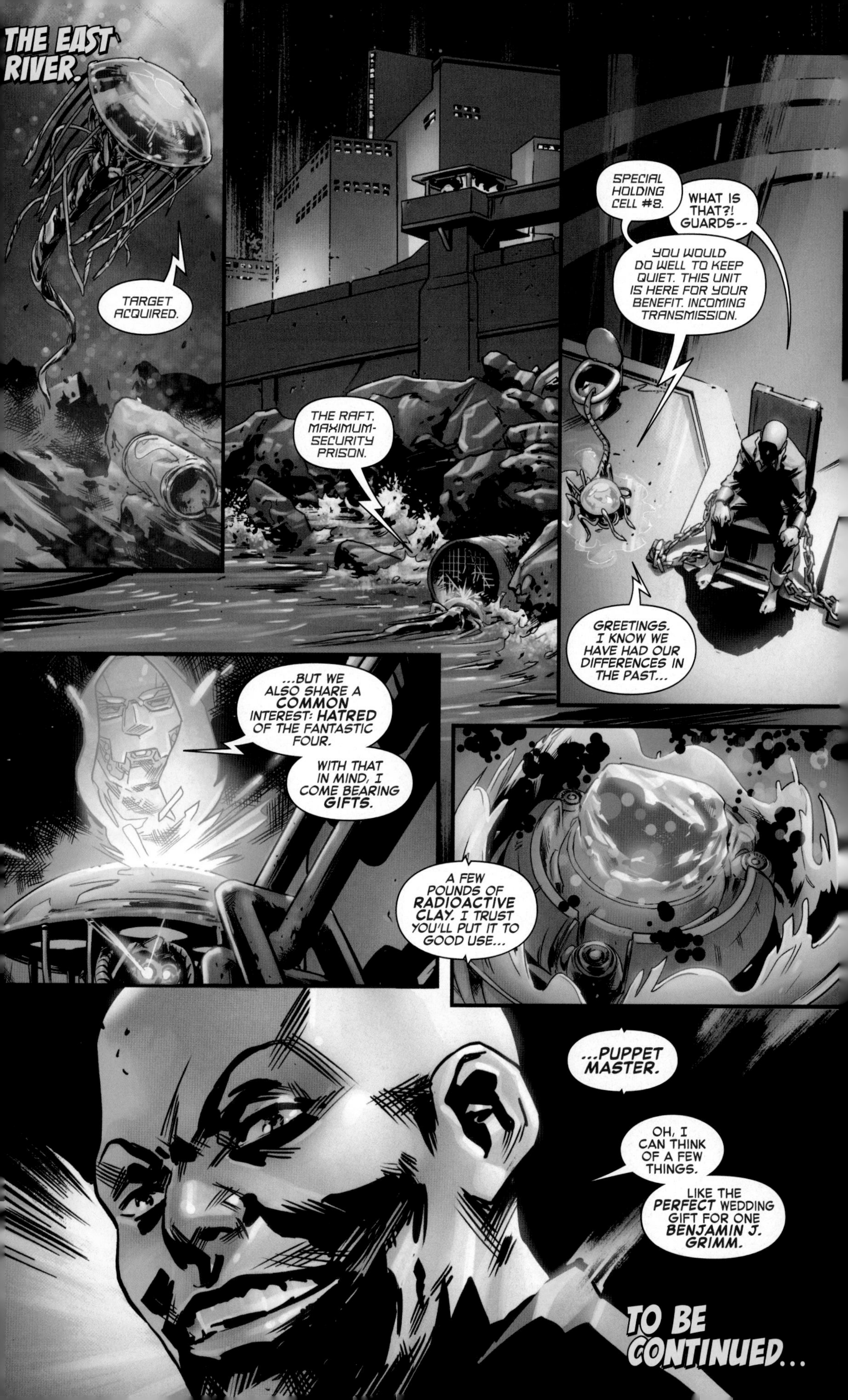
THE EAST RIVER.
TARGET ACQUIRED.
THE RAFT, MAXIMUM-SECURITY PRISON.
SPECIAL HOLDING CELL #8.
WHAT IS THAT?! GUARDS--
YOU WOULD DO WELL TO KEEP QUIET. THIS UNIT IS HERE FOR YOUR BENEFIT. INCOMING TRANSMISSION.
GREETINGS. I KNOW WE HAVE HAD OUR DIFFERENCES IN THE PAST...
...BUT WE ALSO SHARE A COMMON INTEREST: HATRED OF THE FANTASTIC FOUR.
WITH THAT IN MIND, I COME BEARING GIFTS.
A FEW POUNDS OF RADIOACTIVE CLAY. I TRUST YOU'LL PUT IT TO GOOD USE...
...PUPPET MASTER.
OH, I CAN THINK OF A FEW THINGS.
LIKE THE PERFECT WEDDING GIFT FOR ONE BENJAMIN J. GRIMM.
TO BE CONTINUED...

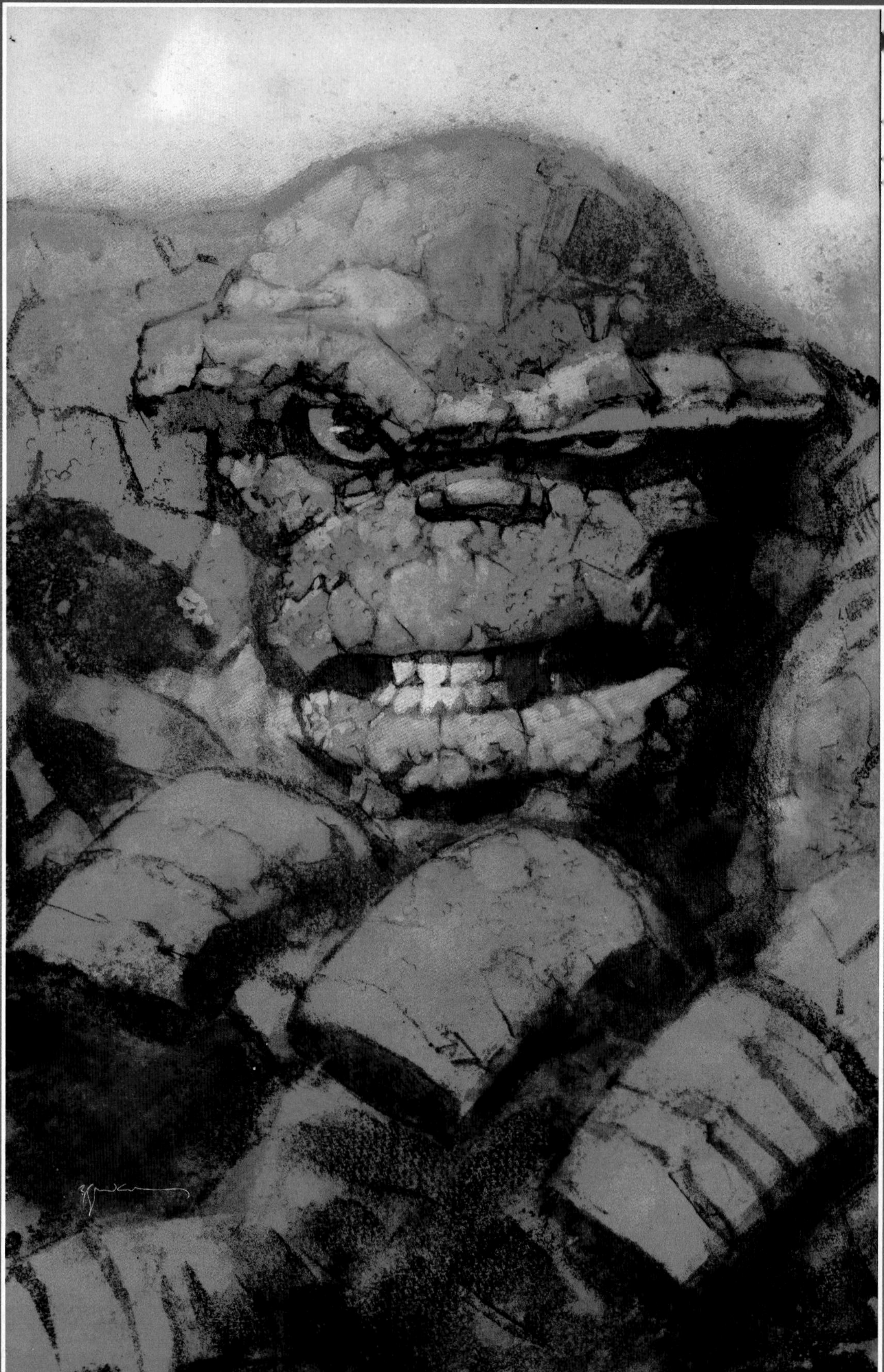

#6 variant by **Bill Sienkiewicz**

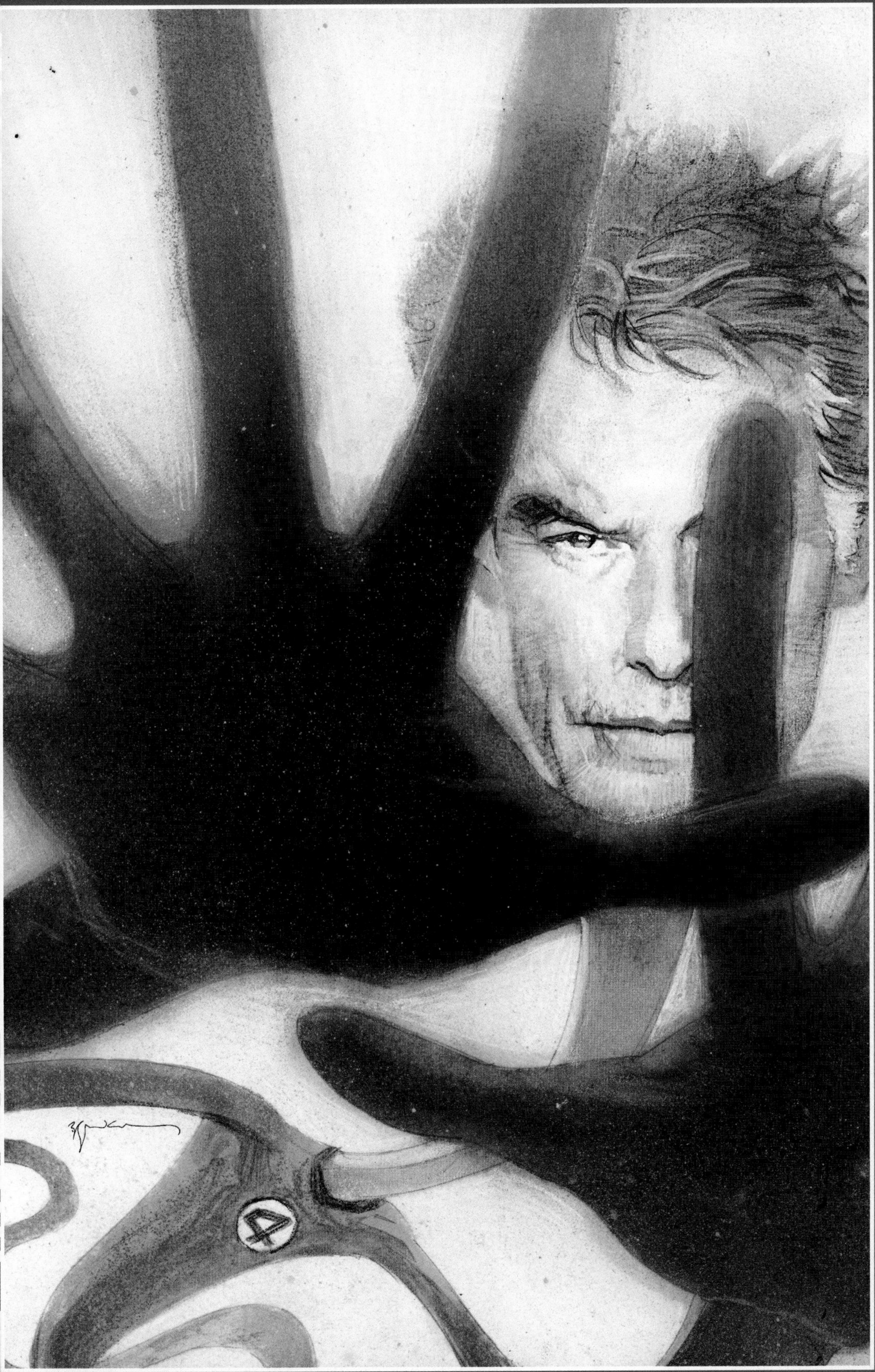

#7 variant by **Bill Sienkiewicz**

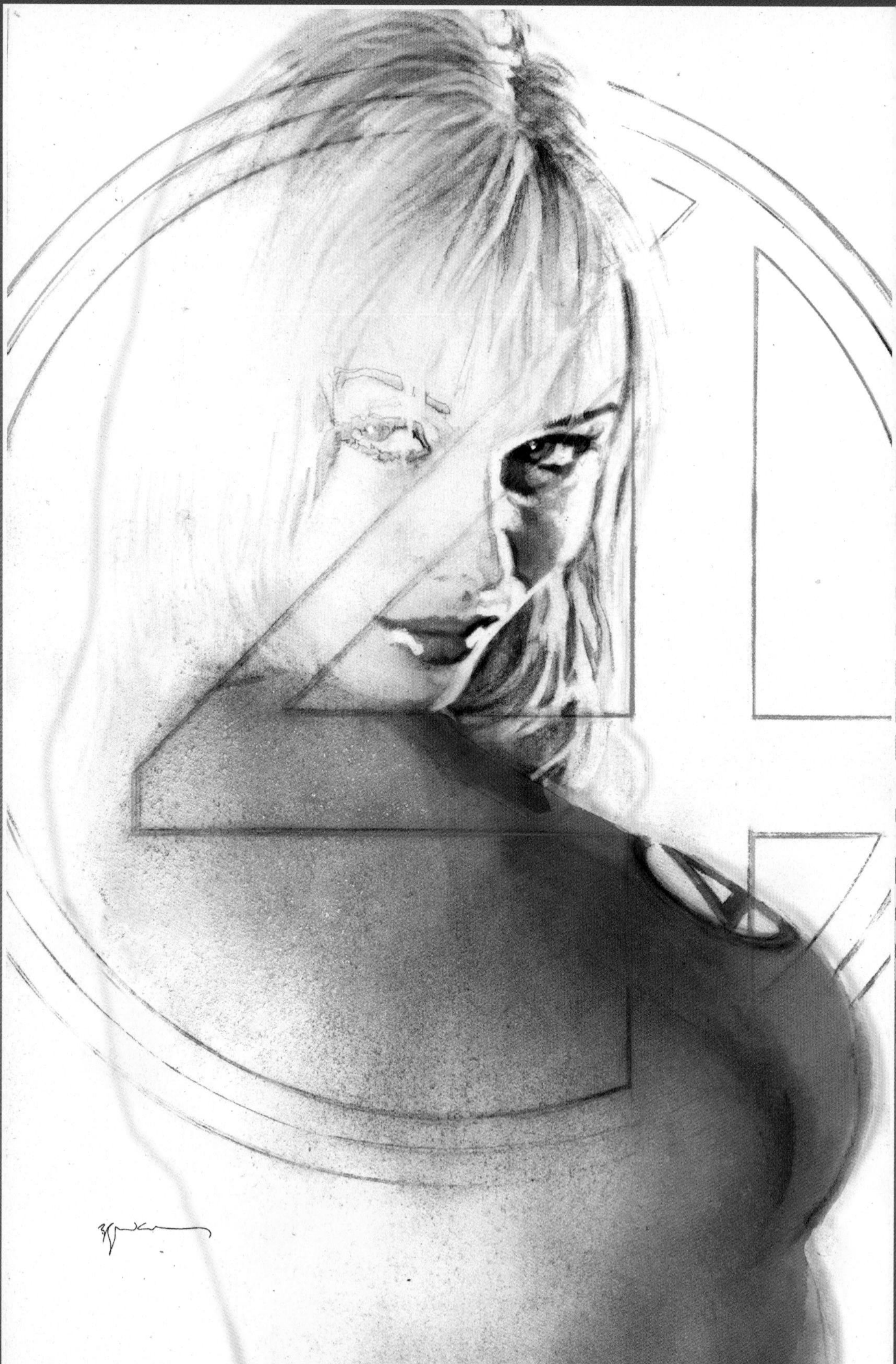

#8 variant by **Bill Sienkiewicz**

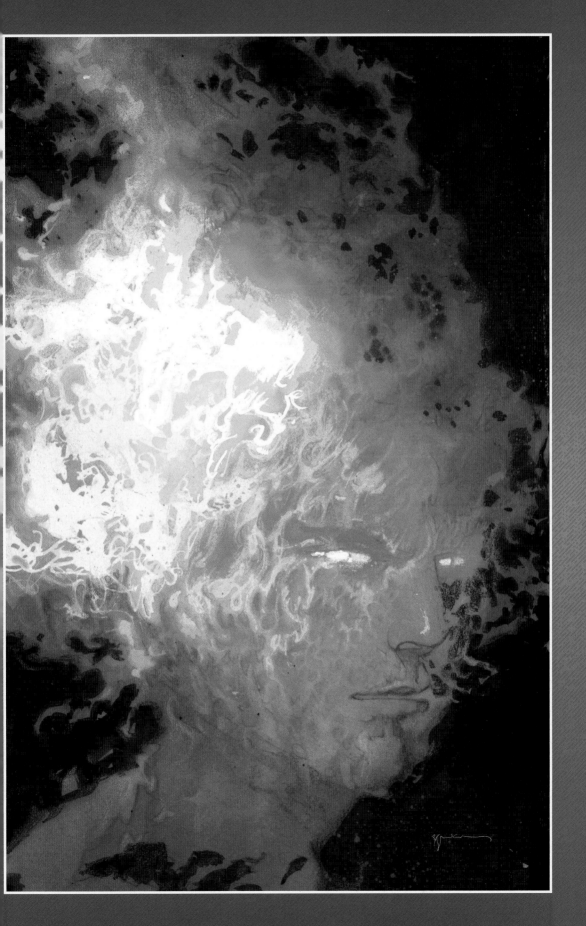

#9 variant by **Bill Sienkiewicz**

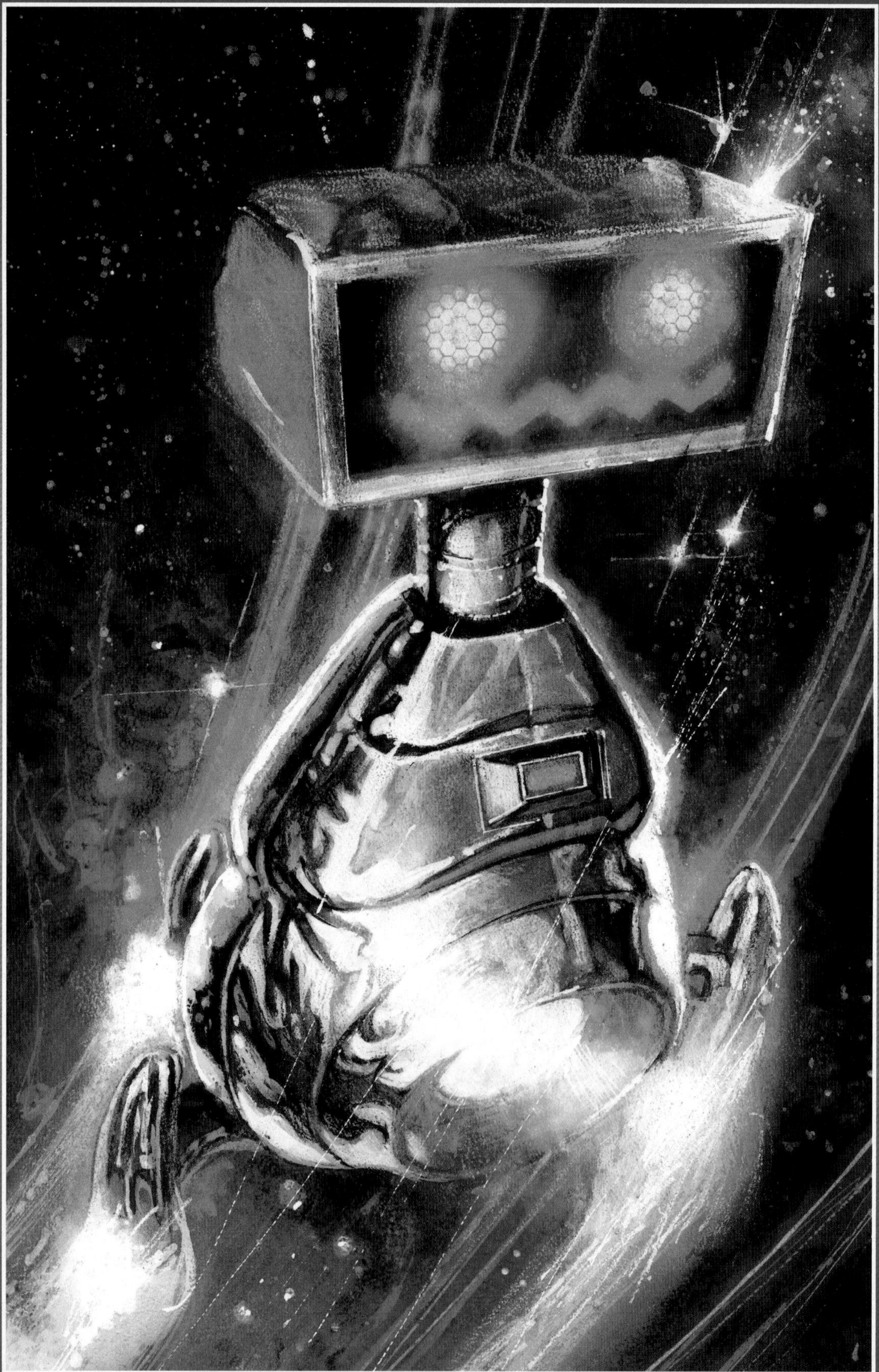

#10 variant by **Bill Sienkiewicz**

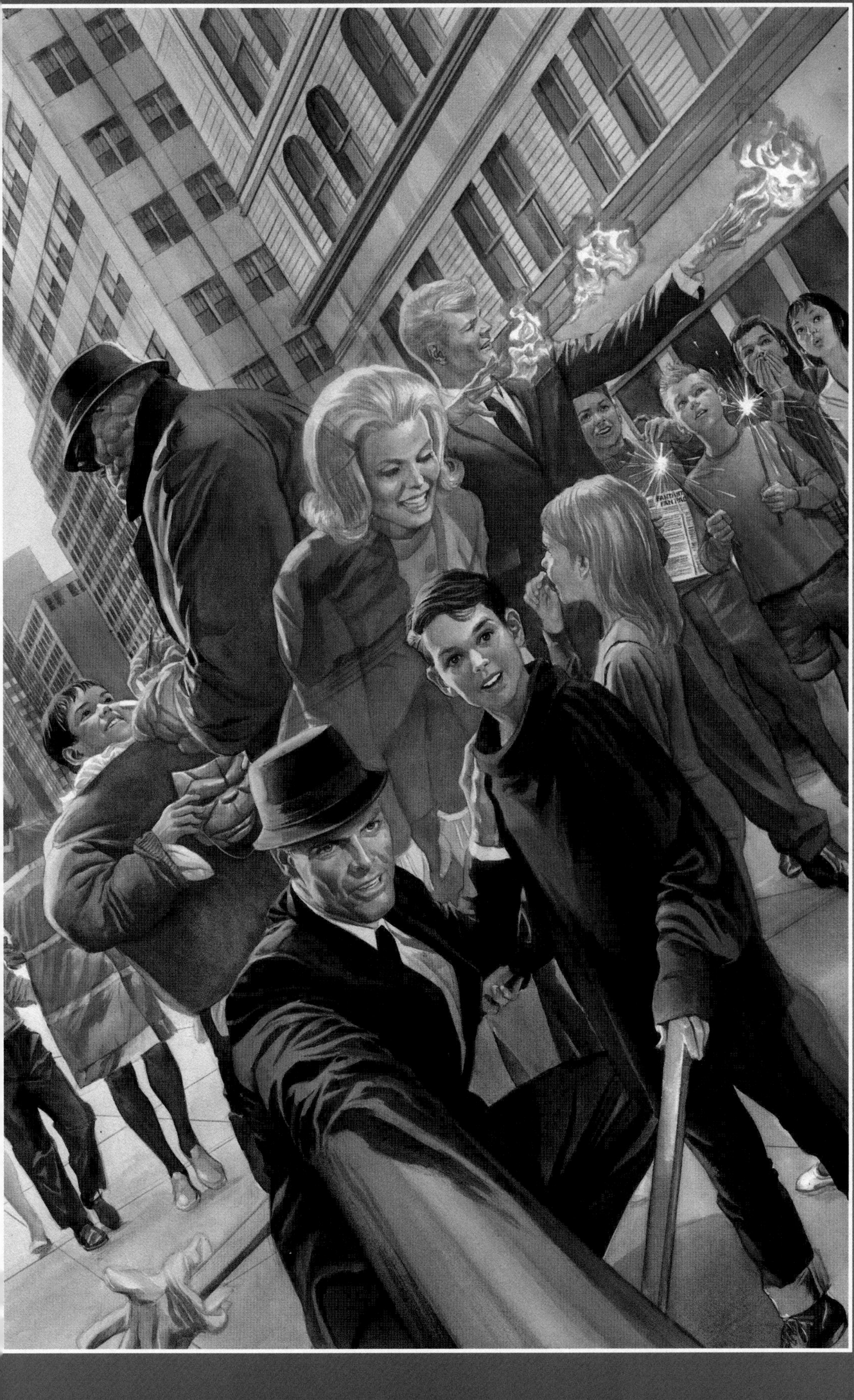

#6 Marvels 25th Anniversary variant by **Alex Ross**

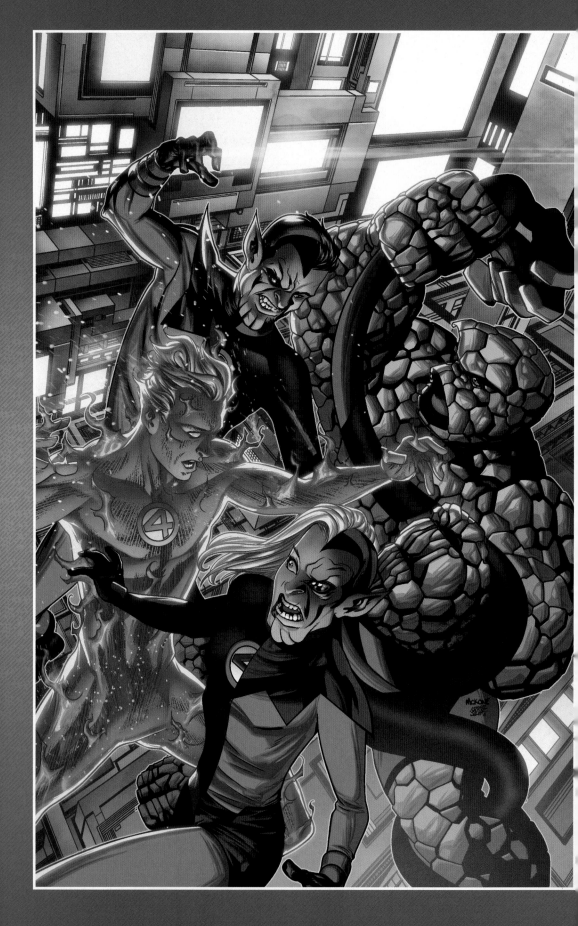

#7 Skrulls variant by **Mike McKone** & **Israel Silva**

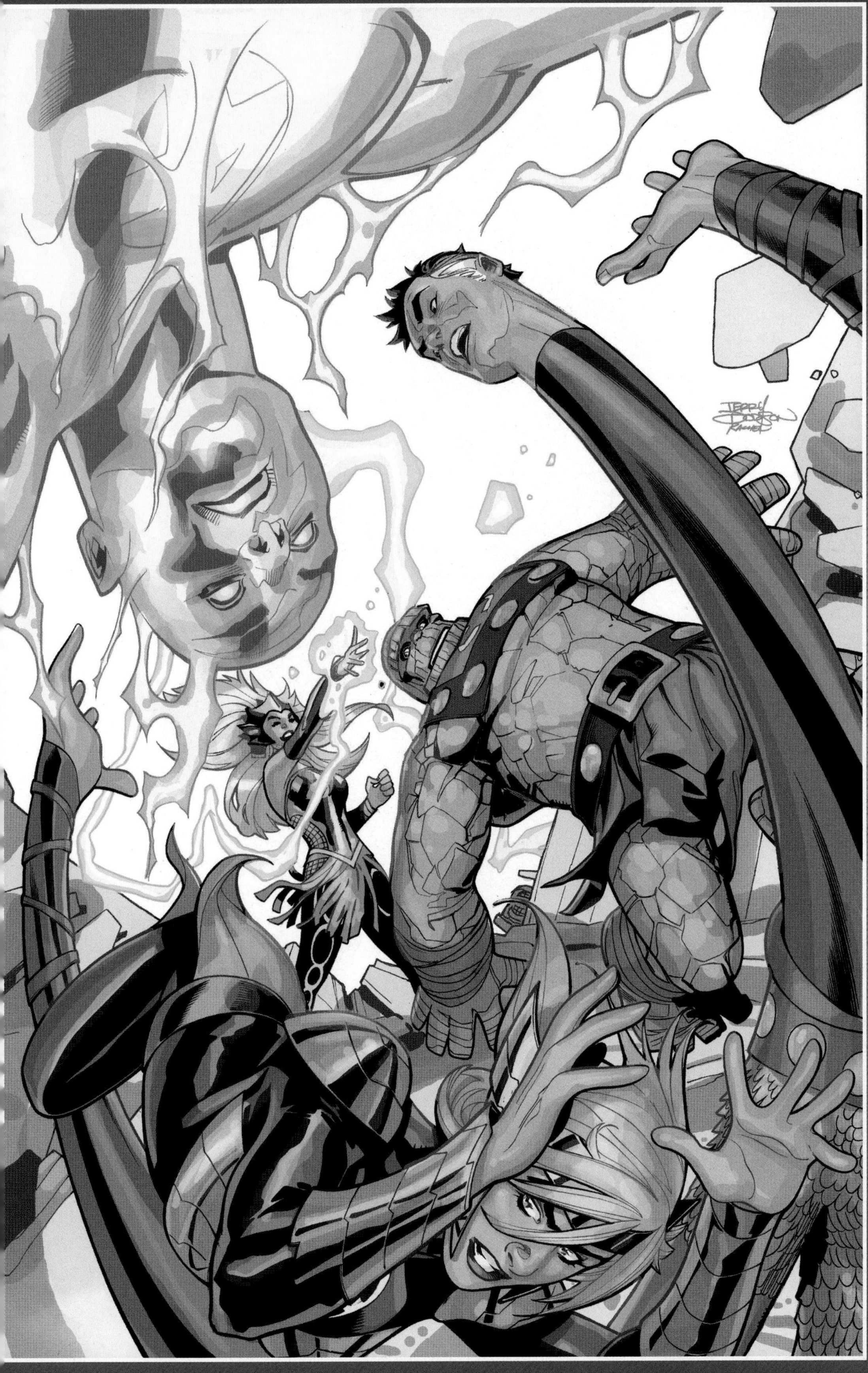

#9 Asgardian variant by **Terry Dodson** & **Rachel Dodson**

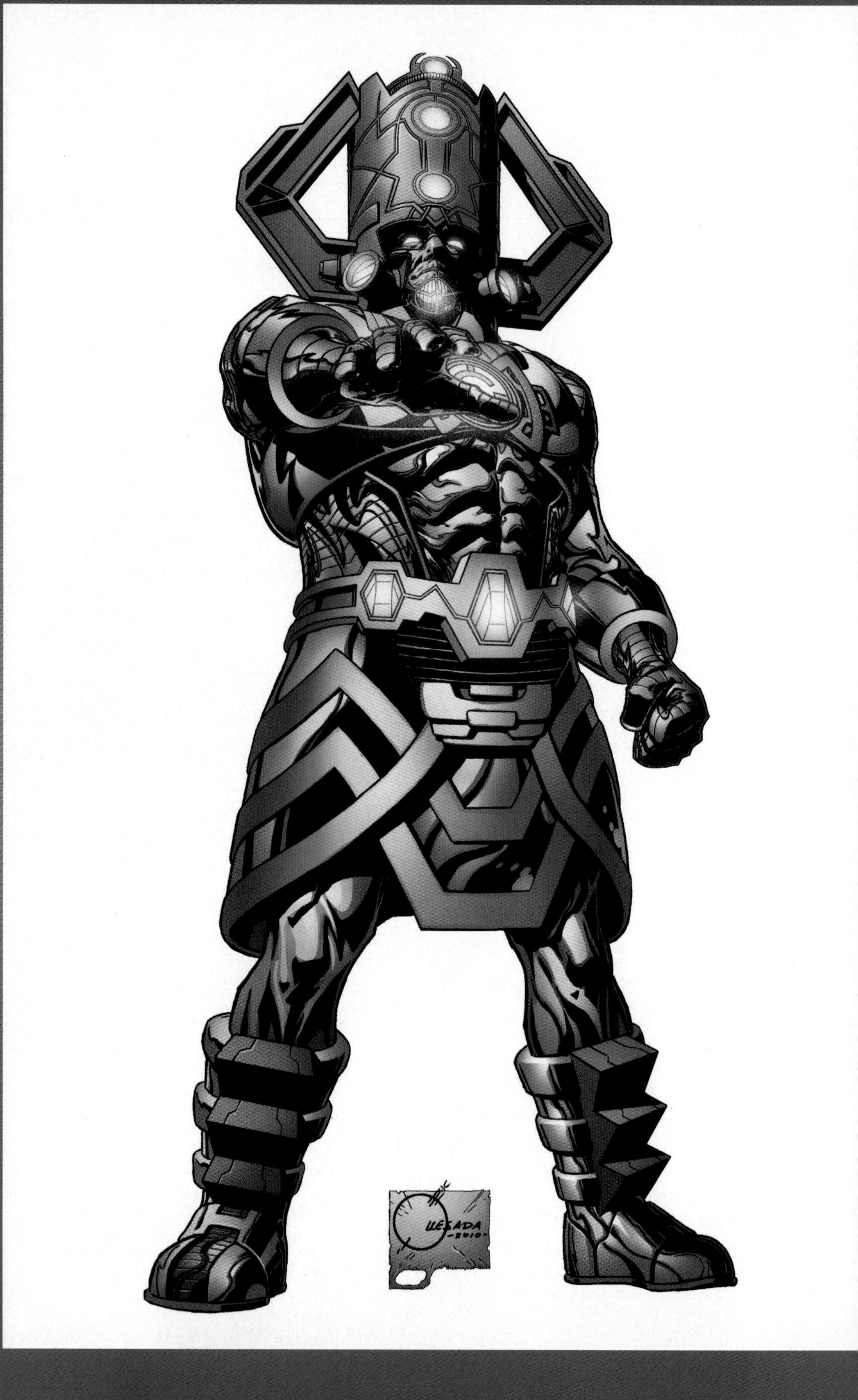

#9 Hidden Gem variant by **Joe Quesada** & **Richard Isanove**

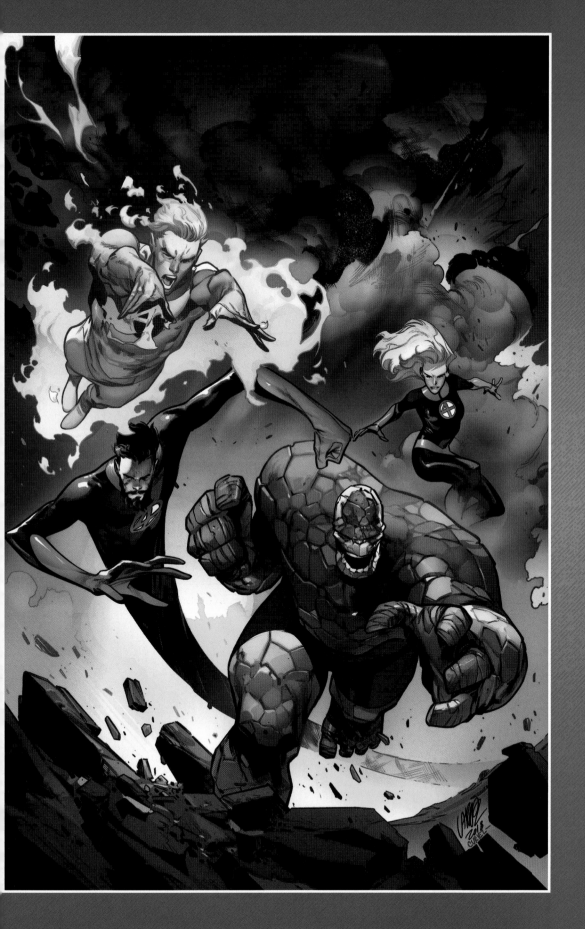

#11 variant by **Pepe Larraz** & **David Curiel**

Victorious designs by **Aaron Kuder**

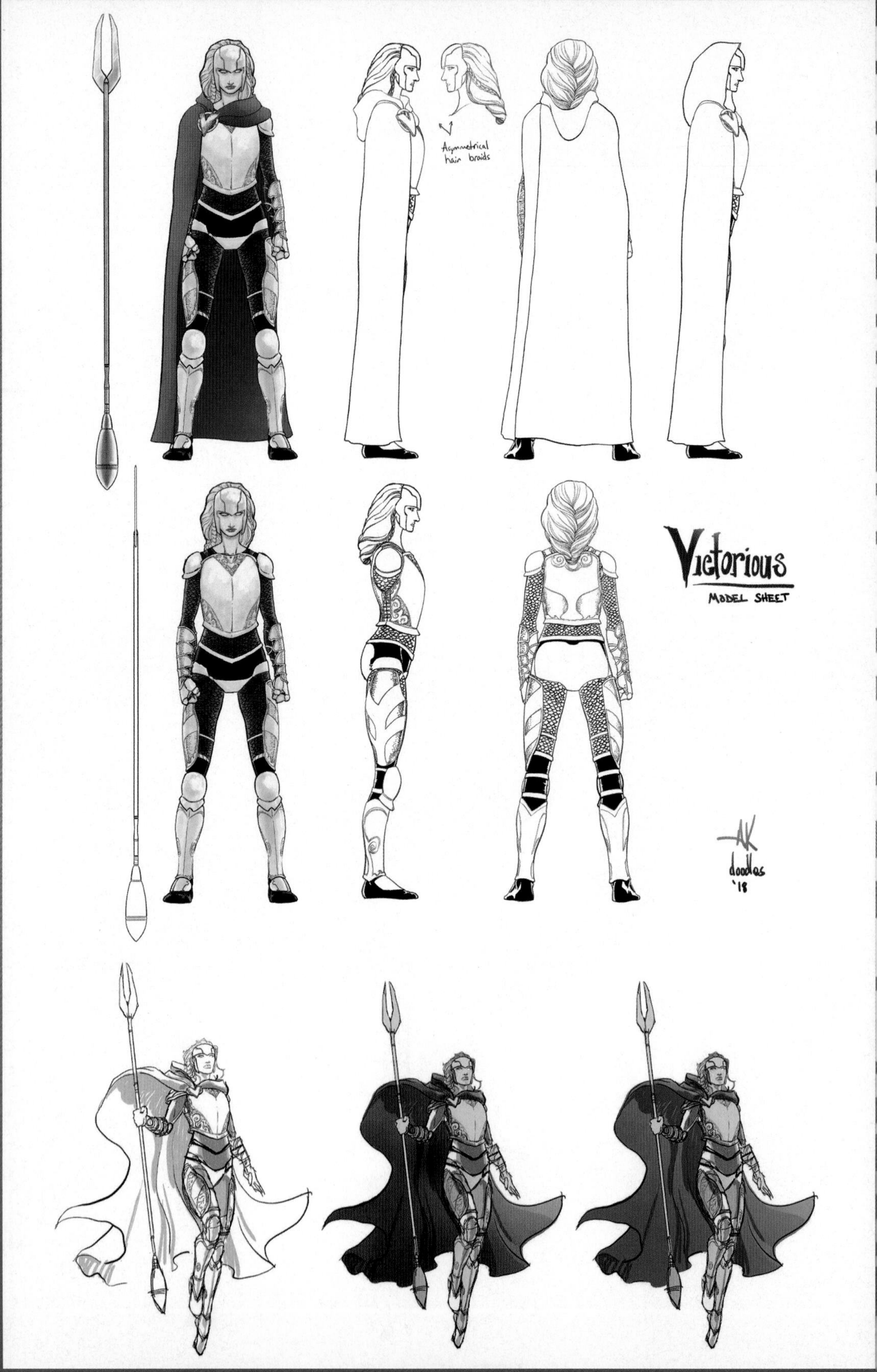
Asymmetrical hair braids
Victorious
MODEL SHEET
AK doodles '18

Gargantua designs by **Paco Medina**

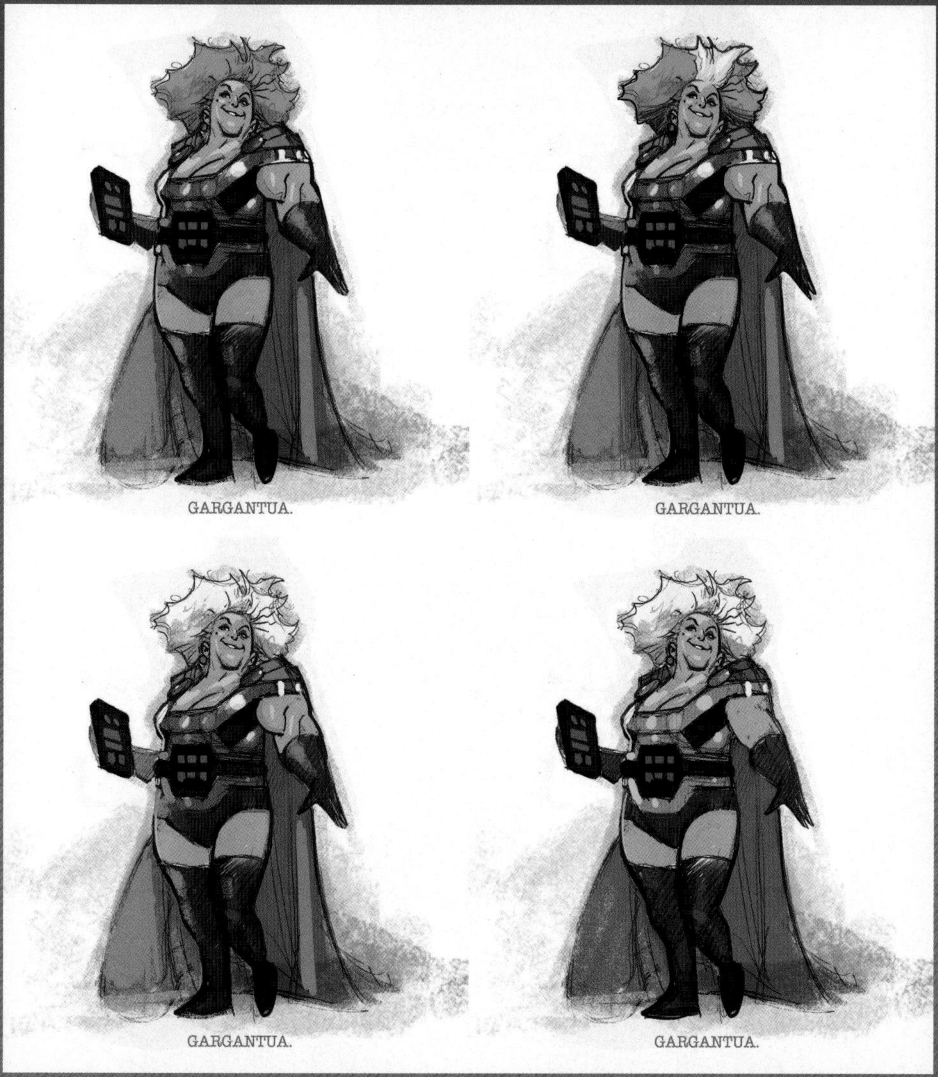
GARGANTUA.
GARGANTUA.
GARGANTUA.
GARGANTUA.

Harriet & Tobias designs by **Kevin Libranda**

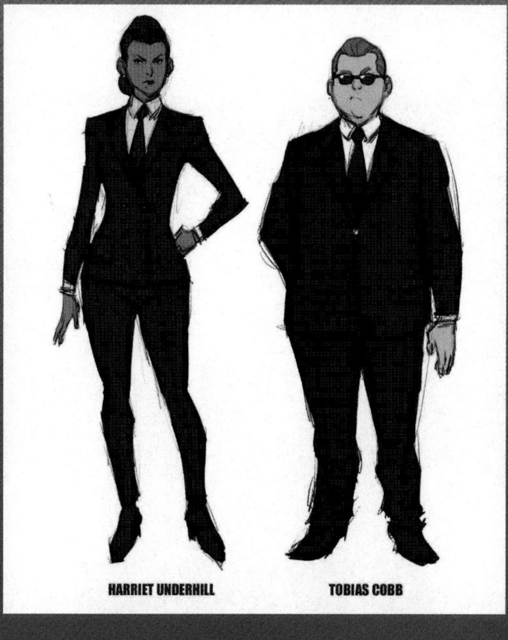
HARRIET UNDERHILL
TOBIAS COBB

#10 cover process by **Matteo Scalera**

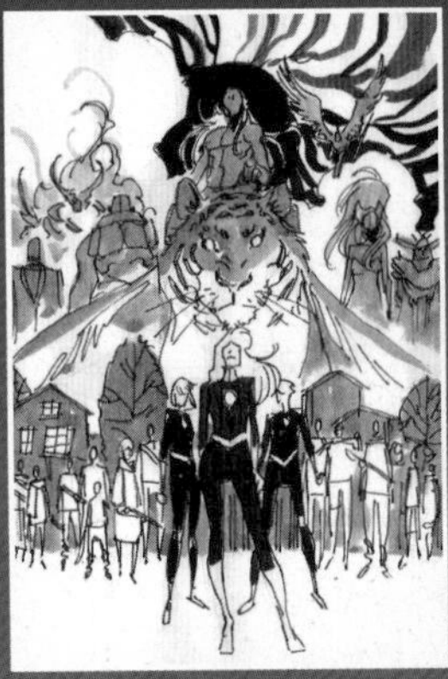

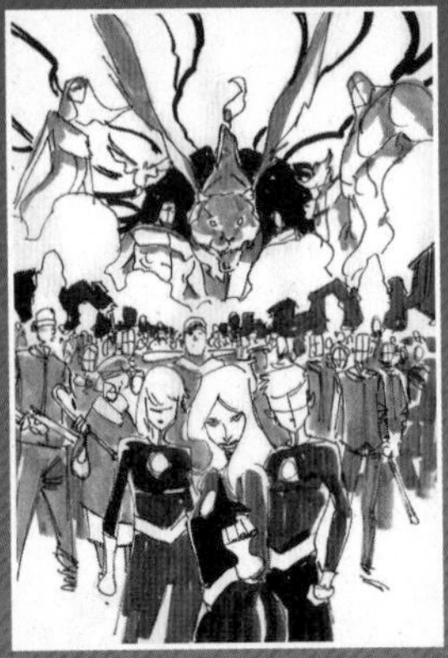

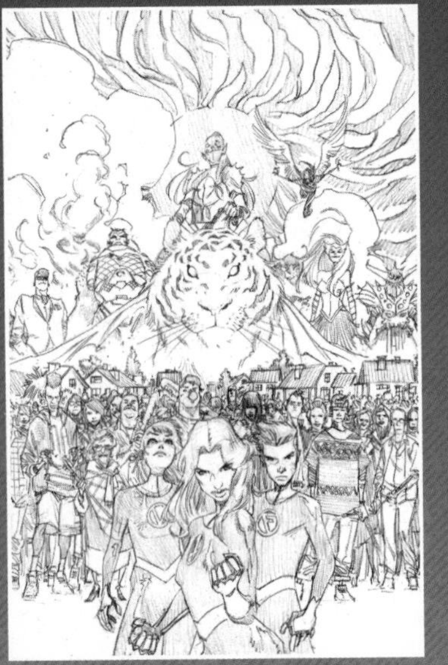

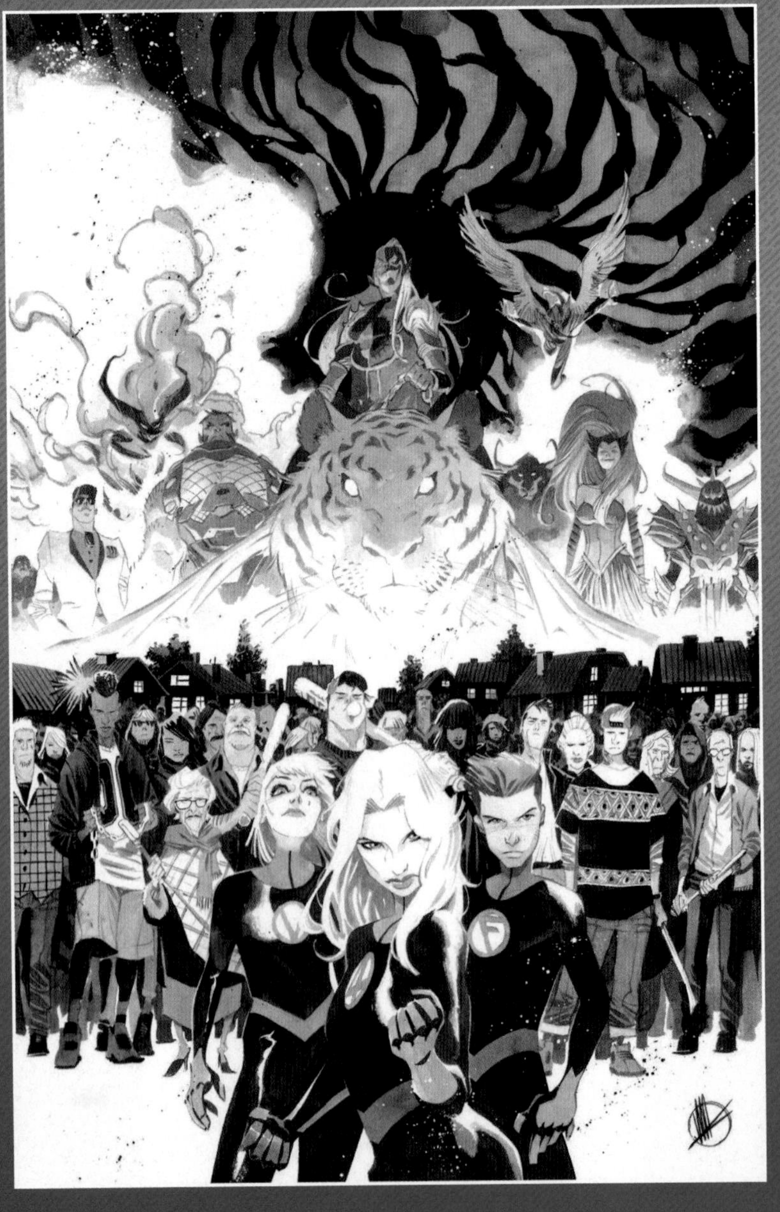

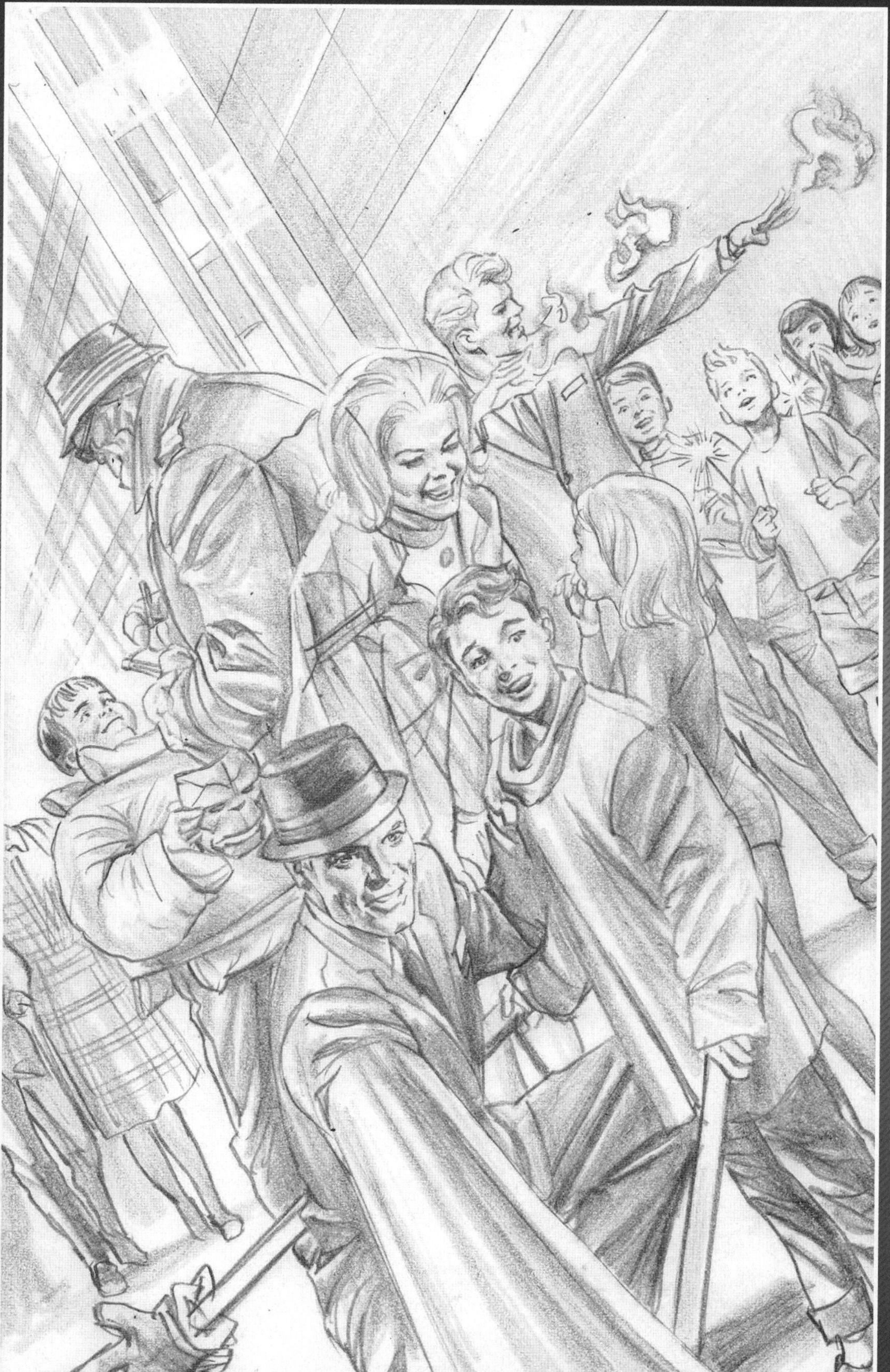

#6 Marvels 25th Anniversary variant pencils by **Alex Ross**

#6, page 9 art process by **Aaron Kuder**

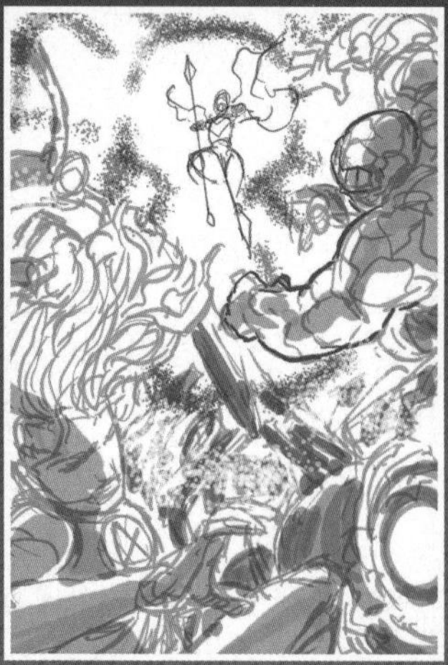

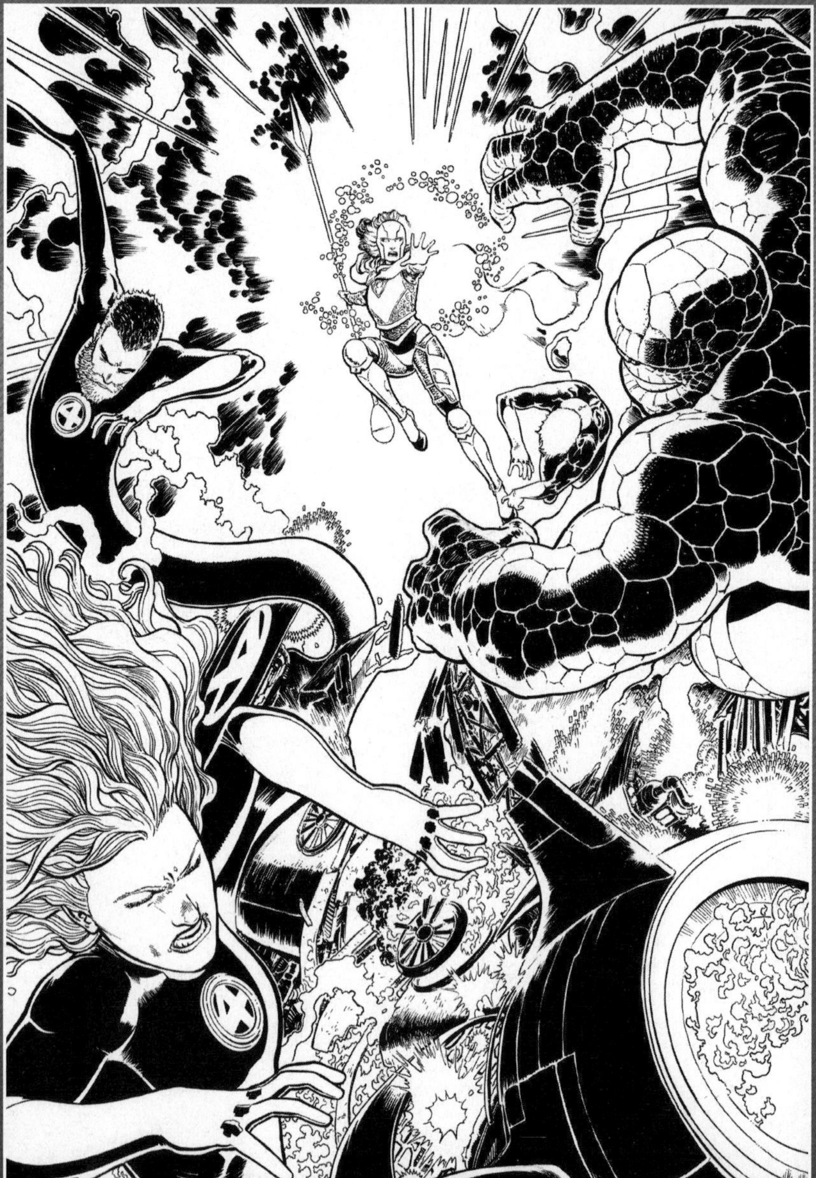